FREE MONEY®
from the Federal Government for Small Businesses and Entrepreneurs
Second Edition

Other Free Money® Books by Laurie Blum

Business

Free Money® for Small Businesses and Entrepreneurs, Fourth Edition
Free Money® When You're Unemployed

Child Care/Education

Free Money® for Athletic Scholarships
Free Money® for College
Free Money® for College from the Government
Free Money® from Colleges and Universities
Free Money® for Day Care
Free Money® for Graduate School
Free Money® for Private Schools
Free Money® for Foreign Study

Health Care

Free Money® for Seniors and Their Families
Free Money® for Childhood Behavioral and Genetic Disorders
Free Money® for Children's Medical/Dental Expenses
Free Money® for Diseases of Aging
Free Money® for Heart Disease and Cancer Care
Free Money® for Infertility Treatments
Free Money® for Mental/Emotional Disorders

FREE MONEY®
from the Federal Government for Small Businesses and Entrepreneurs
Second Edition

Laurie Blum

John Wiley & Sons, Inc.
New York · Chichester · Brisbane · Toronto · Singapore

Contents

Introduction

This is a book that many of my readers have asked me to write. It is the federal version of my popular book *Free Money® for Small Businesses and Entrepreneurs*.

According to the Catalog of Federal Domestic Assistance, over $117 billion and nearly 1,370 federal assistance programs (administered by 52 federal agencies) were available in 1994. Approximately 71 percent of these monies and programs offer eligibility through direct payments (including entitlements such as veterans benefits, social security, etc.), direct loans, project grants, and "other." Although these figures do not directly reflect the exact number of grant dollars and programs available specifically to individuals, they are an indication of the billions of dollars provided through the thousands of funding programs existing at the federal level.

HOW TO USE THIS BOOK

Substantial funding is available from agencies at the various levels of government: federal, state, county, and city.

Because the nature of many government publications and other reference guides makes accessing this information nearly impossible, I have written this book as an easy-to-use directory listing grant programs in seven general areas. Available grants are organized by field of interest: community development, real estate, minorities, and so on. Underneath the grant or government program (where appropriate) are individual state or regional offices through which an individual from a given state should apply.

Check these seven general grants "subject" areas to see which grants apply to you. Remember, regardless of what type of business or enterprise you have or want to undertake, there should be a government funding source that's right for you.

I have also included an important section on how to write a proposal. Unlike private funders, government agencies almost always use a printed application form. Detailed instructions are usually provided, with little room for free-form creative writing. However, from my own experience in writing many successful proposals for government grants, I have found a number of rules that must be adhered to in order to produce a successful proposal.

I am also including a bibliography that lists government source books, private foundation source books, and some books on how to go about seeking government grants that I thought the reader would find helpful.

HOW TO WRITE A PROPOSAL

Once you have identified which government programs are likely prospects for support, your next step is to contact them directly. Request any information that they make available to prospective applicants, including the application form and instruction booklet. (You may apply for more than one grant. Because federal grants are much more complicated and labor-intensive than private foundation or corporate grants, however, I would not recommend applying for more than two or three grants.) In addition, try to identify the contact person at the funding program for which you are applying. After you receive information about the program and determine that you are eligible for funding, try to speak with the contact person; if that is not possible, write to the contact person. Ask what the government official's agency is looking for in proposals or applications. Are there particular types of projects it wants? Don't hesitate to ask questions about completing the application. The government does not expect you to be totally knowledgeable in government grantsmanship.

Most government funding boards make available application forms or formats for proposals. The proposal or the application is a very important document, for it is your opportunity to demonstrate who you are, what you hope to accomplish, and how you are especially qualified to work toward the objectives that you have set forth. Again, if you have any questions that arise while you are preparing your written materials, speak or write to the government official you have previously contacted.

Begin your proposal with a title page. Include:

- The amount requested
- The name of the agency
- The purpose of the grant
- A short descriptive title
- The time frame of the project
- Your full name and affiliation, if any
- Your address and phone number
- The date of submission

The title page should be followed by a clear and precise statement of purpose. Your statement of purpose should answer these three questions:

1. What do you hope to accomplish?

2. How do you plan to obtain your goals? (What activities, programs, or services will you undertake to accomplish your goals? Would you characterize these efforts as service-related, advocacy-focused, or public-education related?)

3. For whose benefit will your project function? (How specifically can you define your prime constituents: by age, sex, geography, minority-group status, or income?)

The proposal should always include an evaluation section that briefly outlines how you intend to show that the proposed results were achieved.

The budget reflects the cost of the project in detail. It should be justified in relation to the tasks. Job descriptions of all staff should be presented, with an outline of the overall organizational structure.

The budget section is followed by a section called "the capability of the contractor," documenting the reasons why you are in a strong position to conduct this project. Your resume, resources, and letters of support should be included.

Frequently, government grant proposals are lengthier than foundation and corporate proposals because of the detail required. Detail does not mean verbosity; rather, clarity and succinct prose are in order.

Don't apply for government grants unless you are willing to play the game by the funders' rules. You must have a certain tolerance for frustration and a willingness to confront red tape. Patience is an absolute necessity to government grant seekers.

Be sure to observe grant deadlines. Like deadlines for tax returns, they require close adherence.

THE YES

Congratulations! You have been awarded a grant. As you will be receiving public tax dollars, make sure you understand all the financial reporting requirements that accompany your award. You may also want to clarify when you will receive your funds. Given the red tape inherent in any bureaucracy, you may have to wait a number of months before you actually receive the monies, so plan accordingly.

THE NO

Don't despair! Inquire why the proposal was rejected. If possible, ask the contact person for a specific reason. Find out the strengths and weaknesses of your proposal. Ask how you can submit an application the next time around that addresses the issues that have been raised during your discussion with the government official. You can always apply again. Persistence will be your best ally as long as any subsequent application demonstrates that you have dealt with the concerns that prompted the rejection.

Be sure that you are on the mailing list of the targeted agency to receive future requests for proposals and any other information that they periodically make available to prospective applications. Thank the official with whom you have been in touch for his or her time and help.

ONE LAST NOTE

By the time this book is published, some of the information contained here will have changed. Names, addresses, dollar amounts, telephone numbers, and other data are always in flux; however, most of the information will not have changed.

Agriculture

Assistance is widely available from the federal government to owners, landlords, or sharecroppers on a farm or ranch for the following:

1. *Assistance* for agricultural conservation programs, such as cotton-production stabilization; emergency livestock assistance; feed grain, rice, and wheat production; or forestry incentive programs
2. *Various loan programs* (i.e., loans for commodity purchases and payments, emergency loans for natural disasters, or soil and water loans)
3. *Assistance* for agricultural research grants

You will need to consult the list of addresses in this chapter for your nearest local or regional Agricultural and Conservation Service office or Farmers Home Administration (FmHA) office.

AGRICULTURE CONSERVATION PROGRAM

Department of Agriculture
Agricultural Stabilization
and Conservation Service
(ASCS)
P.O. Box 2415
Washington, DC 20013
(202) 720-6221

Description: Direct payments for specified use to any owner, landlord, tenant, or sharecropper on a farm or ranch (including associated groups) who agrees to bear part of the cost of an approved conservation practice.
$ Given: Not available
Application Information: Not available
Deadline: Application for payment must be filed with county ASCS committee after the practice is completed.
Contact: Your local, state, and/or regional ASCS office

Alabama
Robert D. Springe
P.O. Box 891
Montgomery, AL 36104-0891
(205) 279-3500

Alaska
Karen O. Lee
Alaska State ASCS Office
800 West Evergreen
Suite 216
Palmer, AK 99654-6539
(907) 745-7982

Arizona
Robert A. Piceno
Arizona State ASCS Office
201 East Indianola
Suite 240
Phoenix, AZ 85012-3118
(602) 640-5200

Arkansas
Wayne Perryman
P.O. Box 2781
New Federal Building
Room 5428
700 West Capitol Street
Little Rock, AR 72201-3225
(501) 324-5220

California
John Smythe
California State ASCS Office
1303 J Street
Suite 300
Sacramento, CA 95814-2916
(916) 551-1801

Colorado
John Stencel
Colorado State ASCS Office
655 Parfet Street
Room E305
Third Floor
Lakewood, CO 80215
(303) 236-2866

Connecticut
Vincent R. Majchier
88 Day Hill Road
Windsor, CT 06095
(203) 285-8483

Delaware
William D. Clifton II
1201 College Park Drive
Suite A
Dover, DE 19901
(302) 678-4912

Florida
Harry McGlin
P.O. Box 141030
4440 NW 25th Place
Suite I
Gainesville, FL 32614-1030
(904) 372-8549

Georgia
Grady (Buck) Johnson
P.O. Box 1907
Federal Building
Room 102
344 East Hancock Avenue
Athens, GA 30601-2775
(404) 546-2266

Hawaii
Jo Ann Nakata
Hawaii State ASCS Office
300 Ala Moana Boulevard
Room 5106
P.O. Box 50008
Honolulu, HI 96850
(808) 551-2644

Idaho
Richard R. Rush
Idaho State ASCS Office
3220 Elder Street
Boise, ID 83705
(208) 334-1486

Illinois
Stephen Scates
P.O. Box 19273
3500 Wabash Avenue
Springfield, IL 62794-9273
(217) 492-4180

Indiana
Kent Yeager
Indiana State ASCS Office
5891 Lakeside Boulevard
Indianapolis, IN 46278
(317) 290-3030

Iowa
Tom Grau
10500 Buena Vista Court
Urbandale, IA 50322
(515) 254-1540, ext. 40

Kansas
Andrian J. Polansky
Kansas State ASCS Office
3600 Anderson Avenue
Manhattan, KS 66502-2511
(913) 539-3531

Kentucky
Hampton (Hoppy) Hinton
Kentucky State ASCS Office
771 Corporate Drive
Suite 100
Lexington, KY 40503-5478
(606) 224-7601

Louisiana
Willie F. Cooper
3737 Government Street
Alexandria, LA 71302-3395
(318) 473-7721

Maine
Arnold Roach
44 Stillwater Avenue
P.O. Box 406
Bangor, ME 04401-0406
(207) 990-9140

Maryland
James M. Voss
8335 East Guilford Road
Columbia, MD 21046
(410) 381-4550

Massachusetts
Charles A. Costa
451 West Street
Amherst, MA 01002-2953
(413) 256-0232

Michigan
Jim Byrum
300 Coolidge Road
Suite 100
East Lansing, MI 48823-6321
(517) 337-6659

Minnesota
Wally Sparby
Minnesota State ASCS
Office
400 Farm Credit Service
Building
375 Jackson Street
St. Paul, MN 55101-1853
(612) 290-3651

Mississippi
Norris Faust
Mississippi State ASCS
Office
6310 I-55 North
Jackson, MS 39236-4995
(601) 965-4300

Missouri
Brad Epperson
601 Parkdale Plaza Business
Loop
70 West
Suite 225
Columbia, MO 65203
(314) 876-0925

Montana
Bruce E. Nelson
P.O. Box 670
10 East Babcock
Room 557
Bozeman, MT 59715
(406) 587-6872

Nebraska
John Frank Johannsen
Nebraska State ASCS Office
P.O. Box 57975
7131 A Street
Lincoln, NE 68510
(402) 437-5581

Nevada
Wendell K. Newman
Nevada State ASCS Office
1755 East Plumb Lane
Suite 202
Reno, NV 89502-3200
(702) 784-5130

New Hampshire
James McConaka
USDA–New Hampshire
State ASCS Office
22 Bridge Street
Fourth Floor
P.O. Box 1398
Concord, NH 03302-1398
(603) 224-7941

New Jersey
Peter de Wilde
Mastoris Professional Plaza
163 Route 130
Building I
Suite E
Bordentown, NJ 08505-2249
(609) 224-7941

New Mexico
Charles Essary
New Mexico State ASCS
Office
P.O. Box 1458
Federal Building
Room 4430
517 Gold Avenue, SW
Albuquerque, NM 87103-
1458
(505) 766-2472

New York
Floyd Duger
811 James H. Hanley
Federal Building
100 South Clinton Street
P.O. Box 7308
Syracuse, NY 13260-7308
(315) 423-5176

North Carolina
Samuel Colney
Federal Building
Suite 175
4407 Bland Road
Raleigh, NC 27609-6296
(919) 790-2957

North Dakota
Scott Stofferahn
North Dakota State ASCS
Office
1025 28th Street, SW
P.O. Box 3046
Fargo, ND 58108-3046
(701) 239-5224

Ohio
Steve Maurer
Federal Building
Room 540
200 North High Street
Columbus, OH 43215
(614) 469-6735

Oklahoma
Terry L. Peach
USDA Agriculture Center
Building
Suite 102
Farm Road and McFarland
Street
Stillwater, OK 74074-2653
(405) 624-4110

Oregon
Jack L. Sainsbury
Oregon State ASCS Office
P.O. Box 1300
Tualatin, OR 97062-1300
(503) 692-6830

Pennsylvania
William H. Baumgartner
One Credit Union Place
Suite 320
Harrisburg, PA 17101-2994
(717) 782-4547

Rhode Island
Paul E. Brule
Aldeic Complex
60 Quaker Lane
West Bay Office Complex
Suite 40
West Warwick, RI 02886
(401) 828-8232

South Carolina
Laurie C. Nelson
Strom Thurmond Mall
Suite 100
Columbia, SC 29201-2375
(803) 765-5186

South Dakota
Michael O'Connor
Federal Building
Room 208
200 Fourth Street, SW
Huron, SD 57350-2478
(605) 353-1092

Tennessee
Walter E. Head
United States Courthouse
Room 579
801 Broadway
Nashville, TN 37203-3816
(615) 736-5555

Texas
Harold B. Bennett
Texas State ASCS Office
P.O. Box 2900
College Station, TX 77841-
0001
(409) 260-9207

Utah
James L. Humlicek
Utah State ASCS Office
P.O. Box 11547
Salt Lake City, UT 84147
(801) 524-5013

Vermont
James L. Monahan
Executive Square Office
Building
346 Shelburne Street
Burlington, VT 05401-4495
(802) 658-2803

Virginia
Donald Davis
Culpeper Building
Suite 138
1606 Santa Rosa Road
Richmond, VA 23229
(804) 287-1500

Washington
Larry R. Albin
Washington State ASCS
Office
Rock Point Tower
Suite 568
316 West Boone Avenue
Spokane, WA 99201-2350
(509) 353-2307

West Virginia
Billy B. Burke
P.O. Box 1049
New Federal Building
Room 239
75 High Street
Morgantown, WV 26505-7558
(304) 291-4351

Wisconsin
Doug Caruso
Wisconsin State ASCS Office
6515 Watts Road
Room 100
Madison, WI 53719-2797
(608) 264-5301

Wyoming
Thomas E. Trowbridge
951 Werner Court
Suite 130
Casper, WY 82601-1307
(307) 261-5231

Caribbean Area
Herberto J. Martinez
Caribbean Area ASCS Office
Cobran's Plaza
Suite 309
1609 Ponce DeLeon Avenue
Santurce, PR 00909-0001
(809) 729-6902

BUSINESS AND INDUSTRIAL LOANS

Department of Agriculture
Farmers Home
Administration (FmHA)
Washington, DC 20250-0700
(202) 690-4730

Description: Guaranteed and insured loans for individuals, cooperatives, corporations, partnerships, trusts, Indian tribes, or subdivisions of states located in rural areas. Applicants must be in rural areas other than cities with populations of 50,000 or more and adjacent to urban areas with a population density of more than 100 persons per square mile.
$ Given: Business and industrial loan range: $30,000–$7.5 million; development loan range: $35,000–$500,000
Application Information: File Form FmHA 449-I for guaranteed loans at your FmHA state office.
Deadline: Contact your local or state FmHA office.
Contact: Consult your local telephone directory under U.S. Government, Department of Agriculture, for FmHA county office number or contact your FmHA state office.

Alabama
Sterling Center
Suite 601
4121 Carmichael Road
Montgomery, AL 36106-3683
(205) 279-3400

Alaska
634 South Bailey
Suite 103
Palmer, AK 99645
(907) 745-2176

Arizona
3003 North Central Avenue
Suite 900
Phoenix, AZ 85012
(602) 280-8700

Arkansas
700 West Capitol
P.O. Box 2778
Little Rock, AR 72203
(501) 324-6281

California
194 West Main Street
Suite F
Woodland, CA 95695-2915
(916) 669-2000

Colorado
655 Parfet Street
Room 31-08
Lakewood, CO 80215
(303) 236-2801

Connecticut
451 West Street
Amherst, MA 01002
(413) 253-4300

Delaware
4611 South Dupont
Highway
P.O. Box 400
Camden, DE 19934-9998
(302) 697-4300

District of Columbia
4611 South Dupont
Highway
P.O. Box 400
Camden, DE 19934-9998
(302) 697-4300

Florida
Federal Building
4440 NW 25th Place
P.O. Box 147010
Gainesville, FL 32614-7010
(904) 338-3400

Georgia
355 East Hancock Avenue
Stephens Federal Building
Athens, GA 30610
(706) 546-2152

Guam
Department of Agriculture
14th Street and
Independence Avenue, SW
Washington, DC 20250
(202) 720-1632

Hawaii
Federal Building
Room 311
154 Waianuenue Avenue
Hilo, HI 96720
(808) 933-3000

Idaho
3232 Elder Street
Boise, ID 83705
(208) 334-1301

Illinois
Illini Plaza
Suite 103
1817 South Neil Street
Champaign, IL 61820
(217) 398-5235

Indiana
5975 Lakeside Boulevard
Indianapolis, IN 46278
(317) 290-3100

Iowa
Federal Building
Room 873
210 Walnut Street
Des Moines, IA 50309
(515) 284-4663

Kansas
1201 SW Summit Executive
Court
P.O. Box 4653
Topeka, KS 66604
(913) 271-2700

Kentucky
771 Corporate Drive
Suite 200
Lexington, KY 40503
(606) 224-7300

Louisiana
3727 Government Street
Alexandria, LA 71302
(318) 473-7920

Maine
444 Stillwater Avenue
Suite 2
P.O. Box 405
Bangor, ME 04402-0405
(207) 990-9106

Maryland
4611 South Dupont
Highway
P.O. Box 400
Camden, DE 19934-9998
(302) 697-4300

Massachusetts
451 West Street
Amherst, MA 01002
(413) 253-4300

Michigan
3001 Coolidge Road
Suite 200
East Lansing, MI 48823
(517) 337-6635

Minnesota
410 Farm Credit Building
375 Jackson Street
St. Paul, MN 55101
(612) 290-3842

Mississippi
Federal Building
Suite 831
100 West Capitol
Jackson, MS 39269
(601) 965-4316

Missouri
601 Business Loop
70 West Parkade Center
Suite 235
Columbia, MO 65203
(314) 768-0976

Montana
900 Technology Boulevard
Suite B
P.O. Box 850
Bozeman, MT 59771
(406) 585-2580

Nebraska
Federal Building
Room 308
100 Centennial Mall
Lincoln, NE 68508
(402) 437-5551

Nevada
1390 South Curry Street
Carson City, NV 89703-
5405
(702) 887-1222

New Hampshire
City Center
89 Main Street
Third Floor
Montpelier, VT 05602
(802) 223-6001

New Jersey
Tarnsfield Plaza
Suite 22
1016 Woodlane Road
Mt. Holly, NJ 08060
(609) 265-3600

New Mexico
Federal Building
Room 3414
517 Gold Avenue, SW
Albuquerque, NM 87102
(505) 766-2462

New York
Federal Building
100 South Clinton Street
Room 871
Syracuse, NY 13261-7318
(315) 423-5290

North Carolina
4405 South Bland Road
Suite 260
Raleigh, NC 27609
(919) 790-2731

North Dakota
Federal Building
Room 208
Third and Rosser
P.O. Box 1737
Bismarck, ND 59502
(701) 250-4781

Ohio
Federal Building
Room 507
200 North High Street
Columbus, OH 43215
(614) 469-5606

Oklahoma
USDA Agricultural Center
Office Building
Stillwater, OK 74074
(405) 624-4250

Oregon
Federal Building
Room 1590
1220 SW Third Avenue
Portland, OR 97204
(503) 326-2731

Pennsylvania
One Credit Union Plaza
Suite 330
Harrisburg, PA 17110-2996
(717) 782-4476

Puerto Rico
New San Juan Center
Building
Room 501
159 Carlos E. Chardon
Street
G.P.O. Box 6106G
Hato Rey, PR 00918-5481
(809) 766-5095

Rhode Island
451 West Street
Amherst, MA 01002
(413) 253-4300

South Carolina
Strom Thurmond Federal
Building
Room 1007
1835 Assembly Street
Columbia, SC 28201
(803) 765-5163

South Dakota
Huron Federal Building
Room 308
200 Fourth Street, SW
Huron, SD 57350
(605) 353-1430

Tennessee
3322 West End Avenue
Suite 300
Nashville, TN 37203-1071
(615) 783-1308

Texas
Federal Building
101 South Main
Suite 102
Temple, TX 76501
(817) 774-1301

Utah
Federal Building
Room 5438
125 South State Street
Salt Lake City, UT 84138
(801) 524-4063

Vermont
City Center
89 Main Street
Third Floor
Montpelier, VT 05602
(802) 828-6001

Virginia
Culpeper Building
1606 Santa Rosa Road
Suite 238
Richmond, VA 23229
(804) 828-1550

Virgin Islands
City Center
89 Main Street
Third Floor
Montpelier, VT 05602
(802) 828-6001

Washington
Federal Building
Room 319
P.O. Box 2427
Wenatchee, WA 98807
(509) 664-0240

West Virginia
75 High Street
P.O. Box 678
Morgantown, WV 26505
(304) 291-4791

Wisconsin
4949 Kirschling Court
Stevens Point, WI 54481
(715) 345-7625

Wyoming
Federal Building Room 1005
100 East B Street
P.O. Box 820
Casper, WY 82602
(307) 261-5271

COLORADO RIVER BASIN SALINITY CONTROL PROGRAM

Department of Agriculture
Agricultural Stabilization
and Conservation Service
(ASCS)
Conservation and
Environmental Protection
Division
P.O. Box 2415
Washington, DC 20013
(202) 720-6221

Description: Direct payments for specified use to individuals, Indian tribes, partnerships, firms, associations, corporations, joint stock companies, and state or local public or nonpublic entities not included in the above, to treat salinity problems caused by agricultural irrigation activities.
$ Given: Not available
Application Information: Complete form at your county ASCS office.
Deadline: None
Contact: Your local, state, and/or regional ASCS office

Alabama
Robert D. Springe
P.O. Box 891
Montgomery, AL 36104-0891
(205) 279-3500

Alaska
Karen O. Lee
Alaska State ASCS Office
800 West Evergreen
Suite 216
Palmer, AK 99654-6539
(907) 745-7982

Arizona
Robert A. Piceno
Arizona State ASCS Office
201 East Indianola
Suite 240
Phoenix, AZ 85012-3118
(602) 640-5200

Arkansas
Wayne Perryman
P.O. Box 2781
New Federal Building
Room 5428
700 West Capitol Street
Little Rock, AR 72201-3225
(501) 324-5220

California
John Smythe
California State ASCS Office
1303 J Street
Suite 300
Sacramento, CA 95814-2916
(916) 551-1801

Colorado
John Stencel
Colorado State ASCS Office
655 Parfet Street
Room E 305
Third Floor
Lakewood, CO 80215
(303) 236-2866

Connecticut
Vincent R. Majchier
88 Day Hill Road
Windsor, CT 06095
(203) 285-8483

Delaware
William D. Clifton II
1201 College Park Drive
Suite A
Dover, DE 19901
(302) 678-4912

Florida
Harry McGlin
P.O. Box 141030
4440 NW 25th Place
Suite I
Gainesville, FL 32614-1030
(904) 372-8549

Georgia
Grady (Buck) Johnson
P.O. Box 1907
Federal Building
Room 102
344 East Hancock Avenue
Athens, GA 30601-2775
(404) 546-2266

Hawaii
Jo Ann Nakata
Hawaii State ASCS Office
300 Ala Moana Boulevard
Room 5106
P.O. Box 50008
Honolulu, HI 96850
(808) 551-2644

Idaho
Richard R. Rush
Idaho State ASCS Office
3220 Elder Street
Boise, ID 83705
(208) 334-1486

Illinois
Stephen Scates
P.O. Box 19273
3500 Wabash Avenue
Springfield, IL 62794-9273
(217) 492-4180

Indiana
Kent Yeager
Indiana State ASCS Office
5891 Lakeside Boulevard
Indianapolis, IN 46278
(317) 290-3030

Iowa
Tom Grau
10500 Buena Vista Court
Urbandale, IA 50322
(515) 254-1540, ext. 40

Kansas
Andrian J. Polansky
Kansas State ASCS Office
3600 Anderson Avenue
Manhattan, KS 66502-2511
(913) 539-3531

Kentucky
Hampton (Hoppy) Hinton
Kentucky State ASCS Office
771 Corporate Drive
Suite 100
Lexington, KY 40503-5478
(606) 224-7601

Louisiana
Willie F. Cooper
3737 Government Street
Alexandria, LA 71302-3395
(318) 473-7721

Maine
Arnold Roach
44 Stillwater Avenue
P.O. Box 406
Bangor, ME 04401-0406
(207) 990-9140

Maryland
James M. Voss
8335 East Guilford Road
Columbia, MD 21046
(410) 381-4550

Massachusetts
Charles A. Costa
451 West Street
Amherst, MA 01002-2953
(413) 256-0232

Michigan
Jim Byrum
300 Coolidge Road
Suite 100
East Lansing, MI 48823-6321
(517) 337-6659

Minnesota
Wally Sparby
Minnesota State ASCS
Office
400 Farm Credit Service
Building
375 Jackson Street
St. Paul, MN 55101-1853
(612) 290-3651

Mississippi
Norris Faust
Mississippi State ASCS
Office
6310 I-55 North
Jackson, MS 39236-4995
(601) 965-4300

Missouri
Brad Epperson
601 Parkdale Plaza Business
Loop
70 West
Suite 225
Columbia, MO 65203
(314) 876-0925

Montana
Bruce E. Nelson
P.O. Box 670
10 East Babcock
Room 557
Bozeman, MT 59715
(406) 587-6872

Nebraska
John Frank Johannsen
Nebraska State ASCS Office
P.O. Box 57975
7131 A Street
Lincoln, NE 68510
(402) 437-5581

Nevada
Wendell K. Newman
Nevada State ASCS Office
1755 East Plumb Lane
Suite 202
Reno, NV 89502-3200
(702) 784-5130

New Hampshire
James McConaka
USDA–New Hampshire
State ASCS Office
22 Bridge Street
Fourth Floor
P.O. Box 1398
Concord, NH 03302-1398
(603) 224-7941

New Jersey
Peter de Wilde
Mastoris Professional Plaza
163 Route 130
Building I
Suite E
Bordentown, NJ 08505-2249
(609) 224-7941

New Mexico
Charles Essary
New Mexico State ASCS
Office
P.O. Box 1458
Federal Building
Room 4430
517 Gold Avenue, SW
Albuquerque, NM 87103-1458
(505) 766-2472

New York
Floyd Duger
811 James H. Hanley
Federal Building
100 South Clinton Street
P.O. Box 7308
Syracuse, NY 13260-7308
(315) 423-5176

North Carolina
Samuel Colney
Federal Building
Suite 175
4407 Bland Road
Raleigh, NC 27609-6296
(919) 790-2957

North Dakota
Scott Stofferahn
North Dakota State ASCS
Office
1025 28th Street, SW
P.O. Box 3046
Fargo, ND 58108-3046
(701) 239-5224

Ohio
Steve Maurer
Federal Building
200 North High Street
Room 540
Columbus, OH 43215
(614) 469-6735

Oklahoma
Terry L. Peach
USDA Agriculture Center
Building
Suite 102
Farm Road and McFarland
Street
Stillwater, OK 74074-2653
(405) 624-4110

Oregon
Jack L. Sainsbury
Oregon State ASCS Office
P.O. Box 1300
Tualatin, OR 97062-1300
(503) 692-6830

Pennsylvania
William H. Baumgartner
One Credit Union Place
Suite 320
Harrisburg, PA 17101-2994
(717) 782-4547

Rhode Island
Paul E. Brule
Aldeic Complex
60 Quaker Lane
West Bay Office Complex
Suite 40
West Warwick, RI 02886
(401) 828-8232

South Carolina
Laurie C. Nelson
Strom Thurmond Mall
Suite 100
Columbia, SC 29201-2375
(803) 765-5186

South Dakota
Michael O'Connor
Federal Building
Room 208
200 Fourth Street, SW
Huron, SD 57350-2478
(605) 353-1092

Tennessee
Walter E. Head
United States Courthouse
Room 579
801 Broadway
Nashville, TN 37203-3816
(615) 736-5555

Texas
Harold B. Bennett
Texas State ASCS Office
P.O. Box 2900
College Station, TX 77841-0001
(409) 260-9207

Utah
James L. Humlicek
Utah State ASCS Office
P.O. Box 11547
Salt Lake City, UT 84147
(801) 524-5013

Vermont
James L. Monahan
Executive Square Office
Building
346 Shelburne Street
Burlington, VT 05401-4495
(802) 658-2803

Virginia
Donald Davis
Culpeper Building
Suite 138
1606 Santa Rosa Road
Richmond, VA 23229
(804) 287-1500

Washington
Larry R. Albin
Washington State ASCS
Office
Rock Point Tower
Suite 568
316 West Boone Avenue
Spokane, WA 99201-2350
(509) 353-2307

West Virginia
Billy B. Burke
P.O. Box 1049
New Federal Building
Room 239
75 High Street
Morgantown, WV 26505-7558
(304) 291-4351

Wisconsin
Doug Caruso
Wisconsin State ASCS Office
6515 Watts Road
Room 100
Madison, WI 53719-2797
(608) 264-5301

Wyoming
Thomas E. Trowbridge
951 Werner Court
Suite 130
Casper, WY 82601-1307
(307) 261-5231

Caribbean Area
Herberto J. Martinez
Caribbean Area ASCS Office
Cobran's Plaza
Suite 309
1609 Ponce DeLeon Avenue
Santurce, PR 00909-0001
(809) 729-6902

COMMODITY LOANS AND PURCHASES

Department of Agriculture
Agricultural Stabilization
and Conservation Service
(ASCS)
Cotton, Grain, and Rice
Support Division
P.O. Box 2415
Washington, DC 20013
(202) 720-7641

Description: Direct loans and payments with unrestricted use to owners, landlords, tenants, or sharecroppers on a farm with a history of producing eligible commodities. Record of farming operation must be on file in the ASCS county office.
$ Given: Loan range: $50–$76 million
Application Information: Write for guidelines.
Deadline: Based on type of crop
Contact: Your state ASCS office

Alabama
Robert D. Springe
P.O. Box 891
Montgomery, AL 36104-
0891
(205) 279-3500

Alaska
Karen O. Lee
Alaska State ASCS Office
800 West Evergreen
Suite 216
Palmer, AK 99654-6539
(907) 745-7982

Arizona
Robert A. Piceno
Arizona State ASCS Office
201 East Indianola
Suite 240
Phoenix, AZ 85012-3118
(602) 640-5200

Arkansas
Wayne Perryman
P.O. Box 2781
New Federal Building
Room 5428
700 West Capitol Street
Little Rock, AR 72201-3225
(501) 324-5220

California
John Smythe
California State ASCS Office
1303 J Street
Suite 300
Sacramento, CA 95814-2916
(916) 551-1801

Colorado
John Stencel
Colorado State ASCS Office
655 Parfet Street
Room E 305
Third Floor
Lakewood, CO 80215
(303) 236-2866

Connecticut
Vincent R. Majchier
88 Day Hill Road
Windsor, CT 06095
(203) 285-8483

Delaware
William D. Clifton II
1201 College Park Drive
Suite A
Dover, DE 19901
(302) 678-4912

Florida
Harry McGlin
P.O. Box 141030
4440 NW 25th Place
Suite I
Gainesville, FL 32614-1030
(904) 372-8549

Georgia
Grady (Buck) Johnson
P.O. Box 1907
Federal Building
Room 102
344 East Hancock Avenue
Athens, GA 30601-2775
(404) 546-2266

Hawaii
Jo Ann Nakata
Hawaii State ASCS Office
300 Ala Moana Boulevard
Room 5106
P.O. Box 50008
Honolulu, HI 96850
(808) 551-2644

Idaho
Richard R. Rush
Idaho State ASCS Office
3220 Elder Street
Boise, ID 83705
(208) 334-1486

Illinois
Stephen Scates
P.O. Box 19273
3500 Wabash Avenue
Springfield, IL 62794-9273
(217) 492-4180

Indiana
Kent Yeager
Indiana State ASCS Office
5891 Lakeside Boulevard
Indianapolis, IN 46278
(317) 290-3030

Iowa
Tom Grau
10500 Buena Vista Court
Urbandale, IA 50322
(515) 254-1540, ext. 40

Kansas
Andrian J. Polansky
Kansas State ASCS Office
3600 Anderson Avenue
Manhattan, KS 66502-2511
(913) 539-3531

Kentucky
Hampton (Hoppy) Hinton
Kentucky State ASCS Office
771 Corporate Drive
Suite 100
Lexington, KY 40503-5478
(606) 224-7601

Louisiana
Willie F. Cooper
3737 Government Street
Alexandria, LA 71302-3395
(318) 473-7721

Maine
Arnold Roach
44 Stillwater Avenue
P.O. Box 406
Bangor, ME 04401-0406
(207) 990-9140

Maryland
James M. Voss
8335 East Guilford Road
Columbia, MD 21046
(410) 381-4550

Massachusetts
Charles A. Costa
451 West Street
Amherst, MA 01002-2953
(413) 256-0232

Michigan
Jim Byrum
300 Coolidge Road
Suite 100
East Lansing, MI 48823-6321
(517) 337-6659

Minnesota
Wally Sparby
Minnesota State ASCS
Office
400 Farm Credit Service
Building
375 Jackson Street
St. Paul, MN 55101-1853
(612) 290-3651

Mississippi
Norris Faust
Mississippi State ASCS
Office
6310 I-55 North
Jackson, MS 39236-4995
(601) 965-4300

Missouri
Brad Epperson
601 Parkdale Plaza Business
Loop
70 West
Suite 225
Columbia, MO 65203
(314) 876-0925

Montana
Bruce E. Nelson
P.O. Box 670
10 East Babcock
Room 557
Bozeman, MT 59715
(406) 587-6872

Nebraska
John Frank Johannsen
Nebraska State ASCS Office
P.O. Box 57975
7131 A Street
Lincoln, NE 68510
(402) 437-5581

Nevada
Wendell K. Newman
Nevada State ASCS Office
1755 East Plumb Lane
Suite 202
Reno, NV 89502-3200
(702) 784-5130

New Hampshire
James McConaka
USDA–New Hampshire
State ASCS Office
22 Bridge Street
Fourth Floor
P.O. Box 1398
Concord, NH 03302-1398
(603) 224-7941

New Jersey
Peter de Wilde
Mastoris Professional Plaza
163 Route 130
Building I
Suite E
Bordentown, NJ 08505-2249
(609) 224-7941

New Mexico
Charles Essary
New Mexico State ASCS
Office
P.O. Box 1458
Federal Building
Room 4430
517 Gold Avenue, SW
Albuquerque, NM 87103-1458
(505) 766-2472

New York
Floyd Duger
811 James H. Hanley
Federal Building
100 South Clinton Street
P.O. Box 7308
Syracuse, NY 13260-7308
(315) 423-5176

North Carolina
Samuel Colney
Federal Building
Suite 175
4407 Bland Road
Raleigh, NC 27609-6296
(919) 790-2957

North Dakota
Scott Stofferahn
North Dakota State ASCS
Office
1025 28th Street, SW
P.O. Box 3046
Fargo, ND 58108-3046
(701) 239-5224

Ohio
Steve Maurer
Federal Building
Room 540
200 North High Street
Columbus, OH 43215
(614) 469-6735

Oklahoma
Terry L. Peach
USDA Agriculture Center
Building
Suite 102
Farm Road and McFarland
Street
Stillwater, OK 74074-2653
(405) 624-4110

Oregon
Jack L. Sainsbury
Oregon State ASCS Office
P.O. Box 1300
Tualatin, OR 97062-1300
(503) 692-6830

Pennsylvania
William H. Baumgartner
One Credit Union Place
Suite 320
Harrisburg, PA 17101-2994
(717) 782-4547

Rhode Island
Paul E. Brule
Aldeic Complex
60 Quaker Lane
West Bay Office Complex
Suite 40
West Warwick, RI 02886
(401) 828-8232

South Carolina
Laurie C. Nelson
Strom Thurmond Mall
Suite 100
Columbia, SC 29201-2375
(803) 765-5186

South Dakota
Michael O'Connor
Federal Building
Room 208
200 Fourth Street, SW
Huron, SD 57350-2478
(605) 353-1092

Tennessee
Walter E. Head
United States Courthouse
Room 579
801 Broadway
Nashville, TN 37203-3816
(615) 736-5555

Texas
Harold B. Bennett
Texas State ASCS Office
P.O. Box 2900
College Station, TX 77841-
0001
(409) 260-9207

Utah
James L. Humlicek
Utah State ASCS Office
P.O. Box 11547
Salt Lake City, UT 84147
(801) 524-5013

Vermont
James L. Monahan
Executive Square Office
Building
346 Shelburne Street
Burlington, VT 05401-4495
(802) 658-2803

Virginia
Donald Davis
Culpeper Building
Suite 138
1606 Santa Rosa Road
Richmond, VA 23229
(804) 287-1500

Washington
Larry R. Albin
Washington State ASCS
Office
Rock Point Tower
Suite 568
316 West Boone Avenue
Spokane, WA 99201-2350
(509) 353-2307

West Virginia
Billy B. Burke
P.O. Box 1049
New Federal Building
Room 239
75 High Street
Morgantown, WV 26505-
7558
(304) 291-4351

Wisconsin
Doug Caruso
Wisconsin State ASCS Office
6515 Watts Road
Room 100
Madison, WI 53719-2797
(608) 264-5301

Wyoming
Thomas E. Trowbridge
951 Werner Court
Suite 130
Casper, WY 82601-1307
(307) 261-5231

Caribbean Area
Herberto J. Martinez
Caribbean Area ASCS Office
Cobran's Plaza
Suite 309
1609 Ponce DeLeon Avenue
Santurce, PR 00909-0001
(809) 729-6902

CONSERVATION RESERVE PROGRAM

Department of Agriculture
Agricultural Stabilization
and Conservation Service
(ASCS)
Conservation and
Environmental Protection
Division
P.O. Box 2415
Washington, DC 20013
(202) 720-6221

Description: Direct payments for specified use to individuals, partnerships, associations, corporations, estates, trusts, and legal entities. Cropland must be owned or operated for at least three years prior to close of annual sign-up period, unless acquired by will or succession, or, if the department determines that ownership was not acquired, to place land in conservation reserve.
$ Given: Payment range: $50–$50,000; average: $5,324
Application Information: Submit rental-rate-per-acre bid to local ASCS office.
Deadline: Submit rental-rate-per-acre bid to local ASCS office.
Contact: Your local, state, and/or regional ASCS office

Alabama
Robert D. Springe
P.O. Box 891
Montgomery, AL 36104-
0891
(205) 279-3500

Alaska
Karen O. Lee
Alaska State ASCS Office
800 West Evergreen
Suite 216
Palmer, AK 99654-6539
(907) 745-7982

Arizona
Robert A. Piceno
Arizona State ASCS Office
201 East Indianola
Suite 240
Phoenix, AZ 85012-3118
(602) 640-5200

Arkansas
Wayne Perryman
P.O. Box 2781
New Federal Building
Room 5428
700 West Capitol Street
Little Rock, AR 72201-3225
(501) 324-5220

California
John Smythe
California State ASCS Office
1303 J Street
Suite 300
Sacramento, CA 95814-
2916
(916) 551-1801

Colorado
John Stencel
Colorado State ASCS Office
655 Parfet Street
Room E 305
Third Floor
Lakewood, CO 80215
(303) 236-2866

Connecticut
Vincent R. Majchier
88 Day Hill Road
Windsor, CT 06095
(203) 285-8483

Delaware
William D. Clifton II
1201 College Park Drive
Suite A
Dover, DE 19901
(302) 678-4912

Florida
Harry McGlin
P.O. Box 141030
4440 NW 25th Place
Suite I
Gainesville, FL 32614-1030
(904) 372-8549

Georgia
Grady (Buck) Johnson
P.O. Box 1907
Federal Building
Room 102
344 East Hancock Avenue
Athens, GA 30601-2775
(404) 546-2266

Hawaii
Jo Ann Nakata
Hawaii State ASCS Office
300 Ala Moana Boulevard
Room 5106
P.O. Box 50008
Honolulu, HI 96850
(808) 551-2644

Idaho
Richard R. Rush
Idaho State ASCS Office
3220 Elder Street
Boise, ID 83705
(208) 334-1486

Illinois
Stephen Scates
P.O. Box 19273
3500 Wabash Avenue
Springfield, IL 62794-9273
(217) 492-4180

Indiana
Kent Yeager
Indiana State ASCS Office
5891 Lakeside Boulevard
Indianapolis, IN 46278
(317) 290-3030

Iowa
Tom Grau
10500 Buena Vista Court
Urbandale, IA 50322
(515) 254-1540, ext. 40

Kansas
Andrian J. Polansky
Kansas State ASCS Office
3600 Anderson Avenue
Manhattan, KS 66502-2511
(913) 539-3531

Kentucky
Hampton (Hoppy) Hinton
Kentucky State ASCS Office
771 Corporate Drive
Suite 100
Lexington, KY 40503-5478
(606) 224-7601

Louisiana
Willie F. Cooper
3737 Government Street
Alexandria, LA 71302-3395
(318) 473-7721

Maine
Arnold Roach
44 Stillwater Avenue
P.O. Box 406
Bangor, ME 04401-0406
(207) 990-9140

Maryland
James M. Voss
8335 East Guilford Road
Columbia, MD 21046
(410) 381-4550

Massachusetts
Charles A. Costa
451 West Street
Amherst, MA 01002-2953
(413) 256-0232

Michigan
Jim Byrum
300 Coolidge Road
Suite 100
East Lansing, MI 48823-6321
(517) 337-6659

Minnesota
Wally Sparby
Minnesota State ASCS
Office
400 Farm Credit Service
Building
375 Jackson Street
St. Paul, MN 55101-1853
(612) 290-3651

Mississippi
Norris Faust
Mississippi State ASCS
Office
6310 I-55 North
Jackson, MS 39236-4995
(601) 965-4300

Missouri
Brad Epperson
601 Parkdale Plaza Business
Loop
70 West
Suite 225
Columbia, MO 65203
(314) 876-0925

Montana
Bruce E. Nelson
P.O. Box 670
10 East Babcock
Room 557
Bozeman, MT 59715
(406) 587-6872

Nebraska
John Frank Johannsen
Nebraska State ASCS Office
P.O. Box 57975
7131 A Street
Lincoln, NE 68510
(402) 437-5581

Nevada
Wendell K. Newman
Nevada State ASCS Office
1755 East Plumb Lane
Suite 202
Reno, NV 89502-3200
(702) 784-5130

New Hampshire
James McConaka
USDA–New Hampshire
State ASCS Office
22 Bridge Street
Fourth Floor
P.O. Box 1398
Concord, NH 03302-1398
(603) 224-7941

New Jersey
Peter de Wilde
Mastoris Professional Plaza
163 Route 130
Building I
Suite E
Bordentown, NJ 08505-2249
(609) 224-7941

New Mexico
Charles Essary
New Mexico State ASCS
Office
P.O. Box 1458
Federal Building
Room 4430
517 Gold Avenue, SW
Albuquerque, NM 87103-
1458
(505) 766-2472

New York
Floyd Duger
811 James H. Hanley
Federal Building
100 South Clinton Street
P.O. Box 7308
Syracuse, NY 13260-7308
(315) 423-5176

North Carolina
Samuel Colney
Federal Building
Suite 175
4407 Bland Road
Raleigh, NC 27609-6296
(919) 790-2957

North Dakota
Scott Stofferahn
North Dakota State ASCS
Office
1025 28th Street, SW
P.O. Box 3046
Fargo, ND 58108-3046
(701) 239-5224

Ohio
Steve Maurer
Federal Building
200 North High Street
Room 540
Columbus, OH 43215
(614) 469-6735

Oklahoma
Terry L. Peach
USDA Agriculture Center
Building
Suite 102
Farm Road and McFarland
Street
Stillwater, OK 74074-2653
(405) 624-4110

Oregon
Jack L. Sainsbury
Oregon State ASCS Office
P.O. Box 1300
Tualatin, OR 97062-1300
(503) 692-6830

Pennsylvania
William H. Baumgartner
One Credit Union Place
Suite 320
Harrisburg, PA 17101-2994
(717) 782-4547

Rhode Island
Paul E. Brule
Aldeic Complex
60 Quaker Lane
West Bay Office Complex
Suite 40
West Warwick, RI 02886
(401) 828-8232

South Carolina
Laurie C. Nelson
Strom Thurmond Mall
Suite 100
Columbia, SC 29201-2375
(803) 765-5186

South Dakota
Michael O'Connor
Federal Building
Room 208
200 Fourth Street, SW
Huron, SD 57350-2478
(605) 353-1092

Tennessee
Walter E. Head
United States Courthouse
Room 579
801 Broadway
Nashville, TN 37203-3816
(615) 736-5555

Texas
Harold B. Bennett
Texas State ASCS Office
P.O. Box 2900
College Station, TX 77841-
0001
(409) 260-9207

Utah
James L. Humlicek
Utah State ASCS Office
P.O. Box 11547
Salt Lake City, UT 84147
(801) 524-5013

Vermont
James L. Monahan
Executive Square Office
Building
346 Shelburne Street
Burlington, VT 05401-4495
(802) 658-2803

Virginia
Donald Davis
Culpeper Building
Suite 138
1606 Santa Rosa Road
Richmond, VA 23229
(804) 287-1500

Washington
Larry R. Albin
Washington State ASCS
Office
Rock Point Tower
Suite 568
316 West Boone Avenue
Spokane, WA 99201-2350
(509) 353-2307

West Virginia
Billy B. Burke
P.O. Box 1049
New Federal Building
Room 239
75 High Street
Morgantown, WV 26505-
7558
(304) 291-4351

Wisconsin
Doug Caruso
Wisconsin State ASCS Office
6515 Watts Road
Room 100
Madison, WI 53719-2797
(608) 264-5301

Wyoming
Thomas E. Trowbridge
951 Werner Court
Suite 130
Casper, WY 82601-1307
(307) 261-5231

Caribbean Area
Herberto J. Martinez
Caribbean Area ASCS Office
Cobran's Plaza
Suite 309
1609 Ponce DeLeon Avenue
Santurce, PR 00909-0001
(809) 729-6902

COTTON PRODUCTION STABILIZATION

Department of Agriculture
Agricultural Stabilization
and Conservation Service
(ASCS)
P.O. Box 2415
Washington, DC 20013
(202) 447-6734

Description: Direct payments with unrestricted use are made
to owners, landlords, tenants, or sharecroppers on a farm
who meet the requirements announced by the Secretary.
Record of farming operation must be on file in the ASCS
county office.
$ Given: Up to $250,000 per person
Application Information: Write for guidelines.
Deadline: Not available
Contact: Your local ASCS office; if unlisted, contact your
state or regional ASCS office.

Alabama
Robert D. Springe
P.O. Box 891
Montgomery, AL 36104-
0891
(205) 279-3500

Alaska
Karen O. Lee
Alaska State ASCS Office
800 West Evergreen
Suite 216
Palmer, AK 99654-6539
(907) 745-7982

Arizona
Robert A. Piceno
Arizona State ASCS Office
201 East Indianola
Suite 240
Phoenix, AZ 85012-3118
(602) 640-5200

Arkansas
Wayne Perryman
P.O. Box 2781
New Federal Building
Room 5428
700 West Capitol Street
Little Rock, AR 72201-3225
(501) 324-5220

California
John Smythe
California State ASCS Office
1303 J Street
Suite 300
Sacramento, CA 95814-2916
(916) 551-1801

Colorado
John Stencel
Colorado State ASCS Office
655 Parfet Street
Room E 305
Third Floor
Lakewood, CO 80215
(303) 236-2866

Connecticut
Vincent R. Majchier
88 Day Hill Road
Windsor, CT 06095
(203) 285-8483

Delaware
William D. Clifton II
1201 College Park Drive
Suite A
Dover, DE 19901
(302) 678-4912

Florida
Harry McGlin
P.O. Box 141030
4440 NW 25th Place
Suite I
Gainesville, FL 32614-1030
(904) 372-8549

Georgia
Grady (Buck) Johnson
P.O. Box 1907
Federal Building
Room 102
344 East Hancock Avenue
Athens, GA 30601-2775
(404) 546-2266

Hawaii
Jo Ann Nakata
Hawaii State ASCS Office
300 Ala Moana Boulevard
Room 5106
P.O. Box 50008
Honolulu, HI 96850
(808) 551-2644

Idaho
Richard R. Rush
Idaho State ASCS Office
3220 Elder Street
Boise, ID 83705
(208) 334-1486

Illinois
Stephen Scates
P.O. Box 19273
3500 Wabash Avenue
Springfield, IL 62794-9273
(217) 492-4180

Indiana
Kent Yeager
Indiana State ASCS Office
5891 Lakeside Boulevard
Indianapolis, IN 46278
(317) 290-3030

Iowa
Tom Grau
10500 Buena Vista Court
Urbandale, IA 50322
(515) 254-1540, ext. 40

Kansas
Andrian J. Polansky
Kansas State ASCS Office
3600 Anderson Avenue
Manhattan, KS 66502-2511
(913) 539-3531

Kentucky
Hampton (Hoppy) Hinton
Kentucky State ASCS Office
771 Corporate Drive
Suite 100
Lexington, KY 40503-5478
(606) 224-7601

Louisiana
Willie F. Cooper
3737 Government Street
Alexandria, LA 71302-3395
(318) 473-7721

Maine
Arnold Roach
44 Stillwater Avenue
P.O. Box 406
Bangor, ME 04401-0406
(207) 990-9140

Maryland
James M. Voss
8335 East Guilford Road
Columbia, MD 21046
(410) 381-4550

Massachusetts
Charles A. Costa
451 West Street
Amherst, MA 01002-2953
(413) 256-0232

Michigan
Jim Byrum
300 Coolidge Road
Suite 100
East Lansing, MI 48823-6321
(517) 337-6659

Minnesota
Wally Sparby
Minnesota State ASCS Office
400 Farm Credit Service Building
375 Jackson Street
St. Paul, MN 55101-1853
(612) 290-3651

Mississippi
Norris Faust
Mississippi State ASCS Office
6310 I-55 North
Jackson, MS 39236-4995
(601) 965-4300

Missouri
Brad Epperson
601 Parkdale Plaza Business Loop
70 West
Suite 225
Columbia, MO 65203
(314) 876-0925

Montana
Bruce E. Nelson
P.O. Box 670
10 East Babcock
Room 557
Bozeman, MT 59715
(406) 587-6872

Nebraska
John Frank Johannsen
Nebraska State ASCS Office
P.O. Box 57975
7131 A Street
Lincoln, NE 68510
(402) 437-5581

Nevada
Wendell K. Newman
Nevada State ASCS Office
1755 East Plumb Lane
Suite 202
Reno, NV 89502-3200
(702) 784-5130

New Hampshire
James McConaka
USDA–New Hampshire
State ASCS Office
22 Bridge Street
Fourth Floor
P.O. Box 1398
Concord, NH 03302-1398
(603) 224-7941

New Jersey
Peter de Wilde
Mastoris Professional Plaza
163 Route 130
Building I
Suite E
Bordentown, NJ 08505-
2249
(609) 224-7941

New Mexico
Charles Essary
New Mexico State ASCS
Office
P.O. Box 1458
Federal Building
Room 4430
517 Gold Avenue, SW
Albuquerque, NM 87103-
1458
(505) 766-2472

New York
Floyd Duger
811 James H. Hanley
Federal Building
100 South Clinton Street
P.O. Box 7308
Syracuse, NY 13260-7308
(315) 423-5176

North Carolina
Samuel Colney
Federal Building
Suite 175
4407 Bland Road
Raleigh, NC 27609-6296
(919) 790-2957

North Dakota
Scott Stofferahn
North Dakota State ASCS
Office
1025 28th Street, SW
P.O. Box 3046
Fargo, ND 58108-3046
(701) 239-5224

Ohio
Steve Maurer
Federal Building
Room 540
200 North High Street
Columbus, OH 43215
(614) 469-6735

Oklahoma
Terry L. Peach
USDA Agriculture Center
Building
Suite 102
Farm Road and McFarland
Street
Stillwater, OK 74074-2653
(405) 624-4110

Oregon
Jack L. Sainsbury
Oregon State ASCS Office
P.O. Box 1300
Tualatin, OR 97062-1300
(503) 692-6830

Pennsylvania
William H. Baumgartner
One Credit Union Place
Suite 320
Harrisburg, PA 17101-2994
(717) 782-4547

Rhode Island
Paul E. Brule
Aldeic Complex
60 Quaker Lane
West Bay Office Complex
Suite 40
West Warwick, RI 02886
(401) 828-8232

South Carolina
Laurie C. Nelson
Strom Thurmond Mall
Suite 100
Columbia, SC 29201-2375
(803) 765-5186

South Dakota
Michael O'Connor
Federal Building
Room 208
200 Fourth Street, SW
Huron, SD 57350-2478
(605) 353-1092

Tennessee
Walter E. Head
United States Courthouse
Room 579
801 Broadway
Nashville, TN 37203-3816
(615) 736-5555

Texas
Harold B. Bennett
Texas State ASCS Office
P.O. Box 2900
College Station, TX 77841-0001
(409) 260-9207

Utah
James L. Humlicek
Utah State ASCS Office
P.O. Box 11547
Salt Lake City, UT 84147
(801) 524-5013

Vermont
James L. Monahan
Executive Square Office
Building
346 Shelburne Street
Burlington, VT 05401-4495
(802) 658-2803

Virginia
Donald Davis
Culpeper Building
Suite 138
1606 Santa Rosa Road
Richmond, VA 23229
(804) 287-1500

Washington
Larry R. Albin
Washington State ASCS
Office
Rock Point Tower
Suite 568
316 West Boone Avenue
Spokane, WA 99201-2350
(509) 353-2307

West Virginia
Billy B. Burke
P.O. Box 1049
New Federal Building
Room 239
75 High Street
Morgantown, WV 26505-7558
(304) 291-4351

Wisconsin
Doug Caruso
Wisconsin State ASCS Office
6515 Watts Road
Room 100
Madison, WI 53719-2797
(608) 264-5301

Wyoming
Thomas E. Trowbridge
951 Werner Court
Suite 130
Casper, WY 82601-1307
(307) 261-5231

Caribbean Area
Herberto J. Martinez
Caribbean Area ASCS Office
Cobran's Plaza
Suite 309
1609 Ponce DeLeon Avenue
Santurce, PR 00909-0001
(809) 729-6902

DAIRY INDEMNITY PROGRAM

Department of Agriculture
Agricultural Stabilization
and Conservation Service
(ASCS)
Emergency Operations and
Livestock Program Division
P.O. Box 2415
Washington, DC 20013
(202) 720-7673

Description: Direct payments with unrestricted use to dairy farmers whose milk has been removed from the market by a public agency because of residue of any violating substance in milk and to manufacturers of dairy products whose product has been removed from the market by a public agency because of pesticide residue.
$ Given: Payment range: $88–$95,000; average: $40,000
Application Information: Producers should file application for payment on Form ASCS-373 with local county ASCS office. Manufacturers must file information on cause and amount of loss with local county ASCS office.
Deadline: Claims must be filed by December 31 following the fiscal year in which the loss is incurred.
Contact: Your local ASCS office or, if not listed, the appropriate state and/or regional office.

Alabama
Robert D. Springe
P.O. Box 891
Montgomery, AL 36104-
0891
(205) 279-3500

Alaska
Karen O. Lee
Alaska State ASCS Office
800 West Evergreen
Suite 216
Palmer, AK 99654-6539
(907) 745-7982

Arizona
Robert A. Piceno
Arizona State ASCS Office
201 East Indianola
Suite 240
Phoenix, AZ 85012-3118
(602) 640-5200

Arkansas
Wayne Perryman
P.O. Box 2781
New Federal Building
Room 5428
700 West Capitol Street
Little Rock, AR 72201-3225
(501) 324-5220

California
John Smythe
California State ASCS Office
1303 J Street
Suite 300
Sacramento, CA 95814-
2916
(916) 551-1801

Colorado
John Stencel
Colorado State ASCS Office
655 Parfet Street
Room E 305
Third Floor
Lakewood, CO 80215
(303) 236-2866

Connecticut
Vincent R. Majchier
88 Day Hill Road
Windsor, CT 06095
(203) 285-8483

Delaware
William D. Clifton II
1201 College Park Drive
Suite A
Dover, DE 19901
(302) 678-4912

Florida
Harry McGlin
P.O. Box 141030
4440 NW 25th Place
Suite I
Gainesville, FL 32614-1030
(904) 372-8549

Georgia
Grady (Buck) Johnson
P.O. Box 1907
Federal Building
Room 102
344 East Hancock Avenue
Athens, GA 30601-2775
(404) 546-2266

Hawaii
Jo Ann Nakata
Hawaii State ASCS Office
300 Ala Moana Boulevard
Room 5106
P.O. Box 50008
Honolulu, HI 96850
(808) 551-2644

Idaho
Richard R. Rush
Idaho State ASCS Office
3220 Elder Street
Boise, ID 83705
(208) 334-1486

Illinois
Stephen Scates
P.O. Box 19273
3500 Wabash Avenue
Springfield, IL 62794-9273
(217) 492-4180

Indiana
Kent Yeager
Indiana State ASCS Office
5891 Lakeside Boulevard
Indianapolis, IN 46278
(317) 290-3030

Iowa
Tom Grau
10500 Buena Vista Court
Urbandale, IA 50322
(515) 254-1540, ext. 40

Kansas
Andrian J. Polansky
Kansas State ASCS Office
3600 Anderson Avenue
Manhattan, KS 66502-2511
(913) 539-3531

Kentucky
Hampton (Hoppy) Hinton
Kentucky State ASCS Office
771 Corporate Drive
Suite 100
Lexington, KY 40503-5478
(606) 224-7601

Louisiana
Willie F. Cooper
3737 Government Street
Alexandria, LA 71302-3395
(318) 473-7721

Maine
Arnold Roach
44 Stillwater Avenue
P.O. Box 406
Bangor, ME 04401-0406
(207) 990-9140

Maryland
James M. Voss
8335 East Guilford Road
Columbia, MD 21046
(410) 381-4550

Massachusetts
Charles A. Costa
451 West Street
Amherst, MA 01002-2953
(413) 256-0232

Michigan
Jim Byrum
300 Coolidge Road
Suite 100
East Lansing, MI 48823-6321
(517) 337-6659

Minnesota
Wally Sparby
Minnesota State ASCS
Office
400 Farm Credit Service
Building
375 Jackson Street
St. Paul, MN 55101-1853
(612) 290-3651

Mississippi
Norris Faust
Mississippi State ASCS
Office
6310 I-55 North
Jackson, MS 39236-4995
(601) 965-4300

Missouri
Brad Epperson
601 Parkdale Plaza Business
Loop
70 West
Suite 225
Columbia, MO 65203
(314) 876-0925

Montana
Bruce E. Nelson
P.O. Box 670
10 East Babcock
Room 557
Bozeman, MT 59715
(406) 587-6872

Nebraska
John Frank Johannsen
Nebraska State ASCS Office
P.O. Box 57975
7131 A Street
Lincoln, NE 68510
(402) 437-5581

Nevada
Wendell K. Newman
Nevada State ASCS Office
1755 East Plumb Lane
Suite 202
Reno, NV 89502-3200
(702) 784-5130

New Hampshire
James McConaka
USDA–New Hampshire
State ASCS Office
22 Bridge Street
Fourth Floor
P.O. Box 1398
Concord, NH 03302-1398
(603) 224-7941

New Jersey
Peter de Wilde
Mastoris Professional Plaza
163 Route 130
Building I
Suite E
Bordentown, NJ 08505-2249
(609) 224-7941

New Mexico
Charles Essary
New Mexico State ASCS
Office
P.O. Box 1458
Federal Building
Room 4430
517 Gold Avenue, SW
Albuquerque, NM 87103-1458
(505) 766-2472

New York
Floyd Duger
811 James H. Hanley
Federal Building
100 South Clinton Street
P.O. Box 7308
Syracuse, NY 13260-7308
(315) 423-5176

North Carolina
Samuel Colney
Federal Building
Suite 175
4407 Bland Road
Raleigh, NC 27609-6296
(919) 790-2957

North Dakota
Scott Stofferahn
North Dakota State ASCS
Office
1025 28th Street, SW
P.O. Box 3046
Fargo, ND 58108-3046
(701) 239-5224

Ohio
Steve Maurer
Federal Building
Room 540
200 North High Street
Columbus, OH 43215
(614) 469-6735

Oklahoma
Terry L. Peach
USDA Agriculture Center
Building
Suite 102
Farm Road and McFarland
Street
Stillwater, OK 74074-2653
(405) 624-4110

Oregon
Jack L. Sainsbury
Oregon State ASCS Office
P.O. Box 1300
Tualatin, OR 97062-1300
(503) 692-6830

Pennsylvania
William H. Baumgartner
One Credit Union Place
Suite 320
Harrisburg, PA 17101-2994
(717) 782-4547

Rhode Island
Paul E. Brule
Aldeic Complex
60 Quaker Lane
West Bay Office Complex
Suite 40
West Warwick, RI 02886
(401) 828-8232

South Carolina
Laurie C. Nelson
Strom Thurmond Mall
Suite 100
Columbia, SC 29201-2375
(803) 765-5186

South Dakota
Michael O'Connor
Federal Building
Room 208
200 Fourth Street, SW
Huron, SD 57350-2478
(605) 353-1092

Tennessee
Walter E. Head
United States Courthouse
Room 579
801 Broadway
Nashville, TN 37203-3816
(615) 736-5555

Texas
Harold B. Bennett
Texas State ASCS Office
P.O. Box 2900
College Station, TX 77841-
0001
(409) 260-9207

Utah
James L. Humlicek
Utah State ASCS Office
P.O. Box 11547
Salt Lake City, UT 84147
(801) 524-5013

Vermont
James L. Monahan
Executive Square Office
Building
346 Shelburne Street
Burlington, VT 05401-4495
(802) 658-2803

Virginia
Donald Davis
Culpeper Building
Suite 138
1606 Santa Rosa Road
Richmond, VA 23229
(804) 287-1500

Washington
Larry R. Albin
Washington State ASCS
Office
Rock Point Tower
Suite 568
316 West Boone Avenue
Spokane, WA 99201-2350
(509) 353-2307

West Virginia
Billy B. Burke
P.O. Box 1049
New Federal Building
Room 239
75 High Street
Morgantown, WV 26505-
7558
(304) 291-4351

Wisconsin
Doug Caruso
Wisconsin State ASCS Office
6515 Watts Road
Room 100
Madison, WI 53719-2797
(608) 264-5301

Wyoming
Thomas E. Trowbridge
951 Werner Court
Suite 130
Casper, WY 82601-1307
(307) 261-5231

Caribbean Area
Herberto J. Martinez
Caribbean Area ASCS Office
Cobran's Plaza
Suite 309
1609 Ponce DeLeon Avenue
Santurce, PR 00909-0001
(809) 729-6902

ECONOMIC INJURY DISASTER LOANS

**Small Business
Administration (SBA)**
Office of Disaster Assistance
409 Third Street, SW
Washington, DC 20416
(202) 205-6734

Description: Direct, guaranteed, and insured loans for small
businesses or agricultural cooperatives that are victims of
drought, to pay liabilities from disaster or to provide
working capital to continue operations until conditions
return to normal.
$ Given: Direct loans: up to $500,000; average: $70,667
Application Information: Write for guidelines.
Deadline: Not available
Contact: Your state and/or regional Small Business
Administration office.

Alabama
1375 Peachtree Street, NE
Fifth Floor
Atlanta, GA 30367-8102
(404) 347-2797

Alaska
2601 Fourth Avenue
Room 440
Seattle, WA 98121-1273
(206) 553-1273

Arizona
71 Stevenson Street, 20th
Floor
San Francisco, CA 94105-
2939
(415) 744-6402

Arkansas
8625 King George Drive
Building C
Dallas, TX 75235-3391
(214) 767-7633

California
71 Stevenson Street
20th Floor
San Francisco, CA 94105-
2939
(415) 744-6402

Colorado
633 17th Street
Seventh Floor
Denver, CO 80202
(303) 294-7186

Connecticut
55 Federal Street
Ninth Floor
Boston, MA 02110
(617) 451-2023

Delaware
475 Allendale Road
Suite 201
King of Prussia, PA 19406
(215) 962-3700

Florida
1375 Peachtree Street, NE
Fifth Floor
Atlanta, GA 30367-8102
(404) 347-2797

Georgia
1375 Peachtree Street, NE
Fifth Floor
Atlanta, GA 30367-8102
(404) 347-2797

Hawaii
71 Stevenson Street
20th Floor
San Francisco, CA 94105-
2939
(415) 744-6402

Idaho
2601 Fourth Avenue
Room 440
Seattle, WA 98121-1273
(206) 553-1273

Illinois
Federal Building
300 South Riverside Plaza
Room 1975
Chicago, IL 60606-6611
(312) 353-5000

Indiana
Federal Building
300 South Riverside Plaza
Room 1975
Chicago, IL 60606-6611
(312) 353-5000

Iowa
911 Walnut Street
13th Floor
Kansas City, MO 64106
(816) 426-3608

Kansas
911 Walnut Street
13th Floor
Kansas City, MO 64106
(816) 426-3608

Kentucky
1375 Peachtree Street, NE
Fifth Floor
Atlanta, GA 30367-8102
(404) 347-2797

Louisiana
8625 King George Drive
Building C
Dallas, TX 75235-3391
(214) 767-7633

Maine
155 Federal Street
Ninth Floor
Boston, MA 02110
(617) 451-2023

Maryland
475 Allendale Road
Suite 201
King of Prussia, PA 19406
(215) 962-3700

Massachusetts
155 Federal Street
Ninth Floor
Boston, MA 02110
(617) 451-2023

Michigan
Federal Building
300 South Riverside Plaza
Room 1975
Chicago, IL 60606-6611
(312) 353-5000

Minnesota
Federal Building
300 South Riverside Plaza
Room 1975
Chicago, IL 60606-6611
(312) 353-5000

Mississippi
1375 Peachtree Street, NE
Fifth Floor
Atlanta, GA 30367-8102
(404) 347-2797

Missouri
911 Walnut Street
13th Floor
Kansas City, MO 64106
(816) 426-3608

Montana
633 17th Street
Seventh Floor
Denver, CO 80202
(303) 294-7186

Nebraska
911 Walnut Street
13th Floor
Kansas City, MO 64106
(816) 426-3608

Nevada
71 Stevenson Street
20th Floor
San Francisco, CA 94105-
29390
(415) 744-6402

New Hampshire
155 Federal Street
Ninth Floor
Boston, MA 02110
(617) 451-2023

New Jersey
26 Federal Plaza
Room 31-08
New York, NY 10278
(212) 264-1450

New Mexico
8625 King George Drive
Building C
Dallas, TX 75235-3391
(214) 767-7633

New York
26 Federal Plaza
Room 31-08
New York, NY 10278
(212) 264-7772

North Carolina
1375 Peachtree Street, NE
Fifth Floor
Atlanta, GA 30367-8102
(404) 347-2797

North Dakota
633 17th Street
Seventh Floor
Denver, CO 80202
(303) 294-7186

Ohio
Federal Building
300 South Riverside Plaza
Room 1975
Chicago, IL 60606-6611
(312) 353-5000

Oklahoma
8625 King George Drive
Building C
Dallas, TX 75235-3391
(214) 767-7633

Oregon
2601 Fourth Avenue
Room 440
Seattle, WA 98121-1273
(206) 553-1273

Pacific Islands
71 Stevenson Street
20th Floor
San Francisco, CA 94105-
2939
(415) 744-6402

Pennsylvania
475 Allendale Road
Suite 201
King of Prussia, PA 19406
(215) 962-3700

Puerto Rico
26 Federal Plaza
Room 31-08
New York, NY 10278
(212) 264-7772

Rhode Island
155 Federal Street
Ninth Floor
Boston, MA 02110
(617) 451-2023

South Carolina
1375 Peachtree Street, NE
Fifth Floor
Atlanta, GA 30367-8102
(404) 347-2797

South Dakota
633 17th Street
Seventh Floor
Denver, CO 80202
(303) 294-7186

Tennessee
1375 Peachtree Street, NE
Fifth Floor
Atlanta, GA 30367-8102
(404) 347-2797

Texas
8625 King George Drive
Building C
Dallas, TX 75235-3391
(214) 767-7633

Utah
633 17th Street
Seventh floor
Denver, CO 80202
(303) 294-7186

Vermont
155 Federal Street
Ninth Floor
Boston, MA 02110
(617) 451-2023

Virginia
475 Allendale Road
Suite 201
King of Prussia, PA 19406
(215) 962-3700

Virgin Islands
26 Federal Plaza
Room 31-08
New York, NY 10278
(212) 264-7772

Washington
2601 Fourth Avenue
Room 440
Seattle, WA 98121-1273
(206) 553-1273

West Virginia
475 Allendale Road
Suite 201
King of Prussia, PA 19406
(215) 962-3700

Wisconsin
Federal Building
300 South Riverside Plaza
Room 1975
Chicago, IL 60606-6611
(312) 353-5000

Wyoming
633 17th Street
Seventh Floor
Denver, CO 80202
(303) 294-7186

EMERGENCY CONSERVATION PROGRAM

Department of Agriculture
Agricultural Stabilization
and Conservation Service
(ASCS)
P.O. Box 2415
Washington, DC 20013
(202) 720-6221

Description: Direct payments for specified use to any owner, landlord, tenant, or sharecropper on a farm or ranch (including associated groups) who agrees to bear part of the cost of an approved conservation practice in a disaster area. Proof of contribution to cost of performing conservation practice must be demonstrated.
$ Given: Payment range: $50–$64,000; average: $1,780
Application Information: File Form ACP-245, for cost sharing, at county ASCS office for county in which the land is located.
Deadline: Not available
Contact: Your local ASCS office or, if not listed, the appropriate state and/or regional office.

Alabama
Robert D. Springe
P.O. Box 891
Montgomery, AL 36104-
0891
(205) 279-3500

Alaska
Karen O. Lee
Alaska State ASCS Office
800 West Evergreen
Suite 216
Palmer, AK 99654-6539
(907) 745-7982

Arizona
Robert A. Piceno
Arizona State ASCS Office
201 East Indianola
Suite 240
Phoenix, AZ 85012-3118
(602) 640-5200

Arkansas
Wayne Perryman
P.O. Box 2781
New Federal Building
Room 5428
700 West Capitol Street
Little Rock, AR 72201-3225
(501) 324-5220

California
John Smythe
California State ASCS Office
1303 J Street
Suite 300
Sacramento, CA 95814-
2916
(916) 551-1801

Colorado
John Stencel
Colorado State ASCS Office
655 Parfet Street
Room E 305
Third Floor
Lakewood, CO 80215
(303) 236-2866

Connecticut
Vincent R. Majchier
88 Day Hill Road
Windsor, CT 06095
(203) 285-8483

Delaware
William D. Clifton II
1201 College Park Drive
Suite A
Dover, DE 19901
(302) 678-4912

Florida
Harry McGlin
P.O. Box 141030
4440 NW 25th Place
Suite I
Gainesville, FL 32614-1030
(904) 372-8549

Georgia
Grady (Buck) Johnson
P.O. Box 1907
Federal Building
Room 102
344 East Hancock Avenue
Athens, GA 30601-2775
(404) 546-2266

Hawaii
Jo Ann Nakata
Hawaii State ASCS Office
300 Ala Moana Boulevard
Room 5106
P.O. Box 50008
Honolulu, HI 96850
(808) 551-2644

Idaho
Richard R. Rush
Idaho State ASCS Office
3220 Elder Street
Boise, ID 83705
(208) 334-1486

Illinois
Stephen Scates
P.O. Box 19273
3500 Wabash Avenue
Springfield, IL 62794-9273
(217) 492-4180

Indiana
Kent Yeager
Indiana State ASCS Office
5891 Lakeside Boulevard
Indianapolis, IN 46278
(317) 290-3030

Iowa
Tom Grau
10500 Buena Vista Court
Urbandale, IA 50322
(515) 254-1540, ext. 40

Kansas
Andrian J. Polansky
Kansas State ASCS Office
3600 Anderson Avenue
Manhattan, KS 66502-2511
(913) 539-3531

Kentucky
Hampton (Hoppy) Hinton
Kentucky State ASCS Office
771 Corporate Drive
Suite 100
Lexington, KY 40503-5478
(606) 224-7601

Louisiana
Willie F. Cooper
3737 Government Street
Alexandria, LA 71302-3395
(318) 473-7721

Maine
Arnold Roach
44 Stillwater Avenue
P.O. Box 406
Bangor, ME 04401-0406
(207) 990-9140

Maryland
James M. Voss
8335 East Guilford Road
Columbia, MD 21046
(410) 381-4550

Massachusetts
Charles A. Costa
451 West Street
Amherst, MA 01002-2953
(413) 256-0232

Michigan
Jim Byrum
300 Coolidge Road
Suite 100
East Lansing, MI 48823-6321
(517) 337-6659

Minnesota
Wally Sparby
Minnesota State ASCS
Office
400 Farm Credit Service
Building
375 Jackson Street
St. Paul, MN 55101-1853
(612) 290-3651

Mississippi
Norris Faust
Mississippi State ASCS
Office
6310 I-55 North
Jackson, MS 39236-4995
(601) 965-4300

Missouri
Brad Epperson
601 Parkdale Plaza Business
Loop
70 West
Suite 225
Columbia, MO 65203
(314) 876-0925

Montana
Bruce E. Nelson
P.O. Box 670
10 East Babcock
Room 557
Bozeman, MT 59715
(406) 587-6872

Nebraska
John Frank Johannsen
Nebraska State ASCS Office
P.O. Box 57975
7131 A Street
Lincoln, NE 68510
(402) 437-5581

Nevada
Wendell K. Newman
Nevada State ASCS Office
1755 East Plumb Lane
Suite 202
Reno, NV 89502-3200
(702) 784-5130

New Hampshire
James McConaka
USDA–New Hampshire
State ASCS Office
22 Bridge Street
Fourth Floor
P.O. Box 1398
Concord, NH 03302-1398
(603) 224-7941

New Jersey
Peter de Wilde
Mastoris Professional Plaza
163 Route 130
Building I
Suite E
Bordentown, NJ 08505-2249
(609) 224-7941

New Mexico
Charles Essary
New Mexico State ASCS
Office
P.O. Box 1458
Federal Building
Room 4430
517 Gold Avenue, SW
Albuquerque, NM 87103-1458
(505) 766-2472

New York
Floyd Duger
811 James H. Hanley
Federal Building
100 South Clinton Street
P.O. Box 7308
Syracuse, NY 13260-7308
(315) 423-5176

North Carolina
Samuel Colney
Federal Building
Suite 175
4407 Bland Road
Raleigh, NC 27609-6296
(919) 790-2957

North Dakota
Scott Stofferahn
North Dakota State ASCS
Office
1025 28th Street, SW
P.O. Box 3046
Fargo, ND 58108-3046
(701) 239-5224

Ohio
Steve Maurer
Federal Building
Room 540
200 North High Street
Columbus, OH 43215
(614) 469-6735

Oklahoma
Terry L. Peach
USDA Agriculture Center
Building
Suite 102
Farm Road and McFarland
Street
Stillwater, OK 74074-2653
(405) 624-4110

Oregon
Jack L. Sainsbury
Oregon State ASCS Office
P.O. Box 1300
Tualatin, OR 97062-1300
(503) 692-6830

Pennsylvania
William H. Baumgartner
One Credit Union Place
Suite 320
Harrisburg, PA 17101-2994
(717) 782-4547

Rhode Island
Paul E. Brule
Aldeic Complex
60 Quaker Lane
West Bay Office Complex
Suite 40
West Warwick, RI 02886
(401) 828-8232

South Carolina
Laurie C. Nelson
Strom Thurmond Mall
Suite 100
Columbia, SC 29201-2375
(803) 765-5186

South Dakota
Michael O'Connor
Federal Building
Room 208
200 Fourth Street, SW
Huron, SD 57350-2478
(605) 353-1092

Tennessee
Walter E. Head
United States Courthouse
Room 579
801 Broadway
Nashville, TN 37203-3816
(615) 736-5555

Texas
Harold B. Bennett
Texas State ASCS Office
P.O. Box 2900
College Station, TX 77841-
0001
(409) 260-9207

Utah
James L. Humlicek
Utah State ASCS Office
P.O. Box 11547
Salt Lake City, UT 84147
(801) 524-5013

Vermont
James L. Monahan
Executive Square Office
Building
346 Shelburne Street
Burlington, VT 05401-4495
(802) 658-2803

Virginia
Donald Davis
Culpeper Building
Suite 138
1606 Santa Rosa Road
Richmond, VA 23229
(804) 287-1500

Washington
Larry R. Albin
Washington State ASCS
Office
Rock Point Tower
Suite 568
316 West Boone Avenue
Spokane, WA 99201-2350
(509) 353-2307

West Virginia
Billy B. Burke
P.O. Box 1049
New Federal Building
Room 239
75 High Street
Morgantown, WV 26505-
7558
(304) 291-4351

Wisconsin
Doug Caruso
Wisconsin State ASCS Office
6515 Watts Road
Room 100
Madison, WI 53719-2797
(608) 264-5301

Wyoming
Thomas E. Trowbridge
951 Werner Court
Suite 130
Casper, WY 82601-1307
(307) 261-5231

Caribbean Area
Herberto J. Martinez
Caribbean Area ASCS Office
Cobran's Plaza
Suite 309
1609 Ponce DeLeon Avenue
Santurce, PR 00909-0001
(809) 729-6902

EMERGENCY LIVESTOCK ASSISTANCE

Department of Agriculture
Agricultural Stabilization
and Conservation Service
(ASCS)
Emergency Operation and
Livestock Program
P.O. Box 2415
Washington, DC 20013
(202) 720-5621

Description: Direct payments with unrestricted use to
individuals, farm cooperatives, private domestic
corporations, partnerships or joint ventures, Indian tribes, or
Indian organizations. Must have annual gross revenue of less
than $2.5 million.
$ Given: Payment range: $10–$50,000; average: $3,411
Application Information: Not available
Deadline: Not available
Contact: Your local, state, and/or regional ASCS office

Alabama
Robert D. Springe
P.O. Box 891
Montgomery, AL
36104-0891
(205) 279-3500

Alaska
Karen O. Lee
Alaska State ASCS Office
800 West Evergreen
Suite 216
Palmer, AK 99654-6539
(907) 745-7982

Arizona
Robert A. Piceno
Arizona State ASCS Office
201 East Indianola
Suite 240
Phoenix, AZ 85012-3118
(602) 640-5200

Arkansas
Wayne Perryman
P.O. Box 2781
New Federal Building
Room 5428
700 West Capitol Street
Little Rock, AR 72201-3225
(501) 324-5220

California
John Smythe
California State ASCS Office
1303 J Street
Suite 300
Sacramento, CA 95814-
2916
(916) 551-1801

Colorado
John Stencel
Colorado State ASCS Office
655 Parfet Street
Room E 305
Third Floor
Lakewood, CO 80215
(303) 236-2866

Connecticut
Vincent R. Majchier
88 Day Hill Road
Windsor, CT 06095
(203) 285-8483

Delaware
William D. Clifton II
1201 College Park Drive
Suite A
Dover, DE 19901
(302) 678-4912

Florida
Harry McGlin
P.O. Box 141030
4440 NW 25th Place
Suite I
Gainesville, FL 32614-1030
(904) 372-8549

Georgia
Grady (Buck) Johnson
P.O. Box 1907
Federal Building
Room 102
344 East Hancock Avenue
Athens, GA 30601-2775
(404) 546-2266

Hawaii
Jo Ann Nakata
Hawaii State ASCS Office
300 Ala Moana Boulevard
Room 5106
P.O. Box 50008
Honolulu, HI 96850
(808) 551-2644

Idaho
Richard R. Rush
Idaho State ASCS Office
3220 Elder Street
Boise, ID 83705
(208) 334-1486

Illinois
Stephen Scates
P.O. Box 19273
3500 Wabash Avenue
Springfield, IL 62794-9273
(217) 492-4180

Indiana
Kent Yeager
Indiana State ASCS Office
5891 Lakeside Boulevard
Indianapolis, IN 46278
(317) 290-3030

Iowa
Tom Grau
10500 Buena Vista Court
Urbandale, IA 50322
(515) 254-1540, ext. 40

Kansas
Andrian J. Polansky
Kansas State ASCS Office
3600 Anderson Avenue
Manhattan, KS 66502-2511
(913) 539-3531

Kentucky
Hampton (Hoppy) Hinton
Kentucky State ASCS Office
771 Corporate Drive
Suite 100
Lexington, KY 40503-5478
(606) 224-7601

Louisiana
Willie F. Cooper
3737 Government Street
Alexandria, LA 71302-3395
(318) 473-7721

Maine
Arnold Roach
44 Stillwater Avenue
P.O. Box 406
Bangor, ME 04401-0406
(207) 990-9140

Maryland
James M. Voss
8335 East Guilford Road
Columbia, MD 21046
(410) 381-4550

Massachusetts
Charles A. Costa
451 West Street
Amherst, MA 01002-2953
(413) 256-0232

Michigan
Jim Byrum
300 Coolidge Road
Suite 100
East Lansing, MI 48823-6321
(517) 337-6659

Minnesota
Wally Sparby
Minnesota State ASCS Office
400 Farm Credit Service Building
375 Jackson Street
St. Paul, MN 55101-1853
(612) 290-3651

Mississippi
Norris Faust
Mississippi State ASCS Office
6310 I-55 North
Jackson, MS 39236-4995
(601) 965-4300

Missouri
Brad Epperson
601 Parkdale Plaza Business Loop
70 West
Suite 225
Columbia, MO 65203
(314) 876-0925

Montana
Bruce E. Nelson
P.O. Box 670
10 East Babcock
Room 557
Bozeman, MT 59715
(406) 587-6872

Nebraska
John Frank Johannsen
Nebraska State ASCS Office
P.O. Box 57975
7131 A Street
Lincoln, NE 68510
(402) 437-5581

Nevada
Wendell K. Newman
Nevada State ASCS Office
1755 East Plumb Lane
Suite 202
Reno, NV 89502-3200
(702) 784-5130

New Hampshire
James McConaka
USDA–New Hampshire State ASCS Office
22 Bridge Street
Fourth Floor
P.O. Box 1398
Concord, NH 03302-1398
(603) 224-7941

New Jersey
Peter de Wilde
Mastoris Professional Plaza
163 Route 130
Building I
Suite E
Bordentown, NJ 08505-2249
(609) 224-7941

New Mexico
Charles Essary
New Mexico State ASCS
Office
P.O. Box 1458
Federal Building
Room 4430
517 Gold Avenue, SW
Albuquerque, NM 87103-
1458
(505) 766-2472

New York
Floyd Duger
811 James H. Hanley
Federal Building
100 South Clinton Street
P.O. Box 7308
Syracuse, NY 13260-7308
(315) 423-5176

North Carolina
Samuel Colney
Federal Building
Suite 175
4407 Bland Road
Raleigh, NC 27609-6296
(919) 790-2957

North Dakota
Scott Stofferahn
North Dakota State ASCS
Office
1025 28th Street, SW
P.O. Box 3046
Fargo, ND 58108-3046
(701) 239-5224

Ohio
Steve Maurer
Federal Building
Room 540
200 North High Street
Columbus, OH 43215
(614) 469-6735

Oklahoma
Terry L. Peach
USDA Agriculture Center
Building
Suite 102
Farm Road and McFarland
Street
Stillwater, OK 74074-2653
(405) 624-4110

Oregon
Jack L. Sainsbury
Oregon State ASCS Office
P.O. Box 1300
Tualatin, OR 97062-1300
(503) 692-6830

Pennsylvania
William H. Baumgartner
One Credit Union Place
Suite 320
Harrisburg, PA 17101-2994
(717) 782-4547

Rhode Island
Paul E. Brule
Aldeic Complex
60 Quaker Lane
West Bay Office Complex
Suite 40
West Warwick, RI 02886
(401) 828-8232

South Carolina
Laurie C. Nelson
Strom Thurmond Mall
Suite 100
Columbia, SC 29201-2375
(803) 765-5186

South Dakota
Michael O'Connor
Federal Building
Room 208
200 Fourth Street, SW
Huron, SD 57350-2478
(605) 353-1092

Tennessee
Walter E. Head
United States Courthouse
Room 579
801 Broadway
Nashville, TN 37203-3816
(615) 736-5555

Texas
Harold B. Bennett
Texas State ASCS Office
P.O. Box 2900
College Station, TX 77841-
0001
(409) 260-9207

Utah
James L. Humlicek
Utah State ASCS Office
P.O. Box 11547
Salt Lake City, UT 84147
(801) 524-5013

Vermont
James L. Monahan
Executive Square Office
Building
346 Shelburne Street
Burlington, VT 05401-4495
(802) 658-2803

Virginia
Donald Davis
Culpeper Building
Suite 138
1606 Santa Rosa Road
Richmond, VA 23229
(804) 287-1500

Washington
Larry R. Albin
Washington State ASCS
Office
Rock Point Tower
Suite 568
316 West Boone Avenue
Spokane, WA 99201-2350
(509) 353-2307

West Virginia
Billy B. Burke
P.O. Box 1049
New Federal Building
Room 239
75 High Street
Morgantown, WV 26505-
7558
(304) 291-4351

Wisconsin
Doug Caruso
Wisconsin State ASCS Office
6515 Watts Road
Room 100
Madison, WI 53719-2797
(608) 264-5301

Wyoming
Thomas E. Trowbridge
951 Werner Court
Suite 130
Casper, WY 82601-1307
(307) 261-5231

Caribbean Area
Herberto J. Martinez
Caribbean Area ASCS Office
Cobran's Plaza
Suite 309
1609 Ponce DeLeon Avenue
Santurce, PR 00909-0001
(809) 729-6902

EMERGENCY LOANS

Department of Agriculture
Farmers Home
Administration (FmHA)
Washington, DC 20250
(202) 720-1632

Description: Direct loans to farmers, ranchers, or aquaculture operators. Must be a U.S. citizen or legal resident alien who was conducting a farming operation at the time of a designated natural disaster and suffered substantial crop loss or physical property damages.
$ Given: Loan range: $500–$500,000
Application Information: Application Form FmHA 410-1 provided by the FmHA must be presented with supporting information to your FmHA county office; FmHA personnel will assist applicants in completing forms.
Deadline: Eight months from date of declaration for losses; consult your local FmHA office.
Contact: Consult your local telephone directory under U.S. Government, Department of Agriculture, for your FmHA county office number or contact your FmHA state office.

Alabama
Sterling Center
Suite 601
4121 Carmichael Road
Montgomery, AL 36106-
3683
(205) 279-3400

Alaska
634 South Bailey
Suite 103
Palmer, AK 99645
(907) 745-2176

Arizona
3003 North Central Avenue
Suite 900
Phoenix, AZ 85012
(602) 280-8700

Arkansas
700 West Capitol
P.O. Box 2778
Little Rock, AR 72203
(501) 324-6281

California
194 West Main Street
Suite F
Woodland, CA 95695-2915
(916) 669-2000

Colorado
655 Parfet Street
Room 31-08
Lakewood, CO 80215
(303) 236-2801

Connecticut
451 West Street
Amherst, MA 01002
(413) 253-4300

Delaware
4611 South Dupont
Highway
P.O. Box 400
Camden, DE 19934-9998
(302) 697-4300

District of Columbia
4611 South Dupont
Highway
P.O. Box 400
Camden, DE 19934-9998
(302) 697-4300

Florida
Federal Building
4440 NW 25th Place
P.O. Box 147010
Gainesville, FL 32614-7010
(904) 338-3400

Georgia
355 East Hancock Avenue
Stephens Federal Building
Athens, GA 30610
(706) 546-2152

Guam
Department of Agriculture
14th Street and
Independence Avenue, SW
Washington, DC 20250
(202) 720-1632

Hawaii
Federal Building
Room 311
154 Waianuenue Avenue
Hilo, HI 96720
(808) 933-3000

Idaho
3232 Elder Street
Boise, ID 83705
(208) 334-1301

Illinois
Illini Plaza
Suite 103
1817 South Neil street
Champaign, IL 61820
(217) 398-5235

Indiana
5975 Lakeside Boulevard
Indianapolis, IN 46278
(317) 290-3100

Iowa
Federal Building
Room 873
210 Walnut Street
Des Moines, IA 50309
(515) 284-4663

Kansas
1201 SW Summit Executive
Court
P.O. Box 4653
Topeka, KS 66604
(913) 271-2700

Kentucky
771 Corporate Drive
Suite 200
Lexington, KY 40503
(606) 224-7300

Louisiana
3727 Government Street
Alexandria, LA 71302
(318) 473-7920

Maine
444 Stillwater Avenue
Suite 2
P.O. Box 405
Bangor, ME 04402-0405
(207) 990-9106

Maryland
4611 South Dupont
Highway
P.O. Box 400
Camden, DE 19934-9998
(302) 697-4300

Massachusetts
451 West Street
Amherst, MA 01002
(413) 253-4300

Michigan
3001 Coolidge Road
Suite 200
East Lansing, MI 48823
(517) 337-6635

Minnesota
410 Farm Credit Service
Building
375 Jackson Street
St. Paul, MN 55101
(612) 290-3842

Mississippi
Federal Building
Suite 831
100 West Capitol
Jackson, MS 39269
(601) 965-4316

Missouri
601 Business Loop
70 West Parkade Center
Suite 235
Columbia, MO 65203
(314) 768-0976

Montana
900 Technology Boulevard
Suite B
P.O. Box 850
Bozeman, MT 59771
(406) 585-2580

Nebraska
Federal Building
Room 308
100 Centennial Mall
Lincoln, NE 68508
(402) 437-5551

Nevada
1390 South Curry Street
Carson City, NV 89703-
5405
(702) 887-1222

New Hampshire
City Center
89 Main Street
Third Floor
Montpelier, VT 05602
(802) 223-6001

New Jersey
Tarnsfield Plaza
Suite 22
1016 Woodlane Road
Mt. Holly, NJ 08060
(609) 265-3600

New Mexico
Federal Building
Room 3414
517 Gold Avenue, SW
Albuquerque, NM 87102
(505) 766-2462

New York
Federal Building
100 South Clinton Street
Room 871
Syracuse, NY 13261-7318
(315) 423-5290

North Carolina
4405 South Bland Road
Suite 260
Raleigh, NC 27609
(919) 790-2731

North Dakota
Federal Building
Room 208
Third and Rosser
P.O. Box 1737
Bismarck, ND 59502
(701) 250-4781

Ohio
Federal Building
Room 507
200 North High Street
Columbus, OH 43215
(614) 469-5606

Oklahoma
USDA Agricultural Center
Office Building
Stillwater, OK 74074
(405) 624-4250

Oregon
Federal Building
Room 1590
1220 SW Third Avenue
Portland, OR 97204
(503) 326-2731

Pennsylvania
One Credit Union Plaza
Suite 330
Harrisburg, PA 17110-2996
(717) 782-4476

Puerto Rico
New San Juan Center
Building
Room 501
159 Carlos E. Chardon
Street
G.P.O. Box 6106G
Hato Rey, PR 00918-5481
(809) 766-5095

Rhode Island
451 West Street
Amherst, MA 01002
(413) 253-4300

South Carolina
Strom Thurmond Federal
Building
Room 1007
1835 Assembly Street
Columbia, SC 28201
(803) 765-5163

South Dakota
Huron Federal Building
Room 308
200 Fourth Street, SW
Huron, SD 57350
(605) 353-1430

Tennessee
3322 West End Avenue
Suite 300
Nashville, TN 37203-1071
(615) 783-1308

Texas
Federal Building
Suite 102
101 South Main
Temple, TX 76501
(817) 774-1301

Utah
Federal Building
Room 5438
125 South State Street
Salt Lake City, UT 84138
(801) 524-4063

Vermont
City Center
89 Main Street
Third Floor
Montpelier, VT 05602
(802) 828-6001

Virginia
Culpeper Building
Suite 238
1606 Santa Rosa Road
Richmond, VA 23229
(804) 828-1550

Virgin Islands
City Center
89 Main Street
Third Floor
Montpelier, VT 05602
(802) 828-6001

Washington
Federal Building
Room 319
P.O. Box 2427
Wenatchee, WA 98807
(509) 664-0240

West Virginia
75 High Street
P.O. Box 678
Morgantown, WV 26505
(304) 291-4791

Wisconsin
4949 Kirschling Court
Stevens Point, WI 54481
(715) 345-7625

Wyoming
Federal Building
Room 1005
100 East B Street
P.O. Box 820
Casper, WY 82602
(307) 261-5271

FARM LABOR HOUSING LOANS AND GRANTS

Department of Agriculture
Farmers Home
Administration (FmHA)
Multifamily Housing
Processing Division
Washington, DC 20250
(202) 720-1604

Description: Project grants and guaranteed and insured loans for farmers; grants given only when there is a pressing need and when it is doubtful that facilities could be provided unless grant assistance is available.
$ Given: Initial grant range: $135,000–$2 million; initial individual loan range: $20,000–$200,000; initial organizational loan range: $165,000–$670,000
Application Information: Write for guidelines.
Deadline: None
Contact: Consult your local telephone directory under U.S. Government, Department of Agriculture, for FmHA county office number, or contact your FmHA state office.

Alabama
Sterling Center
Suite 601
4121 Carmichael Road
Montgomery, AL 36106-3683
(205) 279-3400

Alaska
634 South Bailey
Suite 103
Palmer, AK 99645
(907) 745-2176

Arizona
3003 North Central Avenue
Suite 900
Phoenix, AZ 85012
(602) 280-8700

Arkansas
700 West Capitol
P.O. Box 2778
Little Rock, AR 72203
(501) 324-6281

California
194 West Main Street
Suite F
Woodland, CA 95695-2915
(916) 669-2000

Colorado
655 Parfet Street
Room 31-08
Lakewood, CO 80215
(303) 236-2801

Connecticut
451 West Street
Amherst, MA 01002
(413) 253-4300

Delaware
4611 South Dupont
Highway
P.O. Box 400
Camden, DE 19934-9998
(302) 697-4300

District of Columbia
4611 South Dupont
Highway
P.O. Box 400
Camden, DE 19934-9998
(302) 697-4300

Florida
Federal Building
4440 NW 25th Place
P.O. Box 147010
Gainesville, FL 32614-7010
(904) 338-3400

Georgia
355 East Hancock Avenue
Stephens Federal Building
Athens, GA 30610
(706) 546-2152

Guam
Department of Agriculture
14th Street and
Independence Avenue, SW
Washington, DC 20250
(202) 720-1632

Hawaii
Federal Building
Room 311
154 Waianuenue Avenue
Hilo, HI 96720
(808) 933-3000

Idaho
3232 Elder Street
Boise, ID 83705
(208) 334-1301

Illinois
Illini Plaza
Suite 103
1817 South Neil Street
Champaign, IL 61820
(217) 398-5235

Indiana
6975 Lakeside Boulevard
Indianapolis, IN 46278
(317) 290-3100

Iowa
Federal Building
Room 873
210 Walnut Street
Des Moines, IA 50309
(515) 284-4663

Kansas
1201 SW Summit Executive
Court
P.O. Box 4653
Topeka, KS 66604
(913) 271-2700

Kentucky
771 Corporate Drive
Suite 200
Lexington, KY 40503
(606) 224-7300

Louisiana
3727 Government Street
Alexandria, LA 71302
(318) 473-7920

Maine
444 Stillwater Avenue
Suite 2
P.O. Box 405
Bangor, ME 04402-0405
(207) 990-9106

Maryland
4611 South Dupont
Highway
P.O. Box 400
Camden, DE 19934-9998
(302) 697-4300

Massachusetts
451 West Street
Amherst, MA 01002
(413) 253-4300

Michigan
3001 Coolidge Road
Suite 200
East Lansing, MI 48823
(517) 337-6635

Minnesota
410 Farm Credit Service
Building
375 Jackson Street
St. Paul, MN 55101
(612) 290-3842

Mississippi
Federal Building
Suite 831
100 West Capitol
Jackson, MS 39269
(601) 965-4316

Missouri
601 Business Loop
70 West Parkade Center
Suite 235
Columbia, MO 65203
(314) 768-0976

Montana
900 Technology Boulevard
Suite B
P.O. Box 850
Bozeman, MT 59771
(406) 585-2580

Nebraska
Federal Building
Room 308
100 Centennial Mall
Lincoln, NE 68508
(402) 437-5551

Nevada
1390 South Curry Street
Carson City, NV 89703-
5405
(702) 887-1222

New Hampshire
City Center
89 Main Street
Third Floor
Montpelier, VT 05602
(802) 828-6001

New Jersey
Tarnsfield Plaza
Suite 22
1016 Woodlane Road
Mt. Holly, NJ 08060
(609) 265-3600

New Mexico
Federal Building
Room 3414
517 Gold Avenue, SW
Albuquerque, NM 87102
(505) 766-2462

New York
Federal Building
100 South Clinton Street
Room 871
Syracuse, NY 13261-7318
(315) 423-5290

North Carolina
4405 South Bland Road
Suite 260
Raleigh, NC 27609
(919) 790-2731

North Dakota
Federal Building
Room 208
Third and Rosser
P.O. Box 1737
Bismarck, ND 59502
(701) 250-4781

Ohio
Federal Building
Room 507
200 North High Street
Columbus, OH 43215
(614) 469-5606

Oklahoma
USDA Agricultural Center
Office Building
Stillwater, OK 74074
(405) 624-4250

Oregon
Federal Building
Room 1590
1220 SW Third Avenue
Portland, OR 97204
(503) 326-2731

Pennsylvania
One Credit Union Plaza
Suite 330
Harrisburg, PA 17110-2996
(717) 782-4476

Puerto Rico
New San Juan Center
Building
Room 501
159 Carlos E. Chardon
Street
G.P.O. Box 6106G
Hato Rey, PR 00918-5481
(809) 766-5095

Rhode Island
451 West Street
Amherst, MA 01002
(413) 253-4300

South Carolina
Strom Thurmond Federal
Building
Room 1007
1835 Assembly Street
Columbia, SC 28201
(803) 765-5163

South Dakota
Huron Federal Building
Room 308
200 Fourth Street, SW
Huron, SD 57350
(605) 353-1430

Tennessee
3322 West End Avenue
Suite 300
Nashville, TN 37203-1071
(615) 783-1308

Texas
Federal Building
101 South Main
Suite 102
Temple, TX 76501
(817) 774-1301

Utah
Federal Building
Room 5438
125 South State Street
Salt Lake City, UT 84138
(801) 524-4063

Vermont
City Center
89 Main Street
Third Floor
Montpelier, VT 05602
(802) 828-6001

Virginia
Culpeper Building
Suite 238
1606 Santa Rosa Road
Richmond, VA 23229
(804) 828-1550

Virgin Islands
City Center
89 Main Street
Third Floor
Montpelier, VT 05602
(802) 828-6001

Washington
Federal Building
Room 319
P.O. Box 2427
Wenatchee, WA 98807
(509) 664-0240

West Virginia
75 High Street
P.O. Box 678
Morgantown, WV 26505
(304) 291-4791

Wisconsin
4949 Kirschling Court
Stevens Point, WI 54481
(715) 345-7625

Wyoming
Federal Building
Room 1005
100 East B Street
P.O. Box 820
Casper, WY 82602
(307) 261-5271

FARM OPERATING LOANS

Department of Agriculture
Farmers Home
Administration (FmHA)
Farmer Programs Loan-
Making Division
Washington, DC 20250
(202) 720-1632

Description: Direct, guaranteed, and insured loans to
individuals, as well as to certain corporations, cooperatives,
partnerships, and joint operations operating family-sized
farms; applicant must have farm experience or training, have
a good credit history, be a U.S. citizen, and comply with the
highly erodible land and wetland conservation provisions.
$ Given: Guaranteed loans up to $400,000; insured loans:
up to $200,000.
Application Information: An informal conference with the
local county staff is recommended. File Form FmHA 1910-1
with supporting information. Form FmHA 449-6 for
guaranteed loans should be filed with the prospective lender.
Deadline: None
Contact: Consult your local telephone directory under U.S.
Government, Department of Agriculture, for FmHA county
office number, or contact your FmHA state office.

Alabama
Sterling Center
Suite 601
4121 Carmichael Road
Montgomery, AL 36106-
3683
(205) 279-3400

Alaska
634 South Bailey
Suite 103
Palmer, AK 99645
(907) 745-2176

Arizona
3003 North Central Avenue
Suite 900
Phoenix, AZ 85012
(602) 280-8700

Arkansas
700 West Capitol
P.O. Box 2778
Little Rock, AR 72203
(501) 324-6281

California
194 West Main Street
Suite F
Woodland, CA 95695-2915
(916) 669-2000

Colorado
655 Parfet Street
Room 31-08
Lakewood, CO 80215
(303) 236-2801

Connecticut
451 West Street
Amherst, MA 01002
(413) 253-4300

Delaware
4611 South Dupont
Highway
P.O. Box 400
Camden, DE 19934-9998
(302) 697-4300

District of Columbia
4611 South Dupont
Highway
P.O. Box 400
Camden, DE 19934-9998
(302) 697-4300

Florida
Federal Building
4440 NW 25th Place
P.O. Box 147010
Gainesville, FL 32614-7010
(904) 338-3400

Georgia
Stephens Federal Building
355 East Hancock Avenue
Athens, GA 30610
(706) 546-2152

Guam
Department of Agriculture
14th Street and
Independence Avenue, SW
Washington, DC 20250
(202) 720-1632

Hawaii
Federal Building
Room 311
154 Waianuenue Avenue
Hilo, HI 96720
(808) 933-3000

Idaho
3232 Elder Street
Boise, ID 83705
(208) 334-1301

Illinois
Illini Plaza
Suite 103
1817 South Neil Street
Champaign, IL 61820
(217) 398-5235

Indiana
5975 Lakeside Boulevard
Indianapolis, IN 46278
(317) 290-3100

Iowa
Federal Building
Room 873
210 Walnut Street
Des Moines, IA 50309
(515) 284-4663

Kansas
1201 SW Summit Executive
Court
P.O. Box 4653
Topeka, KS 66604
(913) 271-2700

Kentucky
771 Corporate Drive
Suite 200
Lexington, KY 40503
(606) 224-7300

Louisiana
3727 Government Street
Alexandria, LA 71302
(318) 473-7920

Maine
444 Stillwater Avenue
Suite 2
P.O. Box 405
Bangor, ME 04402-0405
(207) 990-9106

Maryland
4611 South Dupont
Highway
P.O. Box 400
Camden, DE 19934-9998
(302) 697-4300

Massachusetts
451 West Street
Amherst, MA 01002
(413) 253-4300

Michigan
3001 Coolidge Road
Suite 200
East Lansing, MI 48823
(517) 337-6635

Minnesota
410 Farm Credit Service
Building
375 Jackson Street
St. Paul, MN 55101
(612) 290-3842

Mississippi
Federal Building
Suite 831
100 West Capitol
Jackson, MS 39269
(601) 965-4316

Missouri
601 Business Loop
70 West Parkade Center
Suite 235
Columbia, MO 65203
(314) 768-0976

Montana
900 Technology Boulevard
Suite B
P.O. Box 850
Bozeman, MT 59771
(406) 585-2580

Nebraska
Federal Building
Room 308
100 Centennial Mall
Lincoln, NE 68508
(402) 437-5551

Nevada
1390 South Curry Street
Carson City, NV 89703-
5405
(702) 887-1222

New Hampshire
City Center
89 Main Street
Third Floor
Montpelier, VT 05602
(802) 828-6001

New Jersey
Tarnsfield Plaza
Suite 22
1016 Woodlane Road
Mt. Holly, NJ 08060
(609) 265-3600

New Mexico
Federal Building
Room 3414
517 Gold Avenue, SW
Albuquerque, NM 87102
(505) 766-2462

New York
Federal Building
100 South Clinton Street
Room 871
Syracuse, NY 13261-7318
(315) 423-5290

North Carolina
4405 South Bland Road
Suite 260
Raleigh, NC 27609
(919) 790-2731

North Dakota
Federal Building
Room 208
Third and Rosser
P.O. Box 1737
Bismarck, ND 59502
(701) 250-4781

Ohio
Federal Building
Room 507
200 North High Street
Columbus, OH 43215
(614) 469-5606

Oklahoma
USDA Agricultural Center
Office Building
Stillwater, OK 74074
(405) 624-4250

Oregon
Federal Building
Room 1590
1220 SW Third Avenue
Portland, OR 97204
(503) 326-2731

Pennsylvania
One Credit Union Plaza
Suite 330
Harrisburg, PA 17110-2996
(717) 782-4476

Puerto Rico
New San Juan Center Building
Room 501
159 Carlos E. Chardon Street
G.P.O. Box 6106G
Hato Rey, PR 00918-5481
(809) 766-5095

Rhode Island
451 West Street
Amherst, MA 01002
(413) 253-4300

South Carolina
Strom Thurmond Federal
Building
Room 1007
1835 Assembly Street
Columbia, SC 28201
(803) 765-5163

South Dakota
Huron Federal Building
Room 308
200 Fourth Street, SW
Huron, SD 57350
(605) 353-1430

Tennessee
3322 West End Avenue
Suite 300
Nashville, TN 37203-1071
(615) 783-1308

Texas
Federal Building
Suite 102
101 South Main
Temple, TX 76501
(817) 774-1301

Utah
Federal Building
Room 5438
125 South State Street
Salt Lake City, UT 84138
(801) 524-4063

Vermont
City Center
89 Main Street
Third Floor
Montpelier, VT 05602
(802) 828-6001

Virginia
Culpeper Building
Suite 238
1606 Santa Rosa Road
Richmond, VA 23229
(804) 828-1550

Virgin Islands
City Center
89 Main Street
Third Floor
Montpelier, VT 05602
(802) 828-6001

Washington
Federal Building
Room 319
P.O. Box 2427
Wenatchee, WA 98807
(509) 664-0240

West Virginia
75 High Street
P.O. Box 678
Morgantown, WV 26505
(304) 291-4791

Wisconsin
4949 Kirschling Court
Stevens Point, WI 54481
(715) 345-7625

Wyoming
Federal Building
Room 1005
100 East B Street
P.O. Box 820
Casper, WY 82602
(307) 261-5271

FARM OWNERSHIP LOANS

Department of Agriculture
Farmers Home
Administration (FmHA)
Washington, DC 20250
(202) 720-1632

Description: Direct, guaranteed, and insured loans to individuals of family-sized farms engaged primarily and directly in farming in the United States, or to cooperatives, corporations, joint operations, or partnerships controlled by U.S. farmers or ranchers. Individual applicants must not have a combined farm-ownership, soil-and-water, and recreation loan indebtedness to FmHA of more than $200,000 for insured loans and $300,000 for guaranteed loans.
$ Given: Insured loans: maximum $200,000; guaranteed loans: maximum $300,000
Application Information: File Form FmHA 410-1, Application for FmHA Services, with supporting information, at your local county office of the Farmers Home Administration for Direct Loans and with the prospective lender for Loan Guarantees.
Deadline: None
Contact: Consult your local telephone directory under U.S. Government, Department of Agriculture, for FmHA county office number, or contact your FmHA state office.

Alabama
Sterling Center
Suite 601
4121 Carmichael Road
Montgomery, AL 36106-3683
(205) 279-3400

Alaska
634 South Bailey
Suite 103
Palmer, AK 99645
(907) 745-2176

Arizona
3003 North Central Avenue
Suite 900
Phoenix, AZ 85012
(602) 280-8700

Arkansas
700 West Capitol
P.O. Box 2778
Little Rock, AR 72203
(501) 324-6281

California
194 West Main Street
Suite F
Woodland, CA 95695-2915
(916) 669-2000

Colorado
655 Parfet Street
Room 31-08
Lakewood, CO 80215
(303) 236-2801

Connecticut
451 West Street
Amherst, MA 01002
(413) 253-4300

Delaware
4611 South Dupont
Highway
P.O. Box 400
Camden, DE 19934-9998
(302) 697-4300

District of Columbia
4611 South Dupont
Highway
P.O. Box 400
Camden, DE 19934-9998
(302) 697-4300

Florida
Federal Building
4440 NW 25th Place
P.O. Box 147010
Gainesville, FL 32614-7010
(904) 338-3400

Georgia
355 East Hancock Avenue
Stephens Federal Building
Athens, GA 30610
(706) 546-2152

Guam
Department of Agriculture
14th Street and
Independence Avenue, SW
Washington, DC 20250
(202) 720-1632

Hawaii
Federal Building
Room 311
154 Waianuenue Avenue
Hilo, HI 96720
(808) 933-3000

Idaho
3232 Elder Street
Boise, ID 83705
(208) 334-1301

Illinois
Illini Plaza
Suite 103
1817 South Neil Street
Champaign, IL 61820
(217) 398-5235

Indiana
5975 Lakeside Boulevard
Indianapolis, IN 46278
(317) 290-3100

Iowa
Federal Building
Room 873
210 Walnut Street
Des Moines, IA 50309
(515) 284-4663

Kansas
1201 SW Summit Executive
Court
P.O. Box 4653
Topeka, KS 66604
(913) 271-2700

Kentucky
771 Corporate Drive
Suite 200
Lexington, KY 40503
(606) 224-7300

Louisiana
3727 Government Street
Alexandria, LA 71302
(318) 473-7920

Maine
444 Stillwater Avenue
Suite 2
P.O. Box 405
Bangor, ME 04402-0405
(207) 990-9106

Maryland
4611 South Dupont
Highway
P.O. Box 400
Camden, DE 19934-9998
(302) 697-4300

Massachusetts
451 West Street
Amherst, MA 01002
(413) 253-4300

Michigan
3001 Coolidge Road
Suite 200
East Lansing, MI 48823
(517) 337-6635

Minnesota
410 Farm Credit Service
Building
375 Jackson Street
St. Paul, MN 55101
(612) 290-3842

Mississippi
Federal Building
Suite 831
100 West Capitol
Jackson, MS 39269
(601) 965-4316

Missouri
601 Business Loop
70 West Parkade Center
Suite 235
Columbia, MO 65203
(314) 768-0976

Montana
900 Technology Boulevard
Suite B
P.O. Box 850
Bozeman, MT 59771
(406) 585-2580

Nebraska
Federal Building
Room 308
100 Centennial Mall
Lincoln, NE 68508
(402) 437-5551

Nevada
1390 South Curry Street
Carson City, NV 89703-
5405
(702) 887-1222

New Hampshire
City Center
89 Main Street
Third Floor
Montpelier, VT 05602
(802) 828-6001

New Jersey
Tarnsfield Plaza
Suite 22
1016 Woodlane Road
Mt. Holly, NJ 08060
(609) 265-3600

New Mexico
Federal Building
Room 3414
517 Gold Avenue, SW
Albuquerque, NM 87102
(505) 766-2462

New York
Federal Building
100 South Clinton Street
Room 871
Syracuse, NY 13261-7318
(315) 423-5290

North Carolina
4405 South Bland Road
Suite 260
Raleigh, NC 27609
(919) 790-2731

North Dakota
Federal Building
Room 208
Third and Rosser
P.O. Box 1737
Bismarck, ND 59502
(701) 250-4781

Ohio
Federal Building
Room 507
200 North High Street
Columbus, OH 43215
(614) 469-5606

Oklahoma
USDA Agricultural Center
Office Building
Stillwater, OK 74074
(405) 624-4250

Oregon
Federal Building
Room 1590
1220 SW Third Avenue
Portland, OR 97204
(503) 326-2731

Pennsylvania
One Credit Union Plaza
Suite 330
Harrisburg, PA 17110-2996
(717) 782-4476

Puerto Rico
New San Juan Center
Building
Room 501
159 Carlos E. Chardon Street
G.P.O. Box 6106G
Hato Rey, PR 00918-5481
(809) 766-5095

Rhode Island
451 West Street
Amherst, MA 01002
(413) 253-4300

South Carolina
Strom Thurmond Federal
Building
Room 1007
1835 Assembly Street
Columbia, SC 28201
(803) 765-5163

South Dakota
Huron Federal Building
Room 308
200 Fourth Street, SW
Huron, SD 57350
(605) 353-1430

Tennessee
3322 West End Avenue
Suite 300
Nashville, TN 37203-1071
(615) 783-1308

Texas
Federal Building
Suite 102
101 South Main
Temple, TX 76501
(817) 774-1301

Utah
Federal Building
Room 5438
125 South State Street
Salt Lake City, UT 84138
(801) 524-4063

Vermont
City Center
89 Main Street
Third Floor
Montpelier, VT 05602
(802) 828-6001

Virginia
Culpeper Building
Suite 238
1606 Santa Rosa Road
Richmond, VA 23229
(804) 828-1550

Virgin Islands
City Center
89 Main Street
Third Floor
Montpelier, VT 05602
(802) 828-6001

Washington
Federal Building
Room 319
P.O. Box 2427
Wenatchee, WA 98807
(509) 664-0240

West Virginia
75 High Street
P.O. Box 678
Morgantown, WV 26505
(304) 291-4791

Wisconsin
4949 Kirschling Court
Stevens Point, WI 54481
(715) 345-7625

Wyoming
Federal Building
Room 1005
100 East B Street
P.O. Box 820
Casper, WY 82602
(307) 261-5271

FEED GRAIN PRODUCTION STABILIZATION
(Feed Grain Direct Payments)

Department of Agriculture
Agriculture Stabilization and
Conservation Service (ASCS)
P.O. Box 2415
Washington, DC 20013
(202) 720-4418

Description: Direct payments with unrestricted use to owners, landlords, tenants, or sharecroppers on farms; commodity planted must meet program requirements as announced by the Secretary.
$ Given: Up to $250,000 per person
Application Information: Farm operator visits ASCS office prior to a prescribed final date to sign Form CCC-477, indicating an intention to participate and to report planted acreage for harvest on Form ASCS-578.
Deadline: Contact state or county ASCS offices for applicable deadlines.
Contact: Your local, state, and/or regional ASCS office.

Alabama
Robert D. Springe
P.O. Box 891
Montgomery, AL
36104-0891
(205) 279-3500

Alaska
Karen O. Lee
Alaska State ASCS Office
800 West Evergreen
Suite 216
Palmer, AK 99654-6539
(907) 745-7982

Arizona
Robert A. Piceno
Arizona State ASCS Office
201 East Indianola
Suite 240
Phoenix, AZ 85012-3118
(602) 640-5200

Arkansas
Wayne Perryman
P.O. Box 2781
New Federal Building
Room 5428
700 West Capitol Street
Little Rock, AR 72201-3225
(501) 324-5220

California
John Smythe
California State ASCS Office
1303 J Street
Suite 300
Sacramento, CA 95814-
2916
(916) 551-1801

Colorado
John Stencel
Colorado State ASCS Office
655 Parfet Street
Room E 305
Third Floor
Lakewood, CO 80215
(303) 236-2866

Connecticut
Vincent R. Majchier
88 Day Hill Road
Windsor, CT 06095
(203) 285-8483

Delaware
William D. Clifton II
1201 College Park Drive
Suite A
Dover, DE 19901
(302) 678-4912

Florida
Harry McGlin
P.O. Box 141030
4440 NW 25th Place
Suite I
Gainesville, FL 32614-1030
(904) 372-8549

Georgia
Grady (Buck) Johnson
P.O. Box 1907
Federal Building
Room 102
344 East Hancock Avenue
Athens, GA 30601-2775
(404) 546-2266

Hawaii
Jo Ann Nakata
Hawaii State ASCS Office
300 Ala Moana Boulevard
Room 5106
P.O. Box 50008
Honolulu, HI 96850
(808) 551-2644

Idaho
Richard R. Rush
Idaho State ASCS Office
3220 Elder Street
Boise, ID 83705
(208) 334-1486

Illinois
Stephen Scates
P.O. Box 19273
3500 Wabash Avenue
Springfield, IL 62794-9273
(217) 492-4180

Indiana
Kent Yeager
Indiana State ASCS Office
5891 Lakeside Boulevard
Indianapolis, IN 46278
(317) 290-3030

Iowa
Tom Grau
10500 Buena Vista Court
Urbandale, IA 50322
(515) 254-1540, ext. 40

Kansas
Andrian J. Polansky
Kansas State ASCS Office
3600 Anderson Avenue
Manhattan, KS 66502-2511
(913) 539-3531

Kentucky
Hampton (Hoppy) Hinton
Kentucky State ASCS Office
771 Corporate Drive
Suite 100
Lexington, KY 40503-5478
(606) 224-7601

Louisiana
Willie F. Cooper
3737 Government Street
Alexandria, LA 71302-3395
(318) 473-7721

Maine
Arnold Roach
44 Stillwater Avenue
P.O. Box 406
Bangor, ME 04401-0406
(207) 990-9140

Maryland
James M. Voss
8335 East Guilford Road
Columbia, MD 21046
(410) 381-4550

Massachusetts
Charles A. Costa
451 West Street
Amherst, MA 01002-2953
(413) 256-0232

Michigan
Jim Byrum
300 Coolidge Road
Suite 100
East Lansing, MI 48823-6321
(517) 337-6659

Minnesota
Wally Sparby
Minnesota State ASCS Office
400 Farm Credit Service Building
375 Jackson Street
St. Paul, MN 55101-1853
(612) 290-3651

Mississippi
Norris Faust
Mississippi State ASCS Office
6310 I-55 North
Jackson, MS 39236-4995
(601) 965-4300

Missouri
Brad Epperson
601 Parkdale Plaza Business Loop
70 West
Suite 225
Columbia, MO 65203
(314) 876-0925

Montana
Bruce E. Nelson
P.O. Box 670
10 East Babcock
Room 557
Bozeman, MT 59715
(406) 587-6872

Nebraska
John Frank Johannsen
Nebraska State ASCS Office
P.O. Box 57975
7131 A Street
Lincoln, NE 68510
(402) 437-5581

Nevada
Wendell K. Newman
Nevada State ASCS Office
1755 East Plumb Lane
Suite 202
Reno, NV 89502-3200
(702) 784-5130

New Hampshire
James McConaka
USDA–New Hampshire State ASCS Office
22 Bridge Street
Fourth Floor
P.O. Box 1398
Concord, NH 03302-1398
(603) 224-7941

New Jersey
Peter de Wilde
Mastoris Professional Plaza
163 Route 130
Building I
Suite E
Bordentown, NJ 08505-2249
(609) 224-7941

New Mexico
Charles Essary
New Mexico State ASCS
Office
P.O. Box 1458
Federal Building
Room 4430
517 Gold Avenue, SW
Albuquerque, NM 87103-
1458
(505) 766-2472

New York
Floyd Duger
811 James H. Hanley
Federal Building
100 South Clinton Street
P.O. Box 7308
Syracuse, NY 13260-7308
(315) 423-5176

North Carolina
Samuel Colney
Federal Building
Suite 175
4407 Bland Road
Raleigh, NC 27609-6296
(919) 790-2957

North Dakota
Scott Stofferahn
North Dakota State ASCS
Office
1025 28th Street, SW
P.O. Box 3046
Fargo, ND 58108-3046
(701) 239-5224

Ohio
Steve Maurer
Federal Building
Room 540
200 North High Street
Columbus, OH 43215
(614) 469-6735

Oklahoma
Terry L. Peach
USDA Agriculture Center
Building
Suite 102
Farm Road and McFarland
Street
Stillwater, OK 74074-2653
(405) 624-4110

Oregon
Jack L. Sainsbury
Oregon State ASCS Office
P.O. Box 1300
Tualatin, OR 97062-1300
(503) 692-6830

Pennsylvania
William H. Baumgartner
One Credit Union Place
Suite 320
Harrisburg, PA 17101-2994
(717) 782-4547

Rhode Island
Paul E. Brule
Aldeic Complex
60 Quaker Lane
West Bay Office Complex
Suite 40
West Warwick, RI 02886
(401) 828-8232

South Carolina
Laurie C. Nelson
Strom Thurmond Mall
Suite 100
Columbia, SC 29201-2375
(803) 765-5186

South Dakota
Michael O'Connor
Federal Building
Room 208
200 Fourth Street, SW
Huron, SD 57350-2478
(605) 353-1092

Tennessee
Walter E. Head
United States Courthouse
Room 579
801 Broadway
Nashville, TN 37203-3816
(615) 736-5555

Texas
Harold B. Bennett
Texas State ASCS Office
P.O. Box 2900
College Station, TX 77841-
0001
(409) 260-9207

Utah
James L. Humlicek
Utah State ASCS Office
P.O. Box 11547
Salt Lake City, UT 84147
(801) 524-5013

Vermont
James L. Monahan
Executive Square Office
Building
346 Shelburne Street
Burlington, VT 05401-4495
(802) 658-2803

Virginia
Donald Davis
Culpeper Building
Suite 138
1606 Santa Rosa Road
Richmond, VA 23229
(804) 287-1500

Washington
Larry R. Albin
Washington State ASCS
Office
Rock Point Tower
Suite 568
316 West Boone Avenue
Spokane, WA 99201-2350
(509) 353-2307

West Virginia
Billy B. Burke
P.O. Box 1049
New Federal Building
Room 239
75 High Street
Morgantown, WV 26505-
7558
(304) 291-4351

Wisconsin
Doug Caruso
Wisconsin State ASCS Office
6515 Watts Road
Room 100
Madison, WI 53719-2797
(608) 264-5301

Wyoming
Thomas E. Trowbridge
951 Werner Court
Suite 130
Casper, WY 82601-1307
(307) 261-5231

Caribbean Area
Herberto J. Martinez
Caribbean Area ASCS Office
Cobran's Plaza
Suite 309
1609 Ponce DeLeon Avenue
Santurce, PR 00909-0001
(809) 729-6902

FORESTRY INCENTIVE PROGRAM

Department of Agriculture
Agricultural Stabilization
and Conservation Service
(ASCS)
P.O. Box 2415
Washington, DC 20013
(202) 720-6221

Description: Direct payment for specified use to individuals, groups, associations, Indian tribes or other native groups, corporations whose stocks are not publicly traded, or other legal entities that own nonindustrial, private forestlands producing industrial wood crops. Limited to ownership of not more than 1,000 acres of nonindustrial, private forestland that can produce at least 50 cubic feet of wood per acre per year, except by special approval. Program is available to eligible landowners in the United States or any U.S. territory.
$ Given: Payment range: $50–$10,000 per year; average: $1,600
Application Information: Form ACP-245 for annual cost sharing or FIP-11 for long-term cost-sharing agreements may be filed at any time of year with your county ASCS office.
Deadline: As announced by the ASC committee
Contact: Your local, state, and/or regional ASCS office

Alabama
Robert D. Springe
P.O. Box 891
Montgomery, AL 36104-
0891
(205) 279-3500

Alaska
Karen O. Lee
Alaska State ASCS Office
800 West Evergreen
Suite 216
Palmer, AK 99654-6539
(907) 745-7982

Arizona
Robert A. Piceno
Arizona State ASCS Office
201 East Indianola
Suite 240
Phoenix, AZ 85012-3118
(602) 640-5200

Arkansas
Wayne Perryman
P.O. Box 2781
New Federal Building
Room 5428
700 West Capitol Street
Little Rock, AR 72201-3225
(501) 324-5220

California
John Smythe
California State ASCS Office
1303 J Street
Suite 300
Sacramento, CA 95814-
2916
(916) 551-1801

Colorado
John Stencel
Colorado State ASCS Office
655 Parfet Street
Room E 305
Third Floor
Lakewood, CO 80215
(303) 236-2866

Connecticut
Vincent R. Majchier
88 Day Hill Road
Windsor, CT 06095
(203) 285-8483

Delaware
William D. Clifton II
1201 College Park Drive
Suite A
Dover, DE 19901
(302) 678-4912

Florida
Harry McGlin
P.O. Box 141030
4440 NW 25th Place
Suite I
Gainesville, FL 32614-1030
(904) 372-8549

Georgia
Grady (Buck) Johnson
P.O. Box 1907
Federal Building
Room 102
344 East Hancock Avenue
Athens, GA 30601-2775
(404) 546-2266

Hawaii
Jo Ann Nakata
Hawaii State ASCS Office
300 Ala Moana Boulevard
Room 5106
P.O. Box 50008
Honolulu, HI 96850
(808) 551-2644

Idaho
Richard R. Rush
Idaho State ASCS Office
3220 Elder Street
Boise, ID 83705
(208) 334-1486

Illinois
Stephen Scates
P.O. Box 19273
3500 Wabash Avenue
Springfield, IL 62794-9273
(217) 492-4180

Indiana
Kent Yeager
Indiana State ASCS Office
5891 Lakeside Boulevard
Indianapolis, IN 46278
(317) 290-3030

Iowa
Tom Grau
10500 Buena Vista Court
Urbandale, IA 50322
(515) 254-1540, ext. 40

Kansas
Andrian J. Polansky
Kansas State ASCS Office
3600 Anderson Avenue
Manhattan, KS 66502-2511
(913) 539-3531

Kentucky
Hampton (Hoppy) Hinton
Kentucky State ASCS Office
771 Corporate Drive
Suite 100
Lexington, KY 40503-5478
(606) 224-7601

Louisiana
Willie F. Cooper
3737 Government Street
Alexandria, LA 71302-3395
(318) 473-7721

Maine
Arnold Roach
44 Stillwater Avenue
P.O. Box 406
Bangor, ME 04401-0406
(207) 990-9140

Maryland
James M. Voss
8335 East Guilford Road
Columbia, MD 21046
(410) 381-4550

Massachusetts
Charles A. Costa
451 West Street
Amherst, MA 01002-2953
(413) 256-0232

Michigan
Jim Byrum
300 Coolidge Road
Suite 100
East Lansing, MI 48823-
6321
(517) 337-6659

Minnesota
Wally Sparby
Minnesota State ASCS
Office
400 Farm Credit Service
Building
375 Jackson Street
St. Paul, MN 55101-1853
(612) 290-3651

Mississippi
Norris Faust
Mississippi State ASCS
Office
6310 I-55 North
Jackson, MS 39236-4995
(601) 965-4300

Missouri
Brad Epperson
601 Parkdale Plaza Business
Loop
70 West
Suite 225
Columbia, MO 65203
(314) 876-0925

Montana
Bruce E. Nelson
P.O. Box 670
10 East Babcock
Room 557
Bozeman, MT 59715
(406) 587-6872

Nebraska
John Frank Johannsen
Nebraska State ASCS Office
P.O. Box 57975
7131 A Street
Lincoln, NE 68510
(402) 437-5581

Nevada
Wendell K. Newman
Nevada State ASCS Office
1755 East Plumb Lane
Suite 202
Reno, NV 89502-3200
(702) 784-5130

New Hampshire
James McConaka
USDA–New Hampshire
State ASCS Office
22 Bridge Street
Fourth Floor
P.O. Box 1398
Concord, NH 03302-1398
(603) 224-7941

New Jersey
Peter de Wilde
Mastoris Professional Plaza
163 Route 130
Building I
Suite E
Bordentown, NJ 08505-2249
(609) 224-7941

New Mexico
Charles Essary
New Mexico State ASCS
Office
P.O. Box 1458
Federal Building
Room 4430
517 Gold Avenue, SW
Albuquerque, NM 87103-1458
(505) 766-2472

New York
Floyd Duger
811 James H. Hanley
Federal Building
100 South Clinton Street
P.O. Box 7308
Syracuse, NY 13260-7308
(315) 423-5176

North Carolina
Samuel Colney
Federal Building
Suite 175
4407 Bland Road
Raleigh, NC 27609-6296
(919) 790-2957

North Dakota
Scott Stofferahn
North Dakota State ASCS
Office
1025 28th Street, SW
P.O. Box 3046
Fargo, ND 58108-3046
(701) 239-5224

Ohio
Steve Maurer
Federal Building
Room 540
200 North High Street
Columbus, OH 43215
(614) 469-6735

Oklahoma
Terry L. Peach
USDA Agriculture Center
Building
Suite 102
Farm Road and McFarland
Street
Stillwater, OK 74074-2653
(405) 624-4110

Oregon
Jack L. Sainsbury
Oregon State ASCS Office
P.O. Box 1300
Tualatin, OR 97062-1300
(503) 692-6830

Pennsylvania
William H. Baumgartner
One Credit Union Place
Suite 320
Harrisburg, PA 17101-2994
(717) 782-4547

Rhode Island
Paul E. Brule
Aldeic Complex
60 Quaker Lane
West Bay Office Complex
Suite 40
West Warwick, RI 02886
(401) 828-8232

South Carolina
Laurie C. Nelson
Strom Thurmond Mall
Suite 100
Columbia, SC 29201-2375
(803) 765-5186

South Dakota
Michael O'Connor
Federal Building
Room 208
200 Fourth Street, SW
Huron, SD 57350-2478
(605) 353-1092

Tennessee
Walter E. Head
United States Courthouse
Room 579
801 Broadway
Nashville, TN 37203-3816
(615) 736-5555

Texas
Harold B. Bennett
Texas State ASCS Office
P.O. Box 2900
College Station, TX 77841-0001
(409) 260-9207

Utah
James L. Humlicek
Utah State ASCS Office
P.O. Box 11547
Salt Lake City, UT 84147
(801) 524-5013

Vermont
James L. Monahan
Executive Square Office
Building
346 Shelburne Street
Burlington, VT 05401-4495
(802) 658-2803

Virginia
Donald Davis
Culpeper Building
Suite 138
1606 Santa Rosa Road
Richmond, VA 23229
(804) 287-1500

Washington
Larry R. Albin
Washington State ASCS
Office
Rock Point Tower
Suite 568
316 West Boone Avenue
Spokane, WA 99201-2350
(509) 353-2307

West Virginia
Billy B. Burke
P.O. Box 1049
New Federal Building
Room 239
75 High Street
Morgantown, WV 26505-7558
(304) 291-4351

Wisconsin
Doug Caruso
Wisconsin State ASCS Office
6515 Watts Road
Room 100
Madison, WI 53719-2797
(608) 264-5301

Wyoming
Thomas E. Trowbridge
951 Werner Court
Suite 130
Casper, WY 82601-1307
(307) 261-5231

Caribbean Area
Herberto J. Martinez
Caribbean Area ASCS Office
Cobran's Plaza
Suite 309
1609 Ponce DeLeon Avenue
Santurce, PR 00909-0001
(809) 729-6902

GRAIN RESERVE PROGRAM

Department of Agriculture
Agricultural Stabilization
and Conservation Service
(ASCS)
Cotton, Grain, and Rice
Price Support Division
P.O. Box 2415
Washington, DC 20013
(202) 720-9886

Description: Direct payments with unrestricted use to
individual producers or approved cooperatives having a
conservation loan on wheat, corn, barley, oats, or sorghum.
$ Given: Payment range: $1-$122,863; average: $2,661
Application Information: Visit, call, or write your county
ASCS office during availability period.
Deadline: Announced time of availability
Contact: Your local, state, and/or regional office

Alabama
Robert D. Springe
P.O. Box 891
Montgomery, AL 36104-0891
(205) 279-3500

Alaska
Karen O. Lee
Alaska State ASCS Office
800 West Evergreen
Suite 216
Palmer, AK 99654-6539
(907) 745-7982

Arizona
Robert A. Piceno
Arizona State ASCS Office
201 East Indianola
Suite 240
Phoenix, AZ 85012-3118
(602) 640-5200

Arkansas
Wayne Perryman
P.O. Box 2781
New Federal Building
Room 5428
700 West Capitol Street
Little Rock, AR 72201-3225
(501) 324-5220

California
John Smythe
California State ASCS Office
1303 J Street
Suite 300
Sacramento, CA 95814-2916
(916) 551-1801

Colorado
John Stencel
Colorado State ASCS Office
655 Parfet Street
Room E 305
Third Floor
Lakewood, CO 80215
(303) 236-2866

Connecticut
Vincent R. Majchier
88 Day Hill Road
Windsor, CT 06095
(203) 285-8483

Delaware
William D. Clifton II
1201 College Park Drive
Suite A
Dover, DE 19901
(302) 678-4912

Florida
Harry McGlin
P.O. Box 141030
4440 NW 25th Place
Suite I
Gainesville, FL 32614-1030
(904) 372-8549

Georgia
Grady (Buck) Johnson
P.O. Box 1907
Federal Building
Room 102
344 East Hancock Avenue
Athens, GA 30601-2775
(404) 546-2266

Hawaii
Jo Ann Nakata
Hawaii State ASCS Office
300 Ala Moana Boulevard
Room 5106
P.O. Box 50008
Honolulu, HI 96850
(808) 551-2644

Idaho
Richard R. Rush
Idaho State ASCS Office
3220 Elder Street
Boise, ID 83705
(208) 334-1486

Illinois
Stephen Scates
P.O. Box 19273
3500 Wabash Avenue
Springfield, IL 62794-9273
(217) 492-4180

Indiana
Kent Yeager
Indiana State ASCS Office
5891 Lakeside Boulevard
Indianapolis, IN 46278
(317) 290-3030

Iowa
Tom Grau
10500 Buena Vista Court
Urbandale, IA 50322
(515) 254-1540, ext. 40

Kansas
Andrian J. Polansky
Kansas State ASCS Office
3600 Anderson Avenue
Manhattan, KS 66502-2511
(913) 539-3531

Kentucky
Hampton (Hoppy) Hinton
Kentucky State ASCS Office
771 Corporate Drive
Suite 100
Lexington, KY 40503-5478
(606) 224-7601

Louisiana
Willie F. Cooper
3737 Government Street
Alexandria, LA 71302-3395
(318) 473-7721

Maine
Arnold Roach
44 Stillwater Avenue
P.O. Box 406
Bangor, ME 04401-0406
(207) 990-9140

Maryland
James M. Voss
8335 East Guilford Road
Columbia, MD 21046
(410) 381-4550

Massachusetts
Charles A. Costa
451 West Street
Amherst, MA 01002-2953
(413) 256-0232

Michigan
Jim Byrum
300 Coolidge Road
Suite 100
East Lansing, MI 48823-
6321
(517) 337-6659

Minnesota
Wally Sparby
Minnesota State ASCS
Office
400 Farm Credit Service
Building
375 Jackson Street
St. Paul, MN 55101-1853
(612) 290-3651

Mississippi
Norris Faust
Mississippi State ASCS
Office
6310 I-55 North
Jackson, MS 39236-4995
(601) 965-4300

Missouri
Brad Epperson
601 Parkdale Plaza Business
Loop
70 West
Suite 225
Columbia, MO 65203
(314) 876-0925

Montana
Bruce E. Nelson
P.O. Box 670
10 East Babcock
Room 557
Bozeman, MT 59715
(406) 587-6872

Nebraska
John Frank Johannsen
Nebraska State ASCS Office
P.O. Box 57975
7131 A Street
Lincoln, NE 68510
(402) 437-5581

Nevada
Wendell K. Newman
Nevada State ASCS Office
1755 East Plumb Lane
Suite 202
Reno, NV 89502-3200
(702) 784-5130

New Hampshire
James McConaka
USDA–New Hampshire
State ASCS Office
22 Bridge Street
Fourth Floor
P.O. Box 1398
Concord, NH 03302-1398
(603) 224-7941

New Jersey
Peter de Wilde
Mastoris Professional Plaza
163 Route 130
Building I
Suite E
Bordentown, NJ 08505-
2249
(609) 224-7941

New Mexico
Charles Essary
New Mexico State ASCS
Office
P.O. Box 1458
Federal Building
Room 4430
517 Gold Avenue, SW
Albuquerque, NM 87103-
1458
(505) 766-2472

New York
Floyd Duger
811 James H. Hanley
Federal Building
100 South Clinton Street
P.O. Box 7308
Syracuse, NY 13260-7308
(315) 423-5176

North Carolina
Samuel Colney
Federal Building
Suite 175
4407 Bland Road
Raleigh, NC 27609-6296
(919) 790-2957

North Dakota
Scott Stofferahn
North Dakota State ASCS
Office
1025 28th Street, SW
P.O. Box 3046
Fargo, ND 58108-3046
(701) 239-5224

Ohio
Steve Maurer
Federal Building
Room 540
200 North High Street
Columbus, OH 43215
(614) 469-6735

Oklahoma
Terry L. Peach
USDA Agriculture Center
Building
Suite 102
Farm Road and McFarland
Street
Stillwater, OK 74074-2653
(405) 624-4110

Oregon
Jack L. Sainsbury
Oregon State ASCS Office
P.O. Box 1300
Tualatin, OR 97062-1300
(503) 692-6830

Pennsylvania
William H. Baumgartner
One Credit Union Place
Suite 320
Harrisburg, PA 17101-2994
(717) 782-4547

Rhode Island
Paul E. Brule
Aldeic Complex
60 Quaker Lane
West Bay Office Complex
Suite 40
West Warwick, RI 02886
(401) 828-8232

South Carolina
Laurie C. Nelson
Strom Thurmond Mall
Suite 100
Columbia, SC 29201-2375
(803) 765-5186

South Dakota
Michael O'Connor
Federal Building
Room 208
200 Fourth Street, SW
Huron, SD 57350-2478
(605) 353-1092

Tennessee
Walter E. Head
United States Courthouse
Room 579
801 Broadway
Nashville, TN 37203-3816
(615) 736-5555

Texas
Harold B. Bennett
Texas State ASCS Office
P.O. Box 2900
College Station, TX 77841-0001
(409) 260-9207

Utah
James L. Humlicek
Utah State ASCS Office
P.O. Box 11547
Salt Lake City, UT 84147
(801) 524-5013

Vermont
James L. Monahan
Executive Square Office
Building
346 Shelburne Street
Burlington, VT 05401-4495
(802) 658-2803

Virginia
Donald Davis
Culpeper Building
Suite 138
1606 Santa Rosa Road
Richmond, VA 23229
(804) 287-1500

Washington
Larry R. Albin
Washington State ASCS
Office
Rock Point Tower
Suite 568
316 West Boone Avenue
Spokane, WA 99201-2350
(509) 353-2307

West Virginia
Billy B. Burke
P.O. Box 1049
New Federal Building
Room 239
75 High Street
Morgantown, WV 26505-7558
(304) 291-4351

Wisconsin
Doug Caruso
Wisconsin State ASCS Office
6515 Watts Road
Room 100
Madison, WI 53719-2797
(608) 264-5301

Wyoming
Thomas E. Trowbridge
951 Werner Court
Suite 130
Casper, WY 82601-1307
(307) 261-5231

Caribbean Area
Herberto J. Martinez
Caribbean Area ASCS Office
Cobran's Plaza
Suite 309
1609 Ponce DeLeon Avenue
Santurce, PR 00909-0001
(809) 729-6902

RICE PRODUCTION STABILIZATION

Department of Agriculture
Agricultural Stabilization
and Conservation Service
(ASCS)
P.O. Box 2415
Washington, DC 20013-
2415
(202) 720-6734

Description: Direct payments with unrestricted use to owners, landlords, tenants, or sharecroppers on farms. Commodity planted must meet program requirements as announced by the Secretary.
$ Given: Up to $250,000 per person
Application Information: Visit your ASCS office prior to prescribed final date to sign application. File Form ASCS-477, indicating an intention to participate and to report planted acreage for harvest on Form ASCS-578
Deadline: Contact state or county ASCS offices for applicable deadlines.
Contact: Your local, state, and/or regional ASCS office.

Alabama
Robert D. Springe
P.O. Box 891
Montgomery, AL 36104-
0891
(205) 279-3500

Alaska
Karen O. Lee
Alaska State ASCS Office
800 West Evergreen
Suite 216
Palmer, AK 99654-6539
(907) 745-7982

Arizona
Robert A. Piceno
Arizona State ASCS Office
201 East Indianola
Suite 240
Phoenix, AZ 85012-3118
(602) 640-5200

Arkansas
Wayne Perryman
P.O. Box 2781
New Federal Building
Room 5428
700 West Capitol Street
Little Rock, AR 72201-3225
(501) 324-5220

California
John Smythe
California State ASCS Office
1303 J Street
Suite 300
Sacramento, CA 95814-
2916
(916) 551-1801

Colorado
John Stencel
Colorado State ASCS Office
655 Parfet Street
Room E 305
Third Floor
Lakewood, CO 80215
(303) 236-2866

Connecticut
Vincent R. Majchier
88 Day Hill Road
Windsor, CT 06095
(203) 285-8483

Delaware
William D. Clifton II
1201 College Park Drive
Suite A
Dover, DE 19901
(302) 678-4912

Florida
Harry McGlin
P.O. Box 141030
4440 NW 25th Place
Suite I
Gainesville, FL 32614-1030
(904) 372-8549

Georgia
Grady (Buck) Johnson
P.O. Box 1907
Federal Building
Room 102
344 East Hancock Avenue
Athens, GA 30601-2775
(404) 546-2266

Hawaii
Jo Ann Nakata
Hawaii State ASCS Office
300 Ala Moana Boulevard
Room 5106
P.O. Box 50008
Honolulu, HI 96850
(808) 551-2644

Idaho
Richard R. Rush
Idaho State ASCS Office
3220 Elder Street
Boise, ID 83705
(208) 334-1486

Illinois
Stephen Scates
P.O. Box 19273
3500 Wabash Avenue
Springfield, IL 62794-9273
(217) 492-4180

Indiana
Kent Yeager
Indiana State ASCS Office
5891 Lakeside Boulevard
Indianapolis, IN 46278
(317) 290-3030

Iowa
Tom Grau
10500 Buena Vista Court
Urbandale, IA 50322
(515) 254-1540, ext. 40

Kansas
Andrian J. Polansky
Kansas State ASCS Office
3600 Anderson Avenue
Manhattan, KS 66502-2511
(913) 539-3531

Kentucky
Hampton (Hoppy) Hinton
Kentucky State ASCS Office
771 Corporate Drive
Suite 100
Lexington, KY 40503-5478
(606) 224-7601

Louisiana
Willie F. Cooper
3737 Government Street
Alexandria, LA 71302-3395
(318) 473-7721

Maine
Arnold Roach
44 Stillwater Avenue
P.O. Box 406
Bangor, ME 04401-0406
(207) 990-9140

Maryland
James M. Voss
8335 East Guilford Road
Columbia, MD 21046
(410) 381-4550

Massachusetts
Charles A. Costa
451 West Street
Amherst, MA 01002-2953
(413) 256-0232

Michigan
Jim Byrum
300 Coolidge Road
Suite 100
East Lansing, MI 48823-6321
(517) 337-6659

Minnesota
Wally Sparby
Minnesota State ASCS Office
400 Farm Credit Service Building
375 Jackson Street
St. Paul, MN 55101-1853
(612) 290-3651

Mississippi
Norris Faust
Mississippi State ASCS Office
6310 I-55 North
Jackson, MS 39236-4995
(601) 965-4300

Missouri
Brad Epperson
601 Parkdale Plaza Business Loop
70 West
Suite 225
Columbia, MO 65203
(314) 876-0925

Montana
Bruce E. Nelson
P.O. Box 670
10 East Babcock
Room 557
Bozeman, MT 59715
(406) 587-6872

Nebraska
John Frank Johannsen
Nebraska State ASCS Office
P.O. Box 57975
7131 A Street
Lincoln, NE 68510
(402) 437-5581

Nevada
Wendell K. Newman
Nevada State ASCS Office
1755 East Plumb Lane
Suite 202
Reno, NV 89502-3200
(702) 784-5130

New Hampshire
James McConaka
USDA–New Hampshire
State ASCS Office
22 Bridge Street
Fourth Floor
P.O. Box 1398
Concord, NH 03302-1398
(603) 224-7941

New Jersey
Peter de Wilde
Mastoris Professional Plaza
163 Route 130
Building I
Suite E
Bordentown, NJ 08505-2249
(609) 224-7941

New Mexico
Charles Essary
New Mexico State ASCS
Office
P.O. Box 1458
Federal Building
Room 4430
517 Gold Avenue, SW
Albuquerque, NM 87103-
1458
(505) 766-2472

New York
Floyd Duger
811 James H. Hanley
Federal Building
100 South Clinton Street
P.O. Box 7308
Syracuse, NY 13260-7308
(315) 423-5176

North Carolina
Samuel Colney
Federal Building
Suite 175
4407 Bland Road
Raleigh, NC 27609-6296
(919) 790-2957

North Dakota
Scott Stofferahn
North Dakota State ASCS
Office
1025 28th Street, SW
P.O. Box 3046
Fargo, ND 58108-3046
(701) 239-5224

Ohio
Steve Maurer
Federal Building
Room 540
200 North High Street
Columbus, OH 43215
(614) 469-6735

Oklahoma
Terry L. Peach
USDA Agriculture Center
Building
Suite 102
Farm Road and McFarland
Street
Stillwater, OK 74074-2653
(405) 624-4110

Oregon
Jack L. Sainsbury
Oregon State ASCS Office
P.O. Box 1300
Tualatin, OR 97062-1300
(503) 692-6830

Pennsylvania
William H. Baumgartner
One Credit Union Place
Suite 320
Harrisburg, PA 17101-2994
(717) 782-4547

Rhode Island
Paul E. Brule
Aldeic Complex
60 Quaker Lane
West Bay Office Complex
Suite 40
West Warwick, RI 02886
(401) 828-8232

South Carolina
Laurie C. Nelson
Strom Thurmond Mall
Suite 100
Columbia, SC 29201-2375
(803) 765-5186

South Dakota
Michael O'Connor
Federal Building
Room 208
200 Fourth Street, SW
Huron, SD 57350-2478
(605) 353-1092

Tennessee
Walter E. Head
United States Courthouse
Room 579
801 Broadway
Nashville, TN 37203-3816
(615) 736-5555

Texas
Harold B. Bennett
Texas State ASCS Office
P.O. Box 2900
College Station, TX 77841-
0001
(409) 260-9207

Utah
James L. Humlicek
Utah State ASCS Office
P.O. Box 11547
Salt Lake City, UT 84147
(801) 524-5013

Vermont
James L. Monahan
Executive Square Office
Building
346 Shelburne Street
Burlington, VT 05401-4495
(802) 658-2803

Virginia
Donald Davis
Culpeper Building
Suite 138
1606 Santa Rosa Road
Richmond, VA 23229
(804) 287-1500

Washington
Larry R. Albin
Washington State ASCS
Office
Rock Point Tower
Suite 568
316 West Boone Avenue
Spokane, WA 99201-2350
(509) 353-2307

West Virginia
Billy B. Burke
P.O. Box 1049
New Federal Building
Room 239
75 High Street
Morgantown, WV 26505-7558
(304) 291-4351

Wisconsin
Doug Caruso
Wisconsin State ASCS Office
6515 Watts Road
Room 100
Madison, WI 53719-2797
(608) 264-5301

Wyoming
Thomas E. Trowbridge
951 Werner Court
Suite 130
Casper, WY 82601-1307
(307) 261-5231

Caribbean Area
Herberto J. Martinez
Caribbean Area ASCS Office
Cobran's Plaza
Suite 309
1609 Ponce DeLeon Avenue
Santurce, PR 00909-0001
(809) 729-6902

RURAL CLEAN WATER PROGRAM

Department of Agriculture
Agricultural Stabilization
and Conservation Service
(ASCS)
Environmental Protection
Service
P.O. Box 2415
Washington, DC 20013-2415
(202) 720-6734

Description: Direct payments for specified use to private landowners and operators, partnerships, cooperatives, and Indian tribes, as well as for technical assistance.
$ Given: Maximum payment: $50,000 per individual for life of contract
Application Information: Eligible persons make application on Form RSWP-1 any time of the year.
Deadlines: Contact local county ASCS office for application dates.
Contact: Your local, state, and/or regional ASCS office

Alabama
Robert D. Springe
P.O. Box 891
Montgomery, AL 36104-0891
(205) 279-3500

Alaska
Karen O. Lee
Alaska State ASCS Office
800 West Evergreen
Suite 216
Palmer, AK 99654-6539
(907) 745-7982

Arizona
Robert A. Piceno
Arizona State ASCS Office
201 East Indianola
Suite 240
Phoenix, AZ 85012-3118
(602) 640-5200

Arkansas
Wayne Perryman
P.O. Box 2781
New Federal Building
Room 5428
700 West Capitol Street
Little Rock, AR 72201-3225
(501) 324-5220

California
John Smythe
California State ASCS Office
1303 J Street
Suite 300
Sacramento, CA 95814-2916
(916) 551-1801

Colorado
John Stencel
Colorado State ASCS Office
655 Parfet Street
Room E 305
Third Floor
Lakewood, CO 80215
(303) 236-2866

Connecticut
Vincent R. Majchier
88 Day Hill Road
Windsor, CT 06095
(203) 285-8483

Delaware
William D. Clifton II
1201 College Park Drive
Suite A
Dover, DE 19901
(302) 678-4912

Florida
Harry McGlin
P.O. Box 141030
4440 NW 25th Place
Suite I
Gainesville, FL 32614-1030
(904) 372-8549

Georgia
Grady (Buck) Johnson
P.O. Box 1907
Federal Building
Room 102
344 East Hancock Avenue
Athens, GA 30601-2775
(404) 546-2266

Hawaii
Jo Ann Nakata
Hawaii State ASCS Office
300 Ala Moana Boulevard
Room 5106
P.O. Box 50008
Honolulu, HI 96850
(808) 551-2644

Idaho
Richard R. Rush
Idaho State ASCS Office
3220 Elder Street
Boise, ID 83705
(208) 334-1486

Illinois
Stephen Scates
P.O. Box 19273
3500 Wabash Avenue
Springfield, IL 62794-9273
(217) 492-4180

Indiana
Kent Yeager
Indiana State ASCS Office
5891 Lakeside Boulevard
Indianapolis, IN 46278
(317) 290-3030

Iowa
Tom Grau
10500 Buena Vista Court
Urbandale, IA 50322
(515) 254-1540, ext. 40

Kansas
Andrian J. Polansky
Kansas State ASCS Office
3600 Anderson Avenue
Manhattan, KS 66502-2511
(913) 539-3531

Kentucky
Hampton (Hoppy) Hinton
Kentucky State ASCS Office
771 Corporate Drive
Suite 100
Lexington, KY 40503-5478
(606) 224-7601

Louisiana
Willie F. Cooper
3737 Government Street
Alexandria, LA 71302-3395
(318) 473-7721

Maine
Arnold Roach
44 Stillwater Avenue
P.O. Box 406
Bangor, ME 04401-0406
(207) 990-9140

Maryland
James M. Voss
8335 East Guilford Road
Columbia, MD 21046
(410) 381-4550

Massachusetts
Charles A. Costa
451 West Street
Amherst, MA 01002-2953
(413) 256-0232

Michigan
Jim Byrum
300 Coolidge Road
Suite 100
East Lansing, MI 48823-6321
(517) 337-6659

Minnesota
Wally Sparby
Minnesota State ASCS
Office
400 Farm Credit Service
Building
375 Jackson Street
St. Paul, MN 55101-1853
(612) 290-3651

Mississippi
Norris Faust
Mississippi State ASCS
Office
6310 I-55 North
Jackson, MS 39236-4995
(601) 965-4300

Missouri
Brad Epperson
601 Parkdale Plaza Business
Loop
70 West
Suite 225
Columbia, MO 65203
(314) 876-0925

Montana
Bruce E. Nelson
P.O. Box 670
10 East Babcock
Room 557
Bozeman, MT 59715
(406) 587-6872

Nebraska
John Frank Johannsen
Nebraska State ASCS Office
P.O. Box 57975
7131 A Street
Lincoln, NE 68510
(402) 437-5581

Nevada
Wendell K. Newman
Nevada State ASCS Office
1755 East Plumb Lane
Suite 202
Reno, NV 89502-3200
(702) 784-5130

New Hampshire
James McConaka
USDA–New Hampshire
State ASCS Office
22 Bridge Street
Fourth Floor
P.O. Box 1398
Concord, NH 03302-1398
(603) 224-7941

New Jersey
Peter de Wilde
Mastoris Professional Plaza
163 Route 130
Building I
Suite E
Bordentown, NJ 08505-
2249
(609) 224-7941

New Mexico
Charles Essary
New Mexico State ASCS
Office
P.O. Box 1458
Federal Building
Room 4430
517 Gold Avenue, SW
Albuquerque, NM 87103-
1458
(505) 766-2472

New York
Floyd Duger
811 James H. Hanley
Federal Building
100 South Clinton Street
P.O. Box 7308
Syracuse, NY 13260-7308
(315) 423-5176

North Carolina
Samuel Colney
Federal Building
Suite 175
4407 Bland Road
Raleigh, NC 27609-6296
(919) 790-2957

North Dakota
Scott Stofferahn
North Dakota State ASCS
Office
1025 28th Street, SW
P.O. Box 3046
Fargo, ND 58108-3046
(701) 239-5224

Ohio
Steve Maurer
Federal Building
Room 540
200 North High Street
Columbus, OH 43215
(614) 469-6735

Oklahoma
Terry L. Peach
USDA Agriculture Center
Building
Suite 102
Farm Road and McFarland
Street
Stillwater, OK 74074-2653
(405) 624-4110

Oregon
Jack L. Sainsbury
Oregon State ASCS Office
P.O. Box 1300
Tualatin, OR 97062-1300
(503) 692-6830

Pennsylvania
William H. Baumgartner
One Credit Union Place
Suite 320
Harrisburg, PA 17101-2994
(717) 782-4547

Rhode Island
Paul E. Brule
Aldeic Complex
60 Quaker Lane
West Bay Office Complex
Suite 40
West Warwick, RI 02886
(401) 828-8232

South Carolina
Laurie C. Nelson
Strom Thurmond Mall
Suite 100
Columbia, SC 29201-2375
(803) 765-5186

South Dakota
Michael O'Connor
Federal Building
Room 208
200 Fourth Street, SW
Huron, SD 57350-2478
(605) 353-1092

Tennessee
Walter E. Head
United States Courthouse
Room 579
801 Broadway
Nashville, TN 37203-3816
(615) 736-5555

Texas
Harold B. Bennett
Texas State ASCS Office
P.O. Box 2900
College Station, TX 77841-
0001
(409) 260-9207

Utah
James L. Humlicek
Utah State ASCS Office
P.O. Box 11547
Salt Lake City, UT 84147
(801) 524-5013

Vermont
James L. Monahan
Executive Square Office
Building
346 Shelburne Street
Burlington, VT 05401-4495
(802) 658-2803

Virginia
Donald Davis
Culpeper Building
Suite 138
1606 Santa Rosa Road
Richmond, VA 23229
(804) 287-1500

Washington
Larry R. Albin
Washington State ASCS
Office
Rock Point Tower
Suite 568
316 West Boone Avenue
Spokane, WA 99201-2350
(509) 353-2307

West Virginia
Billy B. Burke
P.O. Box 1049
New Federal Building
Room 239
75 High Street
Morgantown, WV 26505-
7558
(304) 291-4351

Wisconsin
Doug Caruso
Wisconsin State ASCS Office
6515 Watts Road
Room 100
Madison, WI 53719-2797
(608) 264-5301

Wyoming
Thomas E. Trowbridge
951 Werner Court
Suite 130
Casper, WY 82601-1307
(307) 261-5231

Caribbean Area
Herberto J. Martinez
Caribbean Area ASCS Office
Cobran's Plaza
Suite 309
1609 Ponce DeLeon Avenue
Santurce, PR 00909-0001
(809) 729-6902

SOIL AND WATER LOANS

Department of Agriculture
Farmers Home
Administration (FmHA)
Washington, DC 20250
(202) 720-1632

Description: Direct, guaranteed, and insured loans for
farming partnerships, joint operators, cooperatives, or
corporations, as well as for individual farm owners or
tenants. Borrower must have or obtain training in financial
and farm-management concepts associated with commercial
farming.
$ Given: Range: $4,000–$300,000; average: $18,200
Application Information: File Form FmHA 410-1, Application for FmHA Services, along with supporting information, with the local county office of the FmHA for insured
loans and with the prospective lender for loan guarantees.
Deadline: None
Contact: Consult your local telephone directory under U.S.
Government, Department of Agriculture, for FmHA county
office number, or contact your FmHA state offices.

Alabama
Sterling Center
Suite 601
4121 Carmichael Road
Montgomery, AL 36106-
3683
(205) 279-3400

Alaska
634 South Bailey
Suite 103
Palmer, AK 99645
(907) 745-2176

Arizona
3003 North Central Avenue
Suite 900
Phoenix, AZ 85012
(602) 280-8700

Arkansas
700 West Capitol
P.O. Box 2778
Little Rock, AR 72203
(501) 324-6281

California
194 West Main Street
Suite F
Woodland, CA 95695-2915
(916) 669-2000

Colorado
655 Parfet Street
Room 31-08
Lakewood, CO 80215
(303) 236-2801

Connecticut
451 West Street
Amherst, MA 01002
(413) 253-4300

Delaware
4611 South Dupont
Highway
P.O. Box 400
Camden, DE 19934-9998
(302) 697-4300

District of Columbia
4611 South Dupont
Highway
P.O. Box 400
Camden, DE 19934-9998
(302) 697-4300

Florida
Federal Building
4440 NW 25th Place
P.O. Box 147010
Gainesville, FL 32614-7010
(904) 338-3400

Georgia
355 East Hancock Avenue
Stephens Federal Building
Athens, GA 30610
(706) 546-2152

Guam
Department of Agriculture
14th Street and
Independence Avenue, SW
Washington, DC 20250
(202) 720-1632

Hawaii
Federal Building
Room 311
154 Waianuenue Avenue
Hilo, HI 96720
(808) 933-3000

Idaho
3232 Elder Street
Boise, ID 83705
(208) 334-1301

Illinois
Illini Plaza
Suite 103
1817 South Neil Street
Champaign, IL 61820
(217) 398-5235

Indiana
5975 Lakeside Boulevard
Indianapolis, IN 46278
(317) 290-3100

Iowa
Federal Building
Room 873
210 Walnut Street
Des Moines, IA 50309
(515) 284-4663

Kansas
1201 SW Summit Executive
Court
P.O. Box 4653
Topeka, KS 66604
(913) 271-2700

Kentucky
771 Corporate Drive
Suite 200
Lexington, KY 40503
(606) 224-7300

Louisiana
3727 Government Street
Alexandria, LA 71302
(318) 473-7920

Maine
444 Stillwater Avenue
Suite 2
P.O. Box 405
Bangor, ME 04402-0405
(207) 990-9106

Maryland
4611 South Dupont
Highway
P.O. Box 400
Camden, DE 19934-9998
(302) 697-4300

Massachusetts
451 West Street
Amherst, MA 01002
(413) 253-4300

Michigan
3001 Coolidge Road
Suite 200
East Lansing, MI 48823
(517) 337-6635

Minnesota
410 Farm Credit Service
Building
375 Jackson Street
St. Paul, MN 55101
(612) 290-3842

Mississippi
Federal Building
Suite 831
100 West Capitol
Jackson, MS 39269
(601) 965-4316

Missouri
601 Business Loop
70 West Parkade Center
Suite 235
Columbia, MO 65203
(314) 768-0976

Montana
900 Technology Boulevard
Suite B
P.O. Box 850
Bozeman, MT 59771
(406) 585-2580

Nebraska
Federal Building
Room 308
100 Centennial Mall
Lincoln, NE 68508
(402) 437-5551

Nevada
1390 South Curry Street
Carson City, NV 89703-
5405
(702) 887-1222

New Hampshire
City Center
89 Main Street
Third Floor
Montpelier, VT 05602
(802) 828-6001

New Jersey
Tarnsfield Plaza
Suite 22
1016 Woodlane Road
Mt. Holly, NJ 08060
(609) 265-3600

New Mexico
Federal Building
Room 3414
517 Gold Avenue, SW
Albuquerque, NM 87102
(505) 766-2462

New York
Federal Building
100 South Clinton Street
Room 871
Syracuse, NY 13261-7318
(315) 423-5290

North Carolina
4405 South Bland Road
Suite 260
Raleigh, NC 27609
(919) 790-2731

North Dakota
Federal Building
Room 208
Third and Rosser
P.O. Box 1737
Bismarck, ND 59502
(701) 250-4781

Ohio
Federal Building
Room 507
200 North High Street
Columbus, OH 43215
(614) 469-5606

Oklahoma
USDA Agricultural Center
Office Building
Stillwater, OK 74074
(405) 624-4250

Oregon
Federal Building
Room 1590
1220 SW Third Avenue
Portland, OR 97204
(503) 326-2731

Pennsylvania
One Credit Union Plaza
Suite 330
Harrisburg, PA 17110-2996
(717) 782-4476

Puerto Rico
New San Juan Center
Building
Room 501
159 Carlos E. Chardon
Street
G.P.O. Box 6106G
Hato Rey, PR 00918-5481
(809) 766-5095

Rhode Island
451 West Street
Amherst, MA 01002
(413) 253-4300

South Carolina
Strom Thurmond Federal
Building
Room 1007
1835 Assembly Street
Columbia, SC 28201
(803) 765-5163

South Dakota
Huron Federal Building
Room 308
200 Fourth Street, SW
Huron, SD 57350
(605) 353-1430

Tennessee
3322 West End Avenue
Suite 300
Nashville, TN 37203-1071
(615) 783-1308

Texas
Federal Building
Suite 102
101 South Main
Temple, TX 76501
(817) 774-1301

Utah
Federal Building
Room 5438
125 South State Street
Salt Lake City, UT 84138
(801) 524-4063

Vermont
City Center
89 Main Street
Third Floor
Montpelier, VT 05602
(802) 828-6001

Virginia
Culpeper Building
Suite 238
1606 Santa Rosa Road
Richmond, VA 23229
(804) 828-1550

Virgin Islands
City Center
89 Main Street
Third Floor
Montpelier, VT 05602
(802) 828-6001

Washington
Federal Building
Room 319
P.O. Box 2427
Wenatchee, WA 98807
(509) 664-0240

West Virginia
75 High Street
P.O. Box 678
Morgantown, WV 26505
(304) 291-4791

Wisconsin
4949 Kirschling Court
Stevens Point, WI 54481
(715) 345-7625

Wyoming
Federal Building
Room 1005
100 East B Street
P.O. Box 820
Casper, WY 82602
(307) 261-5271

VERY LOW INCOME HOUSING-REPAIR LOANS AND GRANTS

Department of Agriculture
Farmers Home
Administration (FmHA)
Washington, DC 20250
(202) 720-1474

Description: Direct loans and project grants to very low income owners-occupants in rural areas for repairing or improving dwellings. Grant recipient must be 62 or older and unable to repay a loan. Very low income limits range from $8,450 to $22,050 for a household.
$ Given: Loan range: $200–$15,000; grant range: $200-$5,000
Application Information: File Form FmHA 1910-4 at your FmHA county office.
Deadline: None
Contact: Consult your local telephone directory under U.S. Government, Department of Agriculture, for FmHA county office number, or contact your FmHA state offices.

Alabama
Sterling Center
Suite 601
4121 Carmichael Road
Montgomery, AL 36106-3683
(205) 279-3400

Alaska
634 South Bailey
Suite 103
Palmer, AK 99645
(907) 745-2176

Arizona
3003 North Central Avenue
Suite 900
Phoenix, AZ 85012
(602) 280-8700

Arkansas
700 West Capitol
P.O. Box 2778
Little Rock, AR 72203
(501) 324-6281

California
194 West Main Street
Suite F
Woodland, CA 95695-2915
(916) 669-2000

Colorado
655 Parfet Street
Room 31-08
Lakewood, CO 80215
(303) 236-2801

Connecticut
451 West Street
Amherst, MA 01002
(413) 253-4300

Delaware
4611 South Dupont
Highway
P.O. Box 400
Camden, DE 19934-9998
(302) 697-4300

District of Columbia
4611 South Dupont
Highway
P.O. Box 400
Camden, DE 19934-9998
(302) 697-4300

Florida
Federal Building
4440 NW 25th Place
P.O. Box 147010
Gainesville, FL 32614-7010
(904) 338-3400

Georgia
355 East Hancock Avenue
Stephens Federal Building
Athens, GA 30610
(706) 546-2152

Guam
Department of Agriculture
14th Street and
Independence Avenue, SW
Washington, DC 20250
(202) 720-1632

Hawaii
Federal Building
Room 311
154 Waianuenue Avenue
Hilo, HI 96720
(808) 933-3000

Idaho
3232 Elder Street
Boise, ID 83705
(208) 334-1301

Illinois
Illini Plaza
Suite 103
1817 South Neil Street
Champaign, IL 61820
(217) 398-5235

Indiana
5975 Lakeside Boulevard
Indianapolis, IN 46278
(317) 290-3100

Iowa
Federal Building
Room 873
210 Walnut Street
Des Moines, IA 50309
(515) 284-4663

Kansas
1201 SW Summit Executive
Court
P.O. Box 4653
Topeka, KS 66604
(913) 271-2700

Kentucky
771 Corporate Drive
Suite 200
Lexington, KY 40503
(606) 224-7300

Louisiana
3727 Government Street
Alexandria, LA 71302
(318) 473-7920

Maine
444 Stillwater Avenue
Suite 2
P.O. Box 405
Bangor, ME 04402-0405
(207) 990-9106

Maryland
4611 South Dupont
Highway
P.O. Box 400
Camden, DE 19934-9998
(302) 697-4300

Massachusetts
451 West Street
Amherst, MA 01002
(413) 253-4300

Michigan
3001 Coolidge Road
Suite 200
East Lansing, MI 48823
(517) 337-6635

Minnesota
410 Farm Credit Service
Building
375 Jackson Street
St. Paul, MN 55101
(612) 290-3842

Mississippi
Federal Building
Suite 831
100 West Capitol
Jackson, MS 39269
(601) 965-4316

Missouri
601 Business Loop
70 West Parkade Center
Suite 235
Columbia, MO 65203
(314) 768-0976

Montana
900 Technology Boulevard
Suite B
P.O. Box 850
Bozeman, MT 59771
(406) 585-2580

Nebraska
Federal Building
Room 308
100 Centennial Mall
Lincoln, NE 68508
(402) 437-5551

Nevada
1390 South Curry Street
Carson City, NV 89703-5405
(702) 887-1222

New Hampshire
City Center
89 Main Street
Third Floor
Montpelier, VT 05602
(802) 828-6001

New Jersey
Tarnsfield Plaza
Suite 22
1016 Woodlane Road
Mt. Holly, NJ 08060
(609) 265-3600

New Mexico
Federal Building
Room 3414
517 Gold Avenue, SW
Albuquerque, NM 87102
(505) 766-2462

New York
Federal Building
100 South Clinton Street
Room 871
Syracuse, NY 13261-7318
(315) 423-5290

North Carolina
4405 South Bland Road
Suite 260
Raleigh, NC 27609
(919) 790-2731

North Dakota
Federal Building
Room 208
Third and Rosser
P.O. Box 1737
Bismarck, ND 59502
(701) 250-4781

Ohio
Federal Building
Room 507
200 North High Street
Columbus, OH 43215
(614) 469-5606

Oklahoma
USDA Agricultural Center
Office Building
Stillwater, OK 74074
(405) 624-4250

Oregon
Federal Building
Room 1590
1220 SW Third Avenue
Portland, OR 97204
(503) 326-2731

Pennsylvania
One Credit Union Plaza
Suite 330
Harrisburg, PA 17110-2996
(717) 782-4476

Puerto Rico
New San Juan Center
Building
Room 501
159 Carlos E. Chardon
Street
G.P.O. Box 6106G
Hato Rey, PR 00918-5481
(809) 766-5095

Rhode Island
451 West Street
Amherst, MA 01002
(413) 253-4300

South Carolina
Strom Thurmond Federal
Building
Room 1007
1835 Assembly Street
Columbia, SC 28201
(803) 765-5163

South Dakota
Huron Federal Building
Room 308
200 Fourth Street, SW
Huron, SD 57350
(605) 353-1430

Tennessee
3322 West End Avenue
Suite 300
Nashville, TN 37203-1071
(615) 783-1308

Texas
Federal Building
Suite 102
101 South Main
Temple, TX 76501
(817) 774-1301

Utah
Federal Building
Room 5438
125 South State Street
Salt Lake City, UT 84138
(801) 524-4063

Vermont
City Center
89 Main Street
Third Floor
Montpelier, VT 05602
(802) 828-6001

Virginia
Culpeper Building
Suite 238
1606 Santa Rosa Road
Richmond, VA 23229
(804) 828-1550

Virgin Islands
City Center
89 Main Street
Third Floor
Montpelier, VT 05602
(802) 828-6001

Washington
Federal Building
Room 319
P.O. Box 2427
Wenatchee, WA 98807
(509) 664-0240

West Virginia
75 High Street
P.O. Box 678
Morgantown, WV 26505
(304) 291-4791

Wisconsin
4949 Kirschling Court
Stevens Point, WI 54481
(715) 345-7625

Wyoming
Federal Building
Room 1005
100 East B Street
P.O. Box 820
Casper, WY 82602
(307) 261-5271

VERY LOW TO MODERATE INCOME HOUSING LOANS

Department of Agriculture
Farmers Home
Administration (FmHA)
Washington, DC 20250
(202) 447-7967

Description: Direct, guaranteed, and insured loans for construction, repair, or housing purchase; adequate sewage-disposal facilities and/or sewage water supply for household; weatherization; essential equipment; purchase site for dwelling; and, under certain conditions, to finance a manufactured home and its site. Housing debts may be refinanced under certain circumstances. Dwelling financed must be modest in size, design, and cost, and located in a rural area with a population of less than 10,000 (25,000 in extreme cases).
$ Given: Loan range: $1,000-$105,000; average for new construction: $57,032; average for existing cost: $48,737
Application Information: For direct loans, file with your FmHA county office. For guaranteed loans, contact a local lender.
Deadline: None
Contact: Consult your local telephone directory under U.S. Government, Department of Agriculture, for FmHA county office number, or contact your FmHA state offices.

Alabama
Sterling Center
Suite 601
4121 Carmichael Road
Montgomery, AL 36106-3683
(205) 279-3400

Alaska
634 South Bailey
Suite 103
Palmer, AK 99645
(907) 745-2176

Arizona
3003 North Central Avenue
Suite 900
Phoenix, AZ 85012
(602) 280-8700

Arkansas
700 West Capitol
P.O. Box 2778
Little Rock, AR 72203
(501) 324-6281

California
194 West Main Street
Suite F
Woodland, CA 95695-2915
(916) 669-2000

Colorado
655 Parfet Street
Room 31-08
Lakewood, CO 80215
(303) 236-2801

Connecticut
451 West Street
Amherst, MA 01002
(413) 253-4300

Delaware
4611 South Dupont
Highway
P.O. Box 400
Camden, DE 19934-9998
(302) 697-4300

District of Columbia
4611 South Dupont
Highway
P.O. Box 400
Camden, DE 19934-9998
(302) 697-4300

Florida
Federal Building
4440 NW 25th Place
P.O. Box 147010
Gainesville, FL 32614-7010
(904) 338-3400

Georgia
355 East Hancock Avenue
Stephens Federal Building
Athens, GA 30610
(706) 546-2152

Guam
Department of Agriculture
14th Street and
Independence Avenue, SW
Washington, DC 20250
(202) 720-1632

Hawaii
Federal Building
Room 311
154 Waianuenue Avenue
Hilo, HI 96720
(808) 933-3000

Idaho
3232 Elder Street
Boise, ID 83705
(208) 334-1301

Illinois
Illini Plaza
Suite 103
1817 South Neil Street
Champaign, IL 61820
(217) 398-5235

Indiana
5975 Lakeside Boulevard
Indianapolis, IN 46278
(317) 290-3100

Iowa
Federal Building
Room 873
210 Walnut Street
Des Moines, IA 50309
(515) 284-4663

Kansas
1201 SW Summit Executive
Court
P.O. Box 4653
Topeka, KS 66604
(913) 271-2700

Kentucky
771 Corporate Drive
Suite 200
Lexington, KY 40503
(606) 224-7300

Louisiana
3727 Government Street
Alexandria, LA 71302
(318) 473-7920

Maine
444 Stillwater Avenue
Suite 2
P.O. Box 405
Bangor, ME 04402-0405
(207) 990-9106

Maryland
4611 South Dupont
Highway
P.O. Box 400
Camden, DE 19934-9998
(302) 697-4300

Massachusetts
451 West Street
Amherst, MA 01002
(413) 253-4300

Michigan
3001 Coolidge Road
Suite 200
East Lansing, MI 48823
(517) 337-6635

Minnesota
410 Farm Credit Service
Building
375 Jackson Street
St. Paul, MN 55101
(612) 290-3842

Mississippi
Federal Building
Suite 831
100 West Capitol
Jackson, MS 39269
(601) 965-4316

Missouri
601 Business Loop
70 West Parkade Center
Suite 235
Columbia, MO 65203
(314) 768-0976

Montana
900 Technology Boulevard
Suite B
P.O. Box 850
Bozeman, MT 59771
(406) 585-2580

Nebraska
Federal Building
Room 308
100 Centennial Mall
Lincoln, NE 68508
(402) 437-5551

Nevada
1390 South Curry Street
Carson City, NV 89703-
5405
(702) 887-1222

New Hampshire
City Center
89 Main Street
Third Floor
Montpelier, VT 05602
(802) 828-6001

New Jersey
Tarnsfield Plaza
Suite 22
1016 Woodlane Road
Mt. Holly, NJ 08060
(609) 265-3600

New Mexico
Federal Building
Room 3414
517 Gold Avenue, SW
Albuquerque, NM 87102
(505) 766-2462

New York
Federal Building
100 South Clinton Street
Room 871
Syracuse, NY 13261-7318
(315) 423-5290

North Carolina
4405 South Bland Road
Suite 260
Raleigh, NC 27609
(919) 790-2731

North Dakota
Federal Building
Room 208
Third and Rosser
P.O. Box 1737
Bismarck, ND 59502
(701) 250-4781

Ohio
Federal Building
Room 507
200 North High Street
Columbus, OH 43215
(614) 469-5606

Oklahoma
USDA Agricultural Center
Office Building
Stillwater, OK 74074
(405) 624-4250

Oregon
Federal Building
Room 1590
1220 SW Third Avenue
Portland, OR 97204
(503) 326-2731

Pennsylvania
One Credit Union Plaza
Suite 330
Harrisburg, PA 17110-2996
(717) 782-4476

Puerto Rico
New San Juan Center
Building
Room 501
159 Carlos E. Chardon
Street
G.P.O. Box 6106G
Hato Rey, PR 00918-5481
(809) 766-5095

Rhode Island
451 West Street
Amherst, MA 01002
(413) 253-4300

South Carolina
Strom Thurmond Federal
Building
Room 1007
1835 Assembly Street
Columbia, SC 28201
(803) 765-5163

South Dakota
Huron Federal Building
Room 308
200 Fourth Street, SW
Huron, SD 57350
(605) 353-1430

Tennessee
3322 West End Avenue
Suite 300
Nashville, TN 37203-1071
(615) 783-1308

Texas
Federal Building
Suite 102
101 South Main
Temple, TX 76501
(817) 774-1301

Utah
Federal Building
Room 5438
125 South State Street
Salt Lake City, UT 84138
(801) 524-4063

Vermont
City Center
89 Main Street
Third Floor
Montpelier, VT 05602
(802) 828-6001

Virginia
Culpeper Building
Suite 238
1606 Santa Rosa Road
Richmond, VA 23229
(804) 828-1550

Virgin Islands
City Center
89 Main Street
Third Floor
Montpelier, VT 05602
(802) 828-6001

Washington
Federal Building
Room 319
P.O. Box 2427
Wenatchee, WA 98807
(509) 664-0240

West Virginia
75 High Street
P.O. Box 678
Morgantown, WV 26505
(304) 291-4791

Wisconsin
4949 Kirschling Court
Stevens Point, WI 54481
(715) 345-7625

Wyoming
Federal Building
Room 1005
100 East B Street
P.O. Box 820
Casper, WY 82602
(307) 261-5271

WATER BANK PROGRAM

Department of Agriculture
Agricultural Stabilization
and Conservation Service
(ASCS)
P.O. Box 2415
Washington, DC 20013-
2415
(202) 720-6734

Description: Direct payments for specified use to landowners
and operators of specified types of wetlands in designated
migratory waterfowl, nesting, breeding, and feeding areas.
$ Given: $7–$75 per acre; average: $13 per acre
Application Information: Apply at your county ASCS office
for the county in which the land is located.
Deadline: None
Contact: Your local, state, and/or regional ASCS office.

Alabama
Robert D. Springe
P.O. Box 891
Montgomery, AL 36104-
0891
(205) 279-3500

Alaska
Karen O. Lee
Alaska State ASCS Office
800 West Evergreen
Suite 216
Palmer, AK 99654-6539
(907) 745-7982

Arizona
Robert A. Piceno
Arizona State ASCS Office
201 East Indianola
Suite 240
Phoenix, AZ 85012-3118
(602) 640-5200

Arkansas
Wayne Perryman
P.O. Box 2781
New Federal Building
Room 5428
700 West Capitol Street
Little Rock, AR 72201-3225
(501) 324-5220

California
John Smythe
California State ASCS Office
1303 J Street
Suite 300
Sacramento, CA 95814-
2916
(916) 551-1801

Colorado
John Stencel
Colorado State ASCS Office
655 Parfet Street
Room E 305
Third Floor
Lakewood, CO 80215
(303) 236-2866

Connecticut
Vincent R. Majchier
88 Day Hill Road
Windsor, CT 06095
(203) 285-8483

Delaware
William D. Clifton II
1201 College Park Drive
Suite A
Dover, DE 19901
(302) 678-4912

Florida
Harry McGlin
P.O. Box 141030
4440 NW 25th Place
Suite I
Gainesville, FL 32614-1030
(904) 372-8549

Georgia
Grady (Buck) Johnson
P.O. Box 1907
Federal Building
Room 102
344 East Hancock Avenue
Athens, GA 30601-2775
(404) 546-2266

Hawaii
Jo Ann Nakata
Hawaii State ASCS Office
300 Ala Moana Boulevard
Room 5106
P.O. Box 50008
Honolulu, HI 96850
(808) 551-2644

Idaho
Richard R. Rush
Idaho State ASCS Office
3220 Elder Street
Boise, ID 83705
(208) 334-1486

Illinois
Stephen Scates
P.O. Box 19273
3500 Wabash Avenue
Springfield, IL 62794-9273
(217) 492-4180

Indiana
Kent Yeager
Indiana State ASCS Office
5891 Lakeside Boulevard
Indianapolis, IN 46278
(317) 290-3030

Iowa
Tom Grau
10500 Buena Vista Court
Urbandale, IA 50322
(515) 254-1540, ext. 40

Kansas
Andrian J. Polansky
Kansas State ASCS Office
3600 Anderson Avenue
Manhattan, KS 66502-2511
(913) 539-3531

Kentucky
Hampton (Hoppy) Hinton
Kentucky State ASCS Office
771 Corporate Drive
Suite 100
Lexington, KY 40503-5478
(606) 224-7601

Louisiana
Willie F. Cooper
3737 Government Street
Alexandria, LA 71302-3395
(318) 473-7721

Maine
Arnold Roach
44 Stillwater Avenue
P.O. Box 406
Bangor, ME 04401-0406
(207) 990-9140

Maryland
James M. Voss
8335 East Guilford Road
Columbia, MD 21046
(410) 381-4550

Massachusetts
Charles A. Costa
451 West Street
Amherst, MA 01002-2953
(413) 256-0232

Michigan
Jim Byrum
300 Coolidge Road
Suite 100
East Lansing, MI 48823-6321
(517) 337-6659

Minnesota
Wally Sparby
Minnesota State ASCS
Office
400 Farm Credit Service
Building
375 Jackson Street
St. Paul, MN 55101-1853
(612) 290-3651

Mississippi
Norris Faust
Mississippi State ASCS
Office
6310 I-55 North
Jackson, MS 39236-4995
(601) 965-4300

Missouri
Brad Epperson
601 Parkdale Plaza Business
Loop
70 West
Suite 225
Columbia, MO 65203
(314) 876-0925

Montana
Bruce E. Nelson
P.O. Box 670
10 East Babcock
Room 557
Bozeman, MT 59715
(406) 587-6872

Nebraska
John Frank Johannsen
Nebraska State ASCS Office
P.O. Box 57975
7131 A Street
Lincoln, NE 68510
(402) 437-5581

Nevada
Wendell K. Newman
Nevada State ASCS Office
1755 East Plumb Lane
Suite 202
Reno, NV 89502-3200
(702) 784-5130

New Hampshire
James McConaka
USDA–New Hampshire
State ASCS Office
22 Bridge Street
Fourth Floor
P.O. Box 1398
Concord, NH 03302-1398
(603) 224-7941

New Jersey
Peter de Wilde
Mastoris Professional Plaza
163 Route 130
Building I
Suite E
Bordentown, NJ 08505-
2249
(609) 224-7941

New Mexico
Charles Essary
New Mexico State ASCS
Office
P.O. Box 1458
Federal Building
Room 4430
517 Gold Avenue, SW
Albuquerque, NM 87103-
1458
(505) 766-2472

New York
Floyd Duger
811 James H. Hanley
Federal Building
100 South Clinton Street
P.O. Box 7308
Syracuse, NY 13260-7308
(315) 423-5176

North Carolina
Samuel Colney
Federal Building
Suite 175
4407 Bland Road
Raleigh, NC 27609-6296
(919) 790-2957

North Dakota
Scott Stofferahn
North Dakota State ASCS
Office
1025 28th Street, SW
P.O. Box 3046
Fargo, ND 58108-3046
(701) 239-5224

Ohio
Steve Maurer
Federal Building
Room 540
200 North High Street
Columbus, OH 43215
(614) 469-6735

Oklahoma
Terry L. Peach
USDA Agriculture Center
Building
Suite 102
Farm Road and McFarland
Street
Stillwater, OK 74074-2653
(405) 624-4110

Oregon
Jack L. Sainsbury
Oregon State ASCS Office
P.O. Box 1300
Tualatin, OR 97062-1300
(503) 692-6830

Pennsylvania
William H. Baumgartner
One Credit Union Place
Suite 320
Harrisburg, PA 17101-2994
(717) 782-4547

Rhode Island
Paul E. Brule
Aldeic Complex
60 Quaker Lane
West Bay Office Complex
Suite 40
West Warwick, RI 02886
(401) 828-8232

South Carolina
Laurie C. Nelson
Strom Thurmond Mall
Suite 100
Columbia, SC 29201-2375
(803) 765-5186

South Dakota
Michael O'Connor
Federal Building
Room 208
200 Fourth Street, SW
Huron, SD 57350-2478
(605) 353-1092

Tennessee
Walter E. Head
United States Courthouse
Room 579
801 Broadway
Nashville, TN 37203-3816
(615) 736-5555

Texas
Harold B. Bennett
Texas State ASCS Office
P.O. Box 2900
College Station, TX 77841-
0001
(409) 260-9207

Utah
James L. Humlicek
Utah State ASCS Office
P.O. Box 11547
Salt Lake City, UT 84147
(801) 524-5013

Vermont
James L. Monahan
Executive Square Office
Building
346 Shelburne Street
Burlington, VT 05401-4495
(802) 658-2803

Virginia
Donald Davis
Culpeper Building
Suite 138
1606 Santa Rosa Road
Richmond, VA 23229
(804) 287-1500

Washington
Larry R. Albin
Washington State ASCS
Office
Rock Point Tower
Suite 568
316 West Boone Avenue
Spokane, WA 99201-2350
(509) 353-2307

West Virginia
Billy B. Burke
P.O. Box 1049
New Federal Building
Room 239
75 High Street
Morgantown, WV 26505-
7558
(304) 291-4351

Wisconsin
Doug Caruso
Wisconsin State ASCS Office
6515 Watts Road
Room 100
Madison, WI 53719-2797
(608) 264-5301

Wyoming
Thomas E. Trowbridge
951 Werner Court
Suite 130
Casper, WY 82601-1307
(307) 261-5231

Caribbean Area
Herberto J. Martinez
Caribbean Area ASCS Office
Cobran's Plaza
Suite 309
1609 Ponce DeLeon Avenue
Santurce, PR 00909-0001
(809) 729-6902

WHEAT-PRODUCTION STABILIZATION

Department of Agriculture
Agricultural Stabilization
and Conservation Service
(ASCS)
P.O. Box 2415
Washington, DC 20013
(202) 720-4418

Alabama
Robert D. Springe
P.O. Box 891
Montgomery, AL 36104-
0891
(205) 279-3500

Description: Direct payments with unrestricted use to
owners, landlords, tenants, or sharecroppers on farms.
Commodity planted must meet program requirements as
announced by the Secretary.
$ Given: Up to $250,000 per person
Deadline: Dates vary from state to state
Contact: Your local, state, and/or regional ASCS office.

Alaska
Karen O. Lee
Alaska State ASCS Office
800 West Evergreen
Suite 216
Palmer, AK 99654-6539
(907) 745-7982

Arizona
Robert A. Piceno
Arizona State ASCS Office
201 East Indianola
Suite 240
Phoenix, AZ 85012-3118
(602) 640-5200

Arkansas
Wayne Perryman
P.O. Box 2781
New Federal Building
Room 5428
700 West Capitol Street
Little Rock, AR 72201-3225
(501) 324-5220

California
John Smythe
California State ASCS Office
1303 J Street
Suite 300
Sacramento, CA 95814-2916
(916) 551-1801

Colorado
John Stencel
Colorado State ASCS Office
655 Parfet Street
Room E 305
Third Floor
Lakewood, CO 80215
(303) 236-2866

Connecticut
Vincent R. Majchier
88 Day Hill Road
Windsor, CT 06095
(203) 285-8483

Delaware
William D. Clifton II
1201 College Park Drive
Suite A
Dover, DE 19901
(302) 678-4912

Florida
Harry McGlin
P.O. Box 141030
4440 NW 25th Place
Suite I
Gainesville, FL 32614-1030
(904) 372-8549

Georgia
Grady (Buck) Johnson
P.O. Box 1907
Federal Building
Room 102
344 East Hancock Avenue
Athens, GA 30601-2775
(404) 546-2266

Hawaii
Jo Ann Nakata
Hawaii State ASCS Office
300 Ala Moana Boulevard
Room 5106
P.O. Box 50008
Honolulu, HI 96850
(808) 551-2644

Idaho
Richard R. Rush
Idaho State ASCS Office
3220 Elder Street
Boise, ID 83705
(208) 334-1486

Illinois
Stephen Scates
P.O. Box 19273
3500 Wabash Avenue
Springfield, IL 62794-9273
(217) 492-4180

Indiana
Kent Yeager
Indiana State ASCS Office
5891 Lakeside Boulevard
Indianapolis, IN 46278
(317) 290-3030

Iowa
Tom Grau
10500 Buena Vista Court
Urbandale, IA 50322
(515) 254-1540, ext. 40

Kansas
Andrian J. Polansky
Kansas State ASCS Office
3600 Anderson Avenue
Manhattan, KS 66502-2511
(913) 539-3531

Kentucky
Hampton (Hoppy) Hinton
Kentucky State ASCS Office
771 Corporate Drive
Suite 100
Lexington, KY 40503-5478
(606) 224-7601

Louisiana
Willie F. Cooper
3737 Government Street
Alexandria, LA 71302-3395
(318) 473-7721

Maine
Arnold Roach
44 Stillwater Avenue
P.O. Box 406
Bangor, ME 04401-0406
(207) 990-9140

Maryland
James M. Voss
8335 East Guilford Road
Columbia, MD 21046
(410) 381-4550

Massachusetts
Charles A. Costa
451 West Street
Amherst, MA 01002-2953
(413) 256-0232

Michigan
Jim Byrum
300 Coolidge Road
Suite 100
East Lansing, MI 48823-6321
(517) 337-6659

Minnesota
Wally Sparby
Minnesota State ASCS
Office
400 Farm Credit Service
Building
375 Jackson Street
St. Paul, MN 55101-1853
(612) 290-3651

Mississippi
Norris Faust
Mississippi State ASCS
Office
6310 1-55 North
Jackson, MS 39236-4995
(601) 965-4300

Missouri
Brad Epperson
601 Parkdale Plaza Business
Loop
70 West
Suite 225
Columbia, MO 65203
(314) 876-0925

Montana
Bruce E. Nelson
P.O. Box 670
10 East Babcock
Room 557
Bozeman, MT 59715
(406) 587-6872

Nebraska
John Frank Johannsen
Nebraska State ASCS Office
P.O. Box 57975
7131 A Street
Lincoln, NE 68510
(402) 437-5581

Nevada
Wendell K. Newman
Nevada State ASCS Office
1755 East Plumb Lane
Suite 202
Reno, NV 89502-3200
(702) 784-5130

New Hampshire
James McConaka
USDA–New Hampshire
State ASCS Office
22 Bridge Street
Fourth Floor
P.O. Box 1398
Concord, NH 03302-1398
(603) 224-7941

New Jersey
Peter de Wilde
Mastoris Professional Plaza
163 Route 130
Building I
Suite E
Bordentown, NJ 08505-
2249
(609) 224-7941

New Mexico
Charles Essary
New Mexico State ASCS
Office
P.O. Box 1458
Federal Building
Room 4430
517 Gold Avenue, SW
Albuquerque, NM 87103-
1458
(505) 766-2472

New York
Floyd Duger
811 James H. Hanley
Federal Building
100 South Clinton Street
P.O. Box 7308
Syracuse, NY 13260-7308
(315) 423-5176

North Carolina
Samuel Colney
Federal Building
Suite 175
4407 Bland Road
Raleigh, NC 27609-6296
(919) 790-2957

North Dakota
Scott Stofferahn
North Dakota State ASCS
Office
1025 28th Street, SW
P.O. Box 3046
Fargo, ND 58108-3046
(701) 239-5224

Ohio
Steve Maurer
Federal Building
Room 540
200 North High Street
Columbus, OH 43215
(614) 469-6735

Oklahoma
Terry L. Peach
USDA Agriculture Center
Building
Suite 102
Farm Road and McFarland
Street
Stillwater, OK 74074-2653
(405) 624-4110

Oregon
Jack L. Sainsbury
Oregon State ASCS Office
P.O. Box 1300
Tualatin, OR 97062-1300
(503) 692-6830

Pennsylvania
William H. Baumgartner
One Credit Union Place
Suite 320
Harrisburg, PA 17101-2994
(717) 782-4547

Rhode Island
Paul E. Brule
Aldeic Complex
60 Quaker Lane
West Bay Office Complex
Suite 40
West Warwick, RI 02886
(401) 828-8232

South Carolina
Laurie C. Nelson
Strom Thurmond Mall
Suite 100
Columbia, SC 29201-2375
(803) 765-5186

South Dakota
Michael O'Connor
Federal Building
Room 208
200 Fourth Street, SW
Huron, SD 57350-2478
(605) 353-1092

Tennessee
Walter E. Head
United States Courthouse
Room 579
801 Broadway
Nashville, TN 37203-3816
(615) 736-5555

Texas
Harold B. Bennett
Texas State ASCS Office
P.O. Box 2900
College Station, TX 77841-0001
(409) 260-9207

Utah
James L. Humlicek
Utah State ASCS Office
P.O. Box 11547
Salt Lake City, UT 84147
(801) 524-5013

Vermont
James L. Monahan
Executive Square Office Building
346 Shelburne Street
Burlington, VT 05401-4495
(802) 658-2803

Virginia
Donald Davis
Culpeper Building
Suite 138
1606 Santa Rosa Road
Richmond, VA 23229
(804) 287-1500

Washington
Larry R. Albin
Washington State ASCS Office
Rock Point Tower
Suite 568
316 West Boone Avenue
Spokane, WA 99201-2350
(509) 353-2307

West Virginia
Billy B. Burke
P.O. Box 1049
New Federal Building
Room 239
75 High Street
Morgantown, WV 26505-7558
(304) 291-4351

Wisconsin
Doug Caruso
Wisconsin State ASCS Office
6515 Watts Road
Room 100
Madison, WI 53719-2797
(608) 264-5301

Wyoming
Thomas E. Trowbridge
951 Werner Court
Suite 130
Casper, WY 82601-1307
(307) 261-5231

Caribbean Area
Herberto J. Martinez
Caribbean Area ASCS Office
Cobran's Plaza
Suite 309
1609 Ponce DeLeon Avenue
Santurce, PR 00909-0001
(809) 729-6902

Community Development

Assistance is widely available from the federal government for community development for the following:

1. *Assistance* for projects that promote long-term economic development and employment, as well as research projects that determine causes of unemployment in the United States
2. *Loans* to businesses for local development, construction, or modernization of buildings; for projects serving low-income areas that have high unemployment or that have experienced natural disasters; or for projects serving disadvantaged individuals

You will need to consult the list of addresses in this chapter for your nearest local or regional Small Business Administration (SBA) office or Economic Development office.

BUSINESS LOANS FOR SBA PROGRAM PARTICIPANTS

Small Business
Administration (SBA)
Loan Policy and Procedures
Branch
409 Third Street, SW
Washington, DC 20416
(202) 205-6570

Description: Direct, guaranteed, and insured loans to small business concerns owned by socially and economically disadvantaged persons for constructing, expanding, or converting facilities; or for acquiring equipment, building materials, or supplies. Loans for working capital limited to manufacturers.
$ Given: Direct loans: up to $150,000; guaranteed loans: up to $750,000; average: $113,636
Application Information: Write for guidelines.
Deadline: None
Contact: Your state and/or regional SBA office

Alabama
1375 Peachtree Street, NE
Fifth Floor
Atlanta, GA 30367-8102
(404) 347-2797

Alaska
2601 Fourth Avenue
Room 440
Seattle, WA 98121-1273
(206) 553-1273

Arizona
71 Stevenson Street
20th Floor
San Francisco, CA 94105-
2939
(415) 744-6402

Arkansas
8625 King George Drive
Building C
Dallas, TX 75235-3391
(214) 767-7633

California
71 Stevenson Street
20th Floor
San Francisco, CA 94105-
2939
(415) 744-6402

Colorado
633 17th Street
Seventh Floor
Denver, CO 80202
(303) 294-7186

Connecticut
155 Federal Street
Ninth Floor
Boston, MA 02110
(617) 451-2023

Delaware
475 Allendale Road
Suite 201
King of Prussia, PA 19406
(215) 962-3700

Florida
1375 Peachtree Street, NE
Fifth Floor
Atlanta, GA 30367-8102
(404) 347-2797

Georgia
1375 Peachtree Street, NE
Fifth Floor
Atlanta, GA 30367-8102
(404) 347-2797

Hawaii
71 Stevenson Street
20th Floor
San Francisco, CA 94105-
2939
(415) 744-6402

Idaho
2601 Fourth Avenue
Room 440
Seattle, WA 98121-1273
(206) 553-1273

Illinois
Federal Building
300 South Riverside Plaza
Room 1975
Chicago, IL 60606-6611
(312) 353-5000

Indiana
Federal Building
300 South Riverside Plaza
Room 1975
Chicago, IL 60606-6611
(312) 353-5000

Iowa
911 Walnut Street
13th Floor
Kansas City, MO 64106
(816) 426-3608

Kansas
911 Walnut Street
13th Floor
Kansas City, MO 64106
(816) 426-3608

Kentucky
1375 Peachtree Street, NE
Fifth Floor
Atlanta, GA 30367-8102
(404) 347-2797

Louisiana
8625 King George Drive
Building C
Dallas, TX 75235-3391
(214) 767-7633

Maine
155 Federal Street
Ninth Floor
Boston, MA 02110
(617) 451-2023

Maryland
475 Allendale Road
Suite 201
King of Prussia, PA 19406
(215) 962-3700

Massachusetts
155 Federal Street
Ninth Floor
Boston, MA 02110
(617) 451-2023

Michigan
Federal Building
300 South Riverside Plaza
Room 1975
Chicago, IL 60606-6611
(312) 353-5000

Minnesota
Federal Building
300 South Riverside Plaza
Room 1975
Chicago, IL 60606-6611
(312) 353-5000

Mississippi
1375 Peachtree Street, NE
Fifth Floor
Atlanta, GA 30367-8102
(404) 347-2797

Missouri
911 Walnut Street
13th Floor
Kansas City, MO 64106
(816) 426-3608

Montana
633 17th Street
Seventh Floor
Denver, CO 80202
(303) 294-7186

Nebraska
911 Walnut Street
13th Floor
Kansas City, MO 64106
(816) 426-3608

Nevada
71 Stevenson Street
20th Floor
San Francisco, CA 94105-2939
(415) 744-6402

New Hampshire
155 Federal Street
Ninth Floor
Boston, MA 02110
(617) 451-2023

New Jersey
26 Federal Plaza
Room 31-08
New York, NY 10278
(212) 264-1450

New Mexico
8625 King George Drive
Building C
Dallas, TX 75235-3391
(214) 767-7633

New York
26 Federal Plaza
Room 31-08
New York, NY 10278
(212) 264-7772

North Carolina
1375 Peachtree Street, NE
Fifth Floor
Atlanta, GA 30367-8102
(404) 347-2797

North Dakota
633 17th Street
Seventh Floor
Denver, CO 80202
(303) 294-7186

Ohio
Federal Building
300 South Riverside Plaza
Room 1975
Chicago, IL 60606-6611
(312) 353-5000

Oklahoma
8625 King George Drive
Building C
Dallas, TX 75235-3391
(214) 767-7633

Oregon
2601 Fourth Avenue
Room 440
Seattle, WA 98121-1273
(206) 553-1273

Pacific Islands
71 Stevenson Street
20th Floor
San Francisco, CA 94105-2939
(415) 744-6402

Pennsylvania
475 Allendale Road
Suite 201
King of Prussia, PA 19406
(215) 962-3700

Puerto Rico
26 Federal Plaza
Room 31-08
New York, NY 10278
(212) 264-7772

Rhode Island
155 Federal Street
Ninth Floor
Boston, MA 02110
(617) 451-2023

South Carolina
1375 Peachtree Street, NE
Fifth Floor
Atlanta, GA 30367-8102
(404) 347-2797

South Dakota
633 17th Street
Seventh Floor
Denver, CO 80202
(303) 294-7186

Tennessee
1375 Peachtree Street, NE
Fifth Floor
Atlanta, GA 30367-8102
(404) 347-2797

Texas
8625 King George Drive
Building C
Dallas, TX 75235-3391
(214) 767-7633

Utah
633 17th Street
Seventh Floor
Denver, CO 80202
(303) 294-7186

Vermont
155 Federal Street
Ninth Floor
Boston, MA 02110
(617) 451-2023

Virgin Islands
26 Federal Plaza
Room 31-08
New York, NY 10278
(212) 264-7772

Virginia
475 Allendale Road
Suite 201
King of Prussia, PA 19406
(215) 962-3700

Washington
2601 Fourth Avenue
Room 440
Seattle, WA 98121-1273
(206) 553-1273

West Virginia
475 Allendale Road
Suite 201
King of Prussia, PA 19406
(215) 962-3700

Wisconsin
Federal Building
300 South Riverside Plaza
Room 1975
Chicago, IL 60606-6611
(312) 353-5000

Wyoming
633 17th Street
Seventh Floor
Denver, CO 80202
(303) 294-7186

ECONOMIC DEVELOPMENT—BUSINESS DEVELOPMENT ASSISTANCE

Department of Commerce
Herbert C. Hoover Building
Room H7830B
Washington, DC 20230
(202) 377-4731

Description: Loan guarantees and grants to businesses for projects when financial assistance is not available from other sources. Business must create or retain permanent jobs, must establish or expand plants in redevelopment areas, must not relocate with a resultant loss of employment, must not produce a product for which there is no market demand, and must not use funds for research and development or marketing.
$ Given: Grant range: $500,000–$111million; average: $2 million
Application Information: Preliminary proposal followed by detailed proposal.
Deadline: June 30
Contact: John McNamee, Director, Credit and Debt Management Division, Economic Development Administration, above address

ECONOMIC DEVELOPMENT—PUBLIC WORKS IMPACT PROGRAM

Economic Development Administration
Public Works Division
Herbert C. Hoover Building
Room H7326
Washington, DC 20230
(202) 482-5265

Description: Project grants for redeveloping an area and promoting long-term economic development and employment. Renovation or construction of public works and development facilities must provide immediate jobs in project area.
$ Given: Priority given to projects of $600,000 or less
Application Information: Contact your Economic Development representative at the appropriate regional office, or contact David L. McIlwain, Director, at the above address.
Deadline: 30 days after formal application has been invited
Contact: Your appropriate regional and/or state office

Alabama
Charles E. Oxley
Regional Director
401 West Peachtree Street, NW
Suite 1820
Atlanta, GA 30308-3510
(404) 730-3002

Alaska
John D. Woodward
Regional Director
915 Second Avenue
Jackson Federal Building
Suite 1856
Seattle, WA 98174
(206) 220-7660

American Samoa
John D. Woodward
Regional Director
915 Second Avenue
Jackson Federal Building
Suite 1856
Seattle, WA 98174
(206) 220-7660

Arizona
John D. Woodward
Regional Director
915 Second Avenue
Jackson Federal Building
Suite 1856
Seattle, WA 98174
(206) 220-7660

Arkansas
Henry N. Troell
Regional Director
Grant Building
Suite 201
611 East Sixth Street
Austin, TX 78701-3748
(512) 482-5461

California
John D. Woodward
Regional Director
915 Second Avenue
Jackson Federal Building
Suite 1856
Seattle, WA 98174
(206) 220-7660

Colorado
Steve R. Brennen
Regional Director
1244 Speer Boulevard
Room 670
Denver, CO 80204
(303) 844-4714

Connecticut
John E. Corrigan
Regional Director
Curtis Center
Independence Square West
Sixth and Walnut Streets
Philadelphia, PA 19106
(215) 597-4603

Delaware
John E. Corrigan
Regional Director
Curtis Center
Independence Square West
Sixth and Walnut Streets
Philadelphia, PA 19106
(215) 597-4603

District of Columbia
John E. Corrigan
Regional Director
Curtis Center
Independence Square West
Sixth and Walnut Streets
Philadelphia, PA 19106
(215) 597-4603

Florida
Charles E. Oxley
Regional Director
401 West Peachtree Street,
NW
Suite 1820
Atlanta, GA 30308-3510
(404) 730-3002

Georgia
Charles E. Oxley
Regional Director
401 West Peachtree Street,
NW
Suite 1820
Atlanta, GA 30308-3510
(404) 730-3002

Guam
John D. Woodward
Regional Director
915 Second Avenue
Jackson Federal Building
Suite 1856
Seattle, WA 98174
(206) 220-7660

Hawaii
John D. Woodward
Regional Director
915 Second Avenue
Jackson Federal Building
Suite 1856
Seattle, WA 98174
(206) 220-7660

Idaho
John D. Woodward
Regional Director
915 Second Avenue
Jackson Federal Building
Suite 1856
Seattle, WA 98174
(206) 220-7660

Illinois
Edward G. Jeep
Regional Director
111 North Canal
Suite 885
Chicago, IL 60606-7204
(312) 353-7706

Indiana
Edward G. Jeep
Regional Director
111 North Canal
Suite 885
Chicago, IL 60606-7204
(312) 353-7706

Iowa
Steven R. Brennen
Regional Director
1244 Speer Boulevard
Room 670
Denver, CO 80204
(303) 844-4714

Kansas
Steven R. Brennen
Regional Director
1244 Speer Boulevard
Room 670
Denver, CO 80204
(303) 844-4714

Kentucky
Charles E. Oxley
Regional Director
401 West Peachtree Street,
NW
Suite 1820
Atlanta, GA 30308-3510
(404) 730-3002

Louisiana
Henry N. Troell
Regional Director
Grant Building
Suite 201
611 East Sixth Street
Austin, TX 78701-3748
(512) 482-5461

Maine
John E. Corrigan
Regional Director
Curtis Center
Independence Square West
Sixth and Walnut Streets
Philadelphia, PA 19106
(215) 597-4603

Marshall Islands
John D. Woodward
Regional Director
915 Second Avenue
Jackson Federal Building
Suite 1856
Seattle, WA 98174
(206) 220-7660

Maryland
John E. Corrigan
Regional Director
Curtis Center
Independence Square West
Sixth and Walnut Streets
Philadelphia, PA 19106
(215) 597-4603

Massachusetts
John E. Corrigan
Regional Director
Curtis Center
Independence Square West
Sixth and Walnut Streets
Philadelphia, PA 19106
(215) 597-4603

Michigan
Edward G. Jeep
Regional Director
111 North Canal
Suite 885
Chicago, IL 60606-7204
(312) 353-7706

Minnesota
Edward G. Jeep
Regional Director
111 North Canal
Suite 885
Chicago, IL 60606-7204
(312) 353-7706

Mississippi
Charles E. Oxley
Regional Director
401 West Peachtree Street,
NW
Suite 1820
Atlanta, GA 30308-3510
(404) 730-3002

Missouri
Steven R. Brennen
Regional Director
1244 Speer Boulevard
Room 670
Denver, CO 80204
(303) 844-4714

Montana
Steven R. Brennen
Regional Director
1244 Speer Boulevard
Room 670
Denver, CO 80204
(303) 844-4714

Nebraska
Steven R. Brennen
Regional Director
1244 Speer Boulevard
Room 670
Denver, CO 80204
(303) 844-4714

Nevada
John D. Woodward
Regional Director
915 Second Avenue
Jackson Federal Building
Suite 1856
Seattle, WA 98174
(206) 220-7660

New Hampshire
John E. Corrigan
Regional Director
Curtis Center
Independence Square West
Sixth and Walnut Streets
Philadelphia, PA 19106
(215) 597-4603

New Jersey
John E. Corrigan
Regional Director
Curtis Center
Independence Square West
Sixth and Walnut Streets
Philadelphia, PA 19106
(215) 597-4603

New Mexico
Henry N. Troell
Regional Director
Grant Building
Suite 201
611 East Sixth Street
Austin, TX 78701-3748
(512) 482-5461

New York
John E. Corrigan
Regional Director
Curtis Center
Independence Square West
Sixth and Walnut Streets
Philadelphia, PA 19106
(215) 597-4603

North Carolina
Charles E. Oxley
Regional Director
401 West Peachtree Street,
NW
Suite 1820
Atlanta, GA 30308-3510
(404) 730-3002

North Dakota
Steven R. Brennen
Regional Director
1244 Speer Boulevard
Room 670
Denver, CO 80204
(303) 844-4714

Northern Mariana Islands
John D. Woodward
Regional Director
915 Second Avenue
Jackson Federal Building
Suite 1856
Seattle, WA 98174
(206) 220-7660

Ohio
Edward G. Jeep
Regional Director
111 North Canal
Suite 885
Chicago, IL 60606-7204
(312) 353-7706

Oklahoma
Henry N. Troell
Regional Director
Grant Building
Suite 201
611 East Sixth Street
Austin, TX 78701-3748
(512) 482-5461

Oregon
John D. Woodward
Regional Director
915 Second Avenue
Jackson Federal Building
Suite 1856
Seattle, WA 98174
(206) 220-7660

Pennsylvania
John E. Corrigan
Regional Director
Curtis Center
Independence Square West
Sixth and Walnut Streets
Philadelphia, PA 19106
(215) 597-4603

Puerto Rico
John E. Corrigan
Regional Director
Curtis Center
Independence Square West
Sixth and Walnut Streets
Philadelphia, PA 19106
(215) 597-4603

Rhode Island
John E. Corrigan
Regional Director
Curtis Center
Independence Square West
Sixth and Walnut Streets
Philadelphia, PA 19106
(215) 597-4603

South Carolina
Charles E. Oxley
Regional Director
401 West Peachtree Street,
NW
Suite 1820
Atlanta, GA 30308-3510
(404) 730-3002

South Dakota
Steven R. Brennen
Regional Director
1244 Speer Boulevard
Room 670
Denver, CO 80204
(303) 844-4714

Tennessee
Charles E. Oxley
Regional Director
401 West Peachtree Street,
NW
Suite 1820
Atlanta, GA 30308-3510
(404) 730-3002

Texas
Henry N. Troell
Regional Director
Grant Building
Suite 201
611 East Sixth Street
Austin, TX 78701-3748
(512) 482-5461

Utah
Steven R. Brennen
Regional Director
1244 Speer Boulevard
Room 670
Denver, CO 80204
(303) 844-4714

Vermont
John E. Corrigan
Regional Director
Curtis Center
Independence Square West
Sixth and Walnut Streets
Philadelphia, PA 19106
(215) 597-4603

Virginia
John E. Corrigan
Regional Director
Curtis Center
Independence Square West
Sixth and Walnut Streets
Philadelphia, PA 19106
(215) 597-4603

Virgin Islands
John E. Corrigan
Regional Director
Curtis Center
Independence Square West
Sixth and Walnut Streets
Philadelphia, PA 19106
(215) 597-4603

Washington
John D. Woodward
Regional Director
915 Second Avenue
Jackson Federal Building
Suite 1856
Seattle, WA 98174
(206) 220-7660

West Virginia
John E. Corrigan
Regional Director
Curtis Center
Independence Square West
Sixth and Walnut Streets
Philadelphia, PA 19106
(215) 597-4603

Wisconsin
Edward G. Jeep
Regional Director
111 North Canal
Suite 885
Chicago, IL 60606-7204
(312) 353-7706

Wyoming
Steven R. Brennen
Regional Director
1244 Speer Boulevard
Room 670
Denver, CO 80204
(303) 844-4714

ECONOMIC INJURY DISASTER

Small Business
Administration (SBA)
Office of Disaster Assistance
409 Third Street, SW
Washington, DC 20416
(202) 205-6734

Description: Direct, guaranteed, and insured loans to small businesses or agricultural cooperatives that are victims of drought, for paying liabilities from disaster or for providing working capital to continue operations until conditions return to normal.
$ Given: Direct loans: up to $1,500,000; average: $50,725
Application Information: Applications are filed with the nearest SBA disaster area office or special disaster office. One copy each of SBA Form 5 and Form 1368 are provided.
Deadline: Deadlines are established for each declaration
Contact: Your state and/or regional office

Alabama
1375 Peachtree Street, NE
Fifth Floor
Atlanta, GA 30367-8102
(404) 347-2797

Alaska
2601 Fourth Avenue
Room 440
Seattle, WA 98121-1273
(206) 553-1273

Arizona
71 Stevenson Street
20th Floor
San Francisco, CA 94105-2939
(415) 744-6402

Arkansas
8625 King George Drive
Building C
Dallas, TX 75235-3391
(214) 767-7633

California
71 Stevenson Street
20th Floor
San Francisco, CA 94105-2939
(415) 744-6402

Colorado
633 17th Street
Seventh Floor
Denver, CO 80202
(303) 294-7186

Connecticut
155 Federal Street
Ninth Floor
Boston, MA 02110
(617) 451-2023

Delaware
475 Allendale Road
Suite 201
King of Prussia, PA 19406
(215) 962-3700

Florida
1375 Peachtree Street, NE
Fifth Floor
Atlanta, GA 30367-8102
(404) 347-2797

Georgia
1375 Peachtree Street, NE
Fifth Floor
Atlanta, GA 30367-8102
(404) 347-2797

Hawaii
71 Stevenson Street
20th Floor
San Francisco, CA 94105-
2939
(415) 744-6402

Idaho
2601 Fourth Avenue
Room 440
Seattle, WA 98121-1273
(206) 553-1273

Illinois
Federal Building
300 South Riverside Plaza
Room 1975
Chicago, IL 60606-6611
(312) 353-5000

Indiana
Federal Building
300 South Riverside Plaza
Room 1975
Chicago, IL 60606-6611
(312) 353-5000

Iowa
911 Walnut Street
13th Floor
Kansas City, MO 64106
(816) 426-3608

Kansas
911 Walnut Street
13th Floor
Kansas City, MO 64106
(816) 426-3608

Kentucky
1375 Peachtree Street, NE
Fifth Floor
Atlanta, GA 30367-8102
(404) 347-2797

Louisiana
8625 King George Drive
Building C
Dallas, TX 75235-3391
(214) 767-7633

Maine
155 Federal Street
Ninth Floor
Boston, MA 02110
(617) 451-2023

Maryland
475 Allendale Road
Suite 201
King of Prussia, PA 19406
(215) 962-3700

Massachusetts
155 Federal Street
Ninth Floor
Boston, MA 02110
(617) 451-2023

Michigan
Federal Building
300 South Riverside Plaza
Room 1975
Chicago, IL 60606-6611
(312) 353-5000

Minnesota
Federal Building
300 South Riverside Plaza
Room 1975
Chicago, IL 60606-6611
(312) 353-5000

Mississippi
1375 Peachtree Street, NE
Fifth Floor
Atlanta, GA 30367-8102
(404) 347-2797

Missouri
911 Walnut Street
13th Floor
Kansas City, MO 64106
(816) 426-3608

Montana
633 17th Street
Seventh Floor
Denver, CO 80202
(303) 294-7186

Nebraska
911 Walnut Street
13th Floor
Kansas City, MO 64106
(816) 426-3608

Nevada
71 Stevenson Street
20th Floor
San Francisco, CA 94105-
2939
(415) 744-6402

New Hampshire
155 Federal Street
Ninth Floor
Boston, MA 02110
(617) 451-2023

New Jersey
26 Federal Plaza
Room 31-08
New York, NY 10278
(212) 264-1450

New Mexico
8625 King George Drive
Building C
Dallas, TX 75235-3391
(214) 767-7633

New York
26 Federal Plaza
Room 31-08
New York, NY 10278
(212) 264-7772

North Carolina
1375 Peachtree Street, NE
Fifth Floor
Atlanta, GA 30367-8102
(404) 347-2797

North Dakota
633 17th Street
Seventh Floor
Denver, CO 80202
(303) 294-7186

Ohio
Federal Building
300 South Riverside Plaza
Room 1975
Chicago, IL 60606-6611
(312) 353-5000

Oklahoma
8625 King George Drive
Building C
Dallas, TX 75235-3391
(214) 767-7633

Oregon
2601 Fourth Avenue
Room 440
Seattle, WA 98121-1273
(206) 553-1273

Pacific Islands
71 Stevenson Street
20th Floor
San Francisco, CA 94105-2939
(415) 744-6402

Pennsylvania
475 Allendale Road
Suite 201
King of Prussia, PA 19406
(215) 962-3700

Puerto Rico
26 Federal Plaza
Room 31-08
New York, NY 10278
(212) 264-7772

Rhode Island
155 Federal Street
Ninth Floor
Boston, MA 02110
(617) 451-2023

South Carolina
1375 Peachtree Street, NE
Fifth Floor
Atlanta, GA 30367-8102
(404) 347-2797

South Dakota
633 17th Street
Seventh Floor
Denver, CO 80202
(303) 294-7186

Tennessee
1375 Peachtree Street, NE
Fifth Floor
Atlanta, GA 30367-8102
(404) 347-2797

Texas
8625 King George Drive
Building C
Dallas, TX 75235-3391
(214) 767-7633

Utah
633 17th Street
Seventh Floor
Denver, CO 80202
(303) 294-7186

Vermont
155 Federal Street
Ninth Floor
Boston, MA 02110
(617) 451-2023

Virgin Islands
26 Federal Plaza
Room 31-08
New York, NY 10278
(212) 264-7772

Virginia
475 Allendale Road
Suite 201
King of Prussia, PA 19406
(215) 962-3700

Washington
2601 Fourth Avenue
Room 440
Seattle, WA 98121-1273
(206) 553-1273

West Virginia
475 Allendale Road
Suite 201
King of Prussia, PA 19406
(215) 962-3700

Wisconsin
Federal Building
300 South Riverside Plaza
Room 1975
Chicago, IL 60606-6611
(312) 353-5000

Wyoming
633 17th Street
Seventh Floor
Denver, CO 80202
(303) 294-7186

LOANS FOR SMALL BUSINESSES

Small Business Administration (SBA)
Loan Policy and Procedures Branch
409 Third Street, SW
Washington, DC 20416
(202) 205-6570

Description: Provides direct loans to small businesses that are owned by low-income persons or that are located in areas with high percentage of unemployment. Business must meet SBA standards and be independently owned and operated and not dominant in its field. Excludes publishing, media, radio and TV, nonprofit, lending, investment or gambling enterprises, speculation in property, and financing real property held for investment.
$ Given: Loans: up to $150,000; average: $67,694
Application Information: Application filed in field office in area in which the business is located.
Deadline: None
Contact: Director

Alabama
Regional Office
1375 Peachtree Street, NE
Fifth Floor
Atlanta, GA 30367-8102
(404) 347-2797

District Office
Birmingham District Office
2121 Eighth Avenue North
Suite 200
Birmingham, AL 35203-2398
(205) 731-1344

Alaska
Regional Office
2601 Fourth Avenue
Room 440
Seattle, WA 98121-1273
(206) 553-1273

District Office
Anchorage District Office
222 West Eighth Avenue
Room 67
Anchorage, AK 99513-7559
(907) 271-4022

Arizona
Regional Office
71 Stevenson Street
20th Floor
San Francisco, CA 94105-2939
(415) 744-6402

District Office
Phoenix District Office
2828 North Central Avenue
Suite 800
Phoenix, AZ 85004-1025
(602) 640-2316

Arkansas
Regional Office
8625 King George Drive
Building C
Dallas, TX 75235-3391
(214) 767-7633

District Office
Little Rock District Office
2120 Riverfront Drive
Suite 100
Little Rock, AR 72202
(501) 324-5278

California
Regional Office
71 Stevenson Street
20th Floor
San Francisco, CA 94105-2939
(415) 744-6402

District Offices
Santa Ana District Office
901 West Civic Center Drive
Suite 160
Santa Ana, CA 92703-2352
(714) 836-2494

San Diego District Office
880 Front Street
Room 4-S-29
San Diego, CA 92188-0270
(619) 557-7252

San Francisco District Office
211 Main Street
Fourth Floor
San Francisco, CA 94105-1988
(415) 744-6820

Fresno District Office
2719 North Air Fresno
Drive
Suite 107
Fresno, CA 93727-1547
(209) 487-5189

Los Angeles District Office
330 North Grand Boulevard
Suite 1200
Glendale, CA 91203-2304
(213) 894-2956

Colorado
Regional Office
633 17th Street
Seventh Floor
Denver, CO 80202
(303) 294-7186

District Office
Denver District Office
721 19th Street
Room 426
Denver, CO 80202-2599
(303) 844-3984

Connecticut
Regional Office
155 Federal Street
Ninth Floor
Boston, MA 02110
(617) 451-2023

District Office
Hartford District Office
Federal Building
Second Floor
330 Main Street
Hartford, CT 06106
(203) 240-4700

Delaware
Regional Office
475 Allendale Road
Suite 201
King of Prussia, PA 19406
(215) 962-3700

District of Columbia
Regional Office
475 Allendale Road
Suite 201
King of Prussia, PA 19406
(215) 962-3700

District Office
1110 Vermont Avenue, NW
Suite 900
Washington, DC 20036
(202) 606-4000

Florida
Regional Office
1375 Peachtree Street, NE
Fifth Floor
Atlanta, GA 30367-8102
(404) 347-2797

District Office
Jacksonville District Office
7825 Baymeadows Way
Suite 100-B
Jacksonville, FL 33146-2911
(904) 443-1900

Georgia
Regional Office
1375 Peachtree Street, NE
Fifth Floor
Atlanta, GA 30367-8102
(404) 347-2797

District Office
Atlanta District Office
1720 Peachtree Road, NW
Sixth Floor
Atlanta, GA 30309
(404) 347-4749

Hawaii
Regional Office
71 Stevenson Street
20th Floor
San Francisco, CA 94105-2939
(415) 744-6402

District Office
Honolulu District Office
300 Ala Moana Boulevard
Room 2213
Honolulu, HI 96850-4981
(808) 541-2990

Idaho
Regional Office
2601 Fourth Avenue
Room 440
Seattle, WA 98121-1273
(206) 553-1273

District Office
Boise District Office
1020 Main Street
Suite 290
Boise, ID 83702
(208) 334-1696

Illinois
Regional Office
Federal Building
300 South Riverside Plaza
Room 1975
Chicago, IL 60606-6611
(312) 353-5000

District Office
Chicago District Office
500 West Madison Street
Room 1250
Chicago, IL 60661-2511
(312) 353-4528

Indiana
Regional Office
Federal Building
300 South Riverside Plaza
Room 1975
Chicago, IL 60606-6611
(312) 353-5000

District Office
Indianapolis District Office
429 North Pennsylvania Street
Suite 100
Indianapolis, IN 46204-1873
(317) 226-7272

Iowa
Regional Office
911 Walnut Street
13th Floor
Kansas City, MO 64106
(816) 426-3608

District Offices
Des Moines District Office
New Federal Building
Room 749
210 Walnut Street
Des Moines, IA 50309
(515) 284-4762

Cedar Rapids District Office
373 Collins Road, NE
Room 100
Cedar Rapids, IA 52402-
3147
(319) 393-8630

Kansas
Regional Office
911 Walnut Street
13th Floor
Kansas City, MO 64106
(816) 426-3608

District Office
Wichita District Office
110 East English Street
Suite 510
Wichita, KS 67202
(316) 269-6273

Kentucky
Regional Office
1375 Peachtree Street, NE
Fifth Floor
Atlanta, GA 30367-8102
(404) 347-2797

District Office
Louisville District Office
Federal Building
Room 188
600 Martin Luther King Jr.
Place
Louisville, KY 40202
(502) 582-5971

Louisiana
Regional Office
8625 King George Drive
Building C
Dallas, TX 75235-3391
(214) 767-7633

District Office
New Orleans District Office
1661 Canal Street
Suite 2000
New Orleans, LA 70112
(504) 589-6685

Maine
Regional Office
155 Federal Street
Ninth Floor
Boston, MA 02110
(617) 451-2023

District Office
Augusta District Office
Federal Building
Room 512
40 Western Avenue
Augusta, ME 04330
(207) 622-8378

Maryland
Regional Office
475 Allendale Road
Suite 201
King of Prussia, PA 19406
(215) 962-3700

Massachusetts
Regional Office
155 Federal Street
Ninth Floor
Boston, MA 02110
(617) 451-2023

District Office
Boston District Office
10 Causeway Street
Room 265
Boston, MA 02222-1093
(617) 565-5590

Michigan
Regional Office
Federal Building
300 South Riverside Plaza
Room 1975
Chicago, IL 60606-6611
(312) 353-5000

District Office
Detroit District Office
477 Michigan Avenue
Room 515
Detroit, MI 48226
(313) 226-6075

Minnesota
Regional Office
Federal Building
300 South Riverside Plaza
Room 1975
Chicago, IL 60606-6611
(312) 353-5000

District Office
Minneapolis District Office
100 North Sixth Street
Suite 610
Minneapolis, MN 55403-
1563
(612) 370-2324

Mississippi
Regional Office
1375 Peachtree Street, NE
Fifth Floor
Atlanta, GA 30367-8102
(404) 347-2797

District Office
Jackson District Office
100 West Capitol Street
Suite 400
Jackson, MS 39201
(601) 965-4378

Missouri
Regional Office
911 Walnut Street
13th Floor
Kansas City, MO 64106
(816) 426-3608

District Offices
St. Louis District Office
815 Olive Street
Room 242
St. Louis, MO 63101
(314) 539-6600

Kansas City District Office
323 West Eighth Street
Suite 501
Kansas City, MO 64105
(816) 374-6708

Montana
Regional Office
633 17th Street
Seventh Floor
Denver, CO 80202
(303) 294-7186

District Office
Helena District Office
301 South Park Avenue
Room 528
Helena, MT 59626
(406) 449-5381

Nebraska
Regional Office
911 Walnut Street
13th Floor
Kansas City, MO 64106
(816) 426-3608

District Office
Omaha District Office
11145 Mill Valley Road
Omaha, NB 64154
(402) 221-4691

Nevada
Regional Office
71 Stevenson Street
20th Floor
San Francisco, CA 94105-2939
(415) 744-6402

District Office
Las Vegas District Office
301 East Steward Street
Room 301
Las Vegas, NV 89125-2527
(702) 388-6611

New Hampshire
Regional Office
155 Federal Street
Ninth Floor
Boston, MA 02110
(617) 451-2023

District Office
Concord District Office
143 North Main Street
Suite 202
Concord, NH 03302-1257
(603) 225-1400

New Jersey
Regional Office
26 Federal Plaza
Room 31-08
New York, NY 10278
(212) 264-1450

District Office
Newark District Office
Military Park Building
Fourth Floor
60 Park Place
Newark, NJ 07102
(201) 645-2434

New Mexico
Regional Office
8625 King George Drive
Building C
Dallas, TX 75235-3391
(214) 767-7633

District Office
Albuquerque District Office
625 Silver Avenue, SW
Suite 320
Albuquerque, NM 87102
(505) 766-1870

New York
Regional Office
26 Federal Plaza
Room 31-08
New York, NY 10278
(212) 264-7772

District Offices
Buffalo District Office
Federal Building 1311
111 West Huron Street
Buffalo, NY 14202
(716) 846-4301

Syracuse District Office
100 South Clinton Street
Room 1070
Syracuse, NY 13260
(315) 423-5383

North Carolina
Regional Office
1375 Peachtree Street, NE
Fifth Floor
Atlanta, GA 30367-8102
(404) 347-2797

District Office
Charlotte District Office
Suite A2015
200 North College Street
Charlotte, NC 28202-2137
(704) 344-6563

North Dakota
Regional Office
633 17th Street
Seventh Floor
Denver, CO 80202
(303) 294-7186

District Office
Federal Building
Room 218
657 Second Avenue, North
Fargo, ND 58108-3086
(701) 239-5131

Ohio
Regional Office
Federal Building
300 South Riverside Plaza
Room 1975
Chicago, IL 60606-6611
(312) 353-5000

District Office
Columbus District Office
2 Nationwide Plaza
Suite 1400
Columbus, OH 43215
(614) 469-6860

Oklahoma
Regional Office
8625 King George Drive
Building C
Dallas, TX 75235-3391
(214) 767-7633

District Office
Oklahoma City District
Office
200 NW Fifth Street
Suite 670
Oklahoma City, OK 73102
(405) 231-4301

Oregon
Regional Office
2601 Fourth Avenue
Room 440
Seattle, WA 98121-1273
(206) 553-1273

District Office
Portland District Office
222 SW Columbia Street
Suite 500
Portland, OR 97201-6605
(503) 326-2682

Pacific Islands
Regional Office
71 Stevenson Street
20th Floor
San Francisco, CA 94105-
2939
(415) 744-6402

District Office
Agana Branch Office
Pacific Daily News Building
Room 508
238 Archbishop R.C.
Flores Street
Agana, GM 96910
(671) 472-7277

Pennsylvania
Regional Office
475 Allendale Road
Suite 201
King of Prussia, PA 19406
(215) 962-3700

District Office
Pittsburgh District Office
960 Penn Avenue
Fifth Floor
Pittsburgh, PA 15222
(412) 644-2780

Puerto Rico
Regional Office
26 Federal Plaza
Room 31-08
New York, NY 10278
(212) 264-7772

District Office
Federico Degetau Federal
Building
Room 691
Carlos Chardon Avenue
Hato Rey, PR 00918
(809) 766-5572

Rhode Island
Regional Office
155 Federal Street
Ninth Floor
Boston, MA 02110
(617) 451-2023

District Office
Providence District Office
380 Westminster Mall
Fifth Floor
Providence, RI 02903
(401) 528-4561

South Carolina
Regional Office
1375 Peachtree Street, NE
Fifth Floor
Atlanta, GA 30367-8102
(404) 347-2797

District Office
Columbia District Office
1835 Assembly Street
Room 358
Columbia, SC 29202
(803) 765-5376

South Dakota
Regional Office
633 17th Street
Seventh Floor
Denver, CO 80202
(303) 294-7186

District Office
Sioux Falls District Office
101 South Main Avenue
Suite 101
Sioux Falls, SD 57102-0527
(605) 330-4231

Tennessee
Regional Office
1375 Peachtree Street, NE
Fifth Floor
Atlanta, GA 30367-8102
(404) 347-2797

District Office
Nashville District Office
50 Vantage Way
Suite 201
Nashville, TN 37228-1500
(615) 736-5881

Texas
Regional Office
8625 King George Drive
Building C
Dallas, TX 75235-3391
(214) 767-7633

District Offices
San Antonio District Office
7400 Blanco Road
Suite 200
San Antonio, TX 78216-
4300
(512) 229-4535

Dallas District Office
4300 Amon Center
Boulevard
Suite 114
Ft. Worth, TX 76155
(817) 885-6500

El Paso District Office
10737 Gateway West
Suite 320
El Paso, TX 79935
(915) 541-5586

Utah
Regional Office
633 17th Street
Seventh Floor
Denver, CO 80202
(303) 294-7186

District Office
Salt Lake City District
Office
Federal Building
Room 2237
125 South State Street
Salt Lake City, UT
84138-1195
(801) 524-5804

Vermont
Regional Office
155 Federal Street
Ninth Floor
Boston, MA 02110
(617) 451-2023

District Office
Montpelier District Office
Federal Building
Room 205
87 State Street
Montpelier, VT 05602
(802) 828-4422

Virgin Islands
Regional Office
26 Federal Plaza
Room 31-08
New York, NY 10278
(212) 264-7772

District Offices
Federico Degetau Federal
Building
Room 691
Carlos Chardon Avenue
Hato Rey, PR 00918
(809) 766-5572

St. Croix Post-of-Duty
Federal Office Building
U.S. Court House and
Building
Room 210
Veterans Drive
St. Thomas, VI 00802
(809) 744-8530

Virginia
Regional Office
475 Allendale Road
Suite 201
King of Prussia, PA 19406
(215) 962-3700

District Office
Richmond District Office
Federal Building
Room 3015
400 North Eighth Street
Richmond, VA 23240
(804) 771-2400

Washington
Regional Office
2601 Fourth Avenue
Room 440
Seattle, WA 98121-1273
(206) 553-1273

District Offices
Spokane District Office
West 601 First Avenue
10th Floor East
Spokane, WA 99204-0317
(509) 353-2800

Seattle District Office
915 Second Avenue
Room 1792
Seattle, WA 98174-1088
(206) 553-1420

West Virginia
Regional Office
475 Allendale Road
Suite 201
King of Prussia, PA 19406
(215) 962-3700

District Office
Clarksburg District Office
168 West Main Street
Fifth Floor
Clarksburg, WV 26301
(304) 623-5631

Wisconsin
Regional Office
Federal Building
300 South Riverside Plaza
Room 1975
Chicago, IL 60606-6611
(312) 353-5000

District Office
Madison District Office
212 East Washington
Avenue
Room 213
Madison, WI 53703
(608) 264-5261

Wyoming
Regional Office
633 17th Street
Seventh Floor
Denver, CO 80202
(303) 294-7186

District Office
Casper District Office
Federal Building
Room 4001
100 East B Street
Casper, WY 82602-2839
(307) 261-5761

LOCAL DEVELOPMENT COMPANY LOANS

Small Business
Administration (SBA)
Office of Rural Affairs and
Economic Development
409 Third Street, SW
Washington, DC 20416
(202) 205-6485

Description: Guaranteed and insured loans to incorporated local development companies for the purchase of land, buildings, machines, and equipment for constructing, expanding, or modernizing building. Loans are not available to provide working capital for refinancing purposes. Loans may not exceed 25 years.
$ Given: Guarantee loans: up to $1,000,000; average: $500,000
Application Information: Applications must be made on SBA Form 1244 for local development company loans and the requirements set forth thereon must be complied with.
Deadline: None
Contact: Your state and/or regional SBA office

Alabama
1375 Peachtree Street, NE
Fifth Floor
Atlanta, GA 30367-8102
(404) 347-2797

Alaska
2601 Fourth Avenue
Room 440
Seattle, WA 98121-1273
(206) 553-1273

Arizona
71 Stevenson Street
20th Floor
San Francisco, CA 94105-
2939
(415) 744-6402

Arkansas
8625 King George Drive
Building C
Dallas, TX 75235-3391
(214) 767-7633

California
71 Stevenson Street
20th Floor
San Francisco, CA 94105-
2939
(415) 744-6402

Colorado
633 17th Street
Seventh Floor
Denver, CO 80202
(303) 294-7186

Connecticut
155 Federal Street
Ninth Floor
Boston, MA 02110
(617) 451-2023

Delaware
475 Allendale Road
Suite 201
King of Prussia, PA 19406
(215) 962-3700

Florida
1375 Peachtree Street, NE
Fifth Floor
Atlanta, GA 30367-8102
(404) 347-2797

Georgia
1375 Peachtree Street, NE
Fifth Floor
Atlanta, GA 30367-8102
(404) 347-2797

Hawaii
71 Stevenson Street
20th Floor
San Francisco, CA 94105-2939
(415) 744-6402

Idaho
2601 Fourth Avenue
Room 440
Seattle, WA 98121-1273
(206) 553-1273

Illinois
Federal Building
300 South Riverside Plaza
Room 1975
Chicago, IL 60606-6611
(312) 353-5000

Indiana
Federal Building
300 South Riverside Plaza
Room 1975
Chicago, IL 60606-6611
(312) 353-5000

Iowa
911 Walnut Street
13th Floor
Kansas City, MO 64106
(816) 426-3608

Kansas
911 Walnut Street
13th Floor
Kansas City, MO 64106
(816) 426-3608

Kentucky
1375 Peachtree Street, NE
Fifth Floor
Atlanta, GA 30367-8102
(404) 347-2797

Louisiana
8625 King George Drive
Building C
Dallas, TX 75235-3391
(214) 767-7633

Maine
155 Federal Street
Ninth Floor
Boston, MA 02110
(617) 451-2023

Maryland
475 Allendale Road
Suite 201
King of Prussia, PA 19406
(215) 962-3700

Massachusetts
155 Federal Street
Ninth Floor
Boston, MA 02110
(617) 451-2023

Michigan
Federal Building
300 South Riverside Plaza
Room 1975
Chicago, IL 60606-6611
(312) 353-5000

Minnesota
Federal Building
300 South Riverside Plaza
Room 1975
Chicago, IL 60606-6611
(312) 353-5000

Mississippi
1375 Peachtree Street, NE
Fifth Floor
Atlanta, GA 30367-8102
(404) 347-2797

Missouri
911 Walnut Street
13th Floor
Kansas City, MO 64106
(816) 426-3608

Montana
633 17th Street
Seventh Floor
Denver, CO 80202
(303) 294-7186

Nebraska
911 Walnut Street
13th Floor
Kansas City, MO 64106
(816) 426-3608

Nevada
71 Stevenson Street
20th Floor
San Francisco, CA 94105-2939
(415) 744-6402

New Hampshire
155 Federal Street
Ninth Floor
Boston, MA 02110
(617) 451-2023

New Jersey
26 Federal Plaza
Room 31-08
New York, NY 10278
(212) 264-1450

New Mexico
8625 King George Drive
Building C
Dallas, TX 75235-3391
(214) 767-7633

New York
26 Federal Plaza
Room 31-08
New York, NY 10278
(212) 264-7772

North Carolina
1375 Peachtree Street, NE
Fifth Floor
Atlanta, GA 30367-8102
(404) 347-2797

North Dakota
633 17th Street
Seventh Floor
Denver, CO 80202
(303) 294-7186

Ohio
Federal Building
300 South Riverside Plaza
Room 1975
Chicago, IL 60606-6611
(312) 353-5000

Oklahoma
8625 King George Drive
Building C
Dallas, TX 75235-3391
(214) 767-7633

Oregon
2601 Fourth Avenue
Room 440
Seattle, WA 98121-1273
(206) 553-1273

Pacific Islands
71 Stevenson Street
20th Floor
San Francisco, CA 94105-2939
(415) 744-6402

Pennsylvania
475 Allendale Road
Suite 201
King of Prussia, PA 19406
(215) 962-3700

Puerto Rico
26 Federal Plaza
Room 31-08
New York, NY 10278
(212) 264-7772

Rhode Island
155 Federal Street
Ninth Floor
Boston, MA 02110
(617) 451-2023

South Carolina
1375 Peachtree Street, NE
Fifth Floor
Atlanta, GA 30367-8102
(404) 347-2797

South Dakota
633 17th Street
Seventh Floor
Denver, CO 80202
(303) 294-7186

Tennessee
1375 Peachtree Street, NE
Fifth Floor
Atlanta, GA 30367-8102
(404) 347-2797

Texas
8625 King George Drive
Building C
Dallas, TX 75235-3391
(214) 767-7633

Utah
633 17th Street
Seventh Floor
Denver, CO 80202
(303) 294-7186

Vermont
155 Federal Street
Ninth Floor
Boston, MA 02110
(617) 451-2023

Virgin Islands
26 Federal Plaza
Room 31-08
New York, NY 10278
(212) 264-7772

Virginia
475 Allendale Road
Suite 201
King of Prussia, PA 19406
(215) 962-3700

Washington
2601 Fourth Avenue
Room 440
Seattle, WA 98121-1273
(206) 553-1273

West Virginia
475 Allendale Road
Suite 201
King of Prussia, PA 19406
(215) 962-3700

Wisconsin
Federal Building
300 South Riverside Plaza
Room 1975
Chicago, IL 60606-6611
(312) 353-5000

Wyoming
633 17th Street
Seventh Floor
Denver, CO 80202
(303) 294-7186

MANAGEMENT TECHNICAL ASSISTANCE FOR SOCIALLY AND ECONOMICALLY DISADVANTAGED BUSINESSES

Small Business Administration (SBA)
409 Third Street, SW
Washington, DC 20416
(202) 205-6420

Description: Grants for providing management and technical assistance to existing or potential businesses that are economically and socially disadvantaged and/or operated in areas of high unemployment or low income.
$ Given: Amount subject to negotiation, commensurate with management and technical assistance to be provided
Application Information: Application or proposal forwarded to Assistant Regional Administrator for Minority Small Businesses and Capitol Ownership Development—SBA regional office for appropriate area.
Deadline: As announced within individual "Request for Application Proposals"
Contact: Appropriate regional SBA office

Alabama
Regional Office
1375 Peachtree Street, NE
Fifth Floor
Atlanta, GA 30367-8102
(404) 347-2797

District Office
Birmingham District Office
2121 Eighth Avenue North
Suite 200
Birmingham, AL 35203-2398
(205) 731-1344

Alaska
Regional Office
2601 Fourth Avenue
Room 440
Seattle, WA 98121-1273
(206) 553-1273

District Office
Anchorage District Office
222 West Eighth Avenue
Room 67
Anchorage, AK 99513-7559
(907) 271-4022

Arizona
Regional Office
71 Stevenson Street
20th Floor
San Francisco, CA 94105-2939
(415) 744-6402

District Office
Phoenix District Office
2828 North Central Avenue
Suite 800
Phoenix, AZ 85004-1025
(602) 640-2316

Arkansas
Regional Office
8625 King George Drive
Building C
Dallas, TX 75235-3391
(214) 767-7633

District Office
Little Rock District Office
2120 Riverfront Drive
Suite 100
Little Rock, AR 72202
(501) 324-5278

California
Regional Office
71 Stevenson Street
20th Floor
San Francisco, CA 94105-2939
(415) 744-6402

District Offices
Santa Ana District Office
901 West Civic Center Drive
Suite 160
Santa Ana, CA 92703-2352
(714) 836-2494

San Diego District Office
880 Front Street
Room 4-S-29
San Diego, CA 92188-0270
(619) 557-7252

San Francisco District Office
211 Main Street
Fourth Floor
San Francisco, CA 94105-1988
(415) 744-6820

Fresno District Office
2719 North Air Fresno
Drive
Suite 107
Fresno, CA 93727-1547
(209) 487-5189

Los Angeles District Office
330 North Grand Boulevard
Suite 1200
Glendale, CA 91203-2304
(213) 894-2956

Colorado
Regional Office
633 17th Street
Seventh Floor
Denver, CO 80202
(303) 294-7186

District Office
Denver District Office
721 19th Street
Room 426
Denver, CO 80202-2599
(303) 844-3984

Connecticut
Regional Office
155 Federal Street
Ninth Floor
Boston, MA 02110
(617) 451-2023

District Office
Hartford District Office
Federal Building
Second Floor
330 Main Street
Hartford, CT 06106
(203) 240-4700

Delaware
Regional Office
475 Allendale Road
Suite 201
King of Prussia, PA 19406
(215) 962-3700

District of Columbia
Regional Office
475 Allendale Road
Suite 201
King of Prussia, PA 19406
(215) 962-3700

District Office
1110 Vermont Avenue, NW
Suite 900
Washington, DC 20036
(202) 606-4000

Florida
Regional Office
1375 Peachtree Street, NE
Fifth Floor
Atlanta, GA 30367-8102
(404) 347-2797

District Office
Jacksonville District Office
7825 Baymeadows Way
Suite 100-B
Jacksonville, FL 33146-2911
(904) 443-1900

Georgia
Regional Office
1375 Peachtree Street, NE
Fifth Floor
Atlanta, GA 30367-8102
(404) 347-2797

District Office
Atlanta District Office
1720 Peachtree Road, NW
Sixth Floor
Atlanta, GA 30309
(404) 347-4749

Hawaii
Regional Office
71 Stevenson Street
20th Floor
San Francisco, CA 94105-
2939
(415) 744-6402

District Office
Honolulu District Office
300 Ala Moana Boulevard
Room 2213
Honolulu, HI 96850-4981
(808) 541-2990

Idaho
Regional Office
2601 Fourth Avenue
Room 440
Seattle, WA 98121-1273
(206) 553-1273

District Office
Boise District Office
1020 Main Street
Suite 290
Boise, ID 83702
(208) 334-1696

Illinois
Regional Office
Federal Building
300 South Riverside Plaza
Room 1975
Chicago, IL 60606-6611
(312) 353-5000

District Office
Chicago District Office
500 West Madison Street
Room 1250
Chicago, IL 60661-2511
(312) 353-4528

Indiana
Regional Office
Federal Building
300 South Riverside Plaza
Room 1975
Chicago, IL 60606-6611
(312) 353-5000

District Office
Indianapolis District Office
429 North Pennsylvania
Street
Suite 100
Indianapolis, IN 46204-
1873
(317) 226-7272

Iowa
Regional Office
911 Walnut Street
13th Floor
Kansas City, MO 64106
(816) 426-3608

District Offices
Des Moines District Office
New Federal Building
Room 749
210 Walnut Street
Des Moines, IA 50309
(515) 284-4762

Cedar Rapids District Office
373 Collins Road, NE
Room 100
Cedar Rapids, IA 52402-
3147
(319) 393-8630

Kansas
Regional Office
911 Walnut Street
13th Floor
Kansas City, MO 64106
(816) 426-3608

District Office
Wichita District Office
110 East English Street
Suite 510
Wichita, KS 67202
(316) 269-6273

Kentucky
Regional Office
1375 Peachtree Street, NE
Fifth Floor
Atlanta, GA 30367-8102
(404) 347-2797

District Office
Louisville District Office
Federal Building
Room 188
600 Martin Luther King Jr.
Place
Louisville, KY 40202
(502) 582-5971

Louisiana
Regional Office
8625 King George Drive
Building C
Dallas, TX 75235-3391
(214) 767-7633

District Office
New Orleans District Office
1661 Canal Street
Suite 2000
New Orleans, LA 70112
(504) 589-6685

Maine
Regional Office
155 Federal Street
Ninth Floor
Boston, MA 02110
(617) 451-2023

District Office
Augusta District Office
Federal Building
Room 512
40 Western Avenue
Augusta, ME 04330
(207) 622-8378

Maryland
Regional Office
475 Allendale Road
Suite 201
King of Prussia, PA 19406
(215) 962-3700

Massachusetts
Regional Office
155 Federal Street
Ninth Floor
Boston, MA 02110
(617) 451-2023

District Office
Boston District Office
10 Causeway Street
Room 265
Boston, MA 02222-1093
(617) 565-5590

Michigan
Regional Office
Federal Building
300 South Riverside Plaza
Room 1975
Chicago, IL 60606-6611
(312) 353-5000

District Office
Detroit District Office
477 Michigan Avenue
Room 515
Detroit, MI 48226
(313) 226-6075

Minnesota
Regional Office
Federal Building
300 South Riverside Plaza
Room 1975
Chicago, IL 60606-6611
(312) 353-5000

District Office
Minneapolis District Office
100 North Sixth Street
Suite 610
Minneapolis, MN 55403-
1563
(612) 370-2324

Mississippi
Regional Office
1375 Peachtree Street, NE
Fifth Floor
Atlanta, GA 30367-8102
(404) 347-2797

District Office
Jackson District Office
100 West Capitol Street
Suite 400
Jackson, MS 39201
(601) 965-4378

Missouri
Regional Office
911 Walnut Street
13th Floor
Kansas City, MO 64106
(816) 426-3608

District Offices
St. Louis District Office
815 Olive Street
Room 242
St. Louis, MO 63101
(314) 539-6600

Kansas City District Office
323 West Eighth Street
Suite 501
Kansas City, MO 64105
(816) 374-6708

Montana
Regional Office
633 17th Street
Seventh Floor
Denver, CO 80202
(303) 294-7186

District Office
Helena District Office
301 South Park Avenue
Room 528
Helena, MT 59626
(406) 449-5381

Nebraska
Regional Office
911 Walnut Street
13th Floor
Kansas City, MO 64106
(816) 426-3608

District Office
Omaha District Office
11145 Mill Valley Road
Omaha, NB 64154
(402) 221-4691

Nevada
Regional Office
71 Stevenson Street
20th Floor
San Francisco, CA 94105-2939
(415) 744-6402

District Office
Las Vegas District Office
301 East Steward Street
Room 301
Las Vegas, NV 89125-2527
(702) 388-6611

New Hampshire
Regional Office
155 Federal Street
Ninth Floor
Boston, MA 02110
(617) 451-2023

District Office
Concord District Office
143 North Main Street
Suite 202
Concord, NH 03302-1257
(603) 225-1400

New Jersey
Regional Office
26 Federal Plaza
Room 31-08
New York, NY 10278
(212) 264-1450

District Office
Newark District Office
Military Park Building
Fourth Floor
60 Park Place
Newark, NJ 07102
(201) 645-2434

New Mexico
Regional Office
8625 King George Drive
Building C
Dallas, TX 75235-3391
(214) 767-7633

District Office
Albuquerque District Office
625 Silver Avenue, SW
Suite 320
Albuquerque, NM 87102
(505) 766-1870

New York
Regional Office
26 Federal Plaza
Room 31-08
New York, NY 10278
(212) 264-7772

District Offices
Buffalo District Office
Federal Building 1311
111 West Huron Street
Buffalo, NY 14202
(716) 846-4301

Syracuse District Office
100 South Clinton Street
Room 1070
Syracuse, NY 13260
(315) 423-5383

North Carolina
Regional Office
1375 Peachtree Street, NE
Fifth Floor
Atlanta, GA 30367-8102
(404) 347-2797

District Office
Charlotte District Office
Suite A2015
200 North College Street
Charlotte, NC 28202-2137
(704) 344-6563

North Dakota
Regional Office
633 17th Street
Seventh Floor
Denver, CO 80202
(303) 294-7186

District Office
Federal Building
Room 218
657 Second Avenue, North
Fargo, ND 58108-3086
(701) 239-5131

Ohio
Regional Office
Federal Building
300 South Riverside Plaza
Room 1975
Chicago, IL 60606-6611
(312) 353-5000

District Office
Columbus District Office
2 Nationwide Plaza
Suite 1400
Columbus, OH 43215
(614) 469-6860

Oklahoma
Regional Office
8625 King George Drive
Building C
Dallas, TX 75235-3391
(214) 767-7633

District Office
Oklahoma City District
Office
200 NW Fifth Street
Suite 670
Oklahoma City, OK 73102
(405) 231-4301

Oregon
Regional Office
2601 Fourth Avenue
Room 440
Seattle, WA 98121-1273
(206) 553-1273

District Office
Portland District Office
222 SW Columbia Street
Suite 500
Portland, OR 97201-6605
(503) 326-2682

Pacific Islands
Regional Office
71 Stevenson Street
20th Floor
San Francisco, CA 94105-2939
(415) 744-6402

District Office
Agana Branch Office
Pacific Daily News Building
Room 508
238 Archbishop R.C.
Flores Street
Agana, GM 96910
(671) 472-7277

Pennsylvania
Regional Office
475 Allendale Road
Suite 201
King of Prussia, PA 19406
(215) 962-3700

District Office
Pittsburgh District Office
960 Penn Avenue
Fifth Floor
Pittsburgh, PA 15222
(412) 644-2780

Puerto Rico
Regional Office
26 Federal Plaza
Room 31-08
New York, NY 10278
(212) 264-7772

District Office
Federico Degetau Federal
Building
Room 691
Carlos Chardon Avenue
Hato Rey, PR 00918
(809) 766-5572

Rhode Island
Regional Office
155 Federal Street
Ninth Floor
Boston, MA 02110
(617) 451-2023

District Office
Providence District Office
380 Westminster Mall
Fifth Floor
Providence, RI 02903
(401) 528-4561

South Carolina
Regional Office
1375 Peachtree Street, NE
Fifth Floor
Atlanta, GA 30367-8102
(404) 347-2797

District Office
Columbia District Office
1835 Assembly Street
Room 358
Columbia, SC 29202
(803) 765-5376

South Dakota
Regional Office
633 17th Street
Seventh Floor
Denver, CO 80202
(303) 294-7186

District Office
Sioux Falls District Office
101 South Main Avenue
Suite 101
Sioux Falls, SD 57102-0527
(605) 330-4231

Tennessee
Regional Office
1375 Peachtree Street, NE
Fifth Floor
Atlanta, GA 30367-8102
(404) 347-2797

District Office
Nashville District Office
50 Vantage Way
Suite 201
Nashville, TN 37228-1500
(615) 736-5881

Texas
Regional Office
8625 King George Drive
Building C
Dallas, TX 75235-3391
(214) 767-7633

District Offices
San Antonio District Office
7400 Blanco Road
Suite 200
San Antonio, TX 78216-
4300
(512) 229-4535

Dallas District Office
4300 Amon Center
Boulevard
Suite 114
Ft. Worth, TX 76155
(817) 885-6500

El Paso District Office
10737 Gateway West
Suite 320
El Paso, TX 79935
(915) 541-5586

Utah
Regional Office
633 17th Street
Seventh Floor
Denver, CO 80202
(303) 294-7186

District Office
Salt Lake City District
Office
Federal Building
Room 2237
125 South State Street
Salt Lake City, UT 84138-
1195
(801) 524-5804

Vermont
Regional Office
155 Federal Street
Ninth Floor
Boston, MA 02110
(617) 451-2023

District Office
Montpelier District Office
Federal Building
Room 205
87 State Street
Montpelier, VT 05602
(802) 828-4422

Virgin Islands
Regional Office
26 Federal Plaza
Room 31-08
New York, NY 10278
(212) 264-7772

District Offices
Federico Degetau Federal
Building
Room 691
Carlos Chardon Avenue
Hato Rey, PR 00918
(809) 766-5572

St. Croix Post-of-Duty
Federal Office Building
U.S. Court House and
Building
Room 210
Veterans Drive
St. Thomas, VI 00802
(809) 744-8530

Virginia
Regional Office
475 Allendale Road
Suite 201
King of Prussia, PA 19406
(215) 962-3700

District Office
Richmond District Office
Federal Building
Room 3015
400 North Eighth Street
Richmond, VA 23240
(804) 771-2400

Washington
Regional Office
2601 Fourth Avenue
Room 440
Seattle, WA 98121-1273
(206) 553-1273

District Offices
Spokane District Office
West 601 First Avenue
10th Floor East
Spokane, WA 99204-0317
(509) 353-2800

Seattle District Office
915 Second Avenue
Room 1792
Seattle, WA 98174-1088
(206) 553-1420

West Virginia
Regional Office
475 Allendale Road
Suite 201
King of Prussia, PA 19406
(215) 962-3700

District Office
Clarksburg District Office
168 West Main Street
Fifth Floor
Clarksburg, WV 26301
(304) 623-5631

Wisconsin
Regional Office
Federal Building
300 South Riverside Plaza
Room 1975
Chicago, IL 60606-6611
(312) 353-5000

District Office
Madison District Office
212 East Washington
Avenue
Room 213
Madison, WI 53703
(608) 264-5261

Wyoming
Regional Office
633 17th Street
Seventh Floor   •
Denver, CO 80202
(303) 294-7186

District Office
Casper District Office
Federal Building
Room 4001
100 East B Street
Casper, WY 82602-2839
(307) 261-5761

PHYSICAL DISASTER LOANS

Small Business
Administration (SBA)
Office of Disaster Assistance
409 Third Street, SW
Washington, DC 20416
(202) 205-6734

Description: Direct, guaranteed, and insured loans to individuals, businesses, and charitable and nonprofit organizations for repairing and/or replacing damaged and/or destroyed real and/or personal property to predisaster conditions.
$ Given: Direct loans: up to $120,000 plus $100,000 additional in special cases; direct business loans: up to $150,000 with additional amounts available for major sources of employment
Application Information: Write for application. When feasible, disaster victims are interviewed and the program is explained.
Deadline: 60 days from date of disaster declaration
Contact: Your state and/or regional office

Alabama
1375 Peachtree Street, NE
Fifth Floor
Atlanta, GA 30367-8102
(404) 347-2797

Alaska
2601 Fourth Avenue
Room 440
Seattle, WA 98121-1273
(206) 553-1273

Arizona
71 Stevenson Street
20th Floor
San Francisco, CA 94105-
2939
(415) 744-6402

Arkansas
8625 King George Drive
Building C
Dallas, TX 75235-3391
(214) 767-7633

California
71 Stevenson Street
20th Floor
San Francisco, CA 94105-
2939
(415) 744-6402

Colorado
633 17th Street
Seventh Floor
Denver, CO 80202
(303) 294-7186

Connecticut
155 Federal Street
Ninth Floor
Boston, MA 02110
(617) 451-2023

Delaware
475 Allendale Road
Suite 201
King of Prussia, PA 19406
(215) 962-3700

Florida
1375 Peachtree Street, NE
Fifth Floor
Atlanta, GA 30367-8102
(404) 347-2797

Georgia
1375 Peachtree Street, NE
Fifth Floor
Atlanta, GA 30367-8102
(404) 347-2797

Hawaii
71 Stevenson Street
20th Floor
San Francisco, CA 94105-
2939
(415) 744-6402

Idaho
2601 Fourth Avenue
Room 440
Seattle, WA 98121-1273
(206) 553-1273

Illinois
Federal Building
300 South Riverside Plaza
Room 1975
Chicago, IL 60606-6611
(312) 353-5000

Indiana
Federal Building
300 South Riverside Plaza
Room 1975
Chicago, IL 60606-6611
(312) 353-5000

Iowa
911 Walnut Street
13th Floor
Kansas City, MO 64106
(816) 426-3608

Kansas
911 Walnut Street
13th Floor
Kansas City, MO 64106
(816) 426-3608

Kentucky
1375 Peachtree Street, NE
Fifth Floor
Atlanta, GA 30367-8102
(404) 347-2797

Louisiana
8625 King George Drive
Building C
Dallas, TX 75235-3391
(214) 767-7633

Maine
155 Federal Street
Ninth Floor
Boston, MA 02110
(617) 451-2023

Maryland
475 Allendale Road
Suite 201
King of Prussia, PA 19406
(215) 962-3700

Massachusetts
155 Federal Street
Ninth Floor
Boston, MA 02110
(617) 451-2023

Michigan
Federal Building
300 South Riverside Plaza
Room 1975
Chicago, IL 60606-6611
(312) 353-5000

Minnesota
Federal Building
300 South Riverside Plaza
Room 1975
Chicago, IL 60606-6611
(312) 353-5000

Mississippi
1375 Peachtree Street, NE
Fifth Floor
Atlanta, GA 30367-8102
(404) 347-2797

Missouri
911 Walnut Street
13th Floor
Kansas City, MO 64106
(816) 426-3608

Montana
633 17th Street
Seventh Floor
Denver, CO 80202
(303) 294-7186

Nebraska
911 Walnut Street
13th Floor
Kansas City, MO 64106
(816) 426-3608

Nevada
71 Stevenson Street
20th Floor
San Francisco, CA 94105-
2939
(415) 744-6402

New Hampshire
155 Federal Street
Ninth Floor
Boston, MA 02110
(617) 451-2023

New Jersey
26 Federal Plaza
Room 31-08
New York, NY 10278
(212) 264-1450

New Mexico
8625 King George Drive
Building C
Dallas, TX 75235-3391
(214) 767-7633

New York
26 Federal Plaza
Room 31-08
New York, NY 10278
(212) 264-7772

North Carolina
1375 Peachtree Street, NE
Fifth Floor
Atlanta, GA 30367-8102
(404) 347-2797

North Dakota
633 17th Street
Seventh Floor
Denver, CO 80202
(303) 294-7186

Ohio
Federal Building
300 South Riverside Plaza
Room 1975
Chicago, IL 60606-6611
(312) 353-5000

Oklahoma
8625 King George Drive
Building C
Dallas, TX 75235-3391
(214)767-7633

Oregon
2601 Fourth Avenue
Room 440
Seattle, WA 98121-1273
(206) 553-1273

Pacific Islands
71 Stevenson Street
20th Floor
San Francisco, CA 94105-2939
(415) 744-6402

Pennsylvania
475 Allendale Road
Suite 201
King of Prussia, PA 19406
(215) 962-3700

Puerto Rico
26 Federal Plaza
Room 31-08
New York, NY 10278
(212) 264-7772

Rhode Island
155 Federal Street
Ninth Floor
Boston, MA 02110
(617) 451-2023

South Carolina
1375 Peachtree Street, NE
Fifth Floor
Atlanta, GA 30367-8102
(404) 347-2797

South Dakota
633 17th Street
Seventh Floor
Denver, CO 80202
(303) 294-7186

Tennessee
1375 Peachtree Street, NE
Fifth Floor
Atlanta, GA 30367-8102
(404) 347-2797

Texas
8625 King George Drive
Building C
Dallas, TX 75235-3391
(214) 767-7633

Utah
633 17th Street
Seventh Floor
Denver, CO 80202
(303) 294-7186

Vermont
155 Federal Street
Ninth Floor
Boston, MA 02110
(617) 451-2023

Virginia
475 Allendale Road
Suite 201
King of Prussia, PA 19406
(215) 962-3700

Virgin Islands
26 Federal Plaza
Room 31-08
New York, NY 10278
(212) 264-7772

Washington
2601 Fourth Avenue
Room 440
Seattle, WA 98121-1273
(206) 553-1273

West Virginia
475 Allendale Road
Suite 201
King of Prussia, PA 19406
(215) 962-3700

Wisconsin
Federal Building
300 South Riverside Plaza
Room 1975
Chicago, IL 60606-6611
(312) 353-5000

Wyoming
633 17th Street
Seventh Floor
Denver, CO 80202
(303) 294-7186

RESEARCH AND EVALUATION PROGRAM

Department of Commerce
Economic Development
Administration (EDA)
Washington, DC 20230
(202) 482-4085

Description: Project grants to individuals, partnerships, corporations, colleges, universities, and for-profit or nonprofit organizations to determine causes of unemployment in various areas of the United States.
$ Given: Range: $7,500–$350,000
Application Information: Write for guidelines.
Deadlines: See Federal Register
Contact: David Geddes, EDA Room H-7315, Washington, DC 20230

Environment/ Conservation

Many funds are available from the federal government for the environment and/or conservation for the following:

1. *Assistance* for projects or for research on pathogenic agents and biological or environmental hazards as well as the health risks associated with these hazards, the toxicology of chemicals, environmental protection, pesticides control, and climate and air-quality research
2. *Assistance* for projects that assess ocean-resource conservation, marine environmental effects, or water pollution controls
3. *Support* for the Superfund Program, which aids environmental technologies

You will need to consult the list of addresses in this chapter for your nearest local or regional Environmental Protection Agency (EPA) office.

AIR POLLUTION CONTROL RESEARCH

Environmental Protection
Agency (EPA)
Grants Administration
Division
Room 216
Washington, DC 20460
(202) 260-7473

Description: Project grants to states, universities and colleges, hospitals, laboratories, state and local health departments, public or private nonprofit institutes, and individuals who have demonstrated unusually high scientific ability.
$ Given: Range: $1,500–$1.8 million; average: $145,198
Application Information: Requests for application forms and completed applications must be submitted to the appropriate EPA Regional Grants Administration branch.
Deadline: None
Contact: Your state and/or regional EPA office

Alabama
William McBride
Grants and Contracts
Administration Section
Management Division
345 Courtland Street, NE
Atlanta, GA 30365
(404) 347-2374

Alaska
Oddvar Aurdal, Chief
Grants Administration
Section
MS 321
1200 Sixth Avenue
Seattle, WA 98101
(206) 442-2930

American Samoa
Mike Schultz, Chief
1235 Hawthorne Street
Grants and Policy Branch
San Francisco, CA 94105
(415) 744-1623

Arizona
Mike Schultz, Chief
1235 Hawthorne Street
Grants and Policy Branch
San Francisco, CA 94105
(415) 744-1623

Arkansas
Beverly Negri, Chief
1445 Ross Avenue
Grants Audit Section
6M-PG
Management Division
Dallas, TX 75270
(214) 655-6525

California
Mike Schultz, Chief
1235 Hawthorne Street
Grants and Policy Branch
San Francisco, CA 94105
(415) 744-1623

Colorado
Martha Nicodemus, Chief
Grants Administration
Branch
8PM-GFM
999 18th Street
Suite 1300
Denver, CO 80202-2413
(303) 293-1672

Connecticut
Robert Goetzel
John F. Kennedy Federal
Building
10th Floor
(PAS-205)
Grants Information and
Management Section
Boston, MA 02203
(617) 565-3395

Delaware
Fred Warren
Grants Management Section
Office of the Comptroller
3PM32
841 Chestnut Building
Philadelphia, PA 19106
(215) 597-6166

Florida
William McBride
Grants and Contracts
Administration Section
Management Division
345 Courtland Street, NE
Atlanta, GA 30365
(404) 347-2374

Georgia
William McBride
Grants and Contracts
Administration Section
Management Division
345 Courtland Street, NE
Atlanta, GA 30365
(404) 347-2374

Hawaii
Mike Schultz, Chief
1235 Hawthorne Street
Grants and Policy Branch
San Francisco, CA 94105
(415) 744-1623

Idaho
Oddvar Aurdal, Chief
Grants Administration
Section
MS 321
1200 Sixth Avenue
Seattle, WA 98101
(206) 442-2930

Illinois
Ivavs Anteus
Contracts and Grants
Branch
230 South Dearborn Street
Chicago, IL 60604
(312) 886-9841

Indiana
Ivavs Anteus
Contracts and Grants
Branch
230 South Dearborn Street
Chicago, IL 60604
(312) 886-9841

Iowa
Carol Rompage
726 Minnesota Avenue
Grants Administration
Branch
Kansas City, MO 66101
(913) 551-7346

Kansas
Carol Rompage
726 Minnesota Avenue
Grants Administration
Branch
Kansas City, MO 66101
(913) 551-7346

Kentucky
William McBride
Grants and Contracts
Administration Section
Management Division
345 Courtland Street, NE
Atlanta, GA 30365
(404) 347-2374

Louisiana
Beverly Negri, Chief
1445 Ross Avenue
Grants Audit Section
6M-PG
Management Division
Dallas, TX 75270
(214) 655-6525

Maine
Robert Goetzel
John F. Kennedy Federal
Building
10th Floor
(PAS-205)
Grants Information and
Management Section
Boston, MA 02203
(617) 565-3395

Maryland
Fred Warren
Grants Management Section
Office of the Comptroller
3PM32
841 Chestnut Building
Philadelphia, PA 19106
(215) 597-6166

Massachusetts
Robert Goetzel
John F. Kennedy Federal
Building
10th Floor
(PAS-205)
Grants Information and
Management Section
Boston, MA 02203
(617) 565-3395

Michigan
Ivavs Anteus
Contracts and Grants
Branch
230 South Dearborn Street
Chicago, IL 60604
(312) 886-9841

Minnesota
Ivavs Anteus
Contracts and Grants
Branch
230 South Dearborn Street
Chicago, IL 60604
(312) 886-9841

Mississippi
William McBride
Grants and Contracts
Administration Section
Management Division
345 Courtland Street, NE
Atlanta, GA 30365
(404) 347-2374

Missouri
Carol Rompage
726 Minnesota Avenue
Grants Administration
Branch
Kansas City, MO 66101
(913) 551-7346

Montana
Martha Nicodemus, Chief
Grants Administration
Branch
8PM-GFM
999 18th Street
Suite 1300
Denver, CO 80202-2413
(303) 293-1672

Nebraska
Carol Rompage
726 Minnesota Avenue
Grants Administration
Branch
Kansas City, MO 66101
(913) 551-7346

Nevada
Mike Schultz, Chief
1235 Hawthorne Street
Grants and Policy Branch
San Francisco, CA 94105
(415) 744-1623

New Hampshire
Robert Goetzel
John F. Kennedy Federal
Building
10th Floor
(PAS-205)
Grants Information and
Management Section
Boston, MA 02203
(617) 565-3395

New Jersey
Dennis Debrowski, Acting
Chief
Grants Administration
Branch
2MGT
26 Federal Plaza
Room 937A
New York, NY 10278
(212) 264-9860

New Mexico
Beverly Negri, Chief
1445 Ross Avenue
Grants Audit Section
6M-PG
Management Division
Dallas, TX 75270
(214) 655-6525

New York
Dennis Debrowski, Acting
Chief
Grants Administration
Branch
2MGT
26 Federal Plaza
Room 937A
New York, NY 10278
(212) 264-9860

North Carolina
William McBride
Grants and Contracts
Administration Section
Management Division
345 Courtland Street, NE
Atlanta, GA 30365
(404) 347-2374

North Dakota
Martha Nicodemus, Chief
Grants Administration
Branch
8PM-GFM
999 18th Street
Suite 1300
Denver, CO 80202-2413
(303) 293-1672

Ohio
Ivavs Anteus
Contracts and Grants
Branch
230 South Dearborn Street
Chicago, IL 60604
(312) 886-9841

Oklahoma
Beverly Negri, Chief
1445 Ross Avenue
Grants Audit Section
6M-PG
Management Division
Dallas, TX 75270
(214) 655-6525

Oregon
Oddvar Aurdal, Chief
Grants Administration
Section
MS 321
1200 Sixth Avenue
Seattle, WA 98101
(206) 442-2930

Pennsylvania
Fred Warren
Grants Management Section
Office of the Comptroller
3PM32
841 Chestnut Building
Philadelphia, PA 19107
(215) 597-6166

Puerto Rico
Dennis Debrowski, Acting
Chief
Grants Administration
Branch
2MGT
26 Federal Plaza
Room 937A
New York, NY 10278
(212) 264-9860

Rhode Island
Robert Goetzel
John F. Kennedy Federal
Building
10th Floor
(PAS-205)
Grants Information and
Management Section
Boston, MA 02203
(617) 565-3395

South Carolina
William McBride
Grants and Contracts
Administration Section
Management Division
345 Courtland Street, NE
Atlanta, GA 30365
(404) 347-2374

South Dakota
Martha Nicodemus, Chief
Grants Administration
Branch
8PM-GFM
999 18th Street
Suite 1300
Denver, CO 80202-2413
(303) 293-1672

Tennessee
William McBride
Grants and Contracts
Administration Section
Management Division
345 Courtland Street, NE
Atlanta, GA 30365
(404) 347-2374

Texas
Beverly Negri, Chief
1445 Ross Avenue
Grants Audit Section
6M-PG
Management Division
Dallas, TX 75270
(214) 655-6525

Utah
Martha Nicodemus, Chief
Grants Administration
Branch
8PM-GFM
999 18th Street
Suite 1300
Denver, CO 80202-2413
(303) 293-1672

Vermont
Robert Goetzel
John F. Kennedy Federal
Building
10th Floor
(PAS-205)
Grants Information and
Management Section
Boston, MA 02203
(617) 565-3395

Virginia
Fred Warren
Grants Management Section
Office of the Comptroller
3PM32
841 Chestnut Building
Philadelphia, PA 19107
(215) 597-6166

Virgin Islands
Dennis Debrowski, Acting
Chief
Grants Administration
Branch
2MGT
26 Federal Plaza
Room 937A
New York, NY 10278
(212) 264-9860

Washington
Oddvar Aurdal, Chief
Grants Administration
Section
MS 321
1200 Sixth Avenue
Seattle, WA 98101
(206) 442-2930

West Virginia
Fred Warren
Grants Management Section
Office of the Comptroller
3PM32
841 Chestnut Building
Philadelphia, PA 19107
(215) 597-6166

Wisconsin
Ivavs Anteus
Contracts and Grants
Branch
230 South Dearborn Street
Chicago, IL 60604
(312) 886-9841

Wyoming
Martha Nicodemus, Chief
Grants Administration
Branch
8PM-GFM
999 18th Street
Suite 1300
Denver, CO 80202-2413
(303) 293-1672

ANADROMOUS FISH CONSERVATION

Department of the Interior
Division of Fish and Wildlife
Management Assistance
Fish and Wildlife Service
Department of the Interior
Washington, DC 20240
(703) 358-1718

Description: Project grants to individual entities with
professional fishery capabilities to conserve resources of
anadromous fish (fish that ascend streams to spawn),
particularly in the Great Lakes and Lake Champlain regions,
and to determine the cause of the drastic decline in the
Atlantic coastal migratory striped bass population. Nineteen
inland states are ineligible.
$ Given: FY 92, average: $100,000
Application Information: Submit standard project application
form to regional office.
Deadline: None
Contact: Regional Fish and Wildlife Service field office.

Alabama
James W. Pulliam Jr.
1875 Century Boulevard
Atlanta, GA 30345
(404) 679-4000

Alaska
Walter O. Stieglitz
1011 East Tudor Road
Anchorage, AK 99503
(907) 786-3542

Arizona
John G. Rogers
P.O. Box 1306
500 Gold Avenue, SW
Room 3018
Albuquerque, NM 87102
(505) 766-2321

Arkansas
James W. Pulliam Jr.
1875 Century Boulevard
Atlanta, GA 30345
(404) 679-4000

California
Marvin L. Plenert
911 NE 11th Avenue
Portland, OR 97232-4181
(503) 231-6118

Colorado
Ralph O. Morgenweck
P.O. Box 25486
Denver Federal Center
Denver, CO 80025
(303) 236-7920

Connecticut
Ronald E. Lambertson
300 Westgate Center Drive
Hadley, MA 01035-9589
(413) 253-8300

Delaware
Ronald E. Lambertson
300 Westgate Center Drive
Hadley, MA 01035-9589
(413) 253-8300

District of Columbia
Ronald E. Lambertson
300 Westgate Center Drive
Hadley, MA 01035-9589
(413) 253-8300

Florida
James W. Pulliam Jr.
1875 Century Boulevard
Atlanta, GA 30345
(404) 679-4000

Georgia
James W. Pulliam Jr.
1875 Century Boulevard
Atlanta, GA 30345
(404) 679-4000

Hawaii
Marvin L. Plenert
911 NE 11th Avenue
Portland, OR 97232-4181
(503) 231-6118

Idaho
Marvin L. Plenert
911 NE 11th Avenue
Portland, OR 97232-4181
(503) 231-6118

Illinois
Joseph S. Marler
Federal Building
Fort Snelling
Twin Cities, MN 55111
(612) 725-3563

Indiana
Joseph S. Marler
Federal Building
Fort Snelling
Twin Cities, MN 55111
(612) 725-3563

Iowa
Joseph S. Marler
Federal Building
Fort Snelling
Twin Cities, MN 55111
(612) 725-3563

Kansas
Ralph O. Morgenweck
P.O. Box 25486
Denver Federal Center
Denver, CO 80025
(303) 236-7920

Kentucky
James W. Pulliam Jr.
1875 Century Boulevard
Atlanta, GA 30345
(404) 679-4000

Louisiana
James W. Pulliam Jr.
1875 Century Boulevard
Atlanta, GA 30345
(404) 679-4000

Maine
Ronald E. Lambertson
300 Westgate Center Drive
Hadley, MA 01035-9589
(413) 253-8300

Maryland
Ronald E. Lambertson
300 Westgate Center Drive
Hadley, MA 01035-9589
(413) 253-8300

Massachusetts
Ronald E. Lambertson
300 Westgate Center Drive
Hadley, MA 01035-9589
(413) 253-8300

Michigan
Joseph S. Marler
Federal Building
Fort Snelling
Twin Cities, MN 55111
(612) 725-3563

Minnesota
Joseph S. Marler
Federal Building
Fort Snelling
Twin Cities, MN 55111
(612) 725-3563

Mississippi
James W. Pulliam Jr.
1875 Century Boulevard
Atlanta, GA 30345
(404) 679-4000

Missouri
Joseph S. Marler
Federal Building
Fort Snelling
Twin Cities, MN 55111
(612) 725-3563

Montana
Ralph O. Morgenweck
P.O. Box 25486
Denver Federal Center
Denver, CO 80025
(303) 236-7920

Nebraska
Ralph O. Morgenweck
P.O. Box 25486
Denver Federal Center
Denver, CO 80025
(303) 236-7920

Nevada
Marvin L. Plenert
911 NE 11th Avenue
Portland, OR 97232-4181
(503) 231-6118

New Hampshire
Ronald E. Lambertson
300 Westgate Center Drive
Hadley, MA 01035-9589
(413) 253-8300

New Jersey
Ronald E. Lambertson
300 Westgate Center Drive
Hadley, MA 01035-9589
(413) 253-8300

New Mexico
John G. Rogers
P.O. Box 1306
500 Gold Avenue, SW
Room 3018
Albuquerque, NM 87102
(505) 766-2321

New York
Ronald E. Lambertson
300 Westgate Center Drive
Hadley, MA 01035-9589
(413) 253-8300

North Carolina
James W. Pulliam Jr.
1875 Century Boulevard
Atlanta, GA 30345
(404) 679-4000

North Dakota
Ralph O. Morgenweck
P.O. Box 25486
Denver Federal Center
Denver, CO 80025
(303) 236-7920

Ohio
Joseph S. Marler
Federal Building
Fort Snelling
Twin Cities, MN 55111
(612) 725-3563

Oklahoma
John G. Rogers
P.O. Box 1306
500 Gold Avenue, SW
Room 3018
Albuquerque, NM 87102
(505) 766-2321

Oregon
Marvin L. Plenert
911 NE 11th Avenue
Portland, OR 97232-4181
(503) 231-6118

Pennsylvania
Ronald E. Lambertson
300 Westgate Center Drive
Hadley, MA 01035-9589
(413) 253-8300

Puerto Rico
James W. Pulliam Jr.
1875 Century Boulevard
Atlanta, GA 30345
(404) 679-4000

Rhode Island
Ronald E. Lambertson
300 Westgate Center Drive
Hadley, MA 01035-9589
(413) 253-8300

South Carolina
James W. Pulliam Jr.
1875 Century Boulevard
Atlanta, GA 30345
(404) 679-4000

South Dakota
Ralph O. Morgenweck
P.O. Box 25486
Denver Federal Center
Denver, CO 80025
(303) 236-7920

Tennessee
James W. Pulliam Jr.
1875 Century Boulevard
Atlanta, GA 30345
(404) 679-4000

Texas
John G. Rogers
P.O. Box 1306
500 Gold Avenue, SW
Room 3018
Albuquerque, NM 87102
(505) 766-2321

Utah
Ralph O. Morgenweck
P.O. Box 25486
Denver Federal Center
Denver, CO 80025
(303) 236-7920

Vermont
Ronald E. Lambertson
300 Westgate Center Drive
Hadley, MA 01035-9589
(413) 253-8300

Virginia
Ronald E. Lambertson
300 Westgate Center Drive
Hadley, MA 01035-9589
(413) 253-8300

Virgin Islands
James W. Pulliam, Jr.
1875 Century Boulevard
Atlanta, GA 30345
(404) 679-4000

Washington
Marvin L. Plenert
911 NE 11th Avenue
Portland, OR 97232-4181
(503) 231-6118

West Virginia
Ronald E. Lambertson
300 Westgate Center Drive
Hadley, MA 01035-9589
(413) 253-8300

Wisconsin
Joseph S. Marler
Federal Building
Fort Snelling
Twin Cities, MN 55111
(612) 725-3563

Wyoming
Ralph O. Morgenweck
P.O. Box 25486
Denver Federal Center
Denver, CO 80025
(303) 236-7920

APPLIED TOXICOLOGICAL RESEARCH AND TESTING
(Bioassay of Chemicals and Test Development)

Department of Health and
Human Services
Division of Extramural
Research and Training
National Institute of
Environmental Health
Sciences
National Institutes of Health
Public Health Service
P.O. Box 12233
Research Triangle Park, NC
27709
(919) 541-7825

Description: Project grants, including Small Business
Innovation Research grants (SBIRs), to for-profit
organizations for research into toxicology of hazardous
chemicals.
$ Given: Est. $6.8 million in total grants nationwide FY 93;
range: $67,920–$436,776; average: $129,000
Application Information: Submit standard applications.
Deadlines: Research grants: February 1, June 1, October 1;
SBIRs: April 15, August 15, December 15
Contact: Dr. Michael Galven, Program Administrator

BIOLOGICAL RESPONSE TO ENVIRONMENTAL
HEALTH HAZARDS

Department of Health and
Human Services
Scientific Programs Branch
Division of Extramural
Research and Training
Environmental Health
Sciences
National Institutes of Health
Public Health Service
P.O. Box 12233
Research Triangle Park, NC
27709
(919) 541-7825

Description: Project grants, including SBIRs, to private for-
profit organizations to foster research on pathogenic agents
and other biological hazards. Special grants to purchase low-
cost research equipment (SBIRs) in two phases: I (feasibility)
and II (continuation). Maximum funds: $50,000 for Phase I,
$500,000 for Phase II. Various other restrictions apply.
Funds to be used in manner consistent with research grants.
$ Given: Est. $76 million in total grants nationwide FY 93;
range (excluding SBIRs): $25,022–$1.6 million
Application Information: Submit standard application.
Deadlines: Research grants: February 1, June 1, October 1;
SBIRs: April 15, August 15, December 15
Contact: Dr. Michael Galven, Program Administration

BIOMETRY AND RISK ESTIMATION

Department of Health and
Human Services
Scientific Programs Branch
Division of Extramural
Research and Training
National Institute of
Environmental Health
Sciences
National Institutes of Health
Public Health Service
P.O. Box 12233
Research Triangle Park, NC
27709
(919) 541-7825

Description: Project grants to for-profit organizations for
research in estimating probable health risks from various
environmental hazards.
$ Given: Est. $6.4 million in total grants nationwide FY 93;
range: $13,751–$481,779
Application Information: Submit standard applications.
Deadlines: Research grants: February 1, June 1, October 1
Contact: Dr. Michael Galven, Program Administrator

CLIMATE AND AIR-QUALITY RESEARCH

Department of Commerce
National Oceanic and
Atmospheric Administration
1335 East West Highway
Silver Spring, MD 20910
(301) 713-2458

Description: Project grants to individuals, technical schools,
and laboratories for developing knowledge required to
predict short-term and long-term fluctuations and trends in
climate and air quality. Funds to be used for research and
development, advisory services, and operational systems.
$ Given: Est. $50,000 nationwide FY 93; range: $2,000–
$10,000
Application Information: Submit standard application with
statement of work to be performed and proposed grant
amount.
Deadline: None
Contact: Alan Thomas or Director, Office of Climate and
Environmental Research Laboratories, Office of Oceanic and
Atmospheric Research, above address

CLIMATE AND ATMOSPHERIC RESEARCH

Department of Commerce
National Oceanic and
Atmospheric Administration
1100 Wayne Avenue
Silver Spring, MD 20910
(301) 427-2089

Description: Project grants to any individual, technical
school, or laboratory for developing ability to predict short-
range and long-range climatic fluctuations and trends. Funds
must be used for research and development, advisory
services, or operational systems.
$ Given: Est. $17.9 million nationwide FY 93; range:
$10,000–$220,000. average: $85,000
Application Information: Submit standard application with
statement of work to be performed and proposed grant
amount.
Deadline: None
Contact: Director, Office of Global Programs, above address.

ENVIRONMENTAL PROTECTION—CONSOLIDATED RESEARCH

**Environmental Protection
Agency (EPA)**
Grants Administration
Division
Room 216
Washington, DC 20460
(202) 620-7473

Description: Project grants to states, universities and colleges,
hospitals, laboratories, public or private nonprofit institutes,
and individuals who have demonstrated unusually high
scientific ability.
$ Given: Range: $2,000–$2.5 million; average: $140,000
Application Information: Request application from above
address.
Deadline: None
Contact: Your state and/or regional EPA office

Alabama
William McBride
Grants and Contracts
Administration Section
Management Division
345 Courtland Street, NE
Atlanta, GA 30365
(404) 347-2374

Alaska
Oddvar Aurdal, Chief
Grants Administration
Section
MS 321
1200 Sixth Avenue
Seattle, WA 98101
(206) 442-2930

American Samoa
Mike Schultz, Chief
1235 Hawthorne Street
Grants and Policy Branch
San Francisco, CA 94105
(415) 744-1623

Arizona
Mike Schultz, Chief
1235 Hawthorne Street
Grants and Policy Branch
San Francisco, CA 94105
(415) 744-1623

Arkansas
Beverly Negri, Chief
1445 Ross Avenue
Grants Audit Section
6M-PG
Management Division
Dallas, TX 75270
(214) 655-6525

California
Mike Schultz, Chief
1235 Hawthorne Street
Grants and Policy Branch
San Francisco, CA 94105
(415) 744-1623

Colorado
Martha Nicodemus, Chief
Grants Administration
Branch
8PM-GFM
999 18th Street
Suite 1300
Denver, CO 80202-2413
(303) 293-1672

Connecticut
Robert Goetzel
John F. Kennedy Federal
Building
10th Floor
(PAS-205)
Grants Information and
Management Section
Boston, MA 02203
(617) 565-3395

Delaware
Fred Warren
Grants Management Section
Office of the Comptroller
3PM32
841 Chestnut Building
Philadelphia, PA 19106
(215) 597-6166

Florida
William McBride
Grants and Contracts
Administration Section
Management Division
345 Courtland Street, NE
Atlanta, GA 30365
(404) 347-2374

Georgia
William McBride
Grants and Contracts
Administration Section
Management Division
345 Courtland Street, NE
Atlanta, GA 30365
(404) 347-2374

Hawaii
Mike Schultz, Chief
1235 Hawthorne Street
Grants and Policy Branch
San Francisco, CA 94105
(415) 744-1623

Idaho
Oddvar Aurdal, Chief
Grants Administration
Section
MS 321
1200 Sixth Avenue
Seattle, WA 98101
(206) 442-2930

Illinois
Ivavs Anteus
Contracts and Grants
Branch
230 South Dearborn Street
Chicago, IL 60604
(312) 886-9841

Indiana
Ivavs Anteus
Contracts and Grants
Branch
230 South Dearborn Street
Chicago, IL 60604
(312) 886-9841

Iowa
Carol Rompage
726 Minnesota Avenue
Grants Administration
Branch
Kansas City, MO 66101
(913) 551-7346

Kansas
Carol Rompage
726 Minnesota Avenue
Grants Administration
Branch
Kansas City, MO 66101
(913) 551-7346

Kentucky
William McBride
Grants and Contracts
Administration Section
Management Division
345 Courtland Street, NE
Atlanta, GA 30365
(404) 347-2374

Louisiana
Beverly Negri, Chief
1445 Ross Avenue
Grants Audit Section
6M-PG
Management Division
Dallas, TX 75270
(214) 655-6525

Maine
Robert Goetzel
John F. Kennedy Federal
Building
10th Floor
(PAS-205)
Grants Information and
Management Section
Boston, MA 02203
(617) 565-3395

Maryland
Fred Warren
Grants Management Section
Office of the Comptroller
3PM32
841 Chestnut Building
Philadelphia, PA 19106
(215) 597-6166

Massachusetts
Robert Goetzel
John F. Kennedy Federal
Building
10th Floor
(PAS-205)
Grants Information and
Management Section
Boston, MA 02203
(617) 565-3395

Michigan
Ivavs Anteus
Contracts and Grants
Branch
230 South Dearborn Street
Chicago, IL 60604
(312) 886-9841

Minnesota
Ivavs Anteus
Contracts and Grants
Branch
230 South Dearborn Street
Chicago, IL 60604
(312) 886-9841

Mississippi
William McBride
Grants and Contracts
Administration Section
Management Division
345 Courtland Street, NE
Atlanta, GA 30365
(404) 347-2374

Missouri
Carol Rompage
726 Minnesota Avenue
Grants Administration
Branch
Kansas City, MO 66101
(913) 551-7346

Montana
Martha Nicodemus, Chief
Grants Administration
Branch
8PM-GFM
999 18th Street
Suite 1300
Denver, CO 80202-2413
(303) 293-1672

Nebraska
Carol Rompage
726 Minnesota Avenue
Grants Administration
Branch
Kansas City, MO 66101
(913) 551-7346

Nevada
Mike Schultz, Chief
1235 Hawthorne Street
Grants and Policy Branch
San Francisco, CA 94105
(415) 744-1623

New Hampshire
Robert Goetzel
John F. Kennedy Federal
Building
10th Floor
(PAS-205)
Grants Information and
Management Section
Boston, MA 02203
(617) 565-3395

New Jersey
Dennis Debrowski, Acting
Chief
Grants Administration
Branch
2MGT
26 Federal Plaza
Room 937A
New York, NY 10278
(212) 264-9860

New Mexico
Beverly Negri, Chief
1445 Ross Avenue
Grants Audit Section
6M-PG
Management Division
Dallas, TX 75270
(214) 655-6525

New York
Dennis Debrowski, Acting
Chief
Grants Administration
Branch
2MGT
26 Federal Plaza
Room 937A
New York, NY 10278
(212) 264-9860

North Carolina
William McBride
Grants and Contracts
Administration Section
Management Division
345 Courtland Street, NE
Atlanta, GA 30365
(404) 347-2374

North Dakota
Martha Nicodemus, Chief
Grants Administration
Branch
8PM-GFM
999 18th Street
Suite 1300
Denver, CO 80202-2413
(303) 293-1672

Ohio
Ivavs Anteus
Contracts and Grants
Branch
230 South Dearborn Street
Chicago, IL 60604
(312) 886-9841

Oklahoma
Beverly Negri, Chief
1445 Ross Avenue
Grants Audit Section
6M-PG
Management Division
Dallas, TX 75270
(214) 655-6525

Oregon
Oddvar Aurdal, Chief
Grants Administration
Section
MS 321
1200 Sixth Avenue
Seattle, WA 98101
(206) 442-2930

Pennsylvania
Fred Warren
Grants Management Section
Office of the Comptroller
3PM32
841 Chestnut Building
Philadelphia, PA 19107
(215) 597-6166

Puerto Rico
Dennis Debrowski, Acting
Chief
Grants Administration
Branch
2MGT
26 Federal Plaza
Room 937A
New York, NY 10278
(212) 264-9860

Rhode Island
Robert Goetzel
John F. Kennedy Federal
Building
10th Floor
(PAS-205)
Grants Information and
Management Section
Boston, MA 02203
(617) 565-3395

South Carolina
William McBride
Grants and Contracts
Administration Section
Management Division
345 Courtland Street, NE
Atlanta, GA 30365
(404) 347-2374

South Dakota
Martha Nicodemus, Chief
Grants Administration
Branch
8PM-GFM
999 18th Street
Suite 1300
Denver, CO 80202-2413
(303) 293-1672

Tennessee
William McBride
Grants and Contracts
Administration Section
Management Division
345 Courtland Street, NE
Atlanta, GA 30365
(404) 347-2374

Texas
Beverly Negri, Chief
1445 Ross Avenue
Grants Audit Section
6M-PG
Management Division
Dallas, TX 75270
(214) 655-6525

Utah
Martha Nicodemus, Chief
Grants Administration
Branch
8PM-GFM
999 18th Street
Suite 1300
Denver, CO 80202-2413
(303) 293-1672

Vermont
Robert Goetzel
John F. Kennedy Federal
Building
10th Floor
(PAS-205)
Grants Information and
Management Section
Boston, MA 02203
(617) 565-3395

Virginia
Fred Warren
Grants Management Section
Office of the Comptroller
3PM32
841 Chestnut Building
Philadelphia, PA 19107
(215) 597-6166

Virgin Islands
Dennis Debrowski, Acting
Chief
Grants Administration
Branch
2MGT
26 Federal Plaza
Room 937A
New York, NY 10278
(212) 264-9860

Washington
Oddvar Aurdal, Chief
Grants Administration
Section
MS 321
1200 Sixth Avenue
Seattle, WA 98101
(206) 442-2930

West Virginia
Fred Warren
Grants Management Section
Office of the Comptroller
3PM32
841 Chestnut Building
Philadelphia, PA 19107
(215) 597-6166

Wisconsin
Ivavs Anteus
Contracts and Grants
Branch
230 South Dearborn Street
Chicago, IL 60604
(312) 886-9841

Wyoming
Martha Nicodemus, Chief
Grants Administration
Branch
8PM-GFM
999 18th Street
Suite 1300
Denver, CO 80202-2413
(303) 293-1672

FINANCIAL ASSISTANCE FOR OCEAN-RESOURCES CONSERVATION AND ASSESSMENT PROGRAM

Department of Commerce
National Ocean Service
1305 East West Highway
Silver Spring, MD 20910

Description: Project grants (cooperative agreements) to individuals and corporations for assessing long-term impact of human activities on coastal and marine environment and for defining and assessing techniques to minimize adverse effects. Recipient must demonstrate expertise in priority objectives and win approval for proposed methods.
$ Given: Est. $850,000 nationwide FY 93; range: $20,000–$200,000; average: $80,000
Application Information: Standard application forms required.
Deadline: None
Contact: Office of Ocean Resources, Conservation and Marine Assessment (N/ORCA), above address

PESTICIDES CONTROL RESEARCH

Environmental Protection
Agency (EPA)
Grants Administration
Division
Room PM216FC
Washington, DC 20460
(202) 260-7473

Description: Project grants to states, universities and colleges, hospitals, laboratories, state and local governments, and individuals.
$ Given: Range: $10,000–$450,000; average: $110,000
Application Information: Request application from above address.
Contact: Your state and/or regional EPA office

Alabama
William McBride
Grants and Contracts
Administration Section
Management Division
345 Courtland Street, NE
Atlanta, GA 30365
(404) 347-2374

Alaska
Oddvar Aurdal, Chief
Grants Administration
Section
MS 321
1200 Sixth Avenue
Seattle, WA 98101
(206) 442-2930

American Samoa
Mike Schultz, Chief
1235 Hawthorne Street
Grants and Policy Branch
San Francisco, CA 94105
(415) 744-1623

Arizona
Mike Schultz, Chief
1235 Hawthorne Street
Grants and Policy Branch
San Francisco, CA 94105
(415) 744-1623

Arkansas
Beverly Negri, Chief
1445 Ross Avenue
Grants Audit Section
6M-PG
Management Division
Dallas, TX 75270
(214) 655-6525

California
Mike Schultz, Chief
1235 Hawthorne Street
Grants and Policy Branch
San Francisco, CA 94105
(415) 744-1623

Colorado
Martha Nicodemus, Chief
Grants Administration
Branch
8PM-GFM
999 18th Street
Suite 1300
Denver, CO 80202-2413
(303) 293-1672

Connecticut
Robert Goetzel
John F. Kennedy Federal
Building
10th Floor
(PAS-205)
Grants Information and
Management Section
Boston, MA 02203
(617) 565-3395

Delaware
Fred Warren
Grants Management Section
Office of the Comptroller
3PM32
841 Chestnut Building
Philadelphia, PA 19106
(215) 597-6166

Florida
William McBride
Grants and Contracts
Administration Section
Management Division
345 Courtland Street, NE
Atlanta, GA 30365
(404) 347-2374

Georgia
William McBride
Grants and Contracts
Administration Section
Management Division
345 Courtland Street, NE
Atlanta, GA 30365
(404) 347-2374

Hawaii
Mike Schultz, Chief
1235 Hawthorne Street
Grants and Policy Branch
San Francisco, CA 94105
(415) 744-1623

Idaho
Oddvar Aurdal, Chief
Grants Administration
Section
MS 321
1200 Sixth Avenue
Seattle, WA 98101
(206) 442-2930

Illinois
Ivavs Anteus
Contracts and Grants
Branch
230 South Dearborn Street
Chicago, IL 60604
(312) 886-9841

Indiana
Ivavs Anteus
Contracts and Grants
Branch
230 South Dearborn Street
Chicago, IL 60604
(312) 886-9841

Iowa
Carol Rompage
726 Minnesota Avenue
Grants Administration
Branch
Kansas City, MO 66101
(913) 551-7346

Kansas
Carol Rompage
726 Minnesota Avenue
Grants Administration
Branch
Kansas City, MO 66101
(913) 551-7346

Kentucky
William McBride
Grants and Contracts
Administration Section
Management Division
345 Courtland Street, NE
Atlanta, GA 30365
(404) 347-2374

Louisiana
Beverly Negri, Chief
1445 Ross Avenue
Grants Audit Section
6M-PG
Management Division
Dallas, TX 75270
(214) 655-6525

Maine
Robert Goetzel
John F. Kennedy Federal
Building
10th Floor
(PAS-205)
Grants Information and
Management Section
Boston, MA 02203
(617) 565-3395

Maryland
Fred Warren
Grants Management Section
Office of the Comptroller
3PM32
841 Chestnut Building
Philadelphia, PA 19106
(215) 597-6166

Massachusetts
Robert Goetzel
John F. Kennedy Federal
Building
10th Floor
(PAS-205)
Grants Information and
Management Section
Boston, MA 02203
(617) 565-3395

Michigan
Ivavs Anteus
Contracts and Grants
Branch
230 South Dearborn Street
Chicago, IL 60604
(312) 886-9841

Minnesota
Ivavs Anteus
Contracts and Grants
Branch
230 South Dearborn Street
Chicago, IL 60604
(312) 886-9841

Mississippi
William McBride
Grants and Contracts
Administration Section
Management Division
345 Courtland Street, NE
Atlanta, GA 30365
(404) 347-2374

Missouri
Carol Rompage
726 Minnesota Avenue
Grants Administration
Branch
Kansas City, MO 66101
(913) 551-7346

Montana
Martha Nicodemus, Chief
Grants Administration
Branch
8PM-GFM
999 18th Street
Suite 1300
Denver, CO 80202-2413
(303) 293-1672

Nebraska
Carol Rompage
726 Minnesota Avenue
Grants Administration
Branch
Kansas City, MO 66101
(913) 551-7346

Nevada
Mike Schultz, Chief
1235 Hawthorne Street
Grants and Policy Branch
San Francisco, CA 94105
(415) 744-1623

New Hampshire
Robert Goetzel
John F. Kennedy Federal
Building
10th Floor
(PAS-205)
Grants Information and
Management Section
Boston, MA 02203
(617) 565-3395

New Jersey
Dennis Debrowski, Acting
Chief
Grants Administration
Branch
2MGT
26 Federal Plaza
Room 937A
New York, NY 10278
(212) 264-9860

New Mexico
Beverly Negri, Chief
1445 Ross Avenue
Grants Audit Section
6M-PG
Management Division
Dallas, TX 75270
(214) 655-6525

New York
Dennis Debrowski, Acting
Chief
Grants Administration
Branch
2MGT
26 Federal Plaza
Room 937A
New York, NY 10278
(212) 264-9860

North Carolina
William McBride
Grants and Contracts
Administration Section
Management Division
345 Courtland Street, NE
Atlanta, GA 30365
(404) 347-2374

North Dakota
Martha Nicodemus, Chief
Grants Administration
Branch
8PM-GFM
999 18th Street
Suite 1300
Denver, CO 80202-2413
(303) 293-1672

Ohio
Ivavs Anteus
Contracts and Grants
Branch
230 South Dearborn Street
Chicago, IL 60604
(312) 886-9841

Oklahoma
Beverly Negri, Chief
1445 Ross Avenue
Grants Audit Section
6M-PG
Management Division
Dallas, TX 75270
(214) 655-6525

Oregon
Oddvar Aurdal, Chief
Grants Administration
Section
MS 321
1200 Sixth Avenue
Seattle, WA 98101
(206) 442-2930

Pennsylvania
Fred Warren
Grants Management Section
Office of the Comptroller
3PM32
841 Chestnut Building
Philadelphia, PA 19107
(215) 597-6166

Puerto Rico
Dennis Debrowski, Acting
Chief
Grants Administration
Branch
2MGT
26 Federal Plaza
Room 937A
New York, NY 10278
(212) 264-9860

Rhode Island
Robert Goetzel
John F. Kennedy Federal
Building
10th Floor
(PAS-205)
Grants Information and
Management Section
Boston, MA 02203
(617) 565-3395

South Carolina
William McBride
Grants and Contracts
Administration Section
Management Division
345 Courtland Street, NE
Atlanta, GA 30365
(404) 347-2374

South Dakota
Martha Nicodemus, Chief
Grants Administration
Branch
8PM-GFM
999 18th Street
Suite 1300
Denver, CO 80202-2413
(303) 293-1672

Tennessee
William McBride
Grants and Contracts
Administration Section
Management Division
345 Courtland Street, NE
Atlanta, GA 30365
(404) 347-2374

Texas
Beverly Negri, Chief
1445 Ross Avenue
Grants Audit Section
6M-PG
Management Division
Dallas, TX 75270
(214) 655-6525

Utah
Martha Nicodemus, Chief
Grants Administration
Branch
8PM-GFM
999 18th Street
Suite 1300
Denver, CO 80202-2413
(303) 293-1672

Vermont
Robert Goetzel
John F. Kennedy Federal
Building
10th Floor
(PAS-205)
Grants Information and
Management Section
Boston, MA 02203
(617) 565-3395

Virginia
Fred Warren
Grants Management Section
Office of the Comptroller
3PM32
841 Chestnut Building
Philadelphia, PA 19107
(215) 597-6166

Virgin Islands
Dennis Debrowski, Acting
Chief
Grants Administration
Branch
2MGT
26 Federal Plaza
Room 937A
New York, NY 10278
(212) 264-9860

Washington
Oddvar Aurdal, Chief
Grants Administration
Section
MS 321
1200 Sixth Avenue
Seattle, WA 98101
(206) 442-2930

West Virginia
Fred Warren
Grants Management Section
Office of the Comptroller
3PM32
841 Chestnut Building
Philadelphia, PA 19107
(215) 597-6166

Wisconsin
Ivavs Anteus
Contracts and Grants
Branch
230 South Dearborn Street
Chicago, IL 60604
(312) 886-9841

Wyoming
Martha Nicodemus, Chief
Grants Administration
Branch
8PM-GFM
999 18th Street
Suite 1300
Denver, CO 80202-2413
(303) 293-1672

POLLUTION PREVENTION GRANTS PROGRAM

Environmental Protection
Agency (EPA)
Pollution Prevention
Division
Office of Pollution
Prevention and Toxics
MC7409
401 M Street, SW
Washington, DC 20460
(202) 260-2237

Description: Provides direct technical assistance to businesses in need of information and training in source-reduction techniques. These programs are administered by the states.
$ Given: Est. $6 million FY 93; range: $50,000–$200,000; average: $160,000
Application Information: Applicants should contact the office designated as the single point of contact for his or her state or the regional EPA office. See contact listed below.
Deadline: N/A
Contact: Lena Hann, regional EPA office, or state single point of contact

Alabama
William McBride
Grants and Contracts
Administration Section
Management Division
345 Courtland Street, NE
Atlanta, GA 30365
(404) 347-2374

Alaska
Oddvar Aurdal, Chief
Grants Administration
Section
MS 321
1200 Sixth Avenue
Seattle, WA 98101
(206) 442-2930

Arizona
Mike Schultz, Chief
1235 Hawthorne Street
Grants and Policy Branch
San Francisco, CA 94105
(415) 744-1623

Arkansas
Tracy L. Copeland, Manager
State Clearinghouse Office
of Intergovernmental
Services
Department of Finance and
Administration
1515 West Seventh Street
Room 412
Little Rock, AR 72210
(501) 682-1074

California
Grants Coordinator
Office of Planning and
Research
1400 10th Street
Room 121
Sacramento, CA 95814
(916) 323-7480

Colorado
State Single Point of Contact
State Clearinghouse
Division of Local
Government
131 Sherman Street
Room 521
Denver, CO 80203
(303) 866-2156

Connecticut
William T. Quiqq
Intergovernmental Review
Coordinator
State Single Point of Contact
Office of Policy and
Management
Intergovernmental Policy
Division
80 Washington Street
Hartford, CT 06106-4459
(203) 566-3410

Delaware
Francine Booth
State Single Point of Contact
Executive Department
Thomas Collins Building
Dover, DE 19903
(302) 736-3326

District of Columbia
Rodney T. Hallman
State Single Point of Contact
Office of Grants
Management and
Development
717 14th Street, SW
Suite 500
Washington, DC 20005
(202) 727-6551

Florida
Suzanne Traub-Metlay
Florida State Clearinghouse
Intergovernment Affairs
Policy Unit
Executive Office of the
Governor
The Capitol
Room 1603
Tallahassee, FL 32399-0001
(904) 488-8441

Georgia
Charles H. Badger,
Administrator
Georgia State Clearinghouse
Room 401J
254 Washington Street, SW
Atlanta, GA 30034
(404) 656-3855

Hawaii
Mary Lou Kobayashi
Planning Program Manager
Office of State Planning
Office of the Governor
P.O. Box 3540
Honolulu, HI 96811
(808) 587-2802

Idaho
Grants Administration
Section
MS 321
1200 Sixth Avenue
Seattle, WA 98101
(206) 442-2930

Illinois
Steve Klokkenga
State Single Point of Contact
Office of the Governor
107 Stratton Building
Springfield, IL 62706
(217) 782-6620

Indiana
Frances E. Williams
State Budget Agency
212 State House
Indianapolis, IN 46204
(317) 232-5610

Iowa
Steven R. McCann
Division for Community
Progress
Iowa Department of
Economic Development
200 East Grand Avenue
Des Moines, IA 50309
(515) 242-4719

Kansas
Carol Rompage
726 Minnesota Avenue
Grants Administration
Branch
Kansas City, MO 66101
(913) 551-7346

Kentucky
Ronald W. Cook
Office of the Governor
Department of Local
Government
1024 Capitol Center Drive
Frankfort, KY 20601
(502) 564-2382

Louisiana
Beverly Negri, Chief
1445 Ross Avenue
Grants Audit Section
6M-PG
Management Division
Dallas, TX 75270
(214) 655-6525

Maine
Joyce Benson
State Planning Office
State Housing Station #38
Augusta, ME 04333
(207) 287-3261

Maryland
State Clearinghouse for
Intergovernmental Assistance
Maryland Office of Planning
301 West Preston Street
Room 1104
Baltimore, MD 21201-2365
(410) 225-4490

Massachusetts
Karen Hirone
State Clearinghouse
Executive Office of
Communities and
Development
100 Cambridge Street
Room 1803
Boston, MA 02202
(617) 727-7001, ext. 443

Michigan
Richard S. Pastula, Director
Office of Federal Grants
Michigan Department of
Commerce
P.O. Box 30225
Lansing, MI 48909
(517) 373-7356

Minnesota
EPA, Region V
77 West Jackson Boulevard
Chicago, IL 60604
(312) 353-2000

Mississippi
Cathy Mallette
Clearinghouse Officer
Office of Federal Grant
Management and Reporting
Department of Finance
301 West Pearl Street
Jackson, MS 39203
(601) 949-2174

Missouri
Louis Pohl
Federal Assistance
Clearinghouse
Office of Administration
P.O. Box 809
Truman Building
Room 760
Jefferson City, MO 65102
(314) 751-4834

Montana
Martha Nicodemus, Chief
Grants Administration
Branch
8PM-GFM
999 18th Street
Suite 1300
Denver, CO 80202-2413
(303) 293-1672

Nebraska
Carol Rompage
726 Minnesota Avenue
Grants Administration
Branch
Kansas City, MO 66101
(913) 551-7346

Nevada
Department of
Administration
State Clearinghouse
Capitol Complex
Carson City, NV 89710
(702) 687-4065

New Hampshire
Jeffrey H. Taylor, Director
New Hampshire Office of
State Planning
Attn: Intergovernmental
Review Process
James E. Bieber
2 1/2 Beacon Street
Concord, NH 03301
(603) 271-2155

New Jersey
Andrew J. Jaskolka
State Review Process
Division of Community
Resources
CN 814
Room 609
Trenton, NJ 08625-0814
(609) 292-9025

New Mexico
George Elliott, Deputy
Director
State Budget Division
Bataan Memorial Building
Room 190
Santa Fe, NM 87503
(505) 827-3640

New York
New York State
Clearinghouse
Division of the Budget
State Capitol
Albany, NY 12224
(518) 474-1605

North Carolina
Chrys Baggett, Director
Intergovernmental Relations
North Carolina Department
of Administration
116 West Jones Street
Raleigh, NC 27611
(919) 733-0499

North Dakota
State Single Point of Contact
Office of Intergovernmental
Assistance
Office of Management and
Budget
600 East Boulevard Avenue
Bismarck, ND 58505-0170
(701) 224-2094

Ohio
Linda Wise
State Single Point of Contact
State/Federal Funds
Coordinator
State Clearinghouse
Office of Budget and
Management
30 East Broad Street
34th Floor
Columbus, OH 43266-0411
(614) 466-0698

Oklahoma
Beverly Negri, Chief
1445 Ross Avenue
Grants Audit Section
6M-PG
Management Division
Dallas, TX 75270
(214) 655-6525

Oregon
Oddvar Aurdal, Chief
Grants Administration
Section
MS 321
1200 Sixth Avenue
Seattle, WA 98101
(206) 442-2930

Pennsylvania
Fred Warren
Grants Management Section
Office of the Comptroller
3PM32
841 Chestnut Building
Philadelphia, PA 19107
(215) 597-6166

Puerto Rico
Norma Burgos, Chairman
Jose E. Caro, Director
Puerto Rico Planning Board
Federal Proposals Review
Office
Manillas Government Center
P.O. Box 41119
San Juan, PR 00940-1119
(809) 727-4444

Rhode Island
Review Coordinator
Office of Strategic Planning
One Capitol Hill
Fourth Floor
Providence, RI 02908-5870
(401) 277-2656

South Carolina
Omeagia Burges
Grant Services
Office of the Governor
1205 Pendleton Street
Room 477
Columbia, SC 29201
(803) 734-0494

South Dakota
Susan Comer
State Clearinghouse
Coordinator
Office of the Government
500 East Capitol
Pierre, SD 57501

Tennessee
Charles Brown
State Single Point of Contact
State Planning Office
500 Charlotte Avenue
309 John Sevier Building
Nashville, TN 37243-0001
(615) 741-1676

Texas
Tom Adams, Director
Intergovernmental
Coordinator
P.O. Box 13005
Austin, TX 78711
(512) 463-1771

Utah
Utah State Clearinghouse
Office of Planning and
Budget
Attn: Carolyn Wright
State Capitol
Room 116
Salt Lake City, UT 84114
(801) 538-1535

Vermont
Nancy McAvoy
Pavilion Office Building
109 State Street
Montpelier, VT 05609
(802) 828-3326

Virginia
Fred Warren
Grants Management Section
Office of the Comptroller
3PM32
841 Chestnut Building
Philadelphia, PA 19107
(215) 597-6166

Virgin Islands
Linda Clarke
Office of Management and
Budget
41 Noregada Emancipation
Garden Station
Second Floor
St. Thomas, VI 00802
(809) 774-0750

Washington
Oddvar Aurdal, Chief
Grants Administration
Section
MS 321
1200 Sixth Avenue
Seattle, WA 98101
(206) 442-2930

West Virginia
Fred Cutlip, Director
Community Development
Division
West Virginia Development
Office
Building #6
Room 553
Charleston, WV 25305
(304) 558-4010

Wisconsin
Martha Kerner, Sectional
Chief
State/Federal Relations
Office
Winconsin Department of
Administration
101 East Wilson
Sixth Floor
P.O. Box 7868
Madison, WI 53707
(608) 266-2125

Wyoming
Cheryl Jeffries
State Single Point of Contact
Herschler Building
Fourth Floor
East Wing
Cheyenne, WY 82002
(307) 777-7574

SUPERFUND INNOVATIVE TECHNOLOGY EVALUATION PROGRAM (SITE)

Environmental Protection
Agency (EPA)
Office of Environmental
Engineering
Technology Demonstration
401 M Street, SW
RD-681
Washington, DC 20460
(202) 260-2583

Description: Aid to environmental technologies that are still in the bench/laboratory stage to bring them up to pilot scale. Provides assistance to developers of new technologies through field demonstrations at hazardous-waste sites. This program is available to any private individual or business that has a new or innovative technology for recycling, separation, detoxification, destruction, stabilization, and handling of hazardous materials.

$ Given: Est. $17.6 million FY 93; the Emerging Technologies Program provides two-year funding at up to $150,000 per year for a maximum of $300,000 over two years.

Application Information: Applications are made to the following listed EPA Headquarters.

Deadline: Applications must be received within 45 days after the EPA's yearly solicitation in the Commerce Business Daily.

Contacts:
John F. Martin
Risk-Reduction Engineering Laboratory
Cincinnati, OH 45268
(513) 569-7696

or

Stephen James, Chief
SITE Demonstration and Evaluation Branch
SITE Program
Office of Research and Development
Risk-Reduction Engineering Laboratory
26 West Martin Luther King Street
Cincinnati, OH 45268
(513) 659-7976

Headquarters contact:
Richard Nalesnik at Office of Environmental Engineering
address given

TOXIC SUBSTANCE RESEARCH

Environmental Protection
Agency (EPA)
Grants Administration
Division
Room 216
Washington, DC 20460
(202) 260-7473

Description: Project grants to states, universities and colleges, hospitals, public or private institutes, and individuals who have demonstrated unusually high scientific ability.
$ Given: Range: $10,000–$700,000; average: $8,600
Application Information: Request application from above address.
Deadline: None
Contact: Your state and/or regional EPA office

Alabama
William McBride
Grants and Contracts
Administration Section
Management Division
345 Courtland Street, NE
Atlanta, GA 30365
(404) 347-2374

Alaska
Oddvar Aurdal, Chief
Grants Administration
Section
MS 321
1200 Sixth Avenue
Seattle, WA 98101
(206) 442-2930

American Samoa
Mike Schultz, Chief
1235 Hawthorne Street
Grants and Policy Branch
San Francisco, CA 94105
(415) 744-1623

Arizona
Mike Schultz, Chief
1235 Hawthorne Street
Grants and Policy Branch
San Francisco, CA 94105
(415) 744-1623

Arkansas
Beverly Negri, Chief
1445 Ross Avenue
Grants Audit Section
6M-PG
Management Division
Dallas, TX 75270
(214) 655-6525

California
Mike Schultz, Chief
1235 Hawthorne Street
Grants and Policy Branch
San Francisco, CA 94105
(415) 744-1623

Colorado
Martha Nicodemus, Chief
Grants Administration
Branch
8PM-GFM
999 18th Street
Suite 1300
Denver, CO 80202-2413
(303) 293-1672

Connecticut
Robert Goetzel
John F. Kennedy Federal
Building
10th Floor
(PAS-205)
Grants Information and
Management Section
Boston, MA 02203
(617) 565-3395

Delaware
Fred Warren
Grants Management Section
Office of the Comptroller
3PM32
841 Chestnut Building
Philadelphia, PA 19106
(215) 597-6166

Florida
William McBride
Grants and Contracts
Administration Section
Management Division
345 Courtland Street, NE
Atlanta, GA 30365
(404) 347-2374

Georgia
William McBride
Grants and Contracts
Administration Section
Management Division
345 Courtland Street, NE
Atlanta, GA 30365
(404) 347-2374

Hawaii
Mike Schultz, Chief
1235 Hawthorne Street
Grants and Policy Branch
San Francisco, CA 94105
(415) 744-1623

Idaho
Oddvar Aurdal, Chief
Grants Administration
Section
MS 321
1200 Sixth Avenue
Seattle, WA 98101
(206) 442-2930

Illinois
Ivavs Anteus
Contracts and Grants
Branch
230 South Dearborn Street
Chicago, IL 60604
(312) 886-9841

Indiana
Ivavs Anteus
Contracts and Grants
Branch
230 South Dearborn Street
Chicago, IL 60604
(312) 886-9841

Iowa
Carol Rompage
726 Minnesota Avenue
Grants Administration
Branch
Kansas City, MO 66101
(913) 551-7346

Kansas
Carol Rompage
726 Minnesota Avenue
Grants Administration
Branch
Kansas City, MO 66101
(913) 551-7346

Kentucky
William McBride
Grants and Contracts
Administration Section
Management Division
345 Courtland Street, NE
Atlanta, GA 30365
(404) 347-2374

Louisiana
Beverly Negri, Chief
1445 Ross Avenue
Grants Audit Section
6M-PG
Management Division
Dallas, TX 75270
(214) 655-6525

Maine
Robert Goetzel
John F. Kennedy Federal
Building
10th Floor
(PAS-205)
Grants Information and
Management Section
Boston, MA 02203
(617) 565-3395

Maryland
Fred Warren
Grants Management Section
Office of the Comptroller
3PM32
841 Chestnut Building
Philadelphia, PA 19106
(215) 597-6166

Massachusetts
Robert Goetzel
John F. Kennedy Federal
Building
10th Floor
(PAS-205)
Grants Information and
Management Section
Boston, MA 02203
(617) 565-3395

Michigan
Ivavs Anteus
Contracts and Grants
Branch
230 South Dearborn Street
Chicago, IL 60604
(312) 886-9841

Minnesota
Ivavs Anteus
Contracts and Grants
Branch
230 South Dearborn Street
Chicago, IL 60604
(312) 886-9841

Mississippi
William McBride
Grants and Contracts
Administration Section
Management Division
345 Courtland Street, NE
Atlanta, GA 30365
(404) 347-2374

Missouri
Carol Rompage
726 Minnesota Avenue
Grants Administration
Branch
Kansas City, MO 66101
(913) 551-7346

Montana
Martha Nicodemus, Chief
Grants Administration
Branch
8PM-GFM
999 18th Street
Suite 1300
Denver, CO 80202-2413
(303) 293-1672

Nebraska
Carol Rompage
726 Minnesota Avenue
Grants Administration
Branch
Kansas City, MO 66101
(913) 551-7346

Nevada
Mike Schultz, Chief
1235 Hawthorne Street
Grants and Policy Branch
San Francisco, CA 94105
(415) 744-1623

New Hampshire
Robert Goetzel
John F. Kennedy Federal
Building
10th Floor
(PAS-205)
Grants Information and
Management Section
Boston, MA 02203
(617) 565-3395

New Jersey
Dennis Debrowski, Acting
Chief
Grants Administration
Branch
2MGT
26 Federal Plaza
Room 937A
New York, NY 10278
(212) 264-9860

New Mexico
Beverly Negri, Chief
1445 Ross Avenue
Grants Audit Section
6M-PG
Management Division
Dallas, TX 75270
(214) 655-6525

New York
Dennis Debrowski, Acting
Chief
Grants Administration
Branch
2MGT
26 Federal Plaza
Room 937A
New York, NY 10278
(212) 264-9860

North Carolina
William McBride
Grants and Contracts
Administration Section
Management Division
345 Courtland Street, NE
Atlanta, GA 30365
(404) 347-2374

North Dakota
Martha Nicodemus, Chief
Grants Administration
Branch
8PM-GFM
999 18th Street
Suite 1300
Denver, CO 80202-2413
(303) 293-1672

Ohio
Ivavs Anteus
Contracts and Grants
Branch
230 South Dearborn Street
Chicago, IL 60604
(312) 886-9841

Oklahoma
Beverly Negri, Chief
1445 Ross Avenue
Grants Audit Section
6M-PG
Management Division
Dallas, TX 75270
(214) 655-6525

Oregon
Oddvar Aurdal, Chief
Grants Administration
Section
MS 321
1200 Sixth Avenue
Seattle, WA 98101
(206) 442-2930

Pennsylvania
Fred Warren
Grants Management Section
Office of the Comptroller
3PM32
841 Chestnut Building
Philadelphia, PA 19107
(215) 597-6166

Puerto Rico
Dennis Debrowski, Acting
Chief
Grants Administration
Branch
2MGT
26 Federal Plaza
Room 937A
New York, NY 10278
(212) 264-9860

Rhode Island
Robert Goetzel
John F. Kennedy Federal
Building
10th Floor
(PAS-205)
Grants Information and
Management Section
Boston, MA 02203
(617) 565-3395

South Carolina
William McBride
Grants and Contracts
Administration Section
Management Division
345 Courtland Street, NE
Atlanta, GA 30365
(404) 347-2374

South Dakota
Martha Nicodemus, Chief
Grants Administration
Branch
8PM-GFM
999 18th Street
Suite 1300
Denver, CO 80202-2413
(303) 293-1672

Tennessee
William McBride
Grants and Contracts
Administration Section
Management Division
345 Courtland Street, NE
Atlanta, GA 30365
(404) 347-2374

Texas
Beverly Negri, Chief
1445 Ross Avenue
Grants Audit Section
6M-PG
Management Division
Dallas, TX 75270
(214) 655-6525

Utah
Martha Nicodemus, Chief
Grants Administration
Branch
8PM-GFM
999 18th Street
Suite 1300
Denver, CO 80202-2413
(303) 293-1672

Vermont
Robert Goetzel
John F. Kennedy Federal
Building
10th Floor
(PAS-205)
Grants Information and
Management Section
Boston, MA 02203
(617) 565-3395

Virginia
Fred Warren
Grants Management Section
Office of the Comptroller
3PM32
841 Chestnut Building
Philadelphia, PA 19107
(215) 597-6166

Virgin Islands
Dennis Debrowski, Acting
Chief
Grants Administration
Branch
2MGT
26 Federal Plaza
Room 937A
New York, NY 10278
(212) 264-9860

Washington
Oddvar Aurdal, Chief
Grants Administration
Section
MS 321
1200 Sixth Avenue
Seattle, WA 98101
(206) 442-2930

West Virginia
Fred Warren
Grants Management Section
Office of the Comptroller
3PM32
841 Chestnut Building
Philadelphia, PA 19107
(215) 597-6166

Wisconsin
Ivavs Anteus
Contracts and Grants
Branch
230 South Dearborn Street
Chicago, IL 60604
(312) 886-9841

Wyoming
Martha Nicodemus, Chief
Grants Administration
Branch
8PM-GFM
999 18th Street
Suite 1300
Denver, CO 80202-2413
(303) 293-1672

WATER POLLUTION CONTROL—RESEARCH, DEVELOPMENT, AND DEMONSTRATION

Environmental Protection
Agency (EPA)
Washington, DC 20460
(202) 260-7473

Description: Nonprofit organizations are usually recipients of grants. Project grants (cooperative agreements) given on an infrequent basis to profit-making organizations to facilitate research in water pollution.
$ Given: N/A
Application Information: Request application forms and return to EPA. Preliminary discussions are advisable.
Deadline: None
Contacts: Communicate with regional EPA offices. For information concerning procedures and applications, contact Grants Administration Division, PM-216, above address; for information concerning program scope, contact Director, Research Grants Staff, RD-675, above address.

Alabama
William McBride
Grants and Contracts
Administration Section
Management Division
345 Courtland Street, NE
Atlanta, GA 30365
(404) 347-2374

Alaska
Oddvar Aurdal, Chief
Grants Administration
Section
MS 321
1200 Sixth Avenue
Seattle, WA 98101
(206) 442-2930

American Samoa
Mike Schultz, Chief
1235 Hawthorne Street
Grants and Policy Branch
San Francisco, CA 94105
(415) 744-1623

Arizona
Mike Schultz, Chief
1235 Hawthorne Street
Grants and Policy Branch
San Francisco, CA 94105
(415) 744-1623

Arkansas
Beverly Negri, Chief
1445 Ross Avenue
Grants Audit Section
6M-PG
Management Division
Dallas, TX 75270
(214) 655-6525

California
Mike Schultz, Chief
1235 Hawthorne Street
Grants and Policy Branch
San Francisco, CA 94105
(415) 744-1623

Colorado
Martha Nicodemus, Chief
Grants Administration
Branch
8PM-GFM
999 18th Street
Suite 1300
Denver, CO 80202-2413
(303) 293-1672

Connecticut
Robert Goetzel
John F. Kennedy Federal
Building
10th Floor
(PAS-205)
Grants Information and
Management Section
Boston, MA 02203
(617) 565-3395

Delaware
Fred Warren
Grants Management Section
Office of the Comptroller
3PM32
841 Chestnut Building
Philadelphia, PA 19106
(215) 597-6166

Florida
William McBride
Grants and Contracts
Administration Section
Management Division
345 Courtland Street, NE
Atlanta, GA 30365
(404) 347-2374

Georgia
William McBride
Grants and Contracts
Administration Section
Management Division
345 Courtland Street, NE
Atlanta, GA 30365
(404) 347-2374

Hawaii
Mike Schultz, Chief
1235 Hawthorne Street
Grants and Policy Branch
San Francisco, CA 94105
(415) 744-1623

Idaho
Oddvar Aurdal, Chief
Grants Administration
Section
MS 321
1200 Sixth Avenue
Seattle, WA 98101
(206) 442-2930

Illinois
Ivavs Anteus
Contracts and Grants
Branch
230 South Dearborn Street
Chicago, IL 60604
(312) 886-9841

Indiana
Ivavs Anteus
Contracts and Grants
Branch
230 South Dearborn Street
Chicago, IL 60604
(312) 886-9841

Iowa
Carol Rompage
726 Minnesota Avenue
Grants Administration
Branch
Kansas City, MO 66101
(913) 551-7346

Kansas
Carol Rompage
726 Minnesota Avenue
Grants Administration
Branch
Kansas City, MO 66101
(913) 551-7346

Kentucky
William McBride
Grants and Contracts
Administration Section
Management Division
345 Courtland Street, NE
Atlanta, GA 30365
(404) 347-2374

Louisiana
Beverly Negri, Chief
1445 Ross Avenue
Grants Audit Section
6M-PG
Management Division
Dallas, TX 75270
(214) 655-6525

Maine
Robert Goetzel
John F. Kennedy Federal
Building
10th Floor
(PAS-205)
Grants Information and
Management Section
Boston, MA 02203
(617) 565-3395

Maryland
Fred Warren
Grants Management Section
Office of the Comptroller
3PM32
841 Chestnut Building
Philadelphia, PA 19106
(215) 597-6166

Massachusetts
Robert Goetzel
John F. Kennedy Federal
Building
10th Floor
(PAS-205)
Grants Information and
Management Section
Boston, MA 02203
(617) 565-3395

Michigan
Ivavs Anteus
Contracts and Grants
Branch
230 South Dearborn Street
Chicago, IL 60604
(312) 886-9841

Minnesota
Ivavs Anteus
Contracts and Grants
Branch
230 South Dearborn Street
Chicago, IL 60604
(312) 886-9841

Mississippi
William McBride
Grants and Contracts
Administration Section
Management Division
345 Courtland Street, NE
Atlanta, GA 30365
(404) 347-2374

Missouri
Carol Rompage
726 Minnesota Avenue
Grants Administration
Branch
Kansas City, MO 66101
(913) 551-7346

Montana
Martha Nicodemus, Chief
Grants Administration
Branch
8PM-GFM
999 18th Street
Suite 1300
Denver, CO 80202-2413
(303) 293-1672

Nebraska
Carol Rompage
726 Minnesota Avenue
Grants Administration
Branch
Kansas City, MO 66101
(913) 551-7346

Nevada
Mike Schultz, Chief
1235 Hawthorne Street
Grants and Policy Branch
San Francisco, CA 94105
(415) 744-1623

New Hampshire
Robert Goetzel
John F. Kennedy Federal
Building
10th Floor
(PAS-205)
Grants Information and
Management Section
Boston, MA 02203
(617) 565-3395

New Jersey
Dennis Debrowski, Acting
Chief
Grants Administration
Branch
2MGT
26 Federal Plaza
Room 937A
New York, NY 10278
(212) 264-9860

New Mexico
Beverly Negri, Chief
1445 Ross Avenue
Grants Audit Section
6M-PG
Management Division
Dallas, TX 75270
(214) 655-6525

New York
Dennis Debrowski, Acting
Chief
Grants Administration
Branch
2MGT
26 Federal Plaza
Room 937A
New York, NY 10278
(212) 264-9860

North Carolina
William McBride
Grants and Contracts
Administration Section
Management Division
345 Courtland Street, NE
Atlanta, GA 30365
(404) 347-2374

North Dakota
Martha Nicodemus, Chief
Grants Administration
Branch
8PM-GFM
999 18th Street
Suite 1300
Denver, CO 80202-2413
(303) 293-1672

Ohio
Ivavs Anteus
Contracts and Grants
Branch
230 South Dearborn Street
Chicago, IL 60604
(312) 886-9841

Oklahoma
Beverly Negri, Chief
1445 Ross Avenue
Grants Audit Section
6M-PG
Management Division
Dallas, TX 75270
(214) 655-6525

Oregon
Oddvar Aurdal, Chief
Grants Administration
Section
MS 321
1200 Sixth Avenue
Seattle, WA 98101
(206) 442-2930

Pennsylvania
Fred Warren
Grants Management Section
Office of the Comptroller
3PM32
841 Chestnut Building
Philadelphia, PA 19107
(215) 597-6166

Puerto Rico
Dennis Debrowski, Acting
Chief
Grants Administration
Branch
2MGT
26 Federal Plaza
Room 937A
New York, NY 10278
(212) 264-9860

Rhode Island
Robert Goetzel
John F. Kennedy Federal
Building
10th Floor
(PAS-205)
Grants Information and
Management Section
Boston, MA 02203
(617) 565-3395

South Carolina
William McBride
Grants and Contracts
Administration Section
Management Division
345 Courtland Street, NE
Atlanta, GA 30365
(404) 347-2374

South Dakota
Martha Nicodemus, Chief
Grants Administration
Branch
8PM-GFM
999 18th Street
Suite 1300
Denver, CO 80202-2413
(303) 293-1672

Tennessee
William McBride
Grants and Contracts
Administration Section
Management Division
345 Courtland Street, NE
Atlanta, GA 30365
(404) 347-2374

Texas
Beverly Negri, Chief
1445 Ross Avenue
Grants Audit Section
6M-PG
Management Division
Dallas, TX 75270
(214) 655-6525

Utah
Martha Nicodemus, Chief
Grants Administration
Branch
8PM-GFM
999 18th Street
Suite 1300
Denver, CO 80202-2413
(303) 293-1672

Vermont
Robert Goetzel
John F. Kennedy Federal
Building
10th Floor
(PAS-205)
Grants Information and
Management Section
Boston, MA 02203
(617) 565-3395

Virginia
Fred Warren
Grants Management Section
Office of the Comptroller
3PM32
841 Chestnut Building
Philadelphia, PA 19107
(215) 597-6166

Virgin Islands
Dennis Debrowski, Acting
Chief
Grants Administration
Branch
2MGT
26 Federal Plaza
Room 937A
New York, NY 10278
(212) 264-9860

Washington
Oddvar Aurdal, Chief
Grants Administration
Section
MS 321
1200 Sixth Avenue
Seattle, WA 98101
(206) 442-2930

West Virginia
Fred Warren
Grants Management Section
Office of the Comptroller
3PM32
841 Chestnut Building
Philadelphia, PA 19107
(215) 597-6166

Wisconsin
Ivavs Anteus
Contracts and Grants
Branch
230 South Dearborn Street
Chicago, IL 60604
(312) 886-9841

Wyoming
Martha Nicodemus, Chief
Grants Administration
Branch
8PM-GFM
999 18th Street
Suite 1300
Denver, CO 80202-2413
(303) 293-1672

General Business

Assistance is widely available from the federal government for general business and individuals operating small businesses for the following:

1. *Assistance* to small businesses for expansion, renovation, or development; to small businesses located in rural areas; to U.S. fishermen or the fishing industry
2. *Advisory services* to small businesses to help them improve their management skills or labor-management relations
3. *Loans* to general business owners, low-income business owners, or businesses owned by handicapped individuals, disabled individuals, or veterans for working capital, construction, or equipment acquisitions; loans to U.S. business investment companies to distribute funds to small businesses

You will need to consult the list of addresses in this chapter for your nearest local or regional Small Business Administration (SBA) office.

BUSINESS DEVELOPMENT ASSISTANCE TO SMALL BUSINESSES

Small Business
Administration (SBA)
Loan Policy and Procedures
Branch
409 Third Street, SW
Washington, DC 20416
(202) 205-6570

Description: Advisory services, counseling, training, and dissemination of technical information to help persons improve skills to manage and operate a prospective or present small business. Limited to creditworthy individuals with income below basic needs or with businesses in areas of high unemployment and/or low income, where business finances have been denied. Business must meet SBA size standards and be independently owned.
$ Given: Not available
Application Information: Application filed in field office serving territory of business location.
Deadline: None
Contact: Director

Alabama
Regional Office
1375 Peachtree Street, NE
Fifth Floor
Atlanta, GA 30367-9102
(404) 347-2797

District Office
Birmingham District Office
2121 Eighth Avenue North
Suite 200
Birmingham, AL 35203-2398
(205) 731-1334

Alaska
Regional Office
2601 Fourth Avenue
Room 440
Seattle, WA 98121-1273
(206) 553-1273

District Office
Anchorage District Office
222 West Eighth Avenue
Room 67
Anchorage, AK 99513
(907) 271-4022

Arizona
Regional Office
71 Stevenson Street
20th Floor
San Francisco, CA 94105-2939
(415) 744-6402

District Office
Phoenix District Office
2828 North Central Avenue
Suite 800
Phoenix, AZ 85004-10257
(602) 640-2316

Arkansas
Regional Office
8625 King George Drive
Building C
Dallas, TX 75235-3391
(214) 767-7633

District Office
Little Rock District Office
2120 Riverfront Drive
Suite 100
Little Rock, AR 72202
(501) 324-5278

California
Regional Office
71 Stevenson Street
20th Floor
San Francisco, CA 94105-2939
(415) 744-6402

District Offices
Santa Ana District Office
901 West Civic Center Drive
Suite 160
Santa Ana, CA 92703-2352
(714) 836-2494

San Diego District Office
880 Front Street
Suite 4-S-29
San Diego, CA 92188-0270
(619) 557-7252

San Francisco District Office
211 Main Street
Fourth Floor
San Francisco, CA 94105-1988
(415) 744-6820

Fresno District Office
2719 North Air Fresno
Drive
Suite 107
Fresno, CA 93727-1547
(209) 487-5189

Los Angeles District Office
330 North Brand Boulevard
Suite 1200
Glendale, CA 91203-2304
(213) 894-2956

Colorado
Regional Office
633 17th Street
Seventh Floor
Denver, CO 80202
(303) 294-7186

District Office
Denver District Office
721 19th Street
Room 426
Denver, CO 80202-2599
(303) 844-3984

Connecticut
Regional Office
155 Federal Street
Ninth Floor
Boston, MA 02110
(617) 451-2023

District Office
Hartford District Office
Federal Building
330 Main Street
Second Floor
Hartford, CT 06106
(203) 240-4700

Delaware
Regional Office
475 Allendale Road
Suite 201
King of Prussia, PA 19406
(215) 962-3700

District of Columbia
Regional Office
475 Allendale Road
Suite 201
King of Prussia, PA 19406
(215) 962-3700

District Office
1110 Vermont Avenue NW
Suite 900
Washington, DC 20036
(202) 606-4000

Florida
Regional Office
1375 Peachtree Street, NE
Fifth Floor
Atlanta, GA 30367-8102
(404) 347-2797

District Offices
Jacksonville District Office
7825 Baymeadows Way
Suite 100-B
Jacksonville, FL 32256-7504
(904) 443-1900

Miami District Office
1320 South District
Highway
Suite 501
Coral Gables, FL 33146-
2911
(305) 536-5521

Georgia
Regional Office
1375 Peachtree Street, NE
Fifth Floor
Atlanta, GA 30367-8102
(404) 347-2797

District Office
Atlanta District Office
1720 Peachtree Road, NW
Sixth Floor
Atlanta, GA 30309
(404) 347-4749

Hawaii
Regional Office
71 Stevenson Street
20th Floor
San Francisco, CA 94105-
2939
(415) 744-6402

District Office
Honolulu District Office
300 Ala Moana Boulevard
Room 2213
Honolulu, HI 96850-4981
(808) 541-2990

Idaho
Regional Office
2601 Fourth Avenue
Room 440
Seattle, WA 98121-1273
(206) 553-1273

District Office
Boise District Office
1020 Main Street
Suite 290
Boise, ID 83702-5745
(208) 334-1696

Illinois
Regional Office
Federal Building
300 South Riverside Plaza
Room 1975
Chicago, IL 60606-6611
(312) 353-5000

District Office
Chicago District Office
500 West Madison Street
Room 1250
Chicago, IL 60661-2511
(312) 353-4528

Indiana
Regional Office
Federal Building
300 South Riverside Plaza
Room 1975
Chicago, IL 60606-6611
(312) 353-5000

District Office
Indianapolis District Office
429 North Pennsylvania Street
Suite 100
Indianapolis, IN 46204-1873
(317) 226-7272

Iowa
Regional Office
911 Walnut Drive
13th Floor
Kansas City, MO 64106
(816) 426-3608

District Offices
Des Moines District Office
New Federal Building
210 Walnut Street
Room 749
Des Moines, IA 50309
(515) 284-4422

Cedar Rapids District Office
373 Collins Road, NE
Room 100
Cedar Rapids, IA 52402-
3147
(319) 393-8630

Kansas
Regional Office
911 Walnut Street
13th Floor
Kansas City, MO 64106
(816) 426-3608

District Office
Wichita District Office
100 East English Street
Suite 510
Wichita, KS 67202
(316) 269-6273

Kentucky
Regional Office
1375 Peachtree Street, NE
Fifth Floor
Atlanta, GA 30367-8102
(404) 347-2797

District Office
Louisville District Office
Federal Building
600 Martin Luther King Jr.
Place
Room 188
Louisville, KY 40202
(502) 582-5971

Louisiana
Regional Office
8625 King George Drive
Building C
Dallas, TX 75235-3391
(214) 767-7633

District Office
New Orleans District Office
1661 Canal Street
Suite 2000
New Orleans, LA 70112
(504) 589-6685

Maine
Regional Office
155 Federal Street
Ninth Floor
Boston, MA 02110
(617) 451-2023

District Office
Augusta District Office
Federal Building
40 Western Avenue
Room 512
Augusta, ME 04330

Massachusetts
Regional Office
155 Federal Street
Ninth Floor
Boston, MA 02110
(617) 451-2023

District Office
Boston District Office
10 Causeway Street
Room 265
Boston, MA 02222-1093
(617) 565-5590

Michigan
Regional Office
Federal Building
300 South Riverside Plaza
Room 1975
Chicago, IL 60606-6611
(312) 353-5000

District Office
Detroit District Office
477 Michigan Avenue
Room 515
Detroit, MI 48226
(313) 226-6075

Minnesota
Regional Office
Federal Building
300 South Riverside Plaza
Room 1975
Chicago, IL 60606-6611
(312) 353-5000

District Office
Minneapolis District Office
100 North Sixth Street
Suite 610
Minneapolis, MN 55403-
1563
(612) 370-2324

Mississippi
Regional Office
1375 Peachtree Street, NE
Fifth Floor
Atlanta, GA 30367-8102
(404) 347-2797

District Office
Jackson District Office
101 West Capitol Street
Suite 400
Jackson, MS 39201
(601) 965-4378

Missouri
Regional Office
911 Walnut Street
13th Floor
Kansas City, MO 64106
(816) 426-3608

District Offices
St. Louis District Office
816 Olive Street
Room 242
St. Louis, MO 63101
(314) 539-6600

Kansas City District Office
323 West Eighth Street
Suite 501
Kansas City, MO 64105
(816) 374-6708

Montana
Regional Office
633 17th Street
Seventh Floor
Denver, CO 80202
(303) 294-7186

District Office
Helena District Office
301 South Park Avenue
Room 528
Helena, MT 59626
(406) 449-5381

Nebraska
Regional Office
911 Walnut Street
13th Floor
Kansas City, MO 64104
(816) 426-3608

District Office
Omaha District Office
11145 Mill Valley Road
Omaha, NE 68154
(402) 221-4691

Nevada
Regional Office
71 Stevenson Street
20th Floor
San Francisco, CA 94105-2939
(415) 744-6402

District Office
Las Vegas District Office
301 East Stewart Street
Room 301
Las Vegas, NV 89125-2527
(702) 388-6611

New Hampshire
Regional Office
155 Federal Street
Ninth Floor
Boston, MA 02110
(617) 451-2023

District Office
Concord District Office
143 North Main Street
Suite 202
Concord, NH 13302-1257
(603) 225-1400

New Jersey
Regional Office
26 Federal Plaza
Room 31-08
New York, NY 10278
(212) 264-1450

District Office
Newark District Office
Military Park Building
60 Park Place
Fourth Floor
Newark, NJ 07102
(201) 645-2434

New Mexico
Regional Office
8625 King George Drive
Building C
Dallas, TX 75235-3391
(214) 767-7633

District Office
Albuquerque District Office
625 Silver Avenue, SW
Suite 320
Albuquerque, NM 87102
(505) 766-1870

New York
Regional Office
26 Federal Plaza
Room 31-08
New York, NY 10278
(212) 264-1450

District Offices
New York District Office
26 Federal Plaza
Room 31-00
New York, NY 10278
(212) 264-2454

Syracuse District Office
100 South Clinton Street
Room 1071
Syracuse, NY 13260
(315) 423-5383

North Carolina
Regional Office
1375 Peachtree Street, NE
Fifth Floor
Atlanta, GA 30367-8102
(404) 347-2797

District Office
Charlotte District Office
200 North College Street
Suite A2015
Charlotte, NC 28202-2137
(704) 344-6563

North Dakota
Regional Office
633 17th Street
Seventh Floor
Denver, CO 80202
(303) 294-7186

District Office
Fargo District Office
Federal Building
657 Second Avenue, North
Room 218
Fargo, ND 58108-3086
(701) 239-5131

Ohio
Regional Office
Federal Building
300 South Riverside Plaza
Room 1975
Chicago, IL 60606-6611
(312) 353-5000

District Office
Cleveland District Office
1111 Superior Avenue
Suite 360
Cleveland, OH 44144-2507
(216) 522-4180

Oklahoma
Regional Office
8625 King George Drive
Building C
Dallas, TX 75235-3391
(214) 767-7633

District Office
Oklahoma City District Office
200 NW Fifth Street
Suite 670
Oklahoma City, OK 73102
(405) 231-4301

Oregon
Regional Office
2601 Fourth Avenue
Room 440
Seattle, WA 98121-1273
(206) 553-1273

District Office
Portland District Office
222 SW Columbia Street
Suite 500
Portland, OR 97201-6605
(503) 326-2682

Pacific Islands
Regional Office
71 Stevenson Street
20th Floor
San Francisco, CA 94105-2939
(415) 744-6402

District Office
Agana Branch Office
Pacific Daily News Building
238 Archbishop F. C. Flores
Street
Room 508
Agana, GM 96910
(671) 472-7277

Pennsylvania
Regional Office
475 Allendale Road
Suite 201
King of Prussia, PA 19406
(215) 962-3700

District Office
Pittsburgh District Office
960 Penn Avenue
Fifth Floor
Pittsburgh, PA 15222
(412) 644-2780

Puerto Rico
Regional Office
26 Federal Plaza
Room 31-08
New York, NY 10278
(212) 264-1450

District Office
Puerto Rico and Virgin
Islands District Office
Federico Degetau Federal
Building
Carlos Chardon Avenue
Room 691
Hato Rey, PR 00918
(809) 766-5572

Rhode Island
Regional Office
155 Federal Street
Ninth Floor
Boston, MA 02110
(617) 451-2023

District Office
Providence District Office
380 Westminster Mall
Fifth Floor
Providence, RI 02903
(401) 528-4561

South Carolina
Regional Office
1375 Peachtree Street, NE
Fifth Floor
Atlanta, GA 30367-8102
(404) 347-2797

District Office
Columbia District Office
1835 Assembly Street
Room 358
Columbia, SC 29202
(803) 765-5376

South Dakota
Regional Office
633 17th Street
Seventh Floor
Denver, CO 80202
(303) 294-7186

District Office
Sioux Falls District Office
101 South Main Avenue
Suite 101
Sioux Falls, SD 57102-0527
(605) 330-4231

Tennessee
Regional Office
1375 Peachtree Street, NE
Fifth Floor
Atlanta, GA 30367-8102
(404) 347-2797

District Office
Nashville District Office
50 Vantage Way
Suite 201
Nashville, TN 37228-1500
(615) 736-5881

Texas
Regional Office
8625 King George Drive
Building C
Dallas, TX 75235-3391
(214) 767-7633

District Offices
San Antonio District Office
7400 Blanco Drive
Suite 200
San Antonio, TX 78216-4300
(210) 229-4535

Dallas District Office
4300 Amon Center
Boulevard
Suite 114
Ft. Worth, TX 76155
(817) 885-6500

El Paso District Office
10737 Gateway West
Suite 320
El Paso, TX 79935
(915) 540-5676

Utah
Regional Office
633 17th Street
Seventh Floor
Denver, CO 80202
(303) 294-7186

District Office
Salt Lake City District Office
Federal Building
125 South State Street
Room 2237
Salt Lake City, UT 84138-
1195
(801) 524-5804

Vermont
Regional Office
155 Federal Street
Ninth Floor
Boston, MA 02110
(617) 451-2023

District Office
Montpelier District Office
Federal Building
87 State Street
Room 205
Montpelier, VT 05602
(802) 828-4422

Virginia
Regional Office
475 Allendale Road
Suite 201
King of Prussia, PA 19406
(215) 962-3700

District Office
Richmond District Office
Federal Building
400 North Eighth Street
Room 3015
Richmond, VA 23240
(804) 771-2400

Virgin Islands
Regional Office
26 Federal Plaza
Room 31-08
New York, NY 10278
(212) 264-1450

District Offices
Federico Degetau Federal
Building
Carlos Chardon Avenue
Room 691
Hato Rey, PR 00918
(809) 766-5572

St. Croix Post-of-Duty
4200 United Shopping Plaza
Suite 7
Christiansted, St. Croix, VI
00820-4487
(809) 778-5380

St. Thomas Post-of-Duty
U.S. Court House and
Building
Federal Office Building
Veterans Drive
Room 210
St. Thomas, VI 00802
(809) 774-8530

Washington
Regional Office
2601 Fourth Avenue
Room 440
Seattle, WA 98121-1273
(206) 553-1273

District Office
Spokane District Office
West 601 First Avenue
10th Floor East
Spokane, WA 99204-0317
(509) 353-2800

West Virginia
Regional Office
475 Allendale Road
Suite 201
King of Prussia, PA 19406
(215) 962-3700

District Office
Clarksburg District Office
168 West Main Street
Fifth Floor
Clarksburg, WV 26301
(304) 623-5631

Wisconsin
Regional Office
Federal Building
300 South Riverside Plaza
Room 1975
Chicago, IL 60606-6611
(312) 353-5000

District Office
Madison District Office
212 East Washington
Avenue
Room 213
Madison, WI 53703
(608) 264-5261

Wyoming
Regional Office
633 17th Street
Seventh Floor
Denver, CO 80202
(303) 294-7186

District Office
Casper District Office
Federal Building
100 East B Street
Room 4001
Casper, WY 82602-2839
(307) 261-5761

BUSINESS LOANS FOR SBA PARTICIPANTS

Small Business
Administration (SBA)
Loan Policy and Procedures
Branch
409 Third Street, SW
Washington, DC 20416
(202) 205-6570

Description: Loans to small businesses for construction, development, expansion, renovation, and acquisition of equipment; limited to small businesses owned by socially and economically disadvantaged persons.
$ Given: $5 million est. nationwide FY 94; average direct loan: $154,839; guaranteed loans: up to $750,000
Application Information: Applications for direct loans are filed by the loan applicant; guaranteed loans are filed by financial institution through SBA field office.
Deadline: Not available
Contact: Regional SBA office for your state

Alabama
1375 Peachtree Street, NE
Fifth Floor
Atlanta, GA 30367-8102
(404) 347-2797

Alaska
2601 Fourth Avenue
Room 440
Seattle, WA 98121-1273
(206) 553-1273

Arizona
71 Stevenson Street
20th Floor
San Francisco, CA 94105-
2939
(415) 744-6402

Arkansas
8625 King George Drive
Building C
Dallas, TX 75235-3391
(214) 767-7633

California
71 Stevenson Street
20th Floor
San Francisco, CA 94105-
2939
(415) 744-6402

Colorado
633 17th Street
Seventh Floor
Denver, CO 80202
(303) 294-7186

Connecticut
155 Federal Street
Ninth Floor
Boston, MA 02110
(617) 451-2023

Delaware
475 Allendale Road
Suite 201
King of Prussia, PA 19406
(215) 962-3700

District of Columbia
475 Allendale Road
Suite 201
King of Prussia, PA 19406
(215) 962-3700

Florida
1375 Peachtree Street, NE
Fifth Floor
Atlanta, GA 30367-8102
(404) 347-2797

Georgia
1375 Peachtree Street, NE
Fifth Floor
Atlanta, GA 30367-8102
(404) 347-2797

Hawaii
71 Stevenson Street
20th Floor
San Francisco, CA 94105-
2939
(415) 744-6402

Idaho
2601 Fourth Avenue
Room 440
Seattle, WA 98121-1273
(206) 553-1273

Illinois
Federal Building
300 South Riverside Plaza
Room 1975
Chicago, IL 60606-6611
(312) 353-5000

Indiana
Federal Building
300 South Riverside Plaza
Room 1975
Chicago, IL 60606-6611
(312) 353-5000

Iowa
911 Walnut Street
13th Floor
Kansas City, MO 64106
(816) 426-3608

Kansas
911 Walnut Street
13th Floor
Kansas City, MO 64106
(816) 426-3608

Kentucky
1375 Peachtree Street, NE
Fifth Floor
Atlanta, GA 30367-8102
(404) 347-2797

Louisiana
8625 King George Drive
Building C
Dallas, TX 75235-3391
(214) 767-7633

Maine
155 Federal Street
Ninth Floor
Boston, MA 02110
(617) 451-2023

Maryland
475 Allendale Road
Suite 201
King of Prussia, PA 19406
(215) 962-3700

Massachusetts
155 Federal Street
Ninth Floor
Boston, MA 02110
(617) 451-2023

Michigan
Federal Building
300 South Riverside Plaza
Room 1975
Chicago, IL 60606-6611
(312) 353-5000

Minnesota
Federal Building
300 South Riverside Plaza
Room 1975
Chicago, IL 60606-6611
(312) 353-5000

Mississippi
1375 Peachtree Street, NE
Fifth Floor
Atlanta, GA 30367-8102
(404) 347-2797

Missouri
911 Walnut Street
13th Floor
Kansas City, MO 64106
(816) 426-3608

Montana
633 17th Street
Seventh Floor
Denver, CO 80202
(303) 294-7186

Nebraska
911 Walnut Street
13th Floor
Kansas City, MO 64106
(816) 426-3608

Nevada
71 Stevenson Street
20th Floor
San Francisco, CA 94105-2939
(415) 744-6402

New Hampshire
155 Federal Street
Ninth Floor
Boston, MA 02110
(617) 451-2023

New Jersey
26 Federal Plaza
Room 31-08
New York, NY 10278
(212) 264-1450

New Mexico
8625 King George Drive
Building C
Dallas, TX 75235-3391
(214) 264-7633

New York
26 Federal Plaza
Room 31-08
New York, NY 10278
(212) 264-1450

North Carolina
1375 Peachtree Street, NE
Fifth Floor
Atlanta, GA 30367-8102
(404) 347-2797

North Dakota
633 17th Street
Seventh Floor
Denver, CO 80202
(303) 294-7186

Ohio
Federal Building
300 South Riverside Plaza
Room 1975
Chicago, IL 60606-6611
(312) 353-5000

Oklahoma
8625 King George Drive
Building C
Dallas, TX 75235-3391
(214) 767-7633

Oregon
2601 Fourth Avenue
Room 440
Seattle, WA 98121-1273
(206) 553-1273

Pennsylvania
475 Allendale Road
Suite 201
King of Prussia, PA 19406
(215) 962-3700

Puerto Rico
26 Federal Plaza
Room 31-08
New York, NY 10278
(212) 264-1450

Rhode Island
155 Federal Street
Ninth Floor
Boston, MA 02110
(617) 451-2023

South Carolina
1375 Peachtree Street, NE
Fifth Floor
Atlanta, GA 30367-8102
(404) 347-2797

South Dakota
633 17th Street
Seventh Floor
Denver, CO 80202
(303) 294-7186

Tennessee
1375 Peachtree Street, NE
Fifth Floor
Atlanta, GA 30367-8102
(404) 347-2797

Texas
8625 King George Drive
Building C
Dallas, TX 75235-3391
(214) 767-7633

Utah
633 17th Street
Seventh Floor
Denver, CO 80202
(303) 294-7186

Vermont
155 Federal Street
Ninth Floor
Boston, MA 02110
(617) 451-2023

Virginia
475 Allendale Road
Suite 201
King of Prussia, PA 19406
(215) 962-3700

Virgin Islands
26 Federal Plaza
Room 31-08
New York, NY 10278
(212) 264-1450

Washington
2601 Fourth Avenue
Room 440
Seattle, WA 98121-1273
(206) 553-1273

West Virginia
475 Allendale Road
Suite 201
King of Prussia, PA 19406
(215) 962-3700

Wisconsin
Federal Building
300 South Riverside Plaza
Room 1975
Chicago, IL 60606-6611
(312) 353-5000

Wyoming
999 18th Street
Suite 701
Denver, CO 80202
(303) 294-7001

CAPITAL CONSTRUCTION FUND (CCF)

Department of
Transportation
Associate Administrator for
Maritime Aids
Maritime Administration
400 Seventh Street, SW
Washington, DC 20590
(202) 366-0364

Description: Direct payments for specified use (in the form of tax deferments) to promote trade-ship construction and reconstruction. Applicant must be a U.S. citizen and own at least one vessel.
$ Given: Tax benefits to applicants not slated; total monies deferred: $5 billion
Application Information: Contact Marine Administration, Office of Ship Financing.
Deadline: Prior to due date for filing federal tax forms
Contact: Local Marine Administration regional office

Alabama
F. X. McNerney
Maritime Administration
365 Canal Street
Suite 2590
New Orleans, LA 70130-
1137
(504) 589-6556

Alaska
Francis X. Johnston
Maritime Administration
211 Main Street
Room 1112
San Francisco, CA 94105
(415) 744-2580

Arizona
Francis X. Johnston
Maritime Administration
211 Main Street
Room 1112
San Francisco, CA 94105
(415) 744-2580

Arkansas
F. X. McNerney
Maritime Administration
365 Canal Street
Suite 2590
New Orleans, LA 70130-
1137
(504) 589-6556

California
Francis X. Johnston
Maritime Administration
211 Main Street
Room 1112
San Francisco, CA 94105
(415) 744-2580

Colorado
Francis X. Johnston
Maritime Administration
211 Main Street
Room 1112
San Francisco, CA 94105
(415) 744-2580

Connecticut
Robert F. McKeon
Maritime Administration
26 Federal Plaza
Room 3737
New York, NY 10278
(212) 264-1300

Delaware
Robert F. McKeon
Maritime Administration
26 Federal Plaza
Room 3737
New York, NY 10278
(212) 264-1300

Florida
(Eastern Half)
Mayank Jain
Maritime Administration
7737 Hampton Boulevard
Building 4D
Room 211
Norfolk, VA 23505
(804) 441-6393

(Western Half)
F. X. McNerney
Maritime Administration
365 Canal Street
Suite 2590
New Orleans, LA 70130-
1137
(504) 589-6556

Georgia
Mayank Jain
Maritime Administration
7737 Hampton Boulevard
Building 4D
Room 211
Norfolk, VA 23505
(804) 441-6393

Hawaii
Francis X. Johnston
Maritime Administration
211 Main Street
Room 1112
San Francisco, CA 94105
(415) 744-2580

Idaho
Francis X. Johnston
Maritime Administration
211 Main Street
Room 1112
San Francisco, CA 94105
(415) 744-2580

Illinois
Alpha H. Ames Jr.
Maritime Administration
2860 South River Road
Suite 185
Des Plaines, IL 60018-4605
(708) 298-2413

Indiana
Alpha H. Ames Jr.
Maritime Administration
2860 South River Road
Suite 185
Des Plaines, IL 60018-4605
(708) 298-2413

Iowa
F. X. McNerney
Maritime Administration
365 Canal Street
Suite 2590
New Orleans, LA 70130-
1137
(504) 589-6556

Kansas
F. X. McNerney
Maritime Administration
365 Canal Street
Suite 2590
New Orleans, LA 70130-
1137
(504) 589-6556

Kentucky
F. X. McNerney
Maritime Administration
365 Canal Street
Suite 2590
New Orleans, LA 70130-
1137
(504) 589-6556

Louisiana
F. X. McNerney
Maritime Administration
365 Canal Street
Suite 2590
New Orleans, LA 70130-
1137
(504) 589-6556

Maine
Robert F. McKeon
Maritime Administration
26 Federal Plaza
Room 3737
New York, NY 10278
(212) 264-1300

Maryland
Robert F. McKeon
Maritime Administration
26 Federal Plaza
Room 3737
New York, NY 10278
(212) 264-1300

Massachusetts
Robert F. McKeon
Maritime Administration
26 Federal Plaza
Room 3737
New York, NY 10278
(212) 264-1300

Michigan
Alpha H. Ames Jr.
Maritime Administration
2860 South River Road
Suite 185
Des Plaines, IL 60018-4605
(708) 298-2413

Minnesota
Alpha H. Ames Jr.
Maritime Administration
2860 South River Road
Suite 185
Des Plaines, IL 60018-4605
(708) 298-2413

Mississippi
F. X. McNerney
Maritime Administration
365 Canal Street
Suite 2590
New Orleans, LA 70130-
1137
(504) 589-6556

Missouri
F. X. McNerney
Maritime Administration
365 Canal Street
Suite 2590
New Orleans, LA 70130-
1137
(504) 589-6556

Montana
Francis X. Johnston
Maritime Administration
211 Main Street
Room 1112
San Francisco, CA 94105
(415) 744-2580

Nebraska
F. X. McNerney
Maritime Administration
365 Canal Street
Suite 2590
New Orleans, LA 70130-
1137
(504) 589-6556

Nevada
Francis X. Johnston
Maritime Administration
211 Main Street
Room 1112
San Francisco, CA 94105
(415) 744-2580

New Hampshire
Robert F. McKeon
Maritime Administration
26 Federal Plaza
Room 3737
New York, NY 10278
(212) 264-1300

New Jersey
Robert F. McKeon
Maritime Administration
26 Federal Plaza
Room 3737
New York, NY 10278
(212) 264-1300

New Mexico
Francis X. Johnston
Maritime Administration
211 Main Street
Room 1112
San Francisco, CA 94105
(415) 744-2580

New York
(Except Lake Coastal Area)
Robert F. McKeon
Maritime Administration
26 Federal Plaza
Room 3737
New York, NY 10278
(212) 264-1300

(Lake Coastal Area)
Alpha H. Ames Jr.
Maritime Administration
2860 South River Road
Suite 185
Des Plaines, IL 60018-4605
(708) 298-2413

North Carolina
Mayank Jain
Maritime Administration
7737 Hampton Boulevard
Building 4D
Room 211
Norfolk, VA 23505
(804) 441-6393

North Dakota
Francis X. Johnston
Maritime Administration
211 Main Street
Room 1112
San Francisco, CA 94105
(415) 744-2580

Ohio
Alpha H. Ames Jr.
Maritime Administration
2860 South River Road
Suite 185
Des Plaines, IL 60018-4605
(708) 298-2413

Oklahoma
F. X. McNerney
Maritime Administration
365 Canal Street
Suite 2590
New Orleans, LA 70130-1137
(504) 589-6556

Oregon
Francis X. Johnston
Maritime Administration
211 Main Street
Room 1112
San Francisco, CA 94105
(415) 744-2580

Pennsylvania
(Except Lake Coastal Area)
Robert F. McKeon
Maritime Administration
26 Federal Plaza
Room 3737
New York, NY 10278
(212) 264-1300

(Lake Coastal Area)
Alpha H. Ames Jr.
Maritime Administration
2860 South River Road
Suite 185
Des Plaines, IL 60018-4605
(708) 298-2413

Puerto Rico
Mayank Jain
Maritime Administration
7737 Hampton Boulevard
Building 4D
Room 211
Norfolk, VA 23505
(804) 441-6393

Rhode Island
Robert F. McKeon
Maritime Administration
26 Federal Plaza
Room 3737
New York, NY 10278
(212) 264-1300

South Carolina
Mayank Jain
Maritime Administration
7737 Hampton Boulevard
Building 4D
Room 211
Norfolk, VA 23505
(804) 441-6393

South Dakota
Francis X. Johnston
Maritime Administration
211 Main Street
Room 1112
San Francisco, CA 94105
(415) 744-2580

Tennessee
F. X. McNerney
Maritime Administration
365 Canal Street
Suite 2590
New Orleans, LA 70130-1137
(504) 589-6556

Texas
F. X. McNerney
Maritime Administration
365 Canal Street
Suite 2590
New Orleans, LA 70130-1137
(504) 589-6556

Utah
Francis X. Johnston
Maritime Administration
211 Main Street
Room 1112
San Francisco, CA 94105
(415) 744-2580

Vermont
Robert F. McKeon
Maritime Administration
26 Federal Plaza
Room 3737
New York, NY 10278
(212) 264-1300

Virginia
Mayank Jain
Maritime Administration
7737 Hampton Boulevard
Building 4D
Room 211
Norfolk, VA 23505
(804) 441-6393

Washington
Francis X. Johnston
Maritime Administration
211 Main Street
Room 1112
San Francisco, CA 94105
(415) 744-2580

West Virginia
Mayank Jain
Maritime Administration
7737 Hampton Boulevard
Building 4D
Room 211
Norfolk, VA 23505
(804) 441-6393

Wisconsin
Alpha H. Ames Jr.
Maritime Administration
2860 South River Road
Suite 185
Des Plaines, IL 60018-4605
(708) 298-2413

Wyoming
Francis X. Johnston
Maritime Administration
211 Main Street
Room 1112
San Francisco, CA 94105
(415) 744-2580

Field Office
Thomas T. Matteson
U.S. Merchant Marine
Academy
Kings Point, NY 11024-
1699
(516) 773-5000

CERTIFIED DEVELOPMENT COMPANY LOANS

**Small Business
Administration (SBA)**
Office of Rural Affairs and
Economic Development
409 Third Street, SW
Washington, DC 20416
(202) 205-6485

Description: Guaranteed and insured loans to small
businesses, independently owned and operated for profit, for
acquiring land and buildings, as well as for construction,
expansion, renovation, and modernization of machinery and
equipment. Loan may have either a 10- or 30-year term.
$ Given: Loans: up to $1 million; average: $307,700
Application Information: Application must be made on SBA
Form 1244, and the requirements set forth thereon must be
complied with.
Deadline: None
Contact: Your state and/or regional office

Alabama
1375 Peachtree Street, NE
Fifth Floor
Atlanta, GA 30367-8102
(404) 347-2797

Alaska
2601 Fourth Avenue
Room 440
Seattle, WA 98121-1273
(206) 553-1273

Arizona
71 Stevenson Street
20th Floor
San Francisco, CA 94105-
2939
(415) 744-6402

Arkansas
8625 King George Drive
Building C
Dallas, TX 75235-3391
(214) 767-7633

California
71 Stevenson Street
20th Floor
San Francisco, CA 94105-
2939
(415) 744-6402

Colorado
633 17th Street
Seventh Floor
Denver, CO 80202
(303) 294-7186

Connecticut
155 Federal Street
Ninth Floor
Boston, MA 02110
(617) 451-2023

Delaware
475 Allendale Road
Suite 201
King of Prussia, PA 19406
(215) 962-3700

District of Columbia
475 Allendale Road
Suite 201
King of Prussia, PA 19406
(215) 962-3700

Florida
1375 Peachtree Street, NE
Fifth Floor
Atlanta, GA 30367-8102
(404) 347-2797

Georgia
1375 Peachtree Street, NE
Fifth Floor
Atlanta, GA 30367-8102
(404) 347-2797

Hawaii
71 Stevenson Street
20th Floor
San Francisco, CA 94105-
2939
(415) 744-6402

Idaho
2601 Fourth Avenue
Room 440
Seattle, WA 98121-1273
(206) 553-1273

Illinois
Federal Building
300 South Riverside Plaza
Room 1975
Chicago, IL 60606-6611
(312) 353-5000

Indiana
Federal Building
300 South Riverside Plaza
Room 1975
Chicago, IL 60606-6611
(312) 353-5000

Iowa
911 Walnut Street
13th Floor
Kansas City, MO 64106
(816) 426-3608

Kansas
911 Walnut Street
13th Floor
Kansas City, MO 64106
(816) 426-3608

Kentucky
1375 Peachtree Street, NE
Fifth Floor
Atlanta, GA 30367-8102
(404) 347-2797

Louisiana
8625 King George Drive
Building C
Dallas, TX 75235-3391
(214) 767-7633

Maine
155 Federal Street
Ninth Floor
Boston, MA 02110
(617) 451-2023

Maryland
475 Allendale Road
Suite 201
King of Prussia, PA 19406
(215) 962-3700

Massachusetts
155 Federal Street
Ninth Floor
Boston, MA 02110
(617) 451-2023

Michigan
Federal Building
300 South Riverside Plaza
Room 1975
Chicago, IL 60606-6611
(312) 353-5000

Minnesota
Federal Building
300 South Riverside Plaza
Room 1975
Chicago, IL 60606-6611
(312) 353-5000

Mississippi
1375 Peachtree Street, NE
Fifth Floor
Atlanta, GA 30367-8102
(404) 347-2797

Missouri
911 Walnut Street
13th Floor
Kansas City, MO 64106
(816) 426-3608

Montana
633 17th Street
Seventh Floor
Denver, CO 80202
(303) 294-7186

Nebraska
911 Walnut Street
13th Floor
Kansas City, MO 64106
(816) 426-3608

Nevada
71 Stevenson Street
20th Floor
San Francisco, CA 94105-
2939
(415) 744-6402

New Hampshire
155 Federal Street
Ninth Floor
Boston, MA 02110
(617) 451-2023

New Jersey
26 Federal Plaza
Room 31-08
New York, NY 10278
(212) 264-1450

New Mexico
8625 King George Drive
Building C
Dallas, TX 75235-3391
(214) 264-7633

New York
26 Federal Plaza
Room 31-08
New York, NY 10278
(212) 264-1450

North Carolina
1375 Peachtree Street, NE
Fifth Floor
Atlanta, GA 30367-8102
(404) 347-2797

North Dakota
633 17th Street
Seventh Floor
Denver, CO 80202
(303) 294-7186

Ohio
Federal Building
300 South Riverside Plaza
Room 1975
Chicago, IL 60606-6611
(312) 353-5000

Oklahoma
8625 King George Drive
Building C
Dallas, TX 75235-3391
(214) 767-7633

Oregon
2601 Fourth Avenue
Room 440
Seattle, WA 98121-1273
(206) 553-1273

Pacific Islands
71 Stevenson Street
20th Floor
San Francisco, CA 94105-
2939
(415) 744-6402

Pennsylvania
475 Allendale Road
Suite 201
King of Prussia, PA 19406
(215) 962-3700

Puerto Rico
26 Federal Plaza
Room 31-08
New York, NY 10278
(212) 264-1450

Rhode Island
155 Federal Street
Ninth Floor
Boston, MA 02110
(617) 451-2023

South Carolina
1375 Peachtree Street, NE
Fifth Floor
Atlanta, GA 30367-8102
(404) 347-2797

South Dakota
633 17th Street
Seventh Floor
Denver, CO 80202
(303) 294-7186

Tennessee
1375 Peachtree Street, NE
Fifth Floor
Atlanta, GA 30367-8102
(404) 347-2797

Texas
8625 King George Drive
Building C
Dallas, TX 75235-3391
(214) 767-7633

Utah
633 17th Street
Seventh Floor
Denver, CO 80202
(303) 294-7186

Vermont
155 Federal Street
Ninth Floor
Boston, MA 02110
(617) 451-2023

Virginia
475 Allendale Road
Suite 201
King of Prussia, PA 19406
(215) 962-3700

Virgin Islands
26 Federal Plaza
Room 31-08
New York, NY 10278
(212) 264-1450

Washington
2601 Fourth Avenue
Room 440
Seattle, WA 98121-1273
(206) 553-1273

West Virginia
475 Allendale Road
Suite 201
King of Prussia, PA 19406
(215) 962-3700

Wisconsin
Federal Building
300 South Riverside Plaza
Room 1975
Chicago, IL 60606-6611
(312) 353-5000

Wyoming
633 17th Street
Seventh Floor
Denver, CO 80202
(303) 294-7186

CONSTRUCTION RESERVE FUND (CRF)

Department of Transportation
Associate Administrator for Maritime Aids
Maritime Administration
400 Seventh Street, SW
Washington, DC 20590
(202) 366-0364

Description: Direct payments for specified use (tax deferments) to promote construction of U.S. maritime trade vessels. In this case, deposited funds are those obtained from sale of vessels or indemnification for lost vessels.
$ Given: Not available
Application Information: Contact Maritime Administration, Office of Ship Financing, prior to formal application.
Deadline: CRF must be established within 60 days after owner's receipt of proceeds of indemnifications.
Contact: Local Maritime Administration regional office

Alabama
F. X. McNerney
Maritime Administration
365 Canal Street
Suite 2590
New Orleans, LA 70130-1137
(504) 589-6556

Alaska
Francis X. Johnston
Maritime Administration
211 Main Street
Room 1112
San Francisco, CA 94105
(415) 744-2580

Arizona
Francis X. Johnston
Maritime Administration
211 Main Street
Room 1112
San Francisco, CA 94105
(415) 744-2580

Arkansas
F. X. McNerney
Maritime Administration
365 Canal Street
Suite 2590
New Orleans, LA 70130-1137
(504) 589-6556

California
Francis X. Johnston
Maritime Administration
211 Main Street
Room 1112
San Francisco, CA 94105
(415) 744-2580

Colorado
Francis X. Johnston
Maritime Administration
211 Main Street
Room 1112
San Francisco, CA 94105
(415) 744-2580

Connecticut
Robert F. McKeon
Maritime Administration
26 Federal Plaza
Room 3737
New York, NY 10278
(212) 264-1300

Delaware
Robert F. McKeon
Maritime Administration
26 Federal Plaza
Room 3737
New York, NY 10278
(212) 264-1300

Florida
(Eastern Half)
Mayank Jain
Maritime Administration
7737 Hampton Boulevard
Building 4D
Room 211
Norfolk, VA 23505
(804) 441-6393

(Western Half)
F. X. McNerney
Maritime Administration
365 Canal Street
Suite 2590
New Orleans, LA 70130-1137
(504) 589-6556

Georgia
Mayank Jain
Maritime Administration
7737 Hampton Boulevard
Building 4D
Room 211
Norfolk, VA 23505
(804) 441-6393

Hawaii
Francis X. Johnston
Maritime Administration
211 Main Street
Room 1112
San Francisco, CA 94105
(415) 744-2580

Idaho
Francis X. Johnston
Maritime Administration
211 Main Street
Room 1112
San Francisco, CA 94105
(415) 744-2580

Illinois
Alpha H. Ames Jr.
Maritime Administration
2860 South River Road
Suite 185
Des Plaines, IL 60018-4605
(708) 298-2413

Indiana
Alpha H. Ames Jr.
Maritime Administration
2860 South River Road
Suite 185
Des Plaines, IL 60018-4605
(708) 298-2413

Iowa
F. X. McNerney
Maritime Administration
365 Canal Street
Suite 2590
New Orleans, LA 70130-1137
(504) 589-6556

Kansas
F. X. McNerney
Maritime Administration
365 Canal Street
Suite 2590
New Orleans, LA 70130-1137
(504) 589-6556

Kentucky
F. X. McNerney
Maritime Administration
365 Canal Street
Suite 2590
New Orleans, LA 70130-1137
(504) 589-6556

Louisiana
F. X. McNerney
Maritime Administration
365 Canal Street
Suite 2590
New Orleans, LA 70130-1137
(504) 589-6556

Maine
Robert F. McKeon
Maritime Administration
26 Federal Plaza
Room 3737
New York, NY 10278
(212) 264-1300

Maryland
Robert F. McKeon
Maritime Administration
26 Federal Plaza
Room 3737
New York, NY 10278
(212) 264-1300

Massachusetts
Robert F. McKeon
Maritime Administration
26 Federal Plaza
Room 3737
New York, NY 10278
(212) 264-1300

Michigan
Alpha H. Ames Jr.
Maritime Administration
2860 South River Road
Suite 185
Des Plaines, IL 60018-4605
(708) 298-2413

Minnesota
Alpha H. Ames Jr.
Maritime Administration
2860 South River Road
Suite 185
Des Plaines, IL 60018-4605
(708) 298-2413

Mississippi
F. X. McNerney
Maritime Administration
365 Canal Street
Suite 2590
New Orleans, LA 70130-1137
(504) 589-6556

Missouri
F. X. McNerney
Maritime Administration
365 Canal Street
Suite 2590
New Orleans, LA 70130-1137
(504) 589-6556

Montana
Francis X. Johnston
Maritime Administration
211 Main Street
Room 1112
San Francisco, CA 94105
(415) 744-2580

Nebraska
F. X. McNerney
Maritime Administration
365 Canal Street
Suite 2590
New Orleans, LA 70130-
1137
(504) 589-6556

Nevada
Francis X. Johnston
Maritime Administration
211 Main Street
Room 1112
San Francisco, CA 94105
(415) 744-2580

New Hampshire
Robert F. McKeon
Maritime Administration
26 Federal Plaza
Room 3737
New York, NY 10278
(212) 264-1300

New Jersey
Robert F. McKeon
Maritime Administration
26 Federal Plaza
Room 3737
New York, NY 10278
(212) 264-1300

New Mexico
Francis X. Johnston
Maritime Administration
211 Main Street
Room 1112
San Francisco, CA 94105
(415) 744-2580

New York
(Except Lake Coastal Area)
Robert F. McKeon
Maritime Administration
26 Federal Plaza
Room 3737
New York, NY 10278
(212) 264-1300

(Lake Coastal Area)
Alpha H. Ames Jr.
Maritime Administration
2860 South River Road
Suite 185
Des Plaines, IL 60018-4605
(708) 298-2413

North Carolina
Mayank Jain
Maritime Administration
7737 Hampton Boulevard
Building 4D
Room 211
Norfolk, VA 23505
(804) 441-6393

North Dakota
Francis X. Johnston
Maritime Administration
211 Main Street
Room 1112
San Francisco, CA 94105
(415) 744-2580

Ohio
Alpha H. Ames Jr.
Maritime Administration
2860 South River Road
Suite 185
Des Plaines, IL 60018-4605
(708) 298-2413

Oklahoma
F. X. McNerney
Maritime Administration
365 Canal Street
Suite 2590
New Orleans, LA 70130-
1137
(504) 589-6556

Oregon
Francis X. Johnston
Maritime Administration
211 Main Street
Room 1112
San Francisco, CA 94105
(415) 744-2580

Pennsylvania
(Except Lake Coastal Area)
Robert F. McKeon
Maritime Administration
26 Federal Plaza
Room 3737
New York, NY 10278
(212) 264-1300

(Lake Coastal Area)
Alpha H. Ames Jr.
Maritime Administration
2860 South River Road
Suite 185
Des Plaines, IL 60018-4605
(708) 298-2413

Puerto Rico
Mayank Jain
Maritime Administration
7737 Hampton Boulevard
Building 4D
Room 211
Norfolk, VA 23505
(804) 441-6393

Rhode Island
Robert F. McKeon
Maritime Administration
26 Federal Plaza
Room 3737
New York, NY 10278
(212) 264-1300

South Carolina
Mayank Jain
Maritime Administration
7737 Hampton Boulevard
Building 4D
Room 211
Norfolk, VA 23505
(804) 441-6393

South Dakota
Francis X. Johnston
Maritime Administration
211 Main Street
Room 1112
San Francisco, CA 94105
(415) 744-2580

Tennessee
F. X. McNerney
Maritime Administration
365 Canal Street
Suite 2590
New Orleans, LA 70130-
1137
(504) 589-6556

Texas
F. X. McNerney
Maritime Administration
365 Canal Street
Suite 2590
New Orleans, LA 70130-
1137
(504) 589-6556

Utah
Francis X. Johnston
Maritime Administration
211 Main Street
Room 1112
San Francisco, CA 94105
(415) 744-2580

Vermont
Robert F. McKeon
Maritime Administration
26 Federal Plaza
Room 3737
New York, NY 10278
(212) 264-1300

Virginia
Mayank Jain
Maritime Administration
7737 Hampton Boulevard
Building 4D
Room 211
Norfolk, VA 23505
(804) 441-6393

Washington
Francis X. Johnston
Maritime Administration
211 Main Street
Room 1112
San Francisco, CA 94105
(415) 744-2580

West Virginia
Mayank Jain
Maritime Administration
7737 Hampton Boulevard
Building 4D
Room 211
Norfolk, VA 23505
(804) 441-6393

Wisconsin
Alpha H. Ames Jr.
Maritime Administration
2860 South River Road
Suite 185
Des Plaines, IL 60018-4605
(708) 298-2413

Wyoming
Francis X. Johnston
Maritime Administration
211 Main Street
Room 1112
San Francisco, CA 94105
(415) 744-2580

Field Office
Thomas T. Matteson
U.S. Merchant Marine
Academy
Kings Point, NY 11024-
1699
(516) 773-5000

DIRECT INVESTMENT LOANS

Overseas Private Investment
Corporation (OPIC)
110 New York Avenue, NW
Washington, DC 20527
(202) 336-8799

Description: Direct loans to small businesses for promoting overseas investment in developing countries. Must be small business (i.e., non-Fortune 1000 size).
$ Given: $30 million est. nationwide FY 94; range: $900,000–$6 million; average: $3 million
Application Information: Request free "Investment Finance Handbook." For application, send letter with required preliminary information.
Deadline: None
Contact: Daven Oswalt, Information Officer, above address

FISHERMEN'S CONTINGENCY FUND

Department of Commerce
National Marine Fisheries
Service
1335 East West Highway
Silver Spring, MD 20910
(301) 713-2396

Description: Direct payments with unrestricted use to compensate U.S. commercial fishermen for damage and loss of fishing gear and 50 percent of resulting economic loss due to oil- and gas-related activities in any area of the Outer Continental Shelf.
$ Given: $600,000 est. nationwide FY 94; range: $500–$25,000; average: $6,000
Application Information: Submit application to above address.
Deadline: Within 90 days of loss; presumption of causation allowed if reported within 15 days of vessel's return to port.
Contact: Chief, Financial Services Division, above address

FISHERMEN'S GUARANTY FUND

Department of State
Office of Fisheries Affairs
Bureau of Oceans
Room 5806
Washington, DC 20520-
7818
(202) 647-2009

Description: Insurance reimbursement for commercial U.S. fishing vessels seized by foreign governments. Vessel must have been seized under territorial claims or on other basis not recognized by the State Department.
$ Given: $900,000 est. nationwide FY 94
Application Information: Obtain standard application forms from above address.
Deadline: None
Contact: Stetson Tinkham, above address

FISHING VESSEL AND GEAR DAMAGE COMPENSATION FUND

National Marine Fisheries
Services
1335 East West Highway
Silver Spring, MD 20910
(301) 713-2396

Description: Direct payments with unrestricted use to compensate U.S. fishermen for loss, damage, or destruction of their vessels by foreign fishing vessels and of their gear by any vessel.
$ Given: $1.3 million est. nationwide FY 94; range: $600–$150,000; average: $7,350
Application Information: Submit application to above address.
Deadline: Within 90 days of loss
Contact: Chief, Financial Services Division, above address

FOREIGN INVESTMENT FINANCING

Overseas Private Investment
Corporation (OPIC)
1100 New York Avenue,
NW
Washington, DC 20527

Description: Guaranteed/insured loans and direct loans to eligible investors in friendly developing countries and areas. Individual must be U.S. citizen; corporation must be substantially owned by U.S. citizens; foreign subsidiary must be 95 percent owned by U.S. citizens.
$ Given: $500 million in guarantees est. nationwide FY 95; range: $10 million–$75 million; average: $20 million
Application Information: Letter followed by discussions with OPIC, which will provide application instructions to eligible applicants.
Deadline: None
Contact: Daven Oswalt, Information Office, above address

FOREIGN INVESTMENT INSURANCE (POLITICAL RISK INSURANCE)

Overseas Private Investment Corporation (OPIC)
1100 New York Avenue, NW
Washington, DC 20527

Description: Insurance to guarantee U.S. investors in friendly foreign countries against risk of war, revolution, and so on. Investors must contribute to welfare of host country without adversely affecting U.S. jobs. Special criteria may be applied to extraction of mineral resources and other large, sensitive projects. Registration with OPIC must be made before investment. Approval of foreign government for the investment must be obtained. Individual must be U.S. citizen; corporation must be created under U.S. law and must be 50 percent owned by U.S. citizens; foreign subsidiary must be 95 percent owned by U.S. citizens.
$ Given: $22.3 million in insurance est. nationwide FY 94.
Application Information: Registration letter followed by formal application.
Deadline: Registration must precede commitment of investment.
Contact: Daven Oswalt, Information Office, above address

HANDICAPPED ASSISTANCE LOANS

Small Business Administration (SBA)
Loan Policy and Procedures Branch
409 Third Street, SW
Washington, DC 20416
(202) 205-6570

Description: Direct loans for construction, expansion, or conversion of facilities; for purchasing buildings, equipment, or materials; and for working capital to independently owned and operated small businesses that are 100 percent owned by handicapped individuals. Excludes speculation, publishing media, radio, television, nonprofit entities, speculators in property lending or investment enterprises, and financing of real property held for sale or investment.
$ Given: Range: $500–$350,000; average: $95,305
Application Information: Write for guidelines.
Deadline: None
Contact: Your state and/or regional office

Alabama
1375 Peachtree Street, NE
Fifth Floor
Atlanta, GA 30367-8102
(404) 347-2797

Alaska
2601 Fourth Avenue
Room 440
Seattle, WA 98121-1273
(206) 553-1273

Arizona
71 Stevenson Street
20th Floor
San Francisco, CA 94105-2939
(415) 744-6402

Arkansas
8625 King George Drive
Building C
Dallas, TX 75235-3391
(214) 767-7633

California
71 Stevenson Street
20th Floor
San Francisco, CA 94105-
2939
(415) 744-6402

Colorado
633 17th Street
Seventh Floor
Denver, CO 80202
(303) 294-7186

Connecticut
155 Federal Street
Ninth Floor
Boston, MA 02110
(617) 451-2023

Delaware
475 Allendale Road
Suite 201
King of Prussia, PA 19406
(215) 962-3700

District of Columbia
475 Allendale Road
Suite 201
King of Prussia, PA 19406
(215) 962-3700

Florida
1375 Peachtree Street, NE
Fifth Floor
Atlanta, GA 30367-8102
(404) 347-2797

Georgia
1375 Peachtree Street, NE
Fifth Floor
Atlanta, GA 30367-8102
(404) 347-2797

Hawaii
71 Stevenson Street
20th Floor
San Francisco, CA 94105-
2939
(415) 744-6402

Idaho
2601 Fourth Avenue
Room 440
Seattle, WA 98121-1273
(206) 553-1273

Illinois
Federal Building
300 South Riverside Plaza
Room 1975
Chicago, IL 60606-6611
(312) 353-5000

Indiana
Federal Building
300 South Riverside Plaza
Room 1975
Chicago, IL 60606-6611
(312) 353-5000

Iowa
911 Walnut Street
13th Floor
Kansas City, MO 64106
(816) 426-3608

Kansas
911 Walnut Street
13th Floor
Kansas City, MO 64106
(816) 426-3608

Kentucky
1375 Peachtree Street, NE
Fifth Floor
Atlanta, GA 30367-8102
(404) 347-2797

Louisiana
8625 King George Drive
Building C
Dallas, TX 75235-3391
(214) 767-7633

Maine
155 Federal Street
Ninth Floor
Boston, MA 02110
(617) 451-2023

Maryland
475 Allendale Road
Suite 201
King of Prussia, PA 19406
(215) 962-3700

Massachusetts
155 Federal Street
Ninth Floor
Boston, MA 02110
(617) 451-2023

Michigan
Federal Building
300 South Riverside Plaza
Room 1975
Chicago, IL 60606-6611
(312) 353-5000

Minnesota
Federal Plaza
300 South Riverside Plaza
Room 1975
Chicago, IL 60606-6611
(312) 353-5000

Mississippi
1375 Peachtree Street, NE
Fifth Floor
Atlanta, GA 30367-8102
(404) 347-2797

Missouri
911 Walnut Street
13th Floor
Kansas City, MO 64106
(816) 426-3608

Montana
633 17th Street
Seventh Floor
Denver, CO 80202
(303) 294-7186

Nebraska
911 Walnut Street
13th Floor
Kansas City, MO 64106
(816) 426-3608

Nevada
71 Stevenson Street
20th Floor
San Francisco, CA 94105-
2939
(415) 744-6402

New Hampshire
155 Federal Street
Ninth Floor
Boston, MA 02110
(617) 451-2023

New Jersey
26 Federal Plaza
Room 31-08
New York, NY 10278
(212) 264-1450

New Mexico
8625 King George Drive
Building C
Dallas, TX 75235-3391
(214) 767-7633

New York
26 Federal Plaza
Room 31-08
New York, NY 10278
(212) 264-1450

North Carolina
1375 Peachtree Street, NE
Fifth Floor
Atlanta, GA 30367-8102
(404) 347-2797

North Dakota
633 17th Street
Seventh Floor
Denver, CO 80202
(303) 294-7186

Ohio
Federal Building
300 South Riverside Plaza
Room 1975
Chicago, IL 60606-6611
(312) 353-5000

Oklahoma
8625 King George Drive
Building C
Dallas, TX 75235-3391
(214) 767-7633

Oregon
2601 Fourth Avenue
Room 440
Seattle, WA 98121-1273
(206) 553-1273

Pacific Islands
71 Stevenson Street
20th Floor
San Francisco, CA 94105-
2939
(415) 744-6402

Pennsylvania
475 Allendale Road
Suite 201
King of Prussia, PA 19406
(215) 962-3700

Puerto Rico
26 Federal Plaza
Room 31-08
New York, NY 10278
(212) 264-1450

Rhode Island
155 Federal Street
Ninth Floor
Boston, MA 02110
(617) 451-2023

South Carolina
1375 Peachtree Street, NE
Fifth Floor
Atlanta, GA 30367-8102
(404) 347-2797

South Dakota
633 17th Street
Seventh Floor
Denver, CO 80202
(303) 294-7186

Tennessee
1375 Peachtree Street, NE
Fifth Floor
Atlanta, GA 30367-8102
(404) 347-2797

Texas
8625 King George Drive
Building C
Dallas, TX 75235-3391
(214) 767-7633

Utah
633 17th Street
Seventh Floor
Denver, CO 80202
(303) 294-7186

Vermont
155 Federal Street
Ninth Floor
Boston, MA 02110
(617) 451-2023

Virginia
475 Allendale Road
Suite 201
King of Prussia, PA 19406
(215) 962-3700

Virgin Islands
26 Federal Plaza
Room 31-08
New York, NY 10278
(212) 264-1450

Washington
2601 Fourth Avenue
Room 440
Seattle, WA 98121-1273
(206) 553-1273

West Virginia
475 Allendale Road
Suite 201
King of Prussia, PA 19406
(215) 962-3700

Wisconsin
Federal Building
300 South Riverside Plaza
Room 1975
Chicago, IL 60606-6611
(312) 353-5000

Wyoming
633 17th Street
Seventh Floor
Denver, CO 80202
(303) 294-7186

IMPORT RELIEF (INDUSTRY) (ESCAPE CLAUSE)

International Trade
Commission (ITC)
500 East Street, SW
Washington, DC 20436
(202) 205-2000

Description: Provision of specialized services (tariffs, import
quotas, and adjustments) to industries and workers adversely
affected by imports. Applicants must be found eligible by the
ITC and the President.
$ Given: Not available
Application Information: Preliminary conference with ITC
staff recommended. Submit petition to Secretary, address
given.
Deadline: None
Contact: Donna R. Koehnke, Secretary, above address

LOCAL DEVELOPMENT COMPANY LOANS

Small Business
Administration (SBA)
Office of Rural Affairs and
Economic Development
409 Third Street, SW
Washington, DC 20416
(202) 205-6485

Description: Loans administered by local development
companies to small businesses for purposes of construction,
land purchases, machinery, and equipment. Limited to small,
independently owned businesses that are not dominant in
their fields. Loans are not provided for working capital or
for financing.
$ Given: $40 million est. nationwide FY 94; range: $62,000–
$1 million; average: $500,000
Application Information: Applicants must contact local agent
or broker of surety bonds. For program particulars, contact
regional SBA office (Program #502 Loans).
Deadline: Not available
Contact: Local regional Small Business Administration office

LOW-INCOME HOME ENERGY ASSISTANCE PROGRAM (LIHEAP)

Department of Health and Human Services
Division of Energy Assistance
Office of Community Services
Administration for Children and Families
370 L'Enfant Promenade, SW
Washington, DC 20447
(202) 401-9351

Description: Technical and training assistance grants to business concerns for helping low-income households meet their home-energy costs. Business concern must apply jointly with a private, nonprofit organization.
$ Given: $750,000 est. nationwide FY 94
Application Information: Submit request. Applicable requirements are published in the Federal Register or Commerce Business Daily.
Deadline: See Federal Register, or contact headquarters office.
Contact: Janet M. Fox, Director, above address

MARITIME WAR RISK INSURANCE

Department of Transportation
Office of Trade Analysis and Insurance
Maritime Administration
Washington, DC 20590
(202) 366-2400

Description: Provision of war risk insurance not available on reasonable terms from insurance companies.
$ Given: Not available
Application Information: File application and supporting documents according to guidelines.
Deadline: None
Contact: Edmond J. Fitzgerald, Director, above address

OPERATING-DIFFERENTIAL SUBSIDIES (ODS)

**Department of
Transportation**
Associate Administrator for
Maritime Aids
Maritime Administration
400 Seventh Street, SW
Washington, DC 20590
(202) 366-0364

Description: Direct payments for specified use to any U.S. citizen able to operate a maritime vessel, to equalize cost of operating a U.S. flag ship with cost of operating a vessel under foreign registry.
$ Given: Subsidies to individual ships: $8,000–$14,200; average: $10,000
Application Information: Submit standard applications.
Deadline: None
Contact: Local Maritime Administration regional office

Alabama
F. X. McNerney
Maritime Administration
365 Canal Street
Suite 2590
New Orleans, LA 70130-
1137
(504) 589-6556

Alaska
Francis X. Johnston
Maritime Administration
211 Main Street
Room 1112
San Francisco, CA 94105
(415) 744-2580

Arizona
Francis X. Johnston
Maritime Administration
211 Main Street
Room 1112
San Francisco, CA 94105
(415) 744-2580

Arkansas
F. X. McNerney
Maritime Administration
365 Canal Street
Suite 2590
New Orleans, LA 70130-
1137
(504) 589-6556

California
Francis X. Johnston
Maritime Administration
211 Main Street
Room 1112
San Francisco, CA 94105
(415) 744-2580

Colorado
Francis X. Johnston
Maritime Administration
211 Main Street
Room 1112
San Francisco, CA 94105
(415) 744-2580

Connecticut
Robert F. McKeon
Maritime Administration
26 Federal Plaza
Room 3737
New York, NY 10278
(212) 264-1300

Delaware
Robert F. McKeon
Maritime Administration
26 Federal Plaza
Room 3737
New York, NY 10278
(212) 264-1300

Florida
(Eastern Half)
Mayank Jain
Maritime Administration
7737 Hampton Boulevard
Building 4D
Room 211
Norfolk, VA 23505
(804) 441-6393

(Western Half)
F. X. McNerney
Maritime Administration
365 Canal Street
Suite 2590
New Orleans, LA 70130-
1137
(504) 589-6556

Georgia
Mayank Jain
Maritime Administration
7737 Hampton Boulevard
Building 4D
Room 211
Norfolk, VA 23505
(804) 441-6393

Hawaii
Francis X. Johnston
Maritime Administration
211 Main Street
Room 1112
San Francisco, CA 94105
(415) 744-2580

Idaho
Francis X. Johnston
Maritime Administration
211 Main Street
Room 1112
San Francisco, CA 94105
(415) 744-2580

Illinois
Alpha H. Ames Jr.
Maritime Administration
2860 South River Road
Suite 185
Des Plaines, IL 60018-4605
(708) 298-2413

Indiana
Alpha H. Ames Jr.
Maritime Administration
2860 South River Road
Suite 185
Des Plaines, IL 60018-4605
(708) 298-2413

Iowa
F. X. McNerney
Maritime Administration
365 Canal Street
Suite 2590
New Orleans, LA 70130-1137
(504) 589-6556

Kansas
F. X. McNerney
Maritime Administration
365 Canal Street
Suite 2590
New Orleans, LA 70130-1137
(504) 589-6556

Kentucky
F. X. McNerney
Maritime Administration
365 Canal Street
Suite 2590
New Orleans, LA 70130-1137
(504) 589-6556

Louisiana
F. X. McNerney
Maritime Administration
365 Canal Street
Suite 2590
New Orleans, LA 70130-1137
(504) 589-6556

Maine
Robert F. McKeon
Maritime Administration
26 Federal Plaza
Room 3737
New York, NY 10278
(212) 264-1300

Maryland
Robert F. McKeon
Maritime Administration
26 Federal Plaza
Room 3737
New York, NY 10278
(212) 264-1300

Massachusetts
Robert F. McKeon
Maritime Administration
26 Federal Plaza
Room 3737
New York, NY 10278
(212) 264-1300

Michigan
Alpha H. Ames Jr.
Maritime Administration
2860 South River Road
Suite 185
Des Plaines, IL 60018-4605
(708) 298-2413

Minnesota
Alpha H. Ames Jr.
Maritime Administration
2860 South River Road
Suite 185
Des Plaines, IL 60018-4605
(708) 298-2413

Mississippi
Alpha H. Ames Jr.
Maritime Administration
2860 South River Road
Suite 185
Des Plaines, IL 60018-4605
(708) 298-2413

Missouri
F. X. McNerney
Maritime Administration
365 Canal Street
Suite 2590
New Orleans, LA 70130-1137
(504) 589-6556

Montana
Francis X. Johnston
Maritime Administration
211 Main Street
Room 1112
San Francisco, CA 94105
(415) 744-2580

Nebraska
F. X. McNerney
Maritime Administration
365 Canal Street
Suite 2590
New Orleans, LA 70130-1137
(504) 589-6556

Nevada
Francis X. Johnston
Maritime Administration
211 Main Street
Room 1112
San Francisco, CA 94105
(415) 744-2580

New Hampshire
Robert F. McKeon
Maritime Administration
26 Federal Plaza
Room 3737
New York, NY 10278
(212) 264-1300

New Jersey
Robert F. McKeon
Maritime Administration
26 Federal Plaza
Room 3737
New York, NY 10278
(212) 264-1300

New Mexico
Francis X. Johnston
Maritime Administration
211 Main Street
Room 1112
San Francisco, CA 94105
(415) 744-2580

New York
(Except Lake Coastal Area)
Robert F. McKeon
Maritime Administration
26 Federal Plaza
Room 3737
New York, NY 10278
(212) 264-1300

(Lake Coastal Area)
Alpha H. Ames Jr.
Maritime Administration
2860 South River Road
Suite 185
Des Plaines, IL 60018-4605
(708) 298-2413

North Carolina
Mayank Jain
Maritime Administration
7737 Hampton Boulevard
Building 4D
Room 211
Norfolk, VA 23505
(804) 441-6393

North Dakota
Francis X. Johnston
Maritime Administration
211 Main Street
Room 1112
San Francisco, CA 94105
(415) 744-2580

Ohio
Alpha H. Ames Jr.
Maritime Administration
2860 South River Road
Suite 185
Des Plaines, IL 60018-4605
(708) 298-2413

Oklahoma
F. X. McNerney
Maritime Administration
365 Canal Street
Suite 2590
New Orleans, LA 70130-1137
(504) 589-6556

Oregon
Francis X. Johnston
Maritime Administration
211 Main Street
Room 1112
San Francisco, CA 94105
(415) 744-2580

Pennsylvania
(Except Lake Coastal Area)
Robert F. McKeon
Maritime Administration
26 Federal Plaza
Room 3737
New York, NY 10278
(212) 264-1300

(Lake Coastal Area)
Alpha H. Ames Jr.
Maritime Administration
2860 South River Road
Suite 185
Des Plaines, IL 60018-4605
(708) 298-2413

Puerto Rico
Mayank Jain
Maritime Administration
7737 Hampton Boulevard
Building 4D
Room 211
Norfolk, VA 23505
(804) 441-6393

Rhode Island
Robert F. McKeon
Maritime Administration
26 Federal Plaza
Room 3737
New York, NY 10278
(212) 264-1300

South Carolina
Mayank Jain
Maritime Administration
7737 Hampton Boulevard
Building 4D
Room 211
Norfolk, VA 23505
(804) 441-6393

South Dakota
Francis X. Johnston
Maritime Administration
211 Main Street
Room 1112
San Francisco, CA 94105
(415) 744-2580

Tennessee
F. X. McNerney
Maritime Administration
365 Canal Street
Suite 2590
New Orleans, LA 70130-1137
(504) 589-6556

Texas
F. X. McNerney
Maritime Administration
365 Canal Street
Suite 2590
New Orleans, LA 70130-1137
(504) 589-6556

Utah
Francis X. Johnston
Maritime Administration
211 Main Street
Room 1112
San Francisco, CA 94105
(415) 744-2580

Vermont
Robert F. McKeon
Maritime Administration
26 Federal Plaza
Room 3737
New York, NY 10278
(212) 264-1300

Virginia
Mayank Jain
Maritime Administration
7737 Hampton Boulevard
Building 4D
Room 211
Norfolk, VA 23505
(804) 441-6393

Washington
Francis X. Johnston
Maritime Administration
211 Main Street
Room 1112
San Francisco, CA 94105
(415) 744-2580

West Virginia
Mayank Jain
Maritime Administration
7737 Hampton Boulevard
Building 4D
Room 211
Norfolk, VA 23505
(804) 441-6393

Wisconsin
Alpha H. Ames Jr.
Maritime Administration
2860 South River Road
Suite 185
Des Plaines, IL 60018-4605
(708) 298-2413

Wyoming
Francis X. Johnston
Maritime Administration
211 Main Street
Room 1112
San Francisco, CA 94105
(415) 744-2580

Field Office
Thomas T. Matteson
U.S. Merchant Marine
Academy
Kings Point, NY 11024-
1699
(516) 773-5000

PENSION PLAN TERMINATION INSURANCE (ERISA)

Pension Benefit Guaranty
Corporation
2020 K Street, NW
Washington, DC 20006-
1806
(202) 778-8800

Description: Insurance to businesses to encourage
establishment and maintenance of voluntary private pension
funds. Employer must prove certain distress criteria.
$ Given: Nationwide FY 95 est. $1,018,100,000 in benefit
payments to retirees; $5.1 million in financial assistance to
plans.
Application Information: Submit application.
Deadline: 60 days prior to termination of distressed plan.
Annual premium must be paid for coverage.
Contact: Regional Pension and Welfare Benefits
Administration offices below or Premium Operation
Division, (202) 326-4000, above address

David Ganz
3660 Wilshire Boulevard
Room 718
Los Angeles, CA 90010
(213) 252-7556

Leonard Garofolo
71 Stevenson Street
Suite 915
P.O. Box 190250
San Francisco, CA 94119-
0250
(415) 744-0250

Rebecca Marshall
Riddell Building
Room 556
1730 K Street, NW
Washington, DC 20006
(202) 254-7013

Jesse Day
Washington Square Building
111 NW 183rd Street
Suite 504
Miami, FL 33169
(305) 651-6464

Howard Marsh
1371 Peachtree Street, NE
Room 205
Atlanta, GA 30367
(404) 347-4090

Kenneth M. Bazar
401 South State Street
Suite 840
Chicago, IL 60605
(312) 353-0900
(312) 353-1023

Joseph Menez
Fort Wright Executive
Building
Suite 210
1885 Dixie Highway
Fort Wright, KY 41011
(606) 292-3121

James Benages
1 Bowdorn Square
Seventh Floor
Boston, MA 02114
(617) 565-8658

Robert Jogan
Federal Building and U.S.
Courthouse
Room 619
231 West Lafayette Street
Detroit, MI 48226
(313) 226-7450

Gregory Egan
Federal Office Building
Room 1700
911 Walnut Street
Kansas City, MO 64106
(816) 426-5131

Roger Schleuter
815 Olive Street
St. Louis, MO 63101
(314) 539-2691

John Wehrum
1633 Broadway
Room 226
New York, NY 10019
(212) 399-5191

Gerard Gumpertz
Gateway Building
Room M300
3535 Market Street
Philadelphia, PA 19104
(215) 596-1134

Bruce Rund
Federal Office Building
Room 707
525 Griffin Street
Dallas, TX 75202
(214) 767-6831

John Scanlon
1111 Third Avenue
Room 860
Seattle, WA 98101
(206) 553-4244

PROCUREMENT AUTOMATED SOURCE SYSTEM (PASS)

Small Business
Administration (SBA)
Associate Administrator for
Procurement Assistance
409 Third Street, SW
Washington, DC 20416
(202) 205-6469

Description: PASS is a computerized database available to government agencies nationwide that lists and profiles small businesses as potential bidders on government contracts. Participation in the program is restricted to small, independently owned businesses as defined by the Small Business Administration.
$ Given: Not available
Application Information: Fill out and submit a Company Profile Form (SBA 1167) available from your regional SBA office.
Deadline: Not available
Contact: Regional SBA office listed below

Alabama
1375 Peachtree Street, NE
Fifth Floor
Atlanta, GA 30367-8102
(404) 347-2797

Alaska
2601 Fourth Avenue
Room 440
Seattle, WA 98121-1273
(206) 442-1273

Arizona
71 Stevenson Street
20th Floor
San Francisco, CA 94105-
2939
(415) 744-6402

Arkansas
8625 King George Drive
Building C
Dallas, TX 75235-3391
(214) 767-7633

California
71 Stevenson Street
20th Floor
San Francisco, CA 94105-
2939
(415) 744-6402

Colorado
633 17th Street
Seventh Floor
Denver, CO 80202
(303) 294-7186

Connecticut
155 Federal Street
Ninth Floor
Boston, MA 02110
(617) 451-2023

Delaware
475 Allendale Road
Suite 201
King of Prussia, PA 19406
(215) 962-3700

District of Columbia
475 Allendale Road
Suite 201
King of Prussia, PA 19406
(215) 962-3700

Florida
1375 Peachtree Street, NE
Fifth Floor
Atlanta, GA 30367-8102
(404) 347-2797

Georgia
1375 Peachtree Street, NE
Fifth Floor
Atlanta, GA 30367-8102
(404) 347-2797

Hawaii
71 Stevenson Street
20th Floor
San Francisco, CA 94105-
2939
(415) 744-6402

Idaho
2601 Fourth Avenue
Room 440
Seattle, WA 98121-1273
(206) 553-1273

Illinois
Federal Building
300 South Riverside Plaza
Room 1975
Chicago, IL 60606-6611
(312) 353-5000

Indiana
Federal Building
300 South Riverside Plaza
Room 1975
Chicago, IL 60606-6611
(312) 353-5000

Iowa
911 Walnut Street
13th Floor
Kansas City, MO 64106
(816) 426-3608

Kansas
911 Walnut Street
13th Floor
Kansas City, MO 64106
(816) 426-3608

Kentucky
1375 Peachtree Street, NE
Fifth Floor
Atlanta, GA 30367-8102
(404) 347-2797

Louisiana
8625 King George Drive
Building C
Dallas, TX 75235-3391
(214) 767-7633

Maine
155 Federal Street
Ninth Floor
Boston, MA 02110
(617) 451-2023

Maryland
475 Allendale Road
Suite 201
King of Prussia, PA 19406
(215) 962-3700

Massachusetts
155 Federal Street
Ninth Floor
Boston, MA 02110
(617) 451-2023

Michigan
Federal Building
300 South Riverside Plaza
Room 1975
Chicago, IL 60606-6611
(312) 353-5000

Minnesota
Federal Building
300 South Riverside Plaza
Room 1975
Chicago, IL 60606-6611
(312) 353-5000

Mississippi
1375 Peachtree Street, NE
Fifth Floor
Atlanta, GA 30367-8102
(404) 347-2797

Missouri
911 Walnut Street
13th Floor
Kansas City, MO 64106
(816) 426-3608

Montana
633 17th Street
Seventh Floor
Denver, CO 80202
(303) 294-7186

Nebraska
911 Walnut Street
13th Floor
Kansas City, MO 64106
(816) 426-3608

Nevada
71 Stevenson Street
20th Floor
San Francisco, CA 94105-
2939
(415) 744-6402

New Hampshire
155 Federal Street
Ninth Floor
Boston, MA 02110
(617) 451-2023

New Jersey
26 Federal Plaza
Room 31-08
New York, NY 10278
(212) 264-1450

New Mexico
8625 King George Drive
Building C
Dallas, TX 75235-3391
(214) 264-7633

New York
26 Federal Plaza
Room 31-08
New York, NY 10278
(212) 264-1450

North Carolina
1375 Peachtree Street, NE
Fifth Floor
Atlanta, GA 30367-8102
(404) 347-2797

North Dakota
633 17th Street
Seventh Floor
Denver, CO 80202
(303) 294-7186

Ohio
Federal Building
300 South Riverside Plaza
Room 1975
Chicago, IL 60606-6611
(312) 353-5000

Oklahoma
8625 King George Drive
Building C
Dallas, TX 75235-3391
(214) 767-7633

Oregon
2601 Fourth Avenue
Room 440
Seattle, WA 98121-1273
(206) 553-1273

Pennsylvania
475 Allendale Road
Suite 201
King of Prussia, PA 19406
(215) 962-3700

Puerto Rico
26 Federal Plaza
Room 31-08
New York, NY 10278
(212) 264-1450

Rhode Island
155 Federal Street
Ninth Floor
Boston, MA 02110
(617) 451-2023

South Carolina
1375 Peachtree Street, NE
Fifth Floor
Atlanta, GA 30367-8102
(404) 347-2797

South Dakota
633 17th Street
Seventh Floor
Denver, CO 80202
(303) 294-7186

Tennessee
1375 Peachtree Street, NE
Fifth Floor
Atlanta, GA 30367-8102
(404) 347-2797

Texas
8625 King George Drive
Building C
Dallas, TX 75235-3391
(214) 767-7633

Utah
633 17th Street
Seventh Floor
Denver, CO 80202
(303) 294-7186

Vermont
155 Federal Street
Ninth Floor
Boston, MA 02110
(617) 451-2023

Virginia
475 Allendale Road
Suite 201
King of Prussia, PA 19406
(215) 962-3700

Virgin Islands
26 Federal Plaza
Room 31-08
New York, NY 10278
(212) 264-1450

Washington
2601 Fourth Avenue
Room 440
Seattle, WA 98121-1273
(206) 553-1273

West Virginia
475 Allendale Road
Suite 201
King of Prussia, PA 19406
(215) 962-3700

Wisconsin
Federal Building
300 South Riverside Plaza
Room 1975
Chicago, IL 60606-6611
(312) 353-5000

Wyoming
633 17th Street
Seventh Floor
Denver, CO 80202
(303) 294-7186

PROTECTION OF SHIPS FROM FOREIGN SEIZURE

Department of State
International Claims and
Investment Disputes
Office of the Legal Adviser
2100 K Street, NW
Suite 402
Washington, DC 20037-
7180
(202) 632-7810

Description: Insurance reimbursement to owners of private fishing vessels seized by a foreign country. Claims must satisfy guidelines of the State Department.
$ Given: Est. $100,000 claims paid nationwide FY 93
Application Information: Submit sworn statement in triplicate with other forms.
Deadline: None
Contact: Ronald J. Bettauer, Assistant Legal Adviser, above address

RURAL DEVELOPMENT GRANTS

Department of Agriculture
Farmers Home
Administration (FmHA)
Community Facilities Loan
Division
Washington, DC 20250-
3222
(202) 720-1490

Description: Grants given to aid development of small private businesses and industries in rural areas. Limited to private businesses that will employ 50 or fewer new employees, will have less than $1.0 million projected gross revenue, and will emphasize technological innovation and commercialization of new products. Priority is given to businesses in communities of less than 25,000, with a large proportion of low-income inhabitants.
$ Given: Est. $50 million total nationwide FY 95; range: $7,000–$1,000,000; average: $166,000
Application Information: Inquire at county or district Farmers Home Administration office or state office listed below.
Deadline: Not available
Contact: Local FmHA office

Alabama
Sterling Center
Suite 601
4121 Carmichael Road
Montgomery, AL 36106-3683
(205) 279-3400

Alaska
634 South Bailey
Suite 103
Palmer, AK 99645
(907) 745-2176

Arizona
3003 North Central Avenue
Suite 900
Phoenix, AZ 85012
(602) 280-8700

Arkansas
700 West Capitol
P.O. Box 2778
Little Rock, AR 72203
(501) 324-6281

California
194 West Main Street
Suite F
Woodland, CA 95695-2915
(916) 666-2000

Colorado
655 Parfet Street
Room 31-08
Lakewood, CO 80215
(303) 236-2801

Connecticut
451 West Street
Amherst, MA 01002
(413) 253-4300

Delaware
4611 South Dupont
Highway
P.O. Box 400
Camden, DE 19934-9998
(302) 697-4300

District of Columbia
4611 South Dupont
Highway
P.O. Box 400
Camden, DE 19934-9998
(302) 697-4300

Florida
Federal Building
4440 NW 25th Place
P.O. Box 147010
Gainesville, FL 32614-7010
(904) 338-3400

Georgia
355 East Hancock Avenue
Stephens Federal Building
Athens, GA 30610
(706) 546-2152

Guam
Department of Agriculture
14th Street and
Independence Avenue, SW
Washington, DC 20250
(202) 720-1632

Hawaii
Federal Building
Room 311
154 Waianuenue Avenue
Hilo, HI 96720
(808) 933-3000

Idaho
3232 Elder Street
Boise, ID 83705
(208) 334-1301

Illinois
Illini Plaza
Suite 103
1817 South Neil Street
Champaign, IL 61820
(217) 398-5235

Indiana
5975 Lakeside Boulevard
Indianapolis, IN 46278
(317) 290-3100

Iowa
Federal Building
Room 873
210 Walnut Street
Des Moines, IA 50309
(515) 284-4663

Kansas
1201 SW Summit Executive
Court
P.O. Box 4653
Topeka, KS 66604
(913) 271-2700

Kentucky
771 Corporate Plaza
Suite 200
Lexington, KY 40503
(606) 224-7300

Louisiana
3727 Government Street
Alexandria, LA 71302
(318) 473-7920

Maine
444 Stillwater Avenue
Suite 2
P.O. Box 405
Bangor, ME 04402-0405
(207) 990-9106

Maryland
4611 South Dupont
Highway
P.O. Box 400
Camden, DE 19934-9998
(302) 697-4300

Massachusetts
451 West Street
Amherst, MA 01002
(413) 253-4300

Michigan
3001 Coolidge Road
Suite 200
East Lansing, MI 48823
(517) 337-6635

Minnesota
410 Farm Credit Building
375 Jackson Street
St. Paul, MN 55101
(612) 290-3842

Mississippi
Federal Building
Suite 831
100 West Capitol
Jackson, MS 39269
(601) 965-4316

Missouri
601 Business Loop
70 West Parkade Center
Suite 235
Columbia, MO 65203
(314) 768-0976

Montana
900 Technology Boulevard
Suite B
P.O. Box 850
Bozeman, MT 59771
(406) 585-2580

Nebraska
Federal Building
Room 308
100 Centennial Mall North
Lincoln, NE 68508
(402) 437-5551

Nevada
1390 South Curry Street
Carson City, NV 89703-
5405
(702) 887-1222

New Hampshire
City Center
Third Floor
89 Main Street
Montpelier, VT 05602
(802) 223-6001

New Jersey
Tarnsfield Plaza
Suite 22
1016 Woodlane Road
Mt. Holly, NJ 08060
(609) 265-3600

New Mexico
Federal Building
Room 3414
517 Gold Avenue, SW
Albuquerque, NM 87102
(505) 766-2462

New York
Federal Building
100 South Clinton Street
Room 871
Syracuse, NY 13261-7318
(315) 423-5290

North Carolina
4405 South Bland Road
Suite 260
Raleigh, NC 27609
(919) 790-2731

North Dakota
Federal Building
Room 208
Third and Rosser
P.O. Box 1737
Bismarck, ND 59502
(701) 250-4781

Ohio
Federal Building
Room 507
200 North High Street
Columbus, OH 43215
(614) 469-5606

Oklahoma
USDA Agricultural Center
Office Building
Stillwater, OK 74074
(405) 624-4250

Oregon
Federal Building
Room 1590
1220 SW Third Avenue
Portland, OR 97204
(503) 326-2731

Pennsylvania
One Credit Union Place
Suite 330
Harrisburg, PA 17110-2996
(717) 782-4476

Puerto Rico
New San Juan Center
Building
Room 501
159 Carlos E. Chardon
Street
G.P.O. Box 6106G
Hato Rey, PR 00918-5481
(809) 766-5095

Rhode Island
451 West Street
Amherst, MA 01002
(413) 253-4300

South Carolina
Strom Thurmond Federal
Building
Room 1007
1835 Assembly Street
Columbia, SC 28201
(803) 765-5163

South Dakota
Huron Federal Building
Room 308
200 Fourth Street, SW
Huron, SD 57350
(605) 353-1430

Tennessee
3322 West End Avenue
Suite 300
Nashville, TN 37203-1071
(615) 783-1308

Texas
Federal Building
Suite 102
101 South Main
Temple, TX 76501
(817) 774-1301

Utah
Federal Building
Room 5438
125 South State Street
Salt Lake City, UT 84138
(801) 524-4063

Vermont
City Center
Third Floor
89 Main Street
Montpelier, VT 05602
(802) 223-6001

Virginia
Culpeper Building
Suite 238
1606 Santa Rosa Road
Richmond, VA 23229
(804) 828-1550

Virgin Islands
City Center
Third Floor
89 Main Street
Montpelier, VT 05602
(802) 223-6001

Washington
Federal Building
Room 319
301 Yakima Street
P.O. Box 2427
Wenatchee, WA 98807
(509) 664-0240

West Virginia
75 High Street
P.O. Box 678
Morgantown, WV 26505
(304) 291-4791

Wisconsin
4949 Kirschling Court
Stevens Point, WI 54481
(715) 345-7625

Wyoming
Federal Building
Room 1005
100 East B Street
P.O. Box 820
Casper, WY 82602
(307) 261-5271

SMALL BUSINESS INNOVATION RESEARCH (SBIR)

Department of Agriculture
Cooperative State Research
Service
AG Box 2243
14th Street and
Independence Avenue, SW
Washington, DC 20250-
2243
(202) 401-6852

Description: Project grants for small businesses. Must be organized for professional, independently owned and operated business that is not dominant in the proposed research field. The principal places of business must be located within the United States and must have no more than 500 employees.
$ Given: Range: $10,000–$240,000
Application Information: Send formal proposals to the SBIR coordinator, Office Research Systems, Cooperative State Research Service.
Deadline: Announced in the Federal Register and the SBIR Program Guidelines
Contact: SBIR coordinator at above address

SMALL BUSINESS INVESTMENT COMPANIES (SBIC)

Small Business
Administration (SBA)
Investment Division
Office of Operations
409 Third Street, SW
Washington, DC 20416
(202) 205-6510

Description: Direct, guaranteed, and insured loans, as well as advisory services and counseling, to any chartered small business investment company having a combined paid-in capital and paid-in surplus of not less than $2.5 million, having qualified management, filing evidence of sound operation, and establishing the need for SBIC financing in geographic area where applicant proposes to operate. Investment company must be chartered as a corporation or limited partnership.
$ Given: Guaranteed loan range: $50,000–$90 million; average: $1.4 million
Application Information: Request information and appropriate forms from SBA office. Complete appropriate requirements and submit with application fee payments of $5,000 to SBA headquarters office.
Deadline: None
Contact: Your state and/or regional SBA offices

Alabama
1375 Peachtree Street, NE
Fifth Floor
Atlanta, GA 30367-8102
(404) 347-2797

Alaska
2601 Fourth Avenue
Room 440
Seattle, WA 98121-1273
(206) 553-1273

Arizona
71 Stevenson Street
20th Floor
San Francisco, CA 94105-
2939
(415) 744-6402

Arkansas
8625 King George Drive
Building C
Dallas, TX 75235-3391
(214) 767-7633

California
71 Stevenson Street
20th Floor
San Francisco, CA 94105-
2939
(415) 744-6402

Colorado
633 17th Street
Seventh Floor
Denver, CO 80202
(303) 294-7186

Connecticut
155 Federal Street
Ninth Floor
Boston, MA 02110
(617) 451-2023

Delaware
475 Allendale Road
Suite 201
King of Prussia, PA 19406
(215) 962-3700

District of Columbia
475 Allendale Road
Suite 201
King of Prussia, PA 19406
(215) 962-3700

Florida
1375 Peachtree Street, NE
Fifth Floor
Atlanta, GA 30367-8102
(404) 347-2797

Georgia
1375 Peachtree Street, NE
Fifth Floor
Atlanta, GA 30367-8102
(404) 347-2797

Hawaii
71 Stevenson Street
20th Floor
San Francisco, CA 94105-
2939
(415) 744-6402

Idaho
2601 Fourth Avenue
Room 440
Seattle, WA 98121-1273
(206) 553-1273

Illinois
Federal Building
300 South Riverside Plaza
Room 1975
Chicago, IL 60606-6611
(312) 353-5000

Indiana
Federal Building
300 South Riverside Plaza
Room 1975
Chicago, IL 60606-6611
(312) 353-5000

Iowa
911 Walnut Street
13th Floor
Kansas City, MO 64106
(816) 426-3608

Kansas
911 Walnut Street
13th Floor
Kansas City, MO 64106
(816) 426-3608

Kentucky
1375 Peachtree Street, NE
Fifth Floor
Atlanta, GA 30367-8102
(404) 347-2797

Louisiana
8625 King George Drive
Building C
Dallas, TX 75235-3391
(214) 767-7633

Maine
155 Federal Street
Ninth Floor
Boston, MA 02110
(617) 451-2023

Maryland
475 Allendale Road
Suite 201
King of Prussia, PA 19406
(215) 962-3700

Massachusetts
155 Federal Street
Ninth Floor
Boston, MA 02110
(617) 451-2023

Michigan
Federal Building
300 South Riverside Plaza
Room 1975
Chicago, IL 60606-6611
(312) 353-5000

Minnesota
Federal Building
300 South Riverside Plaza
Room 1975
Chicago, IL 60606-6611
(312) 353-5000

Mississippi
1375 Peachtree Street, NE
Fifth Floor
Atlanta, GA 30367-8102
(404) 347-2797

Missouri
911 Walnut Street
13th Floor
Kansas City, MO 64106
(816) 426-3608

Montana
633 17th Street
Seventh Floor
Denver, CO 80202
(303) 294-7186

Nebraska
911 Walnut Street
13th Floor
Kansas City, MO 64106
(816) 426-3608

Nevada
71 Stevenson Street
20th Floor
San Francisco, CA 94105-
2939
(415) 744-6402

New Hampshire
155 Federal Street
Ninth Floor
Boston, MA 02110
(617) 451-2023

New Jersey
26 Federal Plaza
Room 31-08
New York, NY 10278
(212) 264-1450

New Mexico
8625 King George Drive
Building C
Dallas, TX 75235-3391
(214) 767-7633

New York
26 Federal Plaza
Room 31-08
New York, NY 10278
(212) 264-1450

North Carolina
1375 Peachtree Street, NE
Fifth Floor
Atlanta, GA 30367-8102
(404) 347-2797

North Dakota
633 17th Street
Seventh Floor
Denver, CO 80202
(303) 294-7186

Ohio
Federal Building
300 South Riverside Plaza
Room 1975
Chicago, IL 60606-6611
(312) 353-5000

Oklahoma
8625 King George Drive
Building C
Dallas, TX 75235-3391
(214) 767-7633

Oregon
2601 Fourth Avenue
Room 440
Seattle, WA 98121-1273
(206) 553-1273

Pacific Islands
71 Stevenson Street
20th Floor
San Francisco, CA 94105-
2939
(415) 744-6402

Pennsylvania
475 Allendale Road
Suite 201
King of Prussia, PA 19406
(215) 962-3700

Puerto Rico
26 Federal Plaza
Room 31-08
New York, NY 10278
(212) 264-1450

Rhode Island
155 Federal Street
Ninth Floor
Boston, MA 02110
(617) 451-2023

South Carolina
1375 Peachtree Street, NE
Fifth Floor
Atlanta, GA 30367-8102
(404) 347-2797

South Dakota
633 17th Street
Seventh Floor
Denver, CO 80202
(303) 294-7186

Tennessee
1375 Peachtree Street, NE
Fifth Floor
Atlanta, GA 30367-8102
(404) 347-2797

Texas
8625 King George Drive
Building C
Dallas, TX 75235-3391
(214) 767-7633

Utah
633 17th Street
Seventh Floor
Denver, CO 80202
(303) 294-7186

Vermont
155 Federal Street
Ninth Floor
Boston, MA 02110
(617) 451-2023

Virginia
475 Allendale Road
Suite 201
King of Prussia, PA 19406
(215) 962-3700

Virgin Islands
26 Federal Plaza
Room 31-08
New York, NY 10278
(212) 264-1450

Washington
2601 Fourth Avenue
Room 440
Seattle, WA 98121-1273
(206) 553-1273

West Virginia
475 Allendale Road
Suite 201
King of Prussia, PA 19406
(215) 962-3700

Wisconsin
Federal Building
300 South Riverside Plaza
Room 1975
Chicago, IL 60606-6611
(312) 353-5000

Wyoming
633 17th Street
Seventh Floor
Denver, CO 80202
(303) 294-7186

SMALL BUSINESS LOANS

Small Business
Administration (SBA)
Loan Policy and Procedures
Branch
409 Third Street, SW
Washington, DC 20416
(202) 205-6570

Description: Guaranteed and insured loans to small,
independently owned businesses not dominant in their field
for constructing, expanding, or converting facilities, for
purchasing building equipment, or for working capital.
Excluded are gambling establishments, publishing media,
nonprofit enterprises, property speculators, lending or
investment enterprises, and financing of real property held
for investment.
$ Given: Loans: up to $750,000; average: $192,126
Application Information: Applications should be filed by
lender in field office serving territory in which applicant's
business is located.
Deadline: None
Contact: Your state and/or regional office

Alabama
1375 Peachtree Street, NE
Fifth Floor
Atlanta, GA 30367-8102
(404) 347-2797

Alaska
2601 Fourth Avenue
Room 440
Seattle, WA 98121-1273
(206) 553-1273

Arizona
71 Stevenson Street
20th Floor
San Francisco, CA 94105-
2939
(415) 744-6402

Arkansas
8625 King George Drive
Building C
Dallas, TX 75235-3391
(214) 767-7633

California
71 Stevenson Street
20th Floor
San Francisco, CA 94105-
2939
(415) 744-6402

Colorado
633 17th Street
Seventh Floor
Denver, CO 80202
(303) 294-7186

Connecticut
155 Federal Street
Ninth Floor
Boston, MA 02110
(617) 451-2023

Delaware
475 Allendale Road
Suite 201
King of Prussia, PA 19406
(215) 962-3700

District of Columbia
475 Allendale Road
Suite 201
King of Prussia, PA 19406
(215) 962-3700

Florida
1375 Peachtree Street, NE
Fifth Floor
Atlanta, GA 30367-8102
(404) 347-2797

Georgia
1375 Peachtree Street, NE
Fifth Floor
Atlanta, GA 30367-8102
(404) 347-2797

Hawaii
71 Stevenson Street
20th Floor
San Francisco, CA 94105-2939
(415) 744-6402

Idaho
2601 Fourth Avenue
Room 440
Seattle, WA 98121-1273
(206) 553-1273

Illinois
Federal Building
300 South Riverside Plaza
Room 1975
Chicago, IL 60606-6611
(312) 353-5000

Indiana
Federal Building
300 South Riverside Plaza
Room 1975
Chicago, IL 60606-6611
(312) 353-5000

Iowa
911 Walnut Street
13th Floor
Kansas City, MO 64106
(816) 426-3608

Kansas
911 Walnut Street
13th Floor
Kansas City, MO 64106
(816) 426-3608

Kentucky
1375 Peachtree Street, NE
Fifth Floor
Atlanta, GA 30367-8102
(404) 347-2797

Louisiana
8625 King George Drive
Building C
Dallas, TX 75235-3391
(214) 767-7633

Maine
155 Federal Street
Ninth Floor
Boston, MA 02110
(617) 451-2023

Maryland
475 Allendale Road
Suite 201
King of Prussia, PA 19406
(215) 962-3700

Massachusetts
155 Federal Street
Ninth Floor
Boston, MA 02110
(617) 451-2023

Michigan
Federal Building
300 South Riverside Plaza
Room 1975
Chicago, IL 60606-6611
(312) 353-5000

Minnesota
Federal Building
300 South Riverside Plaza
Room 1975
Chicago, IL 60606-6611
(312) 353-5000

Mississippi
1375 Peachtree Street, NE
Fifth Floor
Atlanta, GA 30367-8102
(404) 347-2797

Missouri
911 Walnut Street
13th Floor
Kansas City, MO 64106
(816) 426-3608

Montana
633 17th Street
Seventh Floor
Denver, CO 80202
(303) 294-7186

Nebraska
911 Walnut Street
13th Floor
Kansas City, MO 64106
(816) 426-3608

Nevada
71 Stevenson Street
20th Floor
San Francisco, CA 94105-2939
(415) 744-6402

New Hampshire
155 Federal Street
Ninth Floor
Boston, MA 02110
(617) 451-2023

New Jersey
26 Federal Plaza
Room 31-08
New York, NY 10278
(212) 264-1450

New Mexico
8625 King George Drive
Building C
Dallas, TX 75235-3391
(214) 767-7633

New York
26 Federal Plaza
Room 31-08
New York, NY 10278
(212) 264-1450

North Carolina
1375 Peachtree Street, NE
Fifth Floor
Atlanta, GA 30367-8102
(404) 347-2797

North Dakota
633 17th Street
Seventh Floor
Denver, CO 80202
(303) 294-7186

Ohio
Federal Building
300 South Riverside Plaza
Room 1975
Chicago, IL 60606-6611
(312) 353-5000

Oklahoma
8625 King George Drive
Building C
Dallas, TX 75235-3391
(214) 767-7633

Oregon
2601 Fourth Avenue
Room 440
Seattle, WA 98121-1273
(206) 553-1273

Pacific Islands
71 Stevenson Street
20th Floor
San Francisco, CA 94105-2939
(415) 744-6402

Pennsylvania
475 Allendale Road
Suite 201
King of Prussia, PA 19406
(215) 962-3700

Puerto Rico
26 Federal Plaza
Room 31-08
New York, NY 10278
(212) 264-1450

Rhode Island
155 Federal Street
Ninth Floor
Boston, MA 02110
(617) 451-2023

South Carolina
1375 Peachtree Street, NE
Fifth Floor
Atlanta, GA 30367-8102
(404) 347-2797

South Dakota
633 17th Street
Seventh Floor
Denver, CO 80202
(303) 294-7186

Tennessee
1375 Peachtree Street, NE
Fifth Floor
Atlanta, GA 30367-8102
(404) 347-2797

Texas
8625 King George Drive
Building C
Dallas, TX 75235-3391
(214) 767-7633

Utah
633 17th Street
Seventh Floor
Denver, CO 80202
(303) 294-7186

Vermont
155 Federal Street
Ninth Floor
Boston, MA 02110
(617) 451-2023

Virginia
475 Allendale Road
Suite 201
King of Prussia, PA 19406
(215) 962-3700

Virgin Islands
26 Federal Plaza
Room 31-08
New York, NY 10278
(212) 264-1450

Washington
2601 Fourth Avenue
Room 440
Seattle, WA 98121-1273
(206) 553-1273

West Virginia
475 Allendale Road
Suite 201
King of Prussia, PA 19406
(215) 962-3700

Wisconsin
Federal Building
300 South Riverside Plaza
Room 1975
Chicago, IL 60606-6611
(312) 353-5000

Wyoming
633 17th Street
Seventh Floor
Denver, CO 80202
(303) 294-7186

TRADE ADJUSTMENT ASSISTANCE

Department of Commerce
Trade Adjustment Division
Economic Development
Administration
14th Street and Constitution
Avenue, NW
Washington, DC 20230
(202) 377-3373

Description: Grants (cooperative agreements) to firms and industries adversely affected by increased imports; funds will be used to render recipient technically competitive. Firms must be certified by Secretary of Commerce as eligible. Industries must demonstrate hardship and have a substantial number of certified firms or worker groups. Firms must share 25 percent of cost; industries, 50 percent.
$ Given: Grants to firms, range: $5,000–$150,000; grants to industries, range: $25,000–500,000
Application Information: Certified firms and eligible industries must submit acceptable adjustment proposals and applications for technical assistance.
Deadline: For firms, within two years of certification. For industries, no deadline, but funds available on first come, first served basis.
Contact: Daniel F. Harrington, above address, for general information

VETERANS LOAN PROGRAM

Small Business
Administration (SBA)
Loan Policy and Procedures
Branch
409 Third Street, SW
Washington, DC 20416
(202) 205-6570

Description: Direct loans given to small businesses owned by Vietnam-era and disabled veterans for construction, working capital, or equipment. Business must be 51 percent owned by eligible veteran(s) who served more than 180 days, any part of which was between 8/5/64 and 5/7/75, and who was discharged other than dishonorably. Also, loans for disabled vets of any era with a minimum compensable disability of 30 percent or a vet of any era discharged for disability.
$ Given: Range: $1,000–150,000; average: $75,845
Application Information: Application filed in SBA field office serving territory in which business is located.
Deadline: None
Contact: Director, above address, or regional or district office below

Alabama
Regional Office
1375 Peachtree Street, NE
Fifth Floor
Atlanta, GA 30367-8102
(404) 347-2797

District Office
2121 Eighth Avenue North
Suite 200
Birmingham, AL 35203-2398
(205) 731-1344

Alaska
Regional Office
2601 Fourth Avenue
Room 440
Seattle, WA 98121-1273
(206) 442-5676

District Office
222 West Eighth Avenue
Room A36
Anchorage, AK 99513-7559
(907) 271-4022

Arizona
Regional Office
71 Stevenson Street
20th Floor
San Francisco, CA 94105-
2939
(415) 744-6402

District Office
2828 North Central Avenue
Suite 800
Phoenix, AZ 85004-1025
(602) 640-2316

Arkansas
Regional Office
8625 King George Drive
Building C
Dallas, TX 75235-3391
(214) 767-7633

District Office
2120 Riverfront Drive
Suite 100
Little Rock, AR 72202
(501) 324-5278

California
Regional Office
71 Stevenson Street
20th Floor
San Francisco, CA 94105-
2939
(415) 744-6402

District Offices
Santa Ana District Office
901 West Civic Center Drive
Suite 160
Santa Ana, CA 92703-2352
(714) 836-2494

San Diego District Office
880 Front Street
Suite 4-S-29
San Diego, CA 92188-0270
(619) 557-7252

San Francisco District Office
211 Main Street
Fourth Floor
San Francisco, CA 94105-
1988
(415) 744-6820

Fresno District Office
2719 North Air Fresno
Drive
Suite 107
Fresno, CA 93727-1547
(209) 487-5189

Los Angeles District Office
330 North Grand Boulevard
Suite 1200
Glendale, CA 91203-2304
(213) 894-2956

Colorado
Regional Office
633 17th Street
Seventh Floor
Denver, CO 80202
(303) 294-7186

District Office
721 19th Street
Room 426
Denver, CO 80202-2599
(303) 844-3984

Connecticut
Regional Office
155 Federal Street
Ninth Floor
Boston, MA 02110
(617) 451-2023

District Office
Federal Building
Second Floor
330 Main Street
Hartford, CT 06106
(203) 240-4700

Delaware
Regional Office
475 Allendale Road
Suite 201
King of Prussia, PA 19406
(215) 962-3700

District of Columbia
Regional Office
475 Allendale Road
Suite 201
King of Prussia, PA 19406
(215) 962-3700

District Office
1110 Vermont Avenue NW
Suite 900
Washington, DC 20036
(202) 606-4000

Florida
Regional Office
1375 Peachtree Street, NE
Fifth Floor
Atlanta, GA 30367-8102
(404) 347-2797

District Offices
Jacksonville District Office
7825 Baymeadows Way
Suite 100-B
Jacksonville, FL 32256-7504
(904) 443-1900

Miami District Office
1320 South
District Highway
Suite 501
Coral Gables, FL 33146-
2911
(305) 536-5521

Georgia
Regional Office
1375 Peachtree Street, NE
Fifth Floor
Atlanta, GA 30367-8102
(404) 347-2797

District Office
1720 Peachtree Road, NW
Sixth Floor
Atlanta, GA 30309
(404) 347-4749

Hawaii
Regional Office
71 Stevenson Street
20th Floor
San Francisco, CA 94105-2939
(415) 744-6402

District Office
300 Ala Moana Boulevard
Room 2213
Honolulu, HI 96850-4981
(808) 541-2990

Idaho
Regional Office
2601 Fourth Avenue
Room 440
Seattle, WA 98121-1273
(206) 553-1273

District Office
1020 Main Street
Suite 290
Boise, ID 83702-5745
(208) 334-1696

Illinois
Regional Office
Federal Building
300 South Riverside Plaza
Room 1975
Chicago, IL 60606-6611
(312) 353-5000

District Office
500 West Madison Street
Room 1250
Chicago, IL 60661-2511
(312) 353-4528

Indiana
Regional Office
Federal Building
300 South Riverside Plaza
Room 1975
Chicago, IL 60606-6611
(312) 353-5000

District Office
429 North Pennsylvania
Street
Suite 100
Indianapolis, IN 46204-1873
(317) 226-7272

Iowa
Regional Office
911 Walnut Street
13th Floor
Kansas City, MO 64106
(816) 426-3608

District Offices
Des Moines District Office
New Federal Building
210 Walnut Street
Room 749
Des Moines, IA 50309
(515) 284-4422

Cedar Rapids District Office
373 Collins Road, NE
Room 100
Cedar Rapids, IA 52402-3147
(319) 393-8630

Kansas
Regional Office
911 Walnut Street
13th Floor
Kansas City, MO 64106
(816) 426-3608

District Office
100 East English Street
Suite 510
Wichita, KS 67202
(316) 269-6273

Kentucky
Regional Office
1375 Peachtree Street, NE
Fifth Floor
Atlanta, GA 30367-8102
(404) 347-2797

District Office
Federal Building
600 Martin Luther King Jr.
Place
Room 188
Louisville, KY 40202
(502) 582-5971

Louisiana
Regional Office
8625 King George Drive
Building C
Dallas, TX 75235-3391
(214) 767-7643

District Office
1661 Canal Street
Suite 2000
New Orleans, LA 70112
(504) 589-6685

Maine
Regional Office
155 Federal Street
Ninth Floor
Boston, MA 02110
(617) 451-2023

District Office
Federal Building
40 Western Avenue
Room 512
Augusta, ME 04330
(207) 622-8378

Massachusetts
Regional Office
155 Federal Street
Ninth Floor
Boston, MA 02110
(617) 451-2023

District Office
10 Causeway Street
Room 265
Boston, MA 02222-1093
(617) 565-5590

Michigan
Regional Office
Federal Building
300 South Riverside Plaza
Room 1975
Chicago, IL 60606-6611
(312) 353-5000

District Office
477 Michigan Avenue
Room 515
Detroit, MI 48226
(313) 226-6075

Minnesota
Regional Office
Federal Building
300 South Riverside Plaza
Room 1975
Chicago, IL 60606-6611
(312) 353-5000

District Office
100 North Sixth Street
Suite 610
Minneapolis, MN 55403-1563
(612) 370-2324

Mississippi
Regional Office
1375 Peachtree Street, NE
Fifth Floor
Atlanta, GA 30367-8102
(404) 347-2797

District Office
100 West Capitol Street
Suite 400
Jackson, MS 39201
(601) 965-4378

Missouri
Regional Office
911 Walnut Street
13th Floor
Kansas City, MO 64106
(816) 426-3608

District Offices
St. Louis District Office
815 Olive Street
Room 242
St. Louis, MO 63101
(314) 539-6600

Kansas City District Office
323 West Eighth Street
Suite 501
Kansas City, MO 64105
(816) 374-6708

Montana
Regional Office
633 17th Street
Seventh Floor
Denver, CO 80202
(303) 294-7186

District Office
301 South Park Avenue
Room 528
Helena, MT 59626
(406) 449-5381

Nebraska
Regional Office
911 Walnut Street
13th Floor
Kansas City, MO 64106
(816) 426-3608

District Office
11145 Mill Valley Road
Omaha, NE 64154
(402) 221-4691

Nevada
Regional Office
71 Stevenson Street
20th Floor
San Francisco, CA 94105-2939
(415) 744-6402

District Office
301 East Stewart Street
Room 301
Las Vegas, NV 89125-2527
(702) 388-6611

New Hampshire
Regional Office
155 Federal Street
Ninth Floor
Boston, MA 02110
(617) 451-2023

District Office
143 North Main Street
Suite 202
Concord, NH 03302-1257
(603) 225-1400

New Jersey
Regional Office
26 Federal Plaza
Room 31-08
New York, NY 10278
(212) 264-1450

District Office
Military Park Building
60 Park Place
Fourth Floor
Newark, NJ 07102
(201) 645-2434

New Mexico
Regional Office
8625 King George Drive
Building C
Dallas, TX 75235-3391
(214) 767-7633

District Office
625 Silver Avenue, SW
Suite 320
Albuquerque, NM 87102
(505) 766-1870

New York
Regional Office
26 Federal Plaza
Room 31-08
New York, NY 10278
(212) 264-1450

District Offices
Buffalo District Office
Federal Building 1311
111 West Huron Street
Buffalo, NY 14202
(716) 846-4301

Syracuse District Office
100 South Clinton Street
Room 1071
Syracuse, NY 13260
(315) 423-5383

North Carolina
Regional Office
1375 Peachtree Street, NE
Fifth Floor
Atlanta, GA 30367-8102
(404) 347-2797

District Office
200 North College Street
Suite A2015
Charlotte, NC 28202-2137
(704) 344-6563

North Dakota
Regional Office
633 17th Street
Seventh Floor
Denver, CO 80202
(303) 294-7186

District Office
Federal Building
657 Second Avenue, North
Room 218
Fargo, ND 58108-3086
(701) 239-5131

Ohio
Regional Office
Federal Building
300 South Riverside Plaza
Room 1975
Chicago, IL 60606-6611
(312) 353-5000

District Office
2 Nationwide Plaza
Suite 1400
Columbus, OH 43215
(614) 469-6860

Oklahoma
Regional Office
8625 King George Drive
Building C
Dallas, TX 75235-3391
(214) 767-7633

District Office
200 NW Fifth Street
Suite 670
Oklahoma City, OK 73102
(405) 231-4301

Oregon
Regional Office
2601 Fourth Avenue
Room 440
Seattle, WA 98121-1273
(206) 553-1273

District Office
222 SW Columbia Street
Suite 500
Portland, OR 97201-6605
(503) 326-2682

Pacific Islands
Regional Office
71 Stevenson Street
20th Floor
San Francisco, CA 94105-2939
(415) 744-6402

District Office
Agana Branch Office
Pacific Daily News Building
238 Archbishop F. C. Flores
Street
Room 508
Agana, GM 96910
(671) 472-7277

Pennsylvania
Regional Office
475 Allendale Road
Suite 201
King of Prussia, PA 19406
(215) 962-3700

District Office
960 Penn Avenue
Fifth Floor
Pittsburgh, PA 15222
(412) 644-2780

Puerto Rico
Regional Office
26 Federal Plaza
Room 31-08
New York, NY 10278
(212) 264-1450

District Office
Federico Degetau Federal
Building
Carlos Chardon Avenue
Room 691
Hato Rey, PR 00918
(809) 766-5572

Rhode Island
Regional Office
155 Federal Street
Ninth Floor
Boston, MA 02110
(617) 451-2023

District Office
380 Westminster Mall
Fifth Floor
Providence, RI 02903
(401) 528-4561

South Carolina
Regional Office
1375 Peachtree Street, NE
Fifth Floor
Atlanta, GA 30367-8102
(404) 347-2797

District Office
1835 Assembly Street
Room 358
Columbia, SC 29202
(803) 765-5376

South Dakota
Regional Office
633 17th Street
Seventh Floor
Denver, CO 80202
(303) 294-7186

District Office
101 South Main Avenue
Suite 101
Sioux Falls, SD 57102-0527
(605) 3360-4231

Tennessee
Regional Office
1375 Peachtree Street, NE
Fifth Floor
Atlanta, GA 30367-8102
(404) 347-2797

District Office
50 Vantage Way
Suite 201
Nashville, TN 37228-1500
(615) 736-5881

Texas
Regional Office
8625 King George Drive
Building C
Dallas, TX 75235-3391
(214) 767-7633

District Offices
San Antonio District Office
7400 Blanco Drive
Suite 200
San Antonio, TX 78216-
4300
(210) 229-4535

Dallas District Office
4300 Amon Center
Boulevard
Suite 114
Ft. Worth, TX 76155
(817) 885-6500

El Paso District Office
10737 Gateway West
Suite 320
El Paso, TX 79935
(915) 540-5676

Utah
Regional Office
633 17th Street
Seventh Floor
Denver, CO 80202
(303) 294-7186

District Office
Federal Building
125 South State Street
Room 2237
Salt Lake City, UT 84138-
1195
(801) 524-5804

Vermont
Regional Office
155 Federal Street
Ninth Floor
Boston, MA 02110
(617) 451-2023

District Office
Federal Building
87 State Street
Room 205
Montpelier, VT 05602
(802) 828-4422

Virginia
Regional Office
475 Allendale Road
Suite 201
King of Prussia, PA 19406
(215) 962-3700

District Office
Federal Building
400 North Eighth Street
Room 3015
Richmond, VA 23240
(804) 771-2400

Virgin Islands
Regional Office
26 Federal Plaza
Room 31-08
New York, NY 10278
(212) 264-1450

District Offices
Federico Degetau Federal
Building
Carlos Chardon Avenue
Room 691
Hato Rey, PR 00918
(809) 766-5572

St. Croix Post-of-Duty
4200 United Shopping Plaza
Suite 7
Christiansted, St. Croix, VI
00820-4487
(809) 778-5380

St. Thomas Post-of-Duty
U.S. Court House and
Building
Federal Office Building
Veterans Drive
Room 210
St. Thomas, VI 00802
(809) 774-8530

Washington
Regional Office
2601 Fourth Avenue
Room 440
Seattle, WA 98121-1273
(206) 553-1273

District Offices
Spokane District Office
West 601 First Avenue
10th Floor East
Spokane, WA 99204-0317
(509) 353-2800

Seattle District Office
915 Second Avenue
Room 1792
Seattle, WA 98174-1088
(206) 553-1420

West Virginia
Regional Office
475 Allendale Road
Suite 201
King of Prussia, PA 19406
(215) 962-3700

District Office
168 West Main Street
Fifth Floor
Clarksburg, WV 26301
(304) 623-5631

Wisconsin
Regional Office
Federal Building
300 South Riverside Plaza
Room 1975
Chicago, IL 60606-6611
(312) 353-5000

District Office
212 East Washington
Avenue
Room 213
Madison, WI 53703
(608) 264-5261

Wyoming
Regional Office
633 17th Street
Seventh Floor
Denver, CO 80202
(303) 294-7186

District Office
Federal Building
100 East B Street
Room 4001
Casper, WY 82602-2839
(307) 261-5761

Research and Development

Many funds are available from the federal government for business research and development for the following:

1. *Assistance* to companies for researching and developing new products or for developing research centers (i.e., support for energy technology, biomedical research, or biomass technology)
2. *Counseling services* to export companies for facilitating trade development

You will need to consult the list of addresses in this chapter for your nearest local Department of Commerce field office.

ADVANCED TECHNOLOGY PROGRAM (ATP)

Department of Commerce
National Institute of
Standards and Technology
(NIST)
Gaithersburg, MD 20899
(301) 975-2636

Description: Project grants to U.S. businesses, joint research-and-development ventures, and independent research organizations for improving U.S. industry competitiveness by assisting in creating and applying precompetitive generic technology and research necessary to commercialize significant new discoveries and to refine manufacturing technologies. Single recipients must pay indirect costs.
$ Given: $228,047,000 est. nationwide FY 95; range: $500,000–$19 million; average: $5.1 million
Application Information: Submit proposals only in response to periodically published program notices.
Deadline: Variable; contact NIST for details.
Contact: Gail Killen, Advanced Technology Program, above address

AGING RESEARCH

Department of Health and
Human Services
National Institute on Aging
National Institutes of Health
Public Health Service
Bethesda, MD 20892

Description: Project grants, including Small Business Innovative Research grants (SBIRs), to profit-making organizations for fostering research and technological innovation related to the biomedical, social, and behavioral aspects of aging. Funds to be used for research. Usual restrictions apply for SBIRs.
$ Given: $418,639,000 est. nationwide FY 95 (SBIRs: $4.2 million); range: $5,000–$3.4 million; average: $262,283
Application Information: Submit formal proposal.
Deadlines: February 1, June 1, October 1; SBIRs: April 15, August 15, December 15
Contacts: Biology: Dr. Richard L. Sprott, (301) 496-4996
Geriatrics/Clinical: Dr. Evan Hadley, (301) 496-6761
Behavioral/Social: Dr. Ronald Abeles, (301) 496-3136
Neuroscience: Dr. Z. Khachaturian, (301) 496-9350
SBIRs: Dr. Miriam F. Kelty, (301) 496-9322

ALLERGY, IMMUNOLOGY, AND TRANSPLANTATION RESEARCH

Department of Health and Human Services
National Institute of Allergy and Infectious Diseases
National Institutes of Health
Public Health Service
Bethesda, MD 20892
(301) 496-7291

Description: Project grants to profit-making organizations (SBIRs included) for fostering research and technological innovation related to allergies and immunological pathologies. Funds to be used for research. Usual restrictions apply for SBIRs.
$ Given: $3.6 million est. nationwide FY 95; range: $1,000–$1.4 million; average: $98,317
Application Information: Submit formal proposal.
Deadlines: February 1, June 1, October 1; SBIRs: April 15, August 15, December 15
Contact: Dr. John T. McGowan, above address

ARTHRITIS, MUSCULOSKELETAL, AND SKIN DISEASES RESEARCH

Department of Health and Human Services
National Institute of Arthritis and Musculoskeletal and Skin Diseases
National Institutes of Health
Public Health Service
Bethesda, MD 20892

Description: Project grants, including Small Business Innovative Research grants (SBIRs), to profit-making organizations for fostering research and technological innovation related to arthritis and musculoskeletal and skin diseases. Funds to be used for research. Usual restrictions apply for SBIRs.
$ Given: $189.9 million est. nationwide FY 95; range: $10,000–$1.5 million; average: $210,016
Application Information: Submit formal application.
Deadlines: February 1, June 1, October 1; SBIRs: April 15, August 15, December 15
Contacts: Dr. M. Lockshin, Director, Extramural Program, Building 31, Room 4C32, above address
SBIRs: Diane Watson, Grants Management Officer, Division of Extramural Activities, Westwood Building, Room 732A, above address

BIOLOGICAL BASIS RESEARCH IN THE NEUROSCIENCES

Department of Health and
Human Services
National Institute of
Neurological Disorders and
Stroke
National Institutes of Health
Public Health Service
Bethesda, MD 20892
(301) 496-4188

Description: Project grants, including Small Business
Innovative Research grants (SBIRs), to profit-making
organizations for fostering research and technological
innovation related to biologic bases of neurological
pathologies. Funds to be used for research. Usual restrictions
apply for SBIRs.
$ Given: $313 million est. nationwide FY 95;
range: $20,000–$1 million; average: $170,000
Application Information: Submit formal proposal.
Deadlines: February 1, June 1, October 1; SBIRs: April 15,
August 15, December 15
Contact: Edward M. Donohue, Division of Extramural
Activities, Federal Building, Room 1016, above address

BIOLOGICAL SCIENCES

National Science Foundation
(NSF)
4201 Wilson Boulevard
Arlington, VA 22230
(703) 306-1400

Description: Project grants to private for-profit organizations
for promoting biological research. Funds must be used for
research, salaries, equipment, travel, and so on.
$ Given: $313.9 million est. nationwide FY 95;
range: $4,000–$3.5 million; average: $93,000
Application Information: Submit formal proposal.
Deadline: Published in NSF bulletin
Contact: Assistant Director, above address

BIOPHYSICS AND PHYSIOLOGICAL SCIENCES

Department of Health and
Human Services
National Institute of General
Medical Sciences
National Institutes of Health
Public Health Service
Bethesda, MD 20892
(301) 594-7800

Description: Project grants, including Small Business
Innovative Research grants (SBIRs), to profit-making
organizations for fostering research in biomedical
engineering and technology. Funds to be used for research.
Usual restrictions apply for SBIRs.
$ Given: $197 million est. nationwide FY 95 (including $10
million for SBIRs); range: $21,000–$1 million;
average: $188,431
Application Information: Submit formal proposal.
Deadlines: February 1, June 1, October 1; SBIRs: April 15,
August 15, December 15
Contacts: Dr. James Cassatt, Program Director, Biophysics
and Physiological Sciences, above address
SBIRs: Dr. W. Sue Shafer, above address

BLOOD DISEASES AND RESOURCES RESEARCH

Department of Health and
Human Services
National Heart, Lung, and
Blood Institute
National Institutes of Health
Public Health Service
Bethesda, MD 20892
(301) 496-4868

Description: Project grants, including Small Business
Innovative Research grants (SBIRs), to profit-making
organizations for fostering research and technological
innovation related to blood diseases and resources. Funds to
be used for research. Usual restrictions apply for SBIRs.
$ Given: $164.3 million (including SBIRs) est. nationwide
FY 95; range: $1,000–$2.3 million; average: $245,654
Application Information: Submit formal proposal.
Deadlines: February 1, June 1, October 1; SBIRs: April 15,
August 15, December 15
Contacts: Director, Program Planning and Prevention
Research, Division of Blood Diseases and Resources, above
address
SBIRs: Deputy Director, Division of Extramural Affairs,
(301) 594-7432, above address

CELLULAR AND MOLECULAR BASIS OF DISEASE RESEARCH

Department of Health and
Human Services
National Institute of General
Medical Sciences
National Institutes of Health
Public Health Service
Bethesda, MD 20892
(301) 594-7748

Description: Project grants, including Small Business Innovative Research grants (SBIRs), to profit-making organizations for fostering research and technological innovation related to disturbed or abnormal cellular activity. Funds to be used for research. Usual restrictions apply for SBIRs.
$ Given: $253.5 million est. nationwide FY 95; range: $21,000–$1 million; average: $165,245
Application Information: Submit formal proposal.
Deadlines: February 1, June 1, October 1; SBIRs: April 15, August 15, December 15
Contacts: Dr. Charles Miller, Program Director, Cellular and Molecular Basis of Disease, above address
SBIRs: Dr. W. Sue Shafer, (301) 594-7751

CLINICAL RESEARCH RELATED TO NEUROLOGICAL DISORDERS

Department of Health and
Human Services
National Institute of
Neurological Disorders and
Stroke
National Institutes of Health
Public Health Service
Bethesda, MD 20892
(301) 496-9231

Description: Project grants, including Small Business Innovative Research grants (SBIRs), to profit-making organizations for fostering research and technological innovation related to neurological pathologies. Funds to be used for research. Usual restrictions apply for SBIRs.
$ Given: $212.7 million est. nationwide FY 95; range: $20,000–$3 million; average: $470,000
Application Information: Submit formal proposal.
Deadlines: February 1, June 1, October 1; SBIRs: April 15, August 15, December 15
Contact: Edward M. Donahue, Division of Extramural Activities, Federal Building, Room 1016, above address

COMPARATIVE MEDICINE PROGRAM (ANIMAL RESEARCH)

Department of Health and
Human Services
National Center for
Research Resources
National Institutes of Health
Public Health Service
Bethesda, MD 20892
(301) 594-7933

Description: Project grants, including Small Business Innovative Research grants (SBIRs), to profit-making organizations for promoting research and technological innovation in comparative medicine (use of animals in human medicinal research). Funds to be used for research. Usual restrictions for SBIRs apply.
$ Given: $73.3 million est. nationwide FY 95; range: $35,300–$697,978; average: $364,586
Application Information: Submit formal applications.
Deadlines: February 1, June 1, October 1; SBIRs: April 15, August 15, December 15
Contacts: Primate Research: Dr. W. Richard Dukelow
Laboratory Animals: Dr. Cynthia L. Pond
AIDS Animal Models: Dr. Milton April
SBIRs: Dr. Judith Vaitukaitis, (301) 496-6023, above address

COMPUTER AND INFORMATION SCIENCE AND ENGINEERING (CISE)

National Science Foundation
(NSF)
Computer and Information
Science and Engineering
4201 Wilson Boulevard
Arlington, VA 22230
(703) 306-1900

Description: Project grants to small businesses and other profit-making organizations for research into computer and information processing. Funds must be used for research, salaries, equipment, travel, access to advanced computer networking, and so on.
$ Given: $273.5 million est. nationwide FY 95; range: $15,000–$5 million; average: $155,000
Application Information: Preliminary discussion with relevant program officer encouraged. Submit formal proposal following guidelines.
Deadline: None in most cases
Contact: Assistant Director, above address

CONSERVATION RESEARCH AND DEVELOPMENT

Department of Energy
(DOE)
Office of Management and
Resources
Conservation and
Renewable Energy
Washington, DC 20585
(202) 586-9262

Description: Project grants (cost-shared contracts and cooperative agreements) to profit-making organizations for conducting research and transferring technology in the areas of buildings, industry, and transportation-energy conservation.
$ Given: $3.7 million est. nationwide FY 95; range: $50,000–$500,000; average: $200,000
Application Information: Preapplication coordination recommended for unsolicited proposals, which are to be submitted in accordance with DOE guidelines. See the department's publication "Guide for the Submission of Unsolicited Proposals."
Deadline: None
Contact: Fred Glatstein

DIABETES, ENDOCRINOLOGY, AND METABOLISM RESEARCH

Department of Health and
Human Services
National Institute of
Diabetes, Digestive, and
Kidney Diseases
National Institutes of Health
Public Health Service
Bethesda, MD 20892
(301) 496-7348

Description: Project grants, including Small Business Innovative Research grants (SBIRs), to profit-making organizations for fostering research and technological innovation related to diabetes and its underlying causes. Funds to be used for research. Usual restrictions apply for SBIRs.
$ Given: $282.7 million est. nationwide FY 95; range: $16,600–$2.1 million; average: $180,000
Application Information: Submit formal proposals.
Deadlines: February 1, June 1, October 1; SBIRs: April 15, August 15, December 15
Contacts: Director, Division of Diabetes, Endocrinology, and Metabolic Diseases, Room 9A16, Building 31, above address
SBIRs: John Garthune, Assistant Director, Division of Extramural Activities, Westwood Building, Room 637, (301) 594-7569 (same for FTS), above address

DIGESTIVE DISEASES AND NUTRITION RESEARCH

**Department of Health and
Human Services
National Institute of
Diabetes, Digestive, and
Kidney Diseases
National Institutes of Health
Public Health Service
Bethesda, MD 20892
(301) 496-1333**

Description: Project grants, including Small Business
Innovative Research grants (SBIRs), to profit-making
organizations for fostering research and technological
innovation related to digestive diseases and allied studies.
Funds to be used for research. Usual restrictions apply for
SBIRs.
$ Given: $282.7 million est. nationwide FY 95; range:
$16,600–$2.1 million; average: $180,000
Application Information: Submit formal proposals.
Deadlines: February 1, June 1, October 1; SBIRs: April 15,
August 15, December 15
Contacts: Dr. Jay Hoofnagle, Director, Division of Digestive
Diseases and Nutrition, Room 9A23, Building 31, above
address
SBIRs: John Garthune, Assistant Director, Division of
Extramural Activities, Westwood Building, Room 637,
(301) 594-7569, above address

EARTHQUAKE HAZARDS REDUCTION PROGRAM

**Department of the Interior
Office of Earthquakes,
Volcanoes, and Engineering
Geologic Division
Geologic Survey
National Center
Mail Stop 905
Reston, VA 22902
(703) 648-6723
(Same number for FTS)**

Description: Project grants (cooperative agreements) to
profit-making organizations for mitigating earthquake losses
by research into prediction, land-use planning, engineering
design, and emergency preparedness. Applicant must prove
qualifications.
$ Given: $12 million est. nationwide FY 95; range: $16,000–
$200,000; average: $50,000
Application Information: Submit formal proposal package.
Deadline: April 15
Contact: Deputy Chief, Grants and Contracts, above address

EDUCATION AND HUMAN RESOURCES (EHR)

National Science Foundation
(NSF)
Education and Human
Resources
4201 Wilson Boulevard
Arlington, VA 22230
(703) 306-1600

Description: Project grants to private organizations for facilitating research aimed at improving the U.S. educational system. Funds must be used for research, salaries, equipment, travel, and so on.
$ Given: $586 million est. nationwide FY 95; range: $7,500–$2 million; average: $157,000
Application Information: Discussion with NSF staff strongly encouraged. Submit formal proposal.
Deadline: Published in NSF bulletin
Contact: Assistant Director, above address

ENERGY-RELATED INVENTIONS

Department of Energy
(DOE)
Office of Technology
Evaluation and Assessment
National Institute of
Standards and Technology
(NIST)
Gaithersburg, MD 20899
(301) 975-5500

or

Department of Energy
(DOE)
Inventions and Innovation
Division
Energy-Related Inventions
Programs
100 Independence Avenue,
SW
Washington, DC 20585
(202) 586-1479

Descriptions: Project grants and advisory services especially to small businesses, individual inventors, and entrepreneurs for developing non-nuclear-energy technology. Funding assistance limited. Mainly evaluation of inventions and advice concerning engineering, and so on.
$ Given: $5.8 million est. nationwide FY 95; average: $83,000
Application Information: Submit new technology or invention to NIST, formerly National Bureau of Standards (NBS).
Deadline: None
Contact: George Lewett, Director, Office of Technology Evaluation and Assessment, above address

ENGINEERING GRANTS

National Science Foundation
(NSF)
Directorate for Engineering
4201 Wilson Boulevard
Arlington, VA 22230
(703) 306-1303

Description: Project grants (cooperative agreements) to small businesses for promoting progress of engineering and technology. Funds must be used for research (salaries, supplies, travel, and so on). Funds must not be used to support inventions (product development, marketing, pilot plants, and so on).
$ Given: $320 million est. nationwide FY 95; range: $1,000–$5 million; average: $94,000
Application Information: Send proposals following standard guidelines. Preliminary conferences with relevant program officer encouraged.
Deadline: None for unsolicited proposals
Contact: Paul Herer, Senior Adviser, above address

EXPORT PROMOTION SERVICES

Department of Commerce
International Trade
Administration (ITA)
Office of the Director
General
U.S. and Foreign
Commercial Service
Room 3804
Washington, DC 20230
(202) 377-5777

Description: Advisory services and counseling to encourage and assist U.S. firms in expanding their export efforts.
$ Given: Not available
Application Information: Not available
Deadline: Not available
Contact: Local Department of Commerce ITA field office

Alabama
Patrick Wall, Director
Berry Building
Room 302
2015 Second Avenue, North
Birmingham, AL 35203
(205) 731-1331

Alaska
Charles Becker, Director
World Trade Center Alaska
4201 Tudor Center Drive
Suite 319
Anchorage, AK 99508
(907) 271-6237

Arizona
Director
2901 Central Avenue
Suite 970
Phoenix, AZ 85012
(602) 640-2513

Arkansas
Lon J. Hardin, Director
425 West Capitol Avenue
Suite 700
Little Rock, AR 72201
(501) 324-5794

California
Steven Arlinghaus, Director
11000 Wilshire Boulevard
Room 9200
Los Angeles, CA 90024
(310) 575-7105

Director
6363 Greenwich Drive
Suite 230
San Diego, CA 92122
(619) 557-5395

Betty D. Neuhart, Director
250 Montgomery Street
14th Floor
San Francisco, CA 94104
(415) 705-2300

Colorado
Neil Hesse, Director
1625 Broadway
Suite 680
Denver, CO 80202
(303) 844-3246

Connecticut
Carl Jacobsen, Director
Room 610-B
Federal Office Building
450 Main Street
Hartford, CT 06103
(203) 240-3530

Delaware
(Philadelphia, Pennsylvania,
District)
Robert E. Kistler, Director
660 American Avenue
Suite 201
King of Prussia, PA 19406
(610) 962-4980

Florida
Peter B. Alois, Acting
Director
Miami USEAC
5600 NW 36th Street
Suite 617
Miami, FL 33166
(305) 526-7425

Mail Address:
P.O. Box 590570
Miami, FL 33159

George L. Martinez, Trade
Specialist
Miami USEAC
128 North Osceola Avenue
Clearwater, FL 34615
(813) 461-0011

Virginia Krevis, Trade
Specialist
Miami USEAC
Eola Park Centre
200 East Robinson Street
Suite 695
Orlando, FL 32801
(407) 648-6235

Michael Higgins, Trade
Specialist
Collins Building
Room 366G
107 West Gaines Street
Tallahassee, FL 32304
(904) 488-6469

Georgia
Barbara H. Prieto, Director
120 Barnard Street
Room A-107
Savannah, GA 31401
(912) 652-4204

George T. Norton Jr.,
Director
Plaza Square North
Suite 310
4360 Chamblee-Dunwoody
Road
Atlanta, GA 30341

Hawaii
George Dolan, Director
P.O. Box 50026
400 Ala Moana Boulevard
Room 4106
Honolulu, HI 86850
(808) 541-1782

Idaho
(Portland, Oregon, District)
Steve Thompson, Trade
Specialist
Joe R. Williams Building
Second Floor
700 West State Street
Boise, ID 83720
(208) 334-3857

Illinois
Brad Dunderman, Director
Xerox Center
55 East Monroe Street
Chicago, IL 60603
(312) 353-8040

Oscar L. Dube, Trade
Specialist
Illinois Institute of
Technology
201 East Loop Road
Wheaton, IL 60187
(312) 353-4332

Thomas J. DeSeve
515 North Court Street
P.O. Box 1747
Rockford, IL 61110-0247
(815) 987-8123

Indiana
Andrew Thress, Director
One North Capitol
Suite 520
Indianapolis, IN 46204
(317) 226-6214

Iowa
John H. Steuber Jr., Director
Federal Building
Room 817
210 Walnut Street
Des Moines, IA 50309
(515) 284-4222

Kansas
(Kansas City, Missouri,
District)
George D. Lavid, Trade
Specialist
151 North Volutsia
Wichita, KS 67214-4695
(316) 269-6160

Kentucky
John Autin, Director
Gene Snyder Courthouse
and Customhouse Building
Room 636 B
601 West Broadway
Louisville, KY 40202
(502) 582-5066

Louisiana
Paul Guidry, Director
432 World Trade Center
#2 Canal Street
New Orleans, LA 70130
(504) 589-6546

Maine
(Boston, Massachusetts,
District)
Stephen N. Nyulaszi, Trade
Specialist
187 State Street
Augusta, ME 04333
(207) 622-8249

Maryland
Roger Fortner, Director
World Trade Center
Suite 2432
401 Pratt Street
Baltimore, MD 21202
(301) 962-4539

David Earle, Trade Specialist
c/o National Institute of
Standards and Technology
Building 411
Gaithersburg, MD 20899
(301) 975-3904

Massachusetts
Francis J. O'Connor,
Director
World Trade Center
Suite 307
Commonwealth Pier Area
Boston, MA 02210-2071
(617) 565-8563

Michigan
Dean Peterson, Director
1140 McNamara Building
477 Michigan Avenue
Detroit, MI 48226
(313) 226-3650

Thomas J. Maquire, Trade
Specialist
300 Monroe Avenue, NW
Room 409
Grand Rapids, MI 49503-
2291
(616) 456-2411

Minnesota
Ronald E. Kramer, Director
Federal Building
Room 108
110 South Fourth Street
Minneapolis, MN 55401
(612) 348-1638

Mississippi
Director
201 West Capitol Street
Suite 310
Jackson, MS 39201-2005
(601) 965-4388

Missouri
Sandra Gerley, Director
8182 Maryland Avenue
Suite 303
St. Louis, MO 63105
(314) 425-3302

John Steuben, Director
601 East 12th Street
Room 635
Kansas City, MO 64106
(816) 426-3141

Montana
(Portland, Oregon, District)
Steve Thompson, Trade
Specialist
Joe R. Williams Building
Second Floor
700 West State Street
Boise, ID 83720
(208) 334-3857

Nebraska
Director
11133 O Street
Omaha, NE 68137
(402) 221-3664

Nevada
James Hellwig, Director
1755 East Plumb Lane
Room 152
Reno, NV 89502
(702) 784-5203

New Hampshire
Harvey Timberlake, Trade
Specialist
601 Spaulding Turnpike
Suite 29
Portsmouth, NH 03801-
2833
(603) 334-6074

New Jersey
Rod Stuart, Acting Director
3131 Princeton Pike
Building #6
Suite 100
Trenton, NJ 08648
(609) 989-2100

New Mexico
(Dallas, Texas, District)
Sandy Necessary, Trade
Specialist
110 St. Francis Drive
Santa Fe, NM 87503
(505) 827-0350

New York
George Buchanan, Director
26 Federal Plaza
Room 3718
111 West Huron Street
Buffalo, NY 14202
(716) 846-4191

Joel Barkan, Director
26 Federal Plaza
Room 3718
New York, NY 10278
(212) 264-0634

William Freiert, Trade
Specialist
111 East Avenue
Room 220
Rochester, NY 14604
(716) 263-6480

North Carolina
Samuel P. Troy, Director
324 West Market Street
Suite 400
Greensboro, NC 27401
(919) 333-5345

North Dakota
Director
11133 O Street
Omaha, NE 68137
(402) 221-3364

Ohio
McCaslin, Deputy Director
Federal Building
Room 9504
550 Main Street
Cincinnati, OH 45202
(513) 684-2944

Toby T. Zettler, Director
Bank One Center
600 Superior Avenue
Suite 700
Cleveland, OH 44114
(216) 522-4750

Oklahoma
Ronald L. Wilson, Director
6601 Broadway Extension
Oklahoma City, OK 73116
(405) 231-5302

Thomas Strauss, Trade
Specialist
440 South Houston Street
Tulsa, OK 74127
(918) 581-7650

Oregon
William Schrage, Director
One World Trade Center
Suite 242
121 SW Salmon
Portland, OR 97204
(503) 326-3001

Pennsylvania
John McCartney, Director
Federal Building
Room 2002
1000 Liberty Avenue
Pittsburgh, PA 15222
(412) 644-2850

Robert E. Kistler, Director
660 American Avenue
Suite 220
King of Prussia, PA 19406
(215) 962-4980

Puerto Rico
(Hato Rey)
J. Enrique Vilella, Director
Federal Building
Room G-55
San Juan, PR 00918
(809) 766-5555

Rhode Island
(Boston, Massachusetts,
District)
Raimond Meerbach, Trade
Specialist
7 Jackson Walkway
Providence, RI 02903
(401) 538-5104

South Carolina
Edgar Rojas, Director
Strom Thurmond Federal
Building
Suite 172
1835 Assembly Street
Columbia, SC 29201
(803) 765-5345

James Fitzgerald
Trident Technical College
P.O. Box 118067, CE-P
66 Columbus Street
Charleston, SC 29423
(803) 727-4051

South Dakota
Director
11133 O Street
Omaha, NE 68137
(402) 221-3664

Tennessee
Jeanne Marie Russell, Trade
Specialist
Falls Building
Suite 200
22 North Front Street
Memphis, TN 38103

Jim E. Charlet Jr., Director
Parkway Towers
Suite 114
404 James Robertson
Parkway
Nashville, TN 37219-1505
(615) 736-5161

Sean Kelley, Trade Specialist
301 East Church Avenue
Knoxville, TN 37915
(615) 549-9268

Texas
Karen C. Parker, Trade
Reference Assistant
410 East Fifth Street
Suite 414-A
P.O. Box 12728
Austin, TX 78711
(512) 482-5939

James D. Cook, Director
#1 Allen Center
500 Dallas
Suite 1160
Houston, TX 77002
(713) 229-2578

Donald Schilke, Director
World Trade Center
P.O. Box 58130
2050 North Stemmons
Freeway
Suite 170
Dallas, TX 75242-0787
(214) 767-0542

Utah
Stephen Smoot, Director
324 South State Street
Suite 105
Salt Lake City, UT 84111
(801) 524-5116

Vermont
James Cox
Vermont Department of
Economic Development
109 State Street
Montpelier, VT 05609
(802) 828-4508

Virginia
Philip A. Ouzts, Director
700 Center
704 East Franklin Street
Suite 550
Richmond, VA 23219
(804) 771-2246

Washington
Lisa Kjaer
3131 Elliot Avenue
Suite 290
Seattle, WA 98121
(206) 553-5615

Mark Weaver, Trade
Specialist
320 North Johnson Street
Suite 350
Kennewick, WA 99336

West Virginia
Director
405 Capitol Street
Suite 807
Charleston, WV 25301
(304) 347-5123

Wisconsin
Director
517 East Wisconsin Avenue
Room 596
Milwaukee, WI 53202
(414) 297-3473

Wyoming
Neil Hesse, Director
1625 Broadway
Suite 680
Denver, CO 80202
(303) 844-3246

FISHERIES DEVELOPMENT AND UTILIZATION RESEARCH—DEVELOPMENT GRANTS AND COOPERATIVE AGREEMENTS PROGRAM

Department of Commerce
Office of Trade and Industry
Services
National Marine Fisheries
Service
National Oceanic and
Atmospheric Administration
1335 East West Highway
Silver Springs, MD 20910
(301) 713-2358

Description: Project grants (cooperative agreements) for fostering development and strengthening of U.S. fishing industry. Recent projects included development of Alaskan bottom-fish resources and shellfish-toxin detection. Any individual or group may apply.
$ Given: $9.3 million est. nationwide FY 95; range: $30,000–$600,000; average: $110,000
Application Information: Submit standard application form, proposal, and budget following guidelines.
Deadline: Generally 60 days after published solicitation
Contact: National Oceanic and Atmospheric Administration regional office

Northeast Region
Allen E. Peterson Jr.,
Director
One Blackburn Drive
Gloucester, MA 01930
(508) 281-9250

Southeast Region
Andrew Kemmerer, Director
9721 Executive Center Drive
St. Petersburg, FL 33702
(813) 570-5301

Northwest Region
G. Will Stelle, Director
7600 Sand Point Way, NE
Seattle, WA 98115
(206) 526-6150

**Southwest Fisheries Science
Center**
Dr. Michael F. Tillman,
Director
P.O. Box 271
La Jolla, CA 92038
(619) 546-7081

Southwest Region
Rodney McImnis, Director
501 West Ocean Boulevard
Suite 4200
Long Beach, CA 90802-
4213
(310) 980-4001

Alaska Region
Steven Pennoyer, Director
P.O. Box 21668
Juneau, AK 99802-1668
(907) 586-7221

Field Areas
Virginia
Atlantic Marine Center
R. Adm. Freddie L. Jeffries,
Director
439 West York Street
Norfolk, VA 23510-1114
(804) 441-6776

Washington
Pacific Marine Center
R. Adm. John C. Albright,
Director
1801 Fairview Avenue East
Seattle, WA 98102
(206) 553-7656

FOOD AND DRUG ADMINISTRATION—RESEARCH

Department of Health and
Human Services
Grants and Assistance
Agreements Section
Division of Food and Drug
Administration
Public Health Service
HFA-520
Room 3-40
Parklawn Building
5600 Fishers Lane
Rockville, MD 20857
(301) 443-6170

Description: Project grants to private businesses for
encouraging medical research (AIDS, poison control, drug
hazards, medical devices, and so on). Conference grants
provide partial support for medical conferences. Small
Business Innovation Research grants (SBIRs) included in
program; funds to be used for salaries, equipment, travel,
and the like. SBIRs in two phases—Phase I to determine
feasibility; Phase II to ensure competitive continuation of
research.
$ Given: $17 million est. nationwide FY 95; range: $10,000–
$425,000; average: $140,000 (Only about three SBIR Phase
I grants are expected to be made in FY 95.)
Application Information: If wished, consult headquarters
staff. Submit formal proposal.
Deadlines: Conference grants: October 15, January 15, April
15 and July 15; SBIRs: December 15; unsolicited
applications: February 1, June 1, October 1
Contact: Robert L. Robins, Chief, above address

FOSSIL ENERGY RESEARCH AND DEVELOPMENT

**Department of Energy
(DOE)**
Fossil Energy Program
FE-122
Germantown, MD 20545
(202) 903-3514

Description: Project grants and cooperative agreements to commercial corporations for funding high-risk research and development of fossil-fuel technologies with high potential payoff; goals are either to increase oil and gas production or to switch to the use of coal and oil shale. Emphasis is on fundamental research and technology development.
$ Given: $86 million in grants and cooperative agreements est. nationwide FY 95; range: $30,000–$26 million
Application Information: Preapplication coordination recommended for unsolicited proposals, which must be submitted in accordance with DOE guidelines.
Deadline: None
Contact: Pittsburgh Energy Technology Center, Supervisor, FE UPC, AD 21, P.O. Box 10940, Mail Stop 921-118, Pittsburgh, PA 15276, or Mary J. Roland, headquarters address above

GENETICS RESEARCH

Department of Health and Human Services
National Institute of General Medical Sciences
National Institutes of Health
Public Health Service
Bethesda, MD 20892
(301) 594-7773

Description: Project grants, including Small Business Innovative Research grants (SBIRs), to profit-making organizations to foster research and technological innovation related to genetics. Funds to be used for research. Usual restrictions apply for SBIRs.
$ Given: $241.6 million est. nationwide FY 95; range: $21,000–$11 million; average: $190,000
Application Information: Submit formal proposal.
Deadlines: February 1, June 1, October 1; SBIRs: April 15, August 15, December 15
Contact: Dr. Judith H. Greenberg, Program Director (Genetics), above address
SBIRs: Dr. W. Sue Shafer, (301) 594-7767, above address

GEOLOGICAL SURVEY—RESEARCH AND DATA ACQUISITION

Department of the Interior
Geological Survey Research
National Center
Mail Stop 104
12201 Sunrise Valley Drive
Reston, VA 22092
(703) 648-4451

Description: Project grants (cooperative agreements) to profit-making organizations to support any research beneficial to the Geological Survey's mission of gathering and interpreting geological, hydrological, and topological data pertaining to water, land, energy resources, and so on. Conferences and symposia not ordinarily supported. Office furniture and equipment, foreign travel not supported.
$ Given: $10 million est. nationwide FY 95; range: $4,000–$200,000; average: $50,000
Application Information: Limited discussion followed by standard application.
Deadline: None
Contact: Regional office for your area

Alaska
Director's Representative,
Alaska
U.S. Geological Survey
4230 University Drive
Suite 201
Anchorage, AK 99508
(907) 271-4138

Pacific Coast Area
Director's Representative,
Western Region
U.S. Geological Survey
345 Middlefield Road
Menlo Park, CA 94025
(415) 323-8111, ext. 2711

Rocky Mountain Area
Director's Representative,
Central Region
U.S. Geological Survey
Federal Center
Denver, CO 80225
(303) 236-5438

All Other States
Assistant Director for
Intergovernmental Affairs
U.S. Geological Survey
National Center
12201 Sunrise Valley Drive
Reston, VA 22092
(703) 648-4427

GEOSCIENCES

National Science Foundation (NSF)
4201 Wilson Boulevard
Arlington, VA 22230

Description: Project grants to private for-profit organizations to promote earth science research. Funds to be used for salaries, equipment, travel costs, and so on.
$ Given: $501.5 million est. nationwide FY 95; range: $1,000–$3 million; average: $153,500
Application Information: Formal submission of proposal required. Preliminary conference with relevant program officer encouraged.
Deadline: Write for specifics, or see information published in NSF Bulletin.
Contacts: Atmospheric: Dr. Richard S. Greenfield, (703) 306-1520, above address
Earth: Dr. James F. Hayes, (703) 306-1550, above address
Ocean: Dr. M. Grant Gross, (703) 306-1580, above address
Polar: Dr. Cornelius W. Sullivan, (703) 306-1030, above address

GRANTS FOR AGRICULTURAL RESEARCH— COMPETITIVE RESEARCH GRANTS (NATIONAL RESEARCH INITIATIVE COMPETITIVE GRANTS PROGRAM)

Department of Agriculture
Ag Box 2241
14th Street and
Independence Avenue, SW
Washington, DC
20250-2241
(201) 401-5022

Description: Grants to individuals or corporations to promote research in food and agriculture, markets, trade and policy, and processes to add value or develop new products.
$ Given: $96.6 million est. FY 95; range: $2,000–$330,000; average: $116,220
Application Information: Send formal proposal.
Deadline: Announced in the Federal Register for each fiscal year.
Contact: Chief Scientist, National Research Initiative Competitive Grants Program, above address

GRANTS FOR AGRICULTURAL RESEARCH, SPECIAL RESEARCH GRANTS

Department of Agriculture
Cooperative State Research
Service (CSRS)
Ag Box 2201
Washington, DC 20250-
2201
(202) 720-4423

Description: Project grants to universities, other research institutions and organizations, federal agencies, private organizations, or corporations and individuals with demonstrable capacity to facilitate promising breakthroughs in areas of food and agricultural science.
$ Given: $63 million est. nationwide FY 95; range: $3,000–$360,000; average: $85,000
Application Information: Submit formal proposals to Grants Administrative Management, CSRS USDA. Application procedures are contained in the research-grant application kit.
Deadline: Announced in the Federal Register for each fiscal year.
Contact: Administrator, above address

HEART AND VASCULAR DISEASES RESEARCH

**Department of Health and
Human Services**
National Heart, Lung, and
Blood Institute
National Institutes of Health
Public Health Service
Bethesda, MD 20892
(301) 496-5656

Description: Project grants, including Small Business Innovative Research grants (SBIRs), to profit-making organizations for fostering research and technological innovation related to heart and vascular diseases. Funds to be used for research. Usual restrictions apply for SBIRs.
$ Given: $542.3 million (including SBIRs) est. nationwide FY 95; range: $8,100–$2.7 million; average: $234,796
Application Information: Submit formal proposals.
Deadlines: February 1, June 1, October 1; SBIRs: April 15, August 15, December 15
Contacts: Dr. David Robinson, Special Assistant to the Director, Division of Heart and Vascular Diseases, above address
SBIRs: Dr. Henry G. Roscoe, Deputy Director, Division of Extramural Affairs, (301) 594-7432, above address

HUMAN GENOME RESEARCH

Department of Health and Human Services
National Center for Genome Research
National Institutes of Health
Public Health Service
Bethesda, MD 20892
(301) 496-7531

Description: Project grants, including Small Business Innovative Research grants (SBIRs), for stimulating research in human genetics (obtain genetic maps, study DNA sequences, etc.). Funds to be used for salaries, equipment, travel, publication costs, and so on. Usual restrictions and deadlines apply for SBIRs.
$ Given: $100.8 million in grants and $1.6 million in SBIRs est. nationwide FY 95; range: $50,000–$7 million; average: $390,000
Application Information: Application forms and information obtainable from Division of Research Grants, above address.
Deadlines: New projects: February 1, June 1, October 1; SBIRs: April 15, August 15, December 15
Contacts: Dr. Mark Guyer, (301) 496-0844, or Dr. Bettie Graham, (301) 496-7531

INJURY PREVENTION AND CONTROL RESEARCH PROJECTS

Department of Health and Human Services
Division of Injury Prevention and Control
National Center for Environmental Health and Injury Control
Centers for Disease Control
Public Health Service
2545 East Paces Ferry Road, NE
Atlanta, GA 30305
(404) 488-4265

Description: Project grants to any for-profit organization for supporting injury-control research and for implementing aspects of all related disciplines in prevention of injuries. Funds to be spent on research only. Grantees may not subgrant, but may contract.
$ Given: $39.3 million est. nationwide FY 95; range: $500,000–$1,000,000; average: $650,000.
Application Information: Preapplication coordination desired but not required. Submit formal application.
Deadline: Contact headquarters office.
Contact: Ted Jones, Research Grants, above address

KIDNEY DISEASES, UROLOGY, AND HEMATOLOGY RESEARCH

Department of Health and
Human Sciences
National Institute of
Diabetes, Digestive, and
Kidney Diseases
National Institutes of Health
Public Health Service
Bethesda, MD 20892
(301) 496-6325

Description: Project grants, including Small Business Innovative Research grants (SBIRs), to profit-making organizations for fostering research and technological innovation related to kidney diseases and blood studies. Funds to be used for research. Usual restrictions apply for SBIRs.
$ Given: $158 million est. nationwide FY 95; range: $15,000–$1.6 million; average: $171,000
Application Information: Submit formal proposal.
Deadlines: February 1, June 1, October 1; SBIRs: April 15, August 15, December 15
Contact: Dr. G. Striker, Director, Division of Kidney, Urologic, and Hematologic Diseases, 31 Center Drive, MSC 2560, above address
SBIRs: John Garthune, Assistant Director, Division of Extramural Activities, 45 Center Drive, MSC 6600, (301) 594-7569, above address

LUNG DISEASES RESEARCH

Department of Health and
Human Services
National Heart, Lung, and
Blood Institute
National Institutes of Health
Public Health Service
Bethesda, MD 20892
(301) 594-7430

Description: Project grants, including Small Business Innovative Research grants (SBIRs), to profit-making organizations for fostering research and technological innovation related to lung diseases. Funds to be used for research. Usual restrictions apply for SBIRs.
$ Given: $191.6 million est. nationwideFY 95; range: $3,800–$2.1 million; average: $220,000
Application Information: Submit formal proposal.
Deadlines: February 1, June 1, October 1; SBIRs: April 15, August 15, December 15
Contacts: Director, Division of Lung Diseases, or Loretta Layton, Administrative Office, (301) 594-7480, above address
SBIRs: Deputy Director, Division of Extramural Affairs, (301) 594-7432, above address

MARINE FISHERIES INITIATIVE (MARFIN)

Department of Commerce
National Marine Fisheries
Service
9721 Executive Center Drive
St. Petersburg, FL 33702
(813) 570-5324

Description: Project grants to individuals or corporations for understanding and enhancing fishery resources in the Gulf of Mexico and the South Atlantic off the states of North Carolina, South Carolina, Georgia, and Florida. Funds not to be used for loans. Funds may be used to develop harvest methods, analyze fishery economics and processing methods, improve stock, and so on.
$ Given: $1.3 million est. nationwide FY 95;
range: $21,000–$157,000; average: $65,000
Application Information: Submit standard application form with detailed standard proposal and line-by-line budget.
Deadline: Contact office for deadlines.
Contact: David Pritchard, above address

MATERNAL AND CHILD HEALTH FEDERAL CONSOLIDATED PROGRAMS (SPECIAL PROJECTS OF REGIONAL AND NATIONAL SIGNIFICANCE—SPRANS)

Department of Health and Human Services (DHHS)
Maternal and Child Health
Bureau
Health Resources and
Services Administration
Public Health Service
5600 Fishers Lane
Room 18-05
Rockville, MD 20857
(301) 443-2170
(301) 443-1440

Description: Project grants to private nonprofit and for-profit entities for fostering genetic disease testing and counseling, for supporting centers for hemophilia diagnosis and treatment, and for other projects that may be shown to benefit mothers and children.
$ Given: $93.4 million est. nationwide FY 95;
range: $50,000–$1.5 million; average: $183,000
Application Information: Informal discussion followed by standard application.
Deadlines: March 1–August 1, depending on program
Contact: Regional DHHS office, or Dr. Audrey Nora, Director, above address

Alabama
Jim Brannon
101 Marietta Tower
Suite 1515
Atlanta, GA 30323
(404) 331-2442

Alaska
Elizabeth G. Healy
2201 Sixth Avenue
RX-01
Seattle, WA 98121
(206) 615-2010

American Samoa
Emory Lee
Federal Office Building
50 United Nations Plaza
Room 431
San Francisco, CA 94102
(415) 556-1961

Arizona
Emory Lee
Federal Office Building
50 United Nations Plaza
Room 431
San Francisco, CA 94102
(415) 556-1961

Arkansas
DHHS Office
1200 Main Tower Building
Room 1100
Dallas, TX 75202
(214) 767-3301

California
Emory Lee
Federal Office Building
50 United Nations Plaza
Room 431
San Francisco, CA 94102
(415) 556-1961

Colorado
Paul Denham
Room 325
Federal Building
1961 Stout Street
Denver, CO 80294-3538
(303) 844-3372

Connecticut
Maureen Osolnik
Room 2100
John F. Kennedy Federal
Building
Government Center
Boston, MA 02203
(617) 565-1500

Delaware
James Mengel
3535 Market Street
Room 11480
Gateway Building
Philadelphia, PA 19104
(215) 596-6492

Mail Address:
P.O. Box 13716
Mail Stop 1
Philadelphia, PA 19101

District of Columbia
James Mengel
3535 Market Street
Room 11480
Gateway Building
Philadelphia, PA 19104
(215) 596-6492

Mail Address:
P.O. Box 13716
Mail Stop 1
Philadelphia, PA 19101

Florida
Jim Brannon
101 Marietta Tower
Suite 1515
Atlanta, GA 30323
(404) 331-2442

Georgia
Jim Brannon
101 Marietta Tower
Suite 1515
Atlanta, GA 30323
(404) 331-2442

Guam
Emory Lee
Federal Office Building
50 United Nations Plaza
Room 431
San Francisco, CA 94102
(415) 556-1961

Hawaii
Emory Lee
Federal Office Building
50 United Nations Plaza
Room 431
San Francisco, CA 94102
(415) 556-1961

Idaho
Elizabeth G. Healy
2201 Sixth Avenue
RX-01
Seattle, WA 98121
(206) 615-2010

Illinois
Jim Brannon
101 Marietta Tower
Suite 1515
Atlanta, GA 30323
(404) 331-2442

Indiana
Jim Brannon
101 Marietta Tower
Suite 1515
Atlanta, GA 30323
(404) 331-2442

Iowa
Danny K. Sakata
601 East 12th Street
Room 210
Kansas City, MO 64106
(816) 426-2829

Kansas
Danny K. Sakata
601 East 12th Street
Room 210
Kansas City, MO 64106
(816) 426-2829

Kentucky
Jim Brannon
101 Marietta Tower
Suite 1515
Atlanta, GA 30323
(404) 331-2442

Louisiana
DHHS Office
1200 Main Tower Building
Room 1100
Dallas, TX 75202
(214) 767-3301

Maine
Maureen Osolnik
Room 2100
John F. Kennedy Federal
Building
Government Center
Boston, MA 02203
(617) 565-1500

Maryland
James Mengel
3535 Market Street
Room 11480
Gateway Building
Philadelphia, PA 19104
(215) 596-6492

Mail Address:
P.O. Box 13716
Mail Stop 1
Philadelphia, PA 19101

Massachusetts
Maureen Osolnik
Room 2100
John F. Kennedy Federal
Building
Government Center
Boston, MA 02203
(617) 565-1500

Michigan
Jim Brannon
101 Marietta Tower
Suite 1515
Atlanta, GA 30323
(404) 331-2442

Minnesota
Jim Brannon
101 Marietta Tower
Suite 1515
Atlanta, GA 30323
(404) 331-2442

Mississippi
Jim Brannon
101 Marietta Tower
Suite 1515
Atlanta, GA 30323
(404) 331-2442

Missouri
Danny K. Sakata
601 East 12th Street
Room 210
Kansas City, MO 64106
(816) 426-2829

Montana
Paul Denham
Room 325
Federal Building
1961 Stout Street
Denver, CO 80294-3538
(303) 844-3372

Nebraska
Danny K. Sakata
601 East 12th Street
Room 210
Kansas City, MO 64106
(816) 426-2829

Nevada
Emory Lee
Federal Office Building
50 United Nations Plaza
Room 431
San Francisco, CA 94102
(415) 556-1961

New Hampshire
Maureen Osolnik
Room 2100
John F. Kennedy Federal
Building
Government Center
Boston, MA 02203
(617) 565-1500

New Jersey
Antony Marra
26 Federal Plaza
Room 3835
New York, NY 10278
(212) 264-4600

New Mexico
DHHS Office
1200 Main Tower Building
Room 1100
Dallas, TX 75202
(214) 767-3301

New York
Antony Marra
26 Federal Plaza
Room 3835
New York, NY 10278
(212) 264-4600

North Carolina
Jim Brannon
101 Marietta Tower
Suite 1515
Atlanta, GA 30323
(404) 331-2442

North Dakota
Paul Denham
Room 325
Federal Building
1961 Stout Street
Denver, CO 80294-3538
(303) 844-3372

Northern Mariana Islands
Emory Lee
Federal Office Building
50 United Nations Plaza
Room 431
San Francisco, CA 94102
(415) 556-1961

Ohio
Jim Brannon
101 Marietta Tower
Suite 1515
Atlanta, GA 30323
(404) 331-2442

Oklahoma
DHHS Office
1200 Main Tower Building
Room 1100
Dallas, TX 75202
(214) 767-3301

Oregon
Elizabeth G. Healy
2201 Sixth Avenue
RX-01
Seattle, WA 98121
(206) 615-2010

Pacific Islands
Emory Lee
Federal Office Building
50 United Nations Plaza
Room 431
San Francisco, CA 94102
(415) 556-1961

Pennsylvania
James Mengel
3535 Market Street
Room 11480
Gateway Building
Philadelphia, PA 19104
(215) 596-6492

Mail Address:
P.O. Box 13716
Mail Stop 1
Philadelphia, PA 19101

Puerto Rico
Antony Marra
26 Federal Plaza
Room 3835
New York, NY 10278
(212) 264-4600

Rhode Island
Maureen Osolnik
Room 2100
John F. Kennedy Federal
Building
Government Center
Boston, MA 02203
(617) 565-1500

South Carolina
Jim Brannon
101 Marietta Tower
Suite 1515
Atlanta, GA 30323
(404) 331-2442

South Dakota
Paul Denham
Room 325
Federal Building
1961 Stout Street
Denver, CO 80294-3538
(303) 844-3372

Tennessee
Jim Brannon
101 Marietta Tower
Suite 1515
Atlanta, GA 30323
(404) 331-2442

Texas
DHHS Office
1200 Main Tower Building
Room 1100
Dallas, TX 75202
(214) 767-3301

Utah
Paul Denham
Room 325
Federal Building
1961 Stout Street
Denver, CO 80294-3538
(303) 844-3372

Vermont
Maureen Osolnik
Room 2100
John F. Kennedy Federal
Building
Government Center
Boston, MA 02203
(617) 565-1500

Virgin Islands
Antony Marra
26 Federal Plaza
Room 3835
New York, NY 10278
(212) 264-4600

Virginia
James Mengel
3535 Market Street
Room 11480
Gateway Building
Philadelphia, PA 19104
(215) 596-6492

Mail Address:
P.O. Box 13716
Mail Stop 1
Philadelphia, PA 19101

Washington
Elizabeth G. Healy
2201 Sixth Avenue
RX-01
Seattle, WA 98121
(206) 615-2010

West Virginia
James Mengel
3535 Market Street
Room 11480
Gateway Building
Philadelphia, PA 19104
(215) 596-6492

Mail Address:
P.O. Box 13716
Mail Stop 1
Philadelphia, PA 19101

Wisconsin
Hiroshi Kanno
105 West Adams
23rd Floor
Chicago, IL 60603
(312) 353-5132

Wyoming
Paul Denham
Room 325
Federal Building
1961 Stout Street
Denver, CO 80294-3538
(303) 844-3372

MATHEMATICAL AND PHYSICAL SCIENCES

National Science Foundation
(NSF)
Mathematical and Physical
Sciences
4201 Wilson Boulevard
Arlington, VA 22230
(703) 306-1800

Description: Project grants (cooperative agreements) to small businesses for promoting progress of science. Funds must be used for research (salaries, supplies, travel, etc.).
$ Given: $658 million est. nationwide FY 95; range: $10,000–$16 million; average: $130,000
Application Information: Send proposals following standard guidelines.
Deadline: None
Contact: Assistant Director, above address

MICROBIOLOGY AND INFECTIOUS DISEASES RESEARCH

Department of Health and
Human Services
National Institute of Allergy
and Infectious Diseases
National Institutes of Health
Public Health Service
Bethesda, MD 20892
(301) 496-7291

Description: Project grants, including Small Business Innovative Research grants (SBIRs), to profit-making organizations for fostering research and technological innovation related to the microbiology of infectious and parasitic diseases. Funds to be used for research. Usual restrictions apply for SBIRs.
$ Given: $550,000 for grants and $15.5 million for SBIRs est. nationwide FY95; range: $1,000–$3 million; average: $235,000 (SBIR Phase I awards average $50,000 and Phase II awards average $500,000.)
Application Information: Submit formal proposal.
Deadlines: February 1, June 1, October 1; SBIRs: April 15, August 15, December 15
Contact: Dr. John G. McGowan, above address

OCCUPATIONAL SAFETY AND HEALTH RESEARCH GRANTS

Department of Health and
Human Services
National Institute for
Occupational Safety and
Health
Centers for Disease Control
Public Health Service
Building 1
Room 3053
1600 Clinton Road, NE
MS-D30
Atlanta, GA 30333
(404) 639-3343

Description: Project grants, including Small Business
Innovative Research grants (SBIRs), to profit-making
organizations for researching occupational health and safety
questions and for fostering technological innovations. Funds
to be used for research purposes only. Usual restrictions
apply to SBIRs.
$ Given: $8.9 million est. nationwide FY 95;
range: $10,000–$300,000; average: $160,000
Application Information: Submit formal applications.
Deadlines: February 1, June 1, October 1;
SBIRs: December 15
Contact: Dr. Roy M. Fleming, Assistant Director for Grants,
above address

ORAL DISEASES AND DISORDERS RESEARCH

Department of Health and
Human Services
Extramural Program
National Institute of Dental
Research
National Institutes of Health
Public Health Service
Bethesda, MD 20892

Description: Project grants, including Small Business
Innovative Research grants (SBIRs) to businesses for
promoting research on oral diseases (including oral cancer)
and disorders. SBIRs in two phases, I and II (feasibility and
continuation): Maximum funds $50,000 for Phase I;
$500,000 for Phase II. Various other restrictions apply.
Funds to be used in manner consistent with research grants.
$ Given: $120 million est. nationwide FY 95; range: $3,000–
$1 million; average: $194,000
Application Information: Request and submit application
form.
Deadlines: Grants: February 1, June 1, October 1;
SBIRs: April 15, August 15, December 15
Contacts: Caries, Nutrition, and Fluoride: Dr. Joseph E.
Ciardi, (301) 594-7648, above address
Periodontal Diseases: Dr. Dennis F. Mangan,
(301) 594-7641, above address
Soft Tissue Diseases and AIDS: Dr. Norman S. Braveman,
(301) 594-7641, above address
Craniofacial Development and Disorders: Dr. Mohandas
Bhat, (301) 594-7648, above address

POPULATION RESEARCH

Department of Health and
Human Services
National Institute of Child
Health and Human
Development
National Institutes of Health
Public Health Service
Bethesda, MD 20892
(301) 496-1848

Description: Project grants, including Small Business
Innovative Research grants (SBIRs), to profit-making
organizations for fostering research and technological
innovation related to population control and contraception.
Funds to be used for research. Usual restrictions apply for
SBIRs.
$ Given: $125.3 million est. nationwide FY 95;
range: $16,500–$1.3 million; average: $175,000
Application Information: Submit formal proposal.
Deadlines: February 1, June 1, October 1; SBIRs: April 15,
August 15, December 15
Contact: Hildegard P. Topper, Building 31, Room 2A04,
above address

REGIONAL BIOMASS PROGRAMS

Department of Energy
(DOE)
Office of National Programs
EE-522
Washington, DC 20585
(202) 586-1480

Description: Project grants to profit-motivated organizations
for developing and transferring to nonfederal sector biomass
technologies relating to feedstock population, conversion
technologies, and municipal solid waste. Regional needs
must be addressed.
$ Given: $4 million est nationwide FY 95
Application Information: Submit standard application forms.
Unsolicited proposals should be submitted in accordance
with DOE guidelines.
Deadline: None
Contact: Office in your area

Mary Harris
Oak Ridge Field Office
P.O. Box 2008
Oak Ridge, TN 37831-8613
(615) 576-0737

Phil Lusk
Northeast Biomass Energy
Program
400 North Capitol Street,
NW
Washington, DC 20001
(202) 624-8450

Phillip Badger
Southeast Biomass Energy
Program
Tennessee Valley Authority
Muscle Shoals, AL 35660
(205) 386-3086

Pat Fox
Northwest Biomass Energy
Program
Bonneville Power
Administration
905 11th Avenue, NE
Portland, OR 97232
(503) 230-3449

David Swanson
Western Biomass Energy
Program
1627 Cole Boulevard,
P.O. Box 3402
Building 18, MS-0450
Golden, CO 80401
(303) 231-1615

Fred Kuzel
Great Lakes Governors
35 East Walker Drive
Chicago, IL 60601
(312) 407-0177

Mike Voorhies
Department of Energy
Office of National Programs
EE-522
Washington, DC 20585
(202) 586-1480

REGULATION OF SURFACE COAL MINING AND SURFACE EFFECTS OF UNDERGROUND COAL MINING

Department of the Interior
Office of Surface Mining
(OSM) Reclamation and
Enforcement
1951 Constitution Avenue,
NW
Washington, DC 20240
(202) 208-2651

Description: Project grants and direct payments for specified use to small-coal-mine operators for contracting with qualified laboratories to provide hydrologic and geologic data.
$ Given: $51.6 million est. nationwide FY 95
Application Information: Consult local OSM office; submit formal application.
Deadline: None
Contact: Nearest local OSM director or field office

Director
Office of Surface Mining
U.S. Department of the
Interior
1951 Constitution Avenue,
NW
Washington, DC 20240
(202) 208-4006

Assistant Directors
Support Centers

Office of Surface Mining
U.S. Department of the
Interior
Assistant Director, Western
Support Center
1999 Broadway
Suite 3320
Denver, CO 80202-5733
(303) 672-5500

Office of Surface Mining
U.S. Department of the
Interior
Assistant Director, Eastern
Support Center
Ten Parkway Center
Pittsburgh, PA 15220
(412) 937-2828

Field Offices

Office of Surface Mining
U.S. Department of the
Interior
Director, Birmingham Field
Office
135 Gemini Circle
Suite 215
Homewood, AL 35209
(205) 290-7282

Office of Surface Mining
U.S. Department of the
Interior
Director, Charleston Field
Office
603 Morris Street
Charleston, WV 25301
(304) 347-7158

Office of Surface Mining
U.S. Department of the
Interior
Director, Knoxville Field
Office
530 Gay Street, SW
Suite 500
Knoxville, TN 37902
(615) 545-4103

Office of Surface Mining
U.S. Department of the
Interior
Director, Indianapolis Field
Office
575 North Pennsylvania
Street
Room 301
Indianapolis, IN 46204
(317) 226-6700

Office of Surface Mining
U.S. Department of the
Interior
Director, Albuquerque Field
Office
505 Marquette Avenue NW
Suite 1200
Albuquerque, NM 87102
(505) 766-1486

Office of Surface Mining
U.S. Department of the
Interior
Director, Tulsa Field Office
5100 East Skelly Drive
Fourth Floor
Tulsa, OK 74135
(918) 581-6430

Office of Surface Mining
U.S. Department of the
Interior
Director, Harrisburg Field
Office
Fourth and Market Streets
Suite 3C
Harrisburg, PA 17101
(717) 782-4036

Office of Surface Mining
U.S. Department of the
Interior
Director, Lexington Field
Office
2675 Regency Road
Lexington, KY 40503-2922
(606) 233-2494

Office of Surface Mining
U.S. Department of the
Interior
Director, Columbus Field
Office
Eastland Professional Plaza
4480 Refugee Road
Suite 201
Columbus, OH 43232
(614) 866-0578

Office of Surface Mining
U.S. Department of the
Interior
Director, Big Stone Gap
Field Office
P.O. Box Drawer 1217
Big Stone Gap, VA 24219
(703) 523-4303

Office of Surface Mining
U.S. Department of the
Interior
Director, Springfield Field
Office
511 West Capitol Avenue
Suite 202
Springfield, IL 62704
(217) 492-4495

Office of Surface Mining
U.S. Department of the
Interior
Director, Kansas City Field
Office
934 Wyandotte Street
Room 500
Kansas City, MO 64105
(816) 374-6405

Office of Surface Mining
U.S. Department of the
Interior
Director, Casper Field Office
Federal Building
100 East B Street
Room 2128
Casper, WY 82601-1918
(307) 261-5776

RENEWABLE ENERGY RESEARCH AND DEVELOPMENT

**Department of Energy
(DOE)
Office of Management and
Resources
Washington, DC 20585
(202) 586-9262**

Description: Project grants to profit organizations for developing and transfering to the nonfederal sector the following energy technologies: solar buildings, photovoltaics, solar thermal, biomass, alcohol fuels, urban waste, wind, ocean, and geothermal.
$ Given: $2.1 million est. nationwide FY 95; range: $10,000–$100,000
Application Information: Preapplication coordination recommended for unsolicited proposals, which must be submitted in accordance with DOE guidelines.
Deadline: None
Contact: Fred Glatstein, above address

RESEARCH AND TECHNOLOGY DEVELOPMENT

**Department of Defense
Advanced Projects Agency
3701 North Fairfax Drive
Arlington, VA 22203
(703) 696-2399**

Description: Project grants (cooperative agreements) to commercial firms for supporting basic and applied research in state-of-the-art military technology. Individuals not eligible. Programs should encourage careers in science, particularly among underrepresented minority groups. Applicants must not appear on Department of Defense debarred or suspended list.
$ Given: $160 million est. nationwide FY 95; range: $100,000–$100 million; average: $1.2 million
Application Information: Submit proposals or white papers in response to relevant Board Agency announcements.
Deadline: See Board Agency announcements in *Commerce Business Daily.*
Contact: Director, Management Office, above address

RESEARCH FOR MOTHERS AND CHILDREN

Department of Health and Human Services
National Institute of Child Health and Human Development
National Institutes of Health
Public Health Service
Bethesda, MD 20892
(301) 496-1848

Description: Project grants, including Small Business Innovative Research grants (SBIRs), to profit-making organizations for fostering research and technological innovation related to childhood development from conception to maturity. Funds to be used for research. Usual restrictions apply for SBIRs.
$ Given: $247.1 million est. nationwide FY 95; range: $36,000–$2 million; average: $213,000
Application Information: Submit formal proposal.
Deadlines: February 1, June 1, October 1; SBIRs: April 15, August 15, December 15
Contact: Hildegard P. Topper, Building 31, Room 2A04, above address

RESEARCH RELATED TO DEAFNESS AND COMMUNICATION DISORDERS

Department of Health and Human Services
National Institute on Deafness and Other Communication Disorders
National Institutes of Health
Public Health Service
Executive Plaza South
Room 400-B
Bethesda, MD 20892
(301) 496-1804

Description: Project grants, including Small Business Innovative Research grants (SBIRs), to businesses for promoting research into deafness and disorders of hearing, balance, smell, taste, voice, speech, language, and so on. Funds to be used for salaries, equipment, travel, publication costs, and so on. Usual restrictions apply to SBIRs. For-profit institutions not eligible for some grants.
$ Given: $140.4 million est. nationwide FY 95; range: $72,486–$458,342; average: $186,000
Application Information: Submit standard application forms.
Deadlines: New grants: February 1, June 1, October 1; SBIRs: April 15, August 15, December 15
Contacts: Dr. Ralph F. Naunton, above address, or Sharon Hunt, (301) 402-0909, for grants management

SEA GRANT SUPPORT

Department of Commerce
National Oceanic and
Atmospheric Administration
1315 East West Highway
Silver Spring, MD 20910
(301) 713-2448

Description: Project grants for supporting the establishment and operation of major university centers for marine resources research, education, and training, and for supporting marine advisory services. Some individual efforts receive funding. Limited to individuals or private corporations. Funds must be used for research, development, education, and so on. Funds must not be used to purchase or construct ships or facilities.
$ Given: $51.4 million est. nationwide FY 95; range: $5,000–$2.6 million
Application Information: Use standard application forms. Submit proposal to headquarters.
Deadline: None
Contact: Director, National Sea Grant College Program, above address

SMALL BUSINESS INNOVATION RESEARCH (SBIR PROGRAM)

Department of Agriculture
Cooperative State Research
Service
Ag Box 2243
14th Street and
Independence Avenue, SW
Washington, DC 20250-
2243
(202) 401-6852

Description: Project grants to small businesses for stimulating technological innovation and research in various fields of development. Grants given in two phases, I and II. Only Phase I grantees eligible for Phase II. Grants of no more than $50,000 and $500,000, respectively. Businesses must be independently owned and operated and not be dominant in their field. Primary employment of principal investigator must be with firm. Minority and disadvantaged firms encouraged.
$ Given: $9.4 million est. nationwide FY 95
Application Information: May consult official Omnibus Solicitation. Submit formal application.
Deadline: Announced in the Federal Register and SBIR Program Solicitation for each fiscal year
Contact: SBIR Coordinator, Office of Grants and Program Systems, above address

SOCIAL, BEHAVIORAL, AND ECONOMIC SCIENCES (SBE)

National Science Foundation
(NSF)
Social, Behavioral, and
Economic Sciences
4201 Wilson Boulevard
Arlington, VA 22230
(703) 306-1700

Description: Project grants to private for-profit organizations for facilitating cooperative activities with foreign scientists, engineers, and institutions. Funds must be used for studies, research, salaries, equipment, travel (on U.S. flag vessels only), and so on.
$ Given: $112.6 million est. nationwide FY 95; range: $1,000–$9 million; average: $57,500
Application Information: Proposals by the applicant and foreign peers should be submitted simultaneously to their respective agencies. Initial inquiries encouraged.
Deadline: Published in NSF bulletin
Contact: Assistant Director, above address

SOCIOECONOMIC AND DEMOGRAPHIC RESEARCH, DATA, AND OTHER INFORMATION

Department of Energy
(DOE)
Forrestal Building
Room 5B-110
Washington, DC 20585
(202) 586-1593

Description: Project grants to energy-related industry (particularly small and disadvantaged businesses) and national laboratories for researching minority energy use. Funds must be used for salaries, materials and supplies, equipment, travel, publication costs, and so on.
$ Given: $780,000 est. nationwide FY 95
Application Information: Proposals to be submitted in accordance with DOE guidelines.
Deadline: None
Contact: Georgia R. Johnson, above address

TRADE DEVELOPMENT

Department of Commerce
International Trade
Administration (ITA)
14th Street and Constitution
Avenue, NW
Washington, DC 20230
(202) 482-1872
(202) 482-5023
(202) 482-5225

Description: Advisory services and counseling to any
individual or corporation for fostering competitiveness and
growth of U.S. industries and for promoting their increased
participation in international markets.
$ Given: $54 million est. nationwide FY 95
Application Information: Inquire in person, write, or call.
Deadline: Not available
Contact: Local Department of Commerce ITA field office

Alabama
Patrick Wall
Berry Building
Room 302
2015 Second Avenue
North Birmingham, AL 35203
(205) 731-1331

Alaska
Charles Becker, Director
World Trade Center Alaska
4201 Tudor Center Drive
Suite 319
Anchorage, AK 99508
(907) 271-6237

Arizona
Director
Phoenix Plaza
2909 Central Avenue
Suite 970
Phoenix, AZ 85012
(602) 640-2513

Arkansas
Lon J. Hardin, Director
425 West Capitol Avenue
Suite 700
Little Rock, AR 72201
(501) 324-5794

California
Steve Morrison, Director
11000 Wilshire Boulevard
Room 9200
Los Angeles, CA 90024
(310) 575-7104

Paul Tambakis, Trade
Specialist
3300 Irvine Avenue
Suite 305
Newport Beach, CA 92660
(714) 660-1688

Joe Sachs, Director
Long Beach USEAC
One World Trade Center
Suite 1670
Long Beach, CA 90831
(310) 980-4550

Mary Delmege, Director
6363 Greenwich Drive
Suite 230
San Diego, CA 92122
(619) 557-5395

Betty D. Neuhart, Director
250 Montgomery Street
14th Floor
San Francisco, CA 94104
(415) 705-2300

James Kennedy, Trade
Specialist
5201 Great American
Parkway
Suite 456
Santa Clara, CA 95054
(408) 970-4610

Colorado
Neil Hesse, Director
1625 Broadway
Suite 680
Denver, CO 80202
(303) 844-6622

Connecticut
Carl Jacobsen, Director
Room 610-B
Federal Office Building
450 Main Street
Hartford, CT 06103
(203) 240-3530

Delaware
(Philadelphia, Pennsylvania,
District)
Robert E. Kistler, Director
660 American Avenue
Suite 201
King of Prussia, PA 19406
(610) 962-4980

Florida
Peter B. Alois, Acting
Director
Miami USEAC
5600 NW 36th Street
Suite 617
Miami, FL 33166
(305) 526-7425

Mail Address:
P.O. Box 590570
Miami, FL 33159

George L. Martinez, Trade
Specialist
Miami USEAC
128 North Osceola Avenue
Clearwater, FL 34615
(813) 461-0011

Virginia Krevis, Trade
Specialist
Miami USEAC
Eola Park Centre
200 East Robinson Street
Suite 695
Orlando, FL 32801
(407) 648-6235

Michael E. Higgins, Trade
Specialist
Miami USEAC
Collins Building
Room 366G
107 West Gaines Street
Tallahassee, FL 32304
(904) 488-6469

Georgia
Barbara H. Prieto, Director
120 Barnard Street
Room A-107
Savannah, GA 31401
(912) 652-4204

George T. Norton Jr.,
Director
Suite 310
Plaza Square North
4360 Chamblee-Dunwoody
Road
Atlanta, GA 30341
(404) 452-9101

Hawaii
George Dolan, Director
P.O. Box 50026
400 Ala Moana Boulevard
Room 4106
Honolulu, HI 96850
(808) 541-1782

Idaho
(Portland, Oregon, District)
Steve Thompson, Trade
Specialist
Joe R. Williams Building
Second Floor
700 West State Street
Boise, ID 83720
(208) 334-3857

Illinois
Stanley Bokota, US&FCS
Director
Chicago USEAC
Xerox Center
55 West Monroe Street
Room 2440
Chicago, IL 60603
(312) 353-8040

Oscar L. Dube, Trade
Specialist
Chicago USEAC
Illinois Institute of
Technology
201 East Loop Road
Wheaton, IL 60187
(312) 353-4332

Chicago USEAC
515 North Court Street
P.O. Box 1747
Rockford, IL 61110-0247
(815) 987-4347

Indiana
Andrew Thress, Director
Pennwood One
Suite 106
11405 North Pennsylvania
Street
Carmel, IN 46032
(317) 582-2300

Iowa
Randall J. LaBounty
Room 817
Federal Building
210 Walnut Street
Des Moines, IA 50309
(515) 284-4222

Kansas
(Kansas City, Missouri,
District)
George D. Lavid, Trade
Specialist
151 North Volutsia
Wichita, KS 67214-4695
(316) 269-6160

Kentucky
John Austin, Director
Marmaduke Building
Third Floor
520 South Fourth Street
Louisville, KY 40202
(502) 582-5066

Louisiana
Paul Guidry, Director
Hale Boggs Federal Building
10th Floor
501 Magazine Street
New Orleans, LA 70130
(504) 589-6546

Maine
(Boston, Massachusetts,
District)
Stephen M. Nyulaszi, Trade
Specialist
187 State Street
Augusta, ME 04333
(207) 622-8249

Maryland
Roger Fortner, Director
Baltimore USEAC
World Trade Center
Suite 2432
401 Pratt Street
Baltimore, MD 21202
(410) 962-4539

David Earle, Environmental
Technology Trade Specialist
c/o National Institute of
Standards and Technology
Building 411
Gaithersburg, MD 20899
(301) 975-3904

Massachusetts
Francis J. O'Connor,
Director
164 Northern Avenue
World Trade Center
Suite 307
Boston, MA 02210-2071
(617) 424-5950

Michigan
Dean Peterson, Director
1140 McNamara Building
477 Michigan Avenue
Detroit, MI 48226
(313) 226-3650

Thomas J. Maquire, Trade
Specialist
300 Monroe Avenue, NW
Room 409
Grand Rapids, MI 49503-
2291
(616) 456-2411

Minnesota
Ronald E. Kramer, Director
Room 108
Federal Building
110 South Fourth Street
Minneapolis, MN 55401
(612) 348-1638

Mississippi
Mark E. Spinney, Director
201 West Capitol Street
Suite 310
Jackson, MS 39201-2005
(601) 965-4388

Missouri
Ricardo Villalobos, Director
8182 Maryland Avenue
Suite 303
St. Louis, MO 63105
(314) 425-3302

John Steuber, Director
Room 635
601 East 12th Street
Kansas City, MO 64106
(816) 426-3141

Montana
(Portland, Oregon, District)
Steve Thompson, Trade
Specialist
Joe R. Williams Building
Second Floor
700 West State Street
Boise, ID 83720
(208) 334-3857

Nebraska
(Des Moines, Iowa, District)
Harvey Roffman, Trade
Specialist
11133 O Street
Omaha, NE 68137
(402) 221-3664

Nevada
James Hellwig, Director
1755 East Plumb Lane
Room 152
Reno, NV 89502
(702) 784-5203

New Hampshire
(Boston, Massachusetts,
District)
601 Spaulding Turnpike
Suite 29
Portsmouth, NH 03801-
2833
(603) 334-6074

New Jersey
Rod Stuart, Acting Director
3131 Princeton Pike
Building #6
Suite 100
Trenton, NJ 08648
(609) 989-2100

New Mexico
(Dallas, Texas, District)
Sandy Necessary, Trade
Specialist
c/o New Mexico
Department of Economic
Development
1100 St. Francis Drive
Santa Fe, NM 87503
(505) 827-0350

New York
George Buchanan, Director
Room 1312
Federal Building
111 West Huron Street
Buffalo, NY 14202
(716) 846-4191

Joel Barkan, Director
26 Federal Plaza
Room 3718
New York, NY 10278
(212) 264-0634

William Freiert, Trade
Specialist
111 East Avenue
Suite 220
Rochester, NY 14604
(716) 263-6480

North Carolina
Samuel P. Troy, Director
400 West Market Street
Suite 400
Greensboro, NC 27401
(919) 333-5345

North Dakota
(Minneapolis, Minnesota,
District)
Ronald E. Kramer, Director
Room 188
Federal Building
110 South Fourth Street
Minneapolis, MN 55401
(612) 348-1638

Ohio
Acting Director
Federal Building
Room 9504
550 Main Street
Cincinnati, OH 45202
(513) 684-2944

Toby T. Zettler, Director
Bank One Center
600 Superior Avenue
Suite 700
Cleveland, OH 44114
(216) 522-4750

Oklahoma
Ronald L. Wilson, Director
6601 Broadway Extension
Oklahoma City, OK 73116
(405) 231-5302

Thomas Strauss, Trade
Specialist
440 South Houston Street
Tulsa, OK 74127
(918) 581-7650

Oregon
William Schrage, Director
One World Trade Center
Suite 242
121 SW Salmon
Portland, OR 97204
(503) 326-3001

Pennsylvania
John McCartney, Director
Room 2002
Federal Building
1000 Liberty Avenue
Pittsburgh, PA 15222
(412) 644-2850

Robert E. Kistler, Director
660 American Avenue
Suite 201
King of Prussia, PA 19406
(610) 962-4980

Puerto Rico
(Hato Rey)
J. Enrique Vilella, Director
Room G-55
Federal Building
Chardon Avenue
San Juan, PR 00918
(809) 766-5555

Rhode Island
(Hartford, Connecticut,
District)
Raimond Meerbach, Trade
Specialist
7 Jackson Walkway
Providence, RI 02903
(401) 528-5104

South Carolina
Ann Watts, Director
Strom Thurmond Federal
Building
Suite 172
1835 Assembly Street
Columbia, SC 29201
(803) 765-5345

Charleston Trident Chamber
of Commerce
P.O. Box 975
81 Mary Street
Charleston, SC 29402
(803) 727-4051

South Dakota
(Des Moines, Iowa, District)
200 North Phillips Avenue
Commerce Center
Suite 302
Sioux Falls, SD 57102
(605) 330-4264

Tennessee
Jeanne Marie Russell, Trade
Specialist
Falls Building
Suite 200
22 North Front Street
Memphis, TN 38103
(901) 544-4137

Jim E. Charlet Jr., Director
Parkway Towers
Suite 114
404 James Robertson
Parkway
Nashville, TN 37219-1505
(615) 736-5161

W. Bryan Smith, Trade
Specialist
301 East Church Avenue
Knoxville, TN 37915
(615) 545-4637

Texas
Karen C. Parker, Trade
Specialist
410 East Fifth Street
Suite 414-A
P.O. Box 12728
Austin, TX 78711
(512) 482-5939

James D. Cook, Director
#1 Allen Center
500 Dallas·
Suite 1160
Houston, TX 77002
(713) 229-2578

Donald Schilke, Director
World Trade Center
P.O. Box 58130
2050 North Stemmons
Freeway
Suite 170
Dallas, TX 75242-0787
(214) 767-0542

Utah
Stephen Smoot, Director
324 South State Street
Suite 105
Salt Lake City, UT 84111
(801) 524-5116

Vermont
James Cox
c/o Vermont Department of
Economic Development
109 State Street
Montpelier, VT 05609
(802) 828-4508

Virginia
Philip A. Ouzts, Director
700 Center
704 East Franklin Street
Suite 550
Richmond, VA 23219
(804) 771-2246

Washington
Lisa Kjaer, Director
3131 Elliott Avenue
Suite 290
Seattle, WA 98121
(206) 553-5615

Mark Weaver, Trade
Specialist
320 North Johnson Street
Suite 350
Kennewick, WA 99336
(509) 735-2751

West Virginia
Davis Coale
405 Capitol Street
Suite 807
Charleston, WV 25301
(304) 347-5123

Wisconsin
Johnny E. Brown, Director
517 East Wisconsin Avenue
Room 596
Milwaukee, WI 53202
(414) 297-3473

Wyoming
(Denver, Colorado, District
Office)
Neil Hesse, Director
1625 Broadway
Suite 680
Denver, CO 80202
(303) 844-6622

UNDERSEA RESEARCH

Department of Commerce
National Oceanic and
Atmospheric Administration
1315 East West Highway
Silver Spring, MD 20910
(301) 713-2427

Description: Project grants for fostering undersea research.
Any individual, technical school, or laboratory may apply.
Must have professional interest in marine science
engineering.
$ Given: $16 million est. nationwide FY 95; range: $6,000–
$4 million; average: $1 million
Application Information: Submit standard application form
and formal proposal.
Deadline: None
Contact: Director, Office of Undersea Research, above
address

WEIGHTS AND MEASURES SERVICE

Department of Commerce
National Institute of
Standards and Technology
Gaithersburg, MD 20899
(301) 975-4004

Description: Advisory services, counseling, and training to individuals and corporations for promoting an accurate system of weights and measures.
$ Given: $1.5 million est. nationwide FY 95
Application Information: Send letter to contact.
Deadline: Not available
Contact: Chief, Weights and Measures Program, above address

Minorities

Assistance is widely available from the federal government for minority-owned businesses or for businesses serving minorities or the disadvantaged (the word *minority* in this book refers to people who are either African American, Hispanic, Asian American, American Indian, or female) for the following:

1. *Assistance* to American Indian–owned businesses, employment and training programs, and to programs that promote the business and economic development of Indian reservations
2. *Advisory* services for promoting the development of businesses owned by economically or socially disadvantaged individuals as well as counseling services for businesses owned by women
3. *Assistance* to minority firms and individuals for business expansion and development

You will need to consult the list of addresses in this chapter for your nearest local or regional Bureau of Indian Affairs office, tribal contract office, or Minority Business Development office.

ACQUIRED IMMUNODEFICIENCY SYNDROME (AIDS) ACTIVITY

Department of Health and
Human Services
Grants Management Branch
Procurement and Grants
Office
Centers for Disease Control
(CDC)
Public Health Service
255 East Paces Ferry Road,
NE
Atlanta, GA 30305
(404) 842-6575

Description: Project grants (cooperative agreements) to
businesses (with emphasis on small, minority-, and women-
owned businesses) for promoting HIV prevention programs
of information and education.
$ Given: $233.7 million est. nationwide FY 95; range:
$20,000—$2.8 million; average: $300,000
Application Information: Submit standard application form
(PHS-5161.1) to CDC.
Deadline: Varies, contact headquarters office.
Contact: Clara Jenkins, above address

INDIAN ARTS AND CRAFTS DEVELOPMENT

Department of Interior
Indian Arts and Crafts
Board
Main Interior Building
Room 4004
Washington, DC 20240
(202) 208-3773

Description: Use of property, facilities, and equipment, along
with advisory services and counseling, given for
encouragement and promotion of development of American
Indian arts and craft. Assistance for development of
economic concepts related to native culture. Limited to
Native Americans, Eskimos, and Aleut individuals and
organizations.
$ Given: Not available
Application Information: Submit request to headquarters
office.
Deadline: None
Contact: Meridith Z. Stanton, General Manager, above
address

INDIAN GRANTS—ECONOMIC DEVELOPMENT (INDIAN GRANT PROGRAM)

Department of the Interior
Bureau of Indian Affairs
Office of Trust and
Economic Development
1849 C Street, NW
Room 2528
Washington, DC 20240
(202) 219-5274

Description: Seed money to attract financing from other sources for developing Indian-owned businesses; to improve reservation economics by providing employment and goods services where needed. Grants must be used for development of profit-oriented businesses that will have positive economic impact on Indian reservations. Grant no more than 25 percent of project costs.
$ Given: $3.9 million est. nationwide FY 95; limited to $100,000 for individuals; to $250,000 for tribes; range: $810—$250,000; average: $39,400
Application Information: Application initiated at local agency and submitted on forms approved by the Office of Management and Budget.
Deadline: None
Contact: Nearest bureau office and/or Ernie Clark, above address

Alaska
Juneau Area Office
P.O. Box 25520
Juneau, AK 99802-5520
(907) 586-7177

Field Agencies
Anchorage Agency
1675 C Street
Anchorage, AK 99501
(907) 271-4088

Bethel Agency
P.O. Box 347
Bethel, AK 99559
(907) 543-2727

Fairbanks Agency
101 12th Avenue
Box 16
Fairbanks, AK 99707
(907) 452-0222

Nome Agency
Box 1108
Nome, AK 99762
(907) 443-2284

Arizona
Phoenix Area Office
1 North First Street
Phoenix, AZ 85001
(602) 379-6600

Field Agencies
Chinle Agency
P.O. Box 7-H
Chinle, AZ 86503
(505) 674-5201

Colorado River Agency
Route 1
Box 9-C
Parker, AZ 85344
(602) 669-7111

Fort Apache Agency
P.O. Box 560
Whiteriver, AZ 85941
(602) 338-5383

Fort Defiance Agency
P.O. Box 110
Fort Defiance, AZ 86504
(602) 729-5041

Fort Yuma Agency
P.O. Box 1591
Yuma, AZ 85364
(602) 572-0248

Hopi Agency
P.O. Box 158
Keams Canyon, AZ 86034
(602) 738-2228

Papago Agency
P.O. Box 578
Sells, AZ 85634
(602) 383-3286

Pima Agency
P.O. Box 8
Sacaton, AZ 85634
(602) 562-3326

Salt River Agency
Route 1
Box 117
Scottsdale, AZ 85256
(602) 640-2842

San Carlos Agency
P.O. Box 209
San Carlos, AZ 85550
(602) 475-2321

Truxton Canon Agency
P.O. Box 37
Valentine, AZ 86437
(602) 769-2286

Western Navajo Agency
P.O. Box 127
Tuba City, AZ 86045
(602) 283-4531

Navajo Area Office
P.O. Box 1060
Gallup, NM 87305
(505) 863-8314

California
(See also Arizona, Phoenix
Area Office)

Sacramento Area Office
Federal Office Building
Room W-2550
2800 Cottage Way
Sacramento, CA 95825-1846
(916) 978-4691

Field Agencies
Central California Agency
1800 Tribute Road
Suite J
Sacramento, CA 95815
(916) 978-4337

Hoopa Agency
P.O. Box 367
Hoopa, CA 95546
(916) 625-4285

Palm Springs Area Field
Station
P.O. Box 2245
441 South Calle Encilla
Suite 8
Palm Springs, CA 92262
(916) 322-3086

Southern California Agency
P.O. Box 2900
Suite 201
5750 Division Street
Riverside, CA 92506
(909) 276-6624

Colorado
(See New Mexico,
Albuquerque Area Office)

Field Agencies
Southern Ute Agency
P.O. Box 315
Ignacio, CO 81137
(303) 563-4511

Ute Mountain Ute Agency
Towaoc, CO 81334
(303)565-8471

District of Columbia
Eastern Area Office
3701 North Fairfax Drive
Suite 260-Mailroom
Arlington, VA 22203
(703) 235-3006

Deputy Commissioner of
Indian Affairs
1849 C Street, NW
Washington, DC 20240
(202) 208-5116

Florida
(See District of Columbia,
Eastern Area Office)

Field Agency
Seminole Agency
6075 Stirling Road
Hollywood, FL 33024
(305) 581-7050

Idaho
(See Arizona, Phoenix Area
Office, and Oregon,
Portland Area Office)

Field Agencies
Fort Hall Agency
P.O. Box 220
Fort Hall, ID 83202
(208) 238-2301

Northern Idaho Agency
P.O. Drawer 277
Lapwai, ID 83540
(208) 843-2300

Iowa
(See Minnesota, Minneapolis
Area Office)

Field Agency
Sac and Fox Agency
Tawa, IA 52339
(515) 484-4041

Kansas
(See Oklahoma, Anadarkol
Area Office)

Field Agencies
Haskell Indian Junior
College
Lawrence, KS 66604
(913) 843-1831

Horton Agency
P.O. Box 31
Horton, KS 66439
(913) 486-2161

Louisiana
(See District of Columbia,
Eastern Area Office)

Michigan
(See Minnesota)

Minnesota
Minneapolis Area Office
331 South Second Avenue
Minneapolis, MN 55401-
2241
(612) 373-1000

Field Agencies
Minnesota Agency
Route 3
Box 112
Cass Lake, MN 56633
(218) 335-6913

Red Lake Agency
Red Lake, MN 56671
(218) 679-3361

Mississippi
(See District of Columbia,
Eastern Area Office)

Field Agency
Choctaw Agency
421 Powell
Philadelphia, MS 39350
(601) 656-1523

Montana
Billings Area Office
316 North 26th Street
Billings, MT 59101-1397
(406) 657-6315

Field Agencies
Blackfeet Agency
P.O. Box 880
Browning, MT 59417
(406) 338-7544

Crow Agency
Crow Agency, MT 59022
(406) 638-2672

Flathead Agency
P.O. Box A
Ronan, MT 59855-5555
(406) 675-7200

Fort Belknap Agency
P.O. Box 98
Harlem, MT 59526
(406) 353-2901, ext. 23

Fort Peck Agency
P.O. Box 637
Poplar, MT 59225
(406) 768-5312

Northern Cheyenne Agency
Lame Deer, MT 59043
(406) 477-6242

Nebraska
(See South Dakota,
Aberdeen Area Office)

Field Agency
Winnebago Agency
Route 1
Box 18
Winnebago, NE 68071
(402) 878-2502

Nevada
(See Arizona, Phoenix Area
Office)

Field Agencies
Western Nevada Agency
1677 Hotsprings Road
Carson City, NV 89706
(702) 887-3500

Eastern Nevada Agency
P.O. Box 5400
Elko, NV 89802
(702) 738-0569

New Mexico
(See also Arizona, Navajo
Area Office)

Albuquerque Area Office
615 First Street
P.O. Box 26567
Albuquerque, NM 87125-
6567
(505) 766-2996

Field Agencies
Eastern Navajo Agency
P.O. Box 328
Crownpoint, NM 87313
(505) 786-5228

Jicarilla Agency
P.O. Box 167
Dulce, NM 87528
(505) 759-3951

Mescalero Agency
P.O. Box 189
Mescalero, NM 88340
(505) 671-4421

Northern Pueblos Agency
P.O. Box 4269
Fairview Station
Espanola, NM 87533
(505) 753-1400

Ramah-Navajo Agency
Route 2
Box 14
Ramah, NM 87321
(505) 775-3235

Shiprock Agency
P.O. Box 966
Shiprock, NM 87420
(505) 368-4427

Southern Pueblos Agency
P.O. Box 1667
Albuquerque, NM 87103
(505) 766-3021

Zuni Agency
P.O. Box 369
Zuni, NM 87327
(505) 782-5591

New York
(See District of Columbia,
Eastern Area Office)

Field Agency
New York Field Office
Federal Building, # 523
100 South Clinton Street
Syracuse, NY 13261-7366
(315) 423-5476

North Carolina
(See District of Columbia,
Eastern Area Office)

Field Agency
Cherokee Agency
Cherokee, NC 28719
(704) 497-9131

North Dakota
(See South Dakota,
Aberdeen Area Office)

Field Agencies
Fort Berthold Agency
P.O. Box 370
New Town, ND 58763
(701) 627-4707

Fort Totten Agency
P.O. Box 270
Fort Totten, ND 58335
(701) 766-4545

Standing Rock Agency
P.O. Box E
Fort Yates, ND 58538
(701) 854-3433

Turtle Mountain Agency
P.O. Box 60
Belcourt, ND 58316
(701) 477-3191

Oklahoma
Anadarko Area Office
P.O. Box 368
Anadarko, OK 73005-0368
(405) 247-6673

Muskogee Area Office
Federal Building
U.S. Courthouse
101 North Fifth Street
Muskogee, OK 74401-4898
(918) 687-2296

Field Agencies
Anadarko Agency
P.O. Box 309
Anadarko, OK 73005
(405) 247-6673

Concho Agency
1635 East Highway 66
El Reno, OK 73036-5769
(405) 262-7481

Miami Agency
P.O. Box 391
Miami, OK 74354
(918) 542-3396

Okmulgee Agency
P.O. Box 370
Okmulgee, OK 74447
(918) 756-3950

Osage Agency
Pawhuska, OK 74056
(918) 287-1032

Pawnee Agency
P.O. Box 440
Pawnee, OK 74058-0440
(918) 762-2585

Shawnee Agency
624 West Independence
Suite 114
Shawnee, OK 74801
(405) 273-0317

Tahlequah Agency
P.O. Box 948
Tahlequah, OK 74465
(918) 456-0671

Talihina Agency
Drawer H
Talihina, OK 74571
(918) 567-2207

Wewoka Agency
P.O. Box 1060
Wewoka, OK 74884
(918) 257-6257

Oregon
(See also Arizona, Phoenix
Area Office)

Portland Area Office
911 NE 11th Avenue
Portland, OR 97232-4169
(503) 231-6702

Field Agencies
Umatilla Agency
P.O. Box 520
Pendleton, OR 97801
(503) 276-3811

Warm Springs Agency
P.O. Box 1239
Warm Springs, OR 97761
(503) 553-2411

South Dakota
Aberdeen Area Office
Federal Building
115 Fourth Avenue, SE
Aberdeen, SD 57401-4382
(605) 226-7343

Field Agencies
Cheyenne River Agency
P.O. Box 325
Eagle Butte, SD 57625
(605) 964-6611

Crow Creek Agency
P.O. Box 139
Fort Thompson, SD 57339
(605) 245-2311

Lower Brule Agency
P.O. Box 190
Lower Brule, SD 57548
(605) 473-5512

Pine Ridge Agency
P.O. Box 1203
Pine Ridge, SD 57770
(605) 867-5125

Rosebud Agency
P.O. Box 550
Rosebud, SD 57570
(605) 747-2224

Sisseton Agency
P.O. Box 688
Agency Village, SD 57262
(605) 698-7676

Yankton Agency
P.O. Box 577
Marty, SD 57361
(605) 384-3651

Utah
(See Arizona, Navajo Area
Office and Phoenix Area
Office, and Oregon,
Portland Area Office)

Field Agencies
Uintah and Ouray Agency
P.O. Box 130
Fort Duchesne, UT 84026
(801) 722-2406

Southern Palate Field Station
P.O. Box 720
St. George, UT 84771
(801) 722-2406

Washington
(See Oregon, Portland Area
Office)

Field Agencies
Colville Agency
P.O. Box 111
Nespelem, WA 99155-0111
(509) 634-4901

Spokane Agency
P.O. Box 389
Wellpinit, WA 99040
(509) 258-4561

Puget Sound Agency
Federal Building
3006 Colby Avenue
Everett, WA 98201
(206) 258-2651

Yakima Agency
P.O. Box 632
Toppenish, WA 98948
(509) 865-2255

Wisconsin
(See Minnesota, Minneapolis
Area Office)

Field Agency
Great Lakes Agency
615 West Main
Ashland, WI 54806
(715) 682-4527

Wyoming
(See Montana, Billings Area
Office)

Field Agency
Wind River Agency
Fort Washakie, WY 82514
(307) 332-7810

INDIAN LOANS—ECONOMIC DEVELOPMENT (INDIAN CREDIT PROGRAM)

Department of the Interior
Bureau of Indian Affairs
Office of Trust and
Economic Development
1849 C Street, NW
Room 2528
Washington, DC 20240
(202) 219-5274

Description: Assistance given to Indians, Alaska natives, tribes, and Indian organizations to obtain financing from private and governmental sources for promoting economic development of federal Indian reservations. Funds must be unavailable from other sources at reasonable terms and conditions. Funds cannot be used for speculation.
$ Given: $46.9 million in guaranteed loans est. nationwide FY 95; range: $1,000 - over $1 million; average: $100,000
Application Information: Application initiated at local agency level and submitted on forms approved by the Deputy to Assistant Secretary, Indian Affairs.
Deadline: None
Contact: Nearest Bureau Office or Jerry Folsom, above address

Alaska
Juneau Area Office
P.O. Box 25520
Juneau, AK 99802-5520
(907) 586-7177

Field Agencies
Anchorage Agency
1675 C Street
Anchorage, AK 99501
(907) 271-4088

Bethel Agency
P.O. Box 347
Bethel, AK 99559
(907) 543-2727

Fairbanks Agency
101 12th Avenue
Box 16
Fairbanks, AK 99707
(907) 452-0222

Nome Agency
Box 1108
Nome, AK 99762
(907) 443-2284

Arizona
Phoenix Area Office
1 North First Street
Phoenix, AZ 85001
(602) 379-6600

Field Agencies
Chinle Agency
P.O. Box 7-H
Chinle, AZ 86503
(505) 674-5201

Colorado River Agency
Route 1
Box 9-C
Parker, AZ 85344
(602) 669-7111

Fort Apache Agency
P.O. Box 560
Whiteriver, AZ 85941
(602) 338-5383

Fort Defiance Agency
P.O. Box 110
Fort Defiance, AZ 86504
(602) 729-5041

Fort Yuma Agency
P.O. Box 1591
Yuma, AZ 85364
(602) 572-0248

Hopi Agency
P.O. Box 158
Keams Canyon, AZ 86034
(602) 738-2228

Papago Agency
P.O. Box 578
Sells, AZ 85634
(602) 383-3286

Pima Agency
P.O. Box 8
Sacaton, AZ 85634
(602) 562-3326

Salt River Agency
Route 1
Box 117
Scottsdale, AZ 85256
(602) 640-2842

San Carlos Agency
P.O. Box 209
San Carlos, AZ 85550
(602) 475-2321

Truxton Canon Agency
P.O. Box 37
Valentine, AZ 86437
(602) 769-2286

Western Navajo Agency
P.O. Box 127
Tuba City, AZ 86045
(602) 283-4531

Navajo Area Office
P.O. Box 1060
Gallup, NM 87305
(505) 863-8314

California
(See also Arizona, Phoenix
Area Office)

Sacramento Area Office
Federal Office Building
Room W-2550
2800 Cottage Way
Sacramento, CA 95825-
1846
(916) 978-4691

Field Agencies
Central California Agency
1800 Tribute Road
Suite J
Sacramento, CA 95815
(916) 978-4337

Hoopa Agency
P.O. Box 367
Hoopa, CA 95546
(916) 625-4285

Palm Springs Area Field
Station
P.O. Box 2245
441 South Calle Encilla
Suite 8
Palm Springs, CA 92262
(916) 322-3086

Southern California Agency
P.O. Box 2900
Suite 201
5750 Division Street
Riverside, CA 92506
(909) 276-6624

Colorado
(See New Mexico,
Albuquerque Area Office)

Field Agencies
Southern Ute Agency
P.O. Box 315
Ignacio, CO 81137
(303) 563-4511

Ute Mountain Ute Agency
Towaoc, CO 81334
(303)565-8471

District of Columbia
Eastern Area Office
3701 North Fairfax Drive
Suite 260-Mailroom
Arlington, VA 22203
(703) 235-3006

Deputy Commissioner of
Indian Affairs
1849 C Street, NW
Washington, DC 20240
(202) 208-5116

Florida
(See District of Columbia,
Eastern Area Office)

Field Agency
Seminole Agency
6075 Stirling Road
Hollywood, FL 33024
(305) 581-7050

Idaho
(See Arizona, Phoenix Area
Office, and Oregon,
Portland Area Office)

Field Agencies
Fort Hall Agency
P.O. Box 220
Fort Hall, ID 83202
(208) 238-2301

Northern Idaho Agency
P.O. Drawer 277
Lapwai, ID 83540
(208) 843-2300

Iowa
(See Minnesota, Minneapolis
Area Office)

Field Agency
Sac and Fox Agency
Tawa, IA 52339
(515) 484-4041

Kansas
(See Oklahoma, Anadarkol
Area Office)

Field Agencies
Haskell Indian Junior
College
Lawrence, KS 66604
(913) 843-1831

Horton Agency
P.O. Box 31
Horton, KS 66439
(913) 486-2161

Louisiana
(See District of Columbia,
Eastern Area Office)

Michigan
(See Minnesota)

Minnesota
Minneapolis Area Office
331 South Second Avenue
Minneapolis, MN 55401-
2241
(612) 373-1000

Field Agencies
Minnesota Agency
Route 3
Box 112
Cass Lake, MN 56633
(218) 335-6913

Red Lake Agency
Red Lake, MN 56671
(218) 679-3361

Mississippi
(See District of Columbia,
Eastern Area Office)

Field Agency
Choctaw Agency
421 Powell
Philadelphia, MS 39350
(601) 656-1523

Montana
Billings Area Office
316 North 26th Street
Billings, MT 59101-1397
(406) 657-6315

Field Agencies
Blackfeet Agency
P.O. Box 880
Browning, MT 59417
(406) 338-7544

Crow Agency
Crow Agency, MT 59022
(406) 638-2672

Flathead Agency
P.O. Box A
Ronan, MT 59855-5555
(406) 675-7200

Fort Belknap Agency
P.O. Box 98
Harlem, MT 59526
(406) 353-2901 x23

Fort Peck Agency
P.O. Box 637
Poplar, MT 59225
(406) 768-5312

Northern Cheyenne Agency
Lame Deer, MT 59043
(406) 477-6242

Nebraska
(See South Dakota,
Aberdeen Area Office)

Field Agency
Winnebago Agency
Route 1
Box 18
Winnebago, NE 68071
(402) 878-2502

Nevada
(See Arizona, Phoenix Area
Office)

Field Agencies
Western Nevada Agency
1677 Hotsprings Road
Carson City, NV 89706
(702) 887-3500

Eastern Nevada Agency
P.O. Box 5400
Elko, NV 89802
(702) 738-0569

New Mexico
(See also Arizona, Navajo
Area Office)

Albuquerque Area Office
615 First Street
P.O. Box 26567
Albuquerque, NM 87125-
6567

Field Agencies
Eastern Navajo Agency
P.O. Box 328
Crownpoint, NM 87313
(505) 786-5228

Jicarilla Agency
P.O. Box 167
Dulce, NM 87528
(505) 759-3951

Mescalero Agency
P.O. Box 189
Mescalero, NM 88340
(505) 671-4421

Northern Pueblos Agency
P.O. Box 4269
Fairview Station
Espanola, NM 87533
(505) 753-1400

Ramah-Navajo Agency
Route 2
Box 14
Ramah, NM 87321
(505) 775-3235

Shiprock Agency
P.O. Box 966
Shiprock, NM 87420
(505) 368-4427

Southern Pueblos Agency
P.O. Box 1667
Albuquerque, NM 87103
(505) 766-3021

Zuni Agency
P.O. Box 369
Zuni, NM 87327
(505) 782-5591

New York
(See District of Columbia,
Eastern Area Office)

Field Agency
New York Field Office
Federal Building, # 523
100 South Clinton Street
Syracuse, NY 13261-7366
(315) 423-5476

North Carolina
(See District of Columbia,
Eastern Area Office)

Field Agency
Cherokee Agency
Cherokee, NC 28719
(704) 497-9131

North Dakota
(See South Dakota,
Aberdeen Area Office)

Field Agencies
Fort Berthold Agency
P.O. Box 370
New Town, ND 58763
(701) 627-4707

Fort Totten Agency
P.O. Box 270
Fort Totten, ND 58335
(701) 766-4545

Standing Rock Agency
P.O. Box E
Fort Yates, ND 58538
(701) 854-3433

Turtle Mountain Agency
P.O. Box 60
Belcourt, ND 58316
(701) 477-3191

Oklahoma
Anadarko Area Office
P.O. Box 368
Anadarko, OK 73005-0368
(405) 247-6673

Muskogee Area Office
Federal Building
U.S. Courthouse
101 North Fifth Street
Muskogee, OK 74401-4898
(918) 687-2296

Field Agencies
Anadarko Agency
P.O. Box 309
Anadarko, OK 73005
(405) 247-6673

Concho Agency
1635 East Highway 66
El Reno, OK 73036-5769
(405) 262-7481

Miami Agency
P.O. Box 391
Miami, OK 74354
(918) 542-3396

Okmulgee Agency
P.O. Box 370
Okmulgee, OK 74447
(918) 756-3950

Osage Agency
Pawhuska, OK 74056
(918) 287-1032

Pawnee Agency
P.O. Box 440
Pawnee, OK 74058-0440
(918) 762-2585

Shawnee Agency
624 West Independence
Suite 114
Shawnee, OK 74801
(405) 273-0317

Tahlequah Agency
P.O. Box 948
Tahlequah, OK 74465
(918) 456-0671

Talihina Agency
Drawer H
Talihina, OK 74571
(918) 567-2207

Wewoka Agency
P.O. Box 1060
Wewoka, OK 74884
(918) 257-6257

Oregon
(See also Arizona, Phoenix
Area Office)

Portland Area Office
911 NE 11th Avenue
Portland, OR 97232-4169
(503) 231-6702

Field Agencies
Umatilla Agency
P.O. Box 520
Pendleton, OR 97801
(503) 276-3811

Warm Springs Agency
P.O. Box 1239
Warm Springs, OR 97761
(503) 553-2411

South Dakota
Aberdeen Area Office
Federal Building
115 Fourth Avenue, SE
Aberdeen, SD 57401-4382
(605) 226-7343

Field Agencies
Cheyenne River Agency
P.O. Box 325
Eagle Butte, SD 57625
(605) 964-6611

Crow Creek Agency
P.O. Box 139
Fort Thompson, SD 57339
(605) 245-2311

Lower Brule Agency
P.O. Box 190
Lower Brule, SD 57548
(605) 473-5512

Pine Ridge Agency
P.O. Box 1203
Pine Ridge, SD 57770
(605) 867-5125

Rosebud Agency
P.O. Box 550
Rosebud, SD 57570
(605) 747-2224

Sisseton Agency
P.O. Box 688
Agency Village, SD 57262
(605) 698-7676

Yankton Agency
P.O. Box 577
Marty, SD 57361
(605) 384-3651

Utah
(See Arizona, Navajo Area
Office and Phoenix Area
Office, and Oregon,
Portland Area Office)

Field Agencies
Uintah and Ouray Agency
P.O. Box 130
Fort Duchesne, UT 84026
(801) 722-2406

Southern Palate Field Station
P.O. Box 720
St. George, UT 84771
(801) 722-2406

Washington
(See Oregon, Portland Area
Office)

Field Agencies
Colville Agency
P.O. Box 111
Nespelem, WA 99155-0111
(509) 634-4901

Spokane Agency
P.O. Box 389
Wellpinit, WA 99040
(509) 258-4561

Puget Sound Agency
Federal Building
3006 Colby Avenue
Everett, WA 98201
(206) 258-2651

Yakima Agency
P.O. Box 632
Toppenish, WA 98948
(509) 865-2255

Wisconsin
(See Minnesota, Minneapolis
Area Office)

Field Agency
Great Lakes Agency
615 West Main
Ashland, WI 54806
(715) 682-4527

Wyoming
(See Montana, Billings Area
Office)

Field Agency
Wind River Agency
Fort Washakie, WY 82514
(307) 332-7810

MENTAL HEALTH SERVICES FOR CUBAN ENTRANTS

Department of Health and
Human Services
Refugee Mental Health
Branch
Substance Abuse and Mental
Health Services
Administration
Public Health Service
Parklawn Building
Room 18-49
5600 Fishers Lane
Rockville, MD 20857
(301) 443-2130

Description: Project grants (cooperative agreements) to for-profit organizations for providing complete range of treatment to mentally ill and developmentally disabled Cuban entrants currently in federal custody. Applicant must demonstrate qualifications and work closely with federal officials.
$ Given: $2.4 million est. nationwide FY 95.
Application Information: Submit standard application to Grants Management Branch above address.
Deadline: None
Contact: Neal Brown, M.P.A., above address

MINORITY BUSINESS DEVELOPMENT

**Small Business
Administration (SBA)**
Office of Minority Small
Business Development
Administration
409 Third Street, SW
Washington, DC 20416
(202) 205-6410

Description: Provision of specialized services to individuals who are both socially and economically disadvantaged for fostering business ownership and competitive viability. Limited to small businesses with at least 51 percent ownership by an American citizen who is disadvantaged but demonstrates potential for success.
$ Given: Not available
Application Information: Submit written application to SBA district offices. Assistance given in completing forms.
Deadline: None
Contact: Nearest field office

Alabama
Regional Office
1375 Peachtree Street, NE
Fifth Floor
Atlanta, GA 30367-8102
(404) 347-2797

District Office
Birmingham District Office
2121 Eighth Avenue North
Suite 200
Birmingham, AL 35203-
2398
(205) 731-1344

Alaska
Regional Office
2615 Fourth Avenue
Room 440
Seattle, WA 98121-1273
(206) 442-5676

District Office
Anchorage District Office
222 West Eighth Avenue
Room A36
Anchorage, AK 99513-7559
(907) 271-4022

Arizona
Regional Office
71 Stevenson Street
20th Floor
San Francisco, CA 94105-
2939
(415) 744-6402

District Office
Phoenix District Office
2828 North Central Avenue
Suite 800
Phoenix, AZ 85004-1025
(602) 640-2316

Arkansas
Regional Office
8625 King George Drive
Building C
Dallas, TX 75235-3391
(214) 767-7633

District Office
Little Rock District Office
2120 Riverfront Drive
Suite 100
Little Rock, AR 72202
(501) 324-5871

California
Regional Office
71 Stevenson Street
20th Floor
San Francisco, CA 94105-
2939
(415) 744-6402

District Offices
Fresno District Office
2719 North Air Fresno
Drive
Suite 107
Fresno, CA 93727-1547
(209) 487-5189

Los Angeles District Office
330 North Brand Boulevard
Suite 1200
Glendale, CA 91203-2304
(818) 552-3210

San Diego District Office
880 Front Street
Room 4-S-29
San Diego, CA 92188-0270
(619) 557-7252

San Francisco District Office
211 Main Street
Fourth Floor
San Francisco, CA 94105-
1988
(415) 744-6820

Santa Ana District Office
901 West Civic Center Drive
Suite 160
Santa Ana, CA 92703-2352
(714) 836-2494

Colorado
Regional Office
633 17th Street
Seventh Floor
Denver, CO 80202
(303) 294-7186

District Office
Denver District Office
721 19th Street
Room 426
Denver, CO 80202-2599
(303) 844-3984

Connecticut
Regional Office
155 Federal Street
Ninth Floor
Boston, MA 02110
(617) 451-2023

District Office
Hartford District Office
Federal Building
Second Floor
330 Main Street
Hartford, CT 06106
(203) 240-4700

Delaware
Regional Office
475 Allendale Road
Suite 201
King of Prussia, PA 19406
(215) 962-3700

District of Columbia
Regional Office
475 Allendale Road
Suite 201
King of Prussia, PA 19406
(215) 962-3700

District Office
Washington District Office
1110 Vermont Avenue, NW
Suite 900
Washington, DC 20036
(202) 606-4000

Florida
Regional Office
1375 Peachtree Street, NE
Fifth Floor
Atlanta, GA 30367-8102
(404) 347-2797

District Offices
Jacksonville District Office
7825 Baymeadows Way
Suite 100-B
Jacksonville, FL 32256-7504
(904) 443-1900

Miami District Office
1320 South Dixie Highway
Suite 501
Coral Gables, FL 33146-
2911
(305) 536-5521

Georgia
Regional Office
1375 Peachtree Street, NE
Fifth Floor
Atlanta, GA 30367-8102
(404) 347-2797

District Office
Atlanta District Office
1720 Peachtree Road, NW
Sixth Floor
Atlanta, GA 30309
(404) 347-4749

Hawaii
Regional Office
71 Stevenson Street
20th Floor
San Francisco, CA 94105-
2939
(415) 744-6402

District Office
Honolulu District Office
300 Ala Moana Boulevard
Room 2213
Honolulu, HI 96850-4981
(808) 541-2990

Idaho
Regional Office
2615 Fourth Avenue
Room 440
Seattle, WA 98121
(206) 442-5676

District Office
Boise District Office
1020 Main Street
Suite 290
Boise, ID 83702-5745
(208) 334-1696

Illinois
Regional Office
Federal Building
Room 1975
300 South Riverside Plaza
Chicago, IL 60606-6611
(312) 353-5000

District Office
Chicago District Office
500 West Madison Street
Room 1250
Chicago, IL 60661-2511
(312) 353-4528

Indiana
Regional Office
Federal Building
Room 1975
300 South Riverside Plaza
Chicago, IL 60606-6611
(312) 353-5000

District Office
Indianapolis District Office
429 North Pennsylvania
Street
Suite 100
Indianapolis, IN 46204-
1873
(317) 226-7272

Iowa
Regional Office
911 Walnut Street
13th Floor
Kansas City, MO 64106
(816) 426-3608

District Offices
Des Moines District Office
New Federal Building
Room 749
210 Walnut Street
Des Moines, IA 50309
(515) 284-4422

Cedar Rapids District Office
215 Fourth Avenue, SE
Suite 200
Cedar Rapids, IA 52401-
1806
(319) 362-6405

Kansas
Regional Office
911 Walnut Street
13th Floor
Kansas City, MO 64106
(816) 426-3608

District Offices
Kansas City District Office
323 West Eighth Street
Suite 501
Kansas City, MO 64105
(816) 374-6708

Wichita District Office
100 East English Street
Suite 510
Wichita, KS 67202
(316) 269-6016

Kentucky
Regional Office
1375 Peachtree Street, NE
Fifth Floor
Atlanta, GA 30367-8102
(404) 347-2797

District Office
Louisville District Office
Federal Building
Room 188
600 Martin Luther King Jr.
Place
Louisville, KY 40202
(502) 582-5971

Louisiana
Regional Office
8625 King George Drive
Building C
Dallas, TX 75235-3391
(214) 767-7643

District Office
New Orleans District Office
365 Canal Street
Suite 3100
New Orleans, LA 70130
(504) 589-6685

Maine
Regional Office
155 Federal Street
Ninth Floor
Boston, MA 02110
(617) 451-2023

District Office
Augusta District Office
Federal Building
Room 512
40 Western Avenue
Augusta, ME 04330
(207) 622-8378

Maryland
Regional Office
475 Allendale Road
Suite 201
King of Prussia, PA 19406
(215) 962-3700

District Office
Baltimore District Office
10 South Howard Street
Suite 6220
Baltimore, MD 21201-2565
(410) 962-4392

Massachusetts
Regional Office
155 Federal Street
Ninth Floor
Boston, MA 02110
(617) 451-2023

District Office
Boston District Office
10 Causeway Street
Room 265
Boston, MA 02222-1093
(617) 565-5590

Michigan
Regional Office
Federal Building
Room 1975
300 South Riverside Plaza
Chicago, IL 60606-6611
(312) 353-0359

District Office
Detroit District Office
477 Michigan Avenue
Room 515
Detroit, MI 48226
(313) 226-6075

Minnesota
Regional Office
Federal Building
Room 1975
300 South Riverside Plaza
Chicago, IL 60606-6611
(312) 353-0359

District Office
Minneapolis District Office
100 North Sixth Street
Suite 610
Minneapolis, MN 55403-
1563
(612) 370-2324

Mississippi
Regional Office
1375 Peachtree Street, NE
Fifth Floor
Atlanta, GA 30367-8102
(404) 347-2797

District Office
Jackson District Office
100 West Capitol Street
Suite 400
Jackson, MS 39201
(601) 965-4378

Missouri
Regional Office
911 Walnut Street
13th Floor
Kansas City, MO 64106
(816) 426-3608

District Offices
St. Louis District Office
815 Olive Street
Room 242
St. Louis, MO 63101
(314) 539-6600

Kansas City District Office
323 West Eighth Street
Suite 501
Kansas City, MO 64105
(816) 374-6762

Montana
Regional Office
999 18th Street
Suite 701
Denver, CO 80202
(303) 294-7001

District Office
Helena District Office
301 South Park Avenue
Room 334
Helena, MT 59626
(406) 449-5381

Nebraska
Regional Office
911 Walnut Street
13th Floor
Kansas City, MO 64106
(816) 426-3608

District Office
Omaha District Office
11145 Mill Valley Road
Omaha, NE 68154
(402) 221-4691

Nevada
Regional Office
71 Stevenson Street
20th Floor
San Francisco, CA 94105-
2939
(415) 744-6402

District Office
Las Vegas District Office
301 East Stewart Street
Room 301
Las Vegas, NY 89125-2527
(702) 388-6611

New Hampshire
Regional Office
155 Federal Street
Ninth Floor
Boston, MA 02110
(617) 451-2023

District Office
Concord District Office
143 North Main Street
Suite 202
Concord, NH 03301-1257
(603) 225-1400

New Jersey
Regional Office
26 Federal Plaza
Suite 31-08
New York, NY 10278
(212) 264-1450

District Office
Newark District Office
Military Park Building
Fourth Floor
60 Park Place
Newark, NJ 07102
(201) 645-2434

New Mexico
Regional Office
8625 King George Drive
Building C
Dallas, TX 75235-3391
(214) 767-7643

District Office
Albuquerque District Office
625 Silver Avenue, SW
Suite 320
Albuquerque, NM 87102
(505) 766-1870

New York
Regional Office
26 Federal Plaza
Suite 31-08
New York, NY 10278
(212) 264-7772

District Offices
Buffalo District Office
Federal Building
Room 1311
111 West Huron Street
Buffalo, NY 14202
(716) 846-4301

New York District Office
26 Federal Plaza
Room 3100
New York, NY 10278
(212) 264-2454

Syracuse District Office
100 South Clinton Street
Room 1071
Syracuse, NY 13260
(315) 423-5383

North Carolina
Regional Office
1375 Peachtree Street, NE
Fifth Floor
Atlanta, GA 30367-8102
(404) 347-2797

District Office
Charlotte District Office
200 North College Street
Suite A2015
Charlotte, NC 28202
(704) 344-6563

North Dakota
Regional Office
999 18th Street
Suite 701
Denver, CO 80202
(303) 294-7001

District Office
Federal Building
Suite 219
657 Second Avenue North
Fargo, ND 58108-3086
(701) 239-5131

Ohio
Regional Office
Federal Building
Room 1975
300 South Riverside Plaza
Chicago, IL 60606-6611
(312) 353-0359

District Offices
Cleveland District Office
1111 Superior Avenue
Suite 360
Cleveland, OH 44144-2507
(216) 522-4180

Columbus District Office
2 Nationwide Plaza
Suite 1400
Columbus, OH 43215-2592
(614) 469-6860

Oklahoma
Regional Office
8625 King George Drive
Building C
Dallas, TX 75235-3391
(214) 767-7643

District Office
Oklahoma City District Office
200 NW Fifth Street
Suite 670
Oklahoma City, OK 73102
(405) 231-5521

Oregon
Regional Office
2615 Fourth Avenue
Room 440
Seattle, WA 98121
(206) 442-5676

District Office
Portland District Office
222 SW Columbia Street
Suite 500
Portland, OR 97201-6695
(503) 326-2682

Pacific Islands
Regional Office
71 Stevenson Street
20th Floor
San Francisco, CA 94105-
2939
(415) 744-6402

District Office
Agana Branch Office
Pacific Daily News Building
Room 508
238 Archbishop F. C. Flores
Street
Agana, GM 69610
(671) 472-7277

Pennsylvania
Regional Office
475 Allendale Road
Suite 201
King of Prussia, PA 19406
(215) 962-3700

District Office
Pittsburgh District Office
960 Penn Avenue
Fifth Floor
Pittsburgh, PA 15222
(412) 644-2780

Puerto Rico
Regional Office
26 Federal Plaza
Room 31-08
New York, NY 10278
(212) 264-7772

District Office
Federico Degetau Federal
Building
Room 691
Carlos Chardon Avenue
Hato Rey, PR 00918
(809) 766-5572

Rhode Island
Regional Office
155 Federal Street
Ninth Floor
Boston, MA 02110
(617) 451-2023

District Office
Providence District Office
380 Westminster Mall
Fifth Floor
Providence, RI 02903
(401) 528-4561

South Carolina
Regional Office
1375 Peachtree Street NE
Fifth Floor
Atlanta, GA 30367-8102
(404) 347-2797

District Office
Columbia District Office
1835 Assembly Street
Room 358
Columbia, SC 29201
(803) 765-5377

South Dakota
Regional Office
999 18th Street
Suite 701
Denver, CO 80202
(303) 294-7001

District Office
Sioux Falls District Office
110 South Phillips Avenue
Suite 200
Sioux Falls, SD 57102-1109
(605) 330-4231

Tennessee
Regional Office
1375 Peachtree Street, NE
Fifth Floor
Atlanta, GA 30367-8102
(404) 347-2797

District Office
Nashville District Office
50 Vantage Way
Suite 201
Nashville, TN 37338-1500
(615) 736-5881

Texas
Regional Office
8625 King George Drive
Building C
Dallas, TX 75235-3391
(214) 767-7643

District Offices
Dallas District Office
4300 Amon Center Building
Suite 114
Fort Worth, TX 76155
(817) 885-6500

El Paso District Office
10737 Gateway West
Suite 320
El Paso, TX 79935
(915) 540-5676

Houston District Office
9301 Southwest Freeway
Suite 550
Houston, TX 77074-1591
(713) 773-6500

Lower Rio Grande Valley
District Office
222 East Van Buren Street
Room 500
Harlingen, TX 78550
(210) 427-6855

Lubbock District Office
1611 10th Street
Suite 200
Lubbock, TX 79401-2693
(806) 743-7462

San Antonio District Office
727 East Durango
Fifth Floor
San Antonio, TX 78206
(210) 229-5900

Utah
Regional Office
999 18th Street
Suite 701
Denver, CO 80202
(303) 294-7001

District Office
Salt Lake City District
Office
Federal Building
Room 2237
125 South State Street
Salt Lake City, UT 84138-
1195
(801) 524-5804

Vermont
Regional Office
155 Federal Street
Ninth Floor
Boston, MA 02110
(617) 451-2023

District Office
Montpelier District Office
Federal Building
Room 205
87 State Street
Montpelier, VT 05602
(802) 828-4422

Virginia
Regional Office
475 Allendale Road
Suite 201
King of Prussia, PA 19406
(215) 962-3700

District Office
Richmond District Office
Federal Building
Room 3015
400 North Eighth Street
Richmond, VA 23240
(804) 771-2400

Virgin Islands
Regional Office
26 Federal Plaza
Room 31-08
New York, NY 10278
(212) 264-7772

District Offices
Federico Degetau Federal
Building
Room 691
Carlos Chardon Avenue
Hato Rey, PR 00918
(809) 766-5572

St. Croix Post-of-Duty
3013 Golden Rock
Suite 165
St. Croix, VI 00820
(809) 778-5380

St. Thomas Post-of-Duty
3800 Crown Bay
St. Thomas, VI 00802
(809) 774-8530

Washington
Regional Office
2615 Fourth Avenue
Room 440
Seattle, WA 98121
(206) 442-5676

District Offices
Spokane District Office
West 601 First Avenue
10th Floor East
Spokane, WA 99204-0317
(509) 353-2800

Seattle District Office
915 Second Avenue
Room 1792
Seattle, WA 98174-1088
(206) 220-6520

West Virginia
Regional Office
475 Allendale Road
Suite 201
King of Prussia, PA 19406
(215) 962-3700

District Office
Clarksburg District Office
168 West Main Street
Fifth Floor
Clarksburg, WV 26301
(304) 623-5631

Wisconsin
Regional Office
Federal Building
Room 1975
300 South Riverside Plaza
Chicago, IL 60606-6611

District Office
Madison District Office
212 East Washington
Avenue
Room 213
Madison, WI 53703
(608) 264-5261

Wyoming
Regional Office
999 18th Street
Suite 701
Denver, CO 80202
(303) 294-7001

District Office
Casper District Office
Federal Building
Room 4001
100 East B Street
Casper, WY 82602-2839
(307) 261-5761

MINORITY BUSINESS DEVELOPMENT CENTERS

Department of Commerce
Minority Business Agency
14th Street and Constitution
Avenue, NW
Washington, DC 20230
(202) 482-5770

Description: Project grants for providing business-development services for a minimal fee to minority firms and individuals interested in entering, expanding, or improving their efforts in the marketplace.
$ Given: $23.9 million est. nationwide FY 95; range: $165,000—$1.0 million; average: $218,000
Application Information: Submit standard application forms as furnished by the federal agency.
Deadline: See Federal Register and Commerce Business Daily.
Contact: C. Howie Hodges, Assistant Director, Program Development, and/or nearest Minority Business Development Agency Regional Office

Alabama
Robert M. Henderson,
Acting Director
401 West Peachtree Street,
NW
Room 1715
Atlanta, GA 30308-3516
(404) 730-3300

Alaska
Melda Cabrera, Director
221 Main Street
Room 1280
San Francisco, CA 94105
(415) 744-3001

Arkansas
Bobby T. Jefferson, Acting
Director
1100 Commerce Street
Room 7B23
Dallas, TX 75242
(214) 767-8001

Arizona
Melda Cabrera, Director
221 Main Street
Room 1280
San Francisco, CA 94105
(415) 744-3001

American Samoa
Melda Cabrera, Director
221 Main Street
Room 1280
San Francisco, CA 94105
(415) 744-3001

California
Melda Cabrera, Director
221 Main Street
Room 1280
San Francisco, CA 94105
(415) 744-3001

Rudy Guerra, District
Officer
977 North Broadway
Suite 201
Los Angeles, CA 90012
(213) 894-7157

Colorado
Bobby T. Jefferson, Acting
Director
1100 Commerce Street
Room 7B23
Dallas, TX 75242
(214) 767-8001

Connecticut
Ronald P. Isler, Director
26 Federal Plaza
Room 3720
New York, NY 10278
(212) 264-3262

District of Columbia
Ronald P. Isler, Director
26 Federal Plaza
Room 3720
New York, NY 10278
(212) 264-3262

Delaware
Ronald P. Isler, Director
26 Federal Plaza
Room 3720
New York, NY 10278
(212) 264-3262

Florida
Robert M. Henderson,
Acting Director
401 West Peachtree Street,
NW
Room 1715
Atlanta, GA 30308-3516
(404) 730-3300

Rudy Suarez, District
Officer
Federal Building
Room 928
51 SW First Avenue
P.O. Box 25
Miami, FL 33130
(305) 536-5054

Georgia
Robert M. Henderson,
Acting Director
401 West Peachtree Street,
NW
Room 1715
Atlanta, GA 30308-3516
(404) 730-3300

Guam
Melda Cabrera, Director
221 Main Street
Room 1280
San Francisco, CA 94105
(415) 744-3001

Hawaii
Melda Cabrera, Director
221 Main Street
Room 1280
San Francisco, CA 94105
(415) 744-3001

Idaho
Melda Cabrera, Director
221 Main Street
Room 1280
San Francisco, CA 94105
(415) 744-3001

Illinois
David Vega, Director
55 East Monroe Street
Suite 1440
Chicago, IL 60603
(312) 353-0182

Indiana
David Vega, Director
55 East Monroe Street
Suite 1440
Chicago, IL 60603
(312) 353-0182

Iowa
David Vega, Director
55 East Monroe Street
Suite 1440
Chicago, IL 60603
(312) 353-0182

Kansas
David Vega, Director
55 East Monroe Street
Suite 1440
Chicago, IL 60603
(312) 353-0182

Kentucky
Robert M. Henderson,
Acting Director
401 West Peachtree Street,
NW
Room 1715
Atlanta, GA 30308-3516
(404) 730-3300

Louisiana
Bobby T. Jefferson, Acting
Director
1100 Commerce Street
Room 7B23
Dallas, TX 75242
(214) 767-8001

Maine
Ronald P. Isler, Director
26 Federal Plaza
Room 3720
New York, NY 10278
(212) 264-3262

Maryland
Ronald P. Isler, Director
26 Federal Plaza
Room 3720
New York, NY 10278
(212) 264-3262

Massachusetts
Ronald P. Isler, Director
26 Federal Plaza
Room 3720
New York, NY 10278
(212) 264-3262

R. K. Schwartz, District
Officer
10 Causeway Street
Room 418
Boston, MA 02222-1041
(617) 565-6850

Michigan
David Vega, Director
55 East Monroe Street
Suite 1440
Chicago, IL 60603
(312) 353-0182

Minnesota
David Vega, Director
55 East Monroe Street
Suite 1440
Chicago, IL 60603
(312) 353-0182

Mississippi
Robert M. Henderson,
Acting Director
401 West Peachtree Street,
NW
Room 1715
Atlanta, GA 30308-3516
(404) 730-3300

Missouri
David Vega, Director
55 East Monroe Street
Suite 1440
Chicago, IL 60603
(312) 353-0182

Montana
Bobby T. Jefferson, Acting
Director
1100 Commerce Street
Room 7B23
Dallas, TX 75242
(214) 767-8001

Nebraska
David Vega, Director
55 East Monroe Street
Suite 1440
Chicago, IL 60603
(312) 353-0182

Nevada
Melda Cabrera, Director
221 Main Street
Room 1280
San Francisco, CA 94105
(415) 744-3001

New Hampshire
Ronald P. Isler, Director
26 Federal Plaza
Room 3720
New York, NY 10278
(212) 264-3262

New Jersey
Ronald P. Isler, Director
26 Federal Plaza
Room 3720
New York, NY 10278
(212) 264-3262

New Mexico
Bobby T. Jefferson, Acting
Director
1100 Commerce Street
Room 7B23
Dallas, TX 75242
(214) 767-8001

New York
Ronald P. Isler, Director
26 Federal Plaza
Room 3720
New York, NY 10278
(212) 264-3262

North Carolina
Robert M. Henderson,
Acting Director
401 West Peachtree Street,
NW
Room 1715
Atlanta, GA 30308-3516
(404) 730-3300

North Dakota
Bobby T. Jefferson, Acting
Director
1100 Commerce Street
Room 7B23
Dallas, TX 75242
(214) 767-8001

Ohio
David Vega, Director
55 East Monroe Street
Suite 1440
Chicago, IL 60603
(312) 353-0182

Oklahoma
Bobby T. Jefferson, Acting
Director
1100 Commerce Street
Room 7B23
Dallas, TX 75242
(214) 767-8001

Oregon
Melda Cabrera, Director
221 Main Street
Room 1280
San Francisco, CA 94105
(415) 744-3001

Pennsylvania
Ronald P. Isler, Director
26 Federal Plaza
Room 3720
New York, NY 10278
(212) 264-3262

Alfonso Jackson, District
Officer
Federal Office Building
Room 10128
600 Arch Street
Philadelphia, PA 19106
(215) 597-9236

Puerto Rico
Ronald P. Isler, Director
26 Federal Plaza
Room 3720
New York, NY 10278
(212) 264-3262

Rhode Island
Ronald P. Isler, Director
26 Federal Plaza
Room 3720
New York, NY 10278
(212) 264-3262

South Carolina
Robert M. Henderson,
Acting Director
401 West Peachtree Street,
NW
Room 1715
Atlanta, GA 30308-3516
(404) 730-3300

South Dakota
Bobby T. Jefferson, Acting
Director
1100 Commerce Street
Room 7B23
Dallas, TX 75242
(214) 767-8001

Tennessee
Robert M. Henderson,
Acting Director
401 West Peachtree Street,
NW
Room 1715
Atlanta, GA 30308-3516
(404) 730-3300

Texas
Bobby T. Jefferson, Acting
Director
1100 Commerce Street
Room 7B23
Dallas, TX 75242
(214) 767-8001

Utah
Bobby T. Jefferson, Acting
Director
1100 Commerce Street
Room 7B23
Dallas, TX 75242
(214) 767-8001

Vermont
Ronald P. Isler, Director
26 Federal Plaza
Room 3720
New York, NY 10278
(212) 264-3262

Virginia
Ronald P. Isler, Director
26 Federal Plaza
Room 3720
New York, NY 10278
(212) 264-3262

Virgin Islands
Ronald P. Isler, Director
26 Federal Plaza
Room 3720
New York, NY 10278
(212) 264-3262

Washington
Melda Cabrera, Director
221 Main Street
Room 1280
San Francisco, CA 94105
(415) 744-3001

West Virginia
Ronald P. Isler, Director
26 Federal Plaza
Room 3720
New York, NY 10278
(212) 264-3262

Wisconsin
David Vega, Director
55 East Monroe Street
Suite 1440
Chicago, IL 60603
(312) 353-0182

Wyoming
Bobby T. Jefferson, Acting
Director
1100 Commerce Street
Room 7B23
Dallas, TX 75242
(214) 767-8001

NATIVE AMERICAN EMPLOYMENT AND TRAINING PROGRAMS

Department of Labor
Employment and Training
Administration
Division of Indian and
Native American Programs
200 Constitution Avenue,
NW
Room N4641
Washington, DC 20210
(202) 219-5502

Description: Funds for employment, training programs, and services given to afford job training to Native Americans facing barriers to employment. Limited to Indian tribes, bands, or groups; Alaska native villages/groups; and Hawaiian native communities.
$ Given: $61.9 million est. nationwide FY 95; average: $331,250
Application Information: Standard application forms as furnished by federal agency required. Grantees must prepare four-year master plan addressing administrative, planning, and operational elements.
Deadline: January 1 for notices of intent to apply
Contact: Thomas M. Dowd, above address

NATIVE AMERICAN PROGRAM (NAP)

Department of Commerce
Minority Business
Development Agency
14th Street and
Constitution Avenue, NW
Washington, DC 20230
(202) 482-5770

Description: Project grants for providing business development service to American Indians interested in entering, expanding, or improving their efforts in the marketplace.
$ Given: $1.9 million est. nationwide FY 95; average: $204,000
Application Information: Submit standard application form as furnished by federal agency.
Deadline: Outlined in the Federal Register and Commerce Business Daily
Contact: Nearest Minority Business Development Agency regional office

Alabama
Robert M. Henderson,
Acting Director
401 West Peachtree Street,
NW
Room 1715
Atlanta, GA 30308-3516
(404) 730-3300

Alaska
Melda Cabrera, Director
221 Main Street
Room 1280
San Francisco, CA 94105
(415) 744-3001

Arkansas
Bobby T. Jefferson, Acting
Director
1100 Commerce Street
Room 7B23
Dallas, TX 75242
(214) 767-8001

Arizona
Melda Cabrera, Director
221 Main Street
Room 1280
San Francisco, CA 94105
(415) 744-3001

American Samoa
Melda Cabrera, Director
221 Main Street
Room 1280
San Francisco, CA 94105
(415) 744-3001

California
Melda Cabrera, Director
221 Main Street
Room 1280
San Francisco, CA 94105
(415) 744-3001

Rudy Guerra, District
Officer
977 North Broadway
Suite 201
Los Angeles, CA 90012
(213) 894-7157

Colorado
Bobby T. Jefferson, Acting
Director
1100 Commerce Street
Room 7B23
Dallas, TX 75242
(214) 767-8001

Connecticut
Ronald P. Isler, Director
26 Federal Plaza
Room 3720
New York, NY 10278
(212) 264-3262

District of Columbia
Ronald P. Isler, Director
26 Federal Plaza
Room 3720
New York, NY 10278
(212) 264-3262

Delaware
Ronald P. Isler, Director
26 Federal Plaza
Room 3720
New York, NY 10278
(212) 264-3262

Florida
Robert M. Henderson,
Acting Director
401 West Peachtree Street,
NW
Room 1715
Atlanta, GA 30308-3516
(404) 730-3300

Rudy Suarez, District
Officer
Federal Building
Room 928
51 SW First Avenue
P.O. Box 25
Miami, FL 33130
(305) 536-5054

Georgia
Robert M. Henderson,
Acting Director
401 West Peachtree Street,
NW
Room 1715
Atlanta, GA 30308-3516
(404) 730-3300

Guam
Melda Cabrera, Director
221 Main Street
Room 1280
San Francisco, CA 94105
(415) 744-3001

Hawaii
Melda Cabrera, Director
221 Main Street
Room 1280
San Francisco, CA 94105
(415) 744-3001

Idaho
Melda Cabrera, Director
221 Main Street
Room 1280
San Francisco, CA 94105
(415) 744-3001

Illinois
David Vega, Director
55 East Monroe Street
Suite 1440
Chicago, IL 60603
(312) 353-0182

Indiana
David Vega, Director
55 East Monroe Street
Suite 1440
Chicago, IL 60603
(312) 353-0182

Iowa
David Vega, Director
55 East Monroe Street
Suite 1440
Chicago, IL 60603
(312) 353-0182

Kansas
David Vega, Director
55 East Monroe Street
Suite 1440
Chicago, IL 60603
(312) 353-0182

Kentucky
Robert M. Henderson,
Acting Director
401 West Peachtree Street,
NW
Room 1715
Atlanta, GA 30308-3516
(404) 730-3300

Louisiana
Bobby T. Jefferson, Acting
Director
1100 Commerce Street
Room 7B23
Dallas, TX 75242
(214) 767-8001

Maine
Ronald P. Isler, Director
26 Federal Plaza
Room 3720
New York, NY 10278
(212) 264-3262

Maryland
Ronald P. Isler, Director
26 Federal Plaza
Room 3720
New York, NY 10278
(212) 264-3262

Massachusetts
Ronald P. Isler, Director
26 Federal Plaza
Room 3720
New York, NY 10278
(212) 264-3262

R. K. Schwartz, District
Officer
10 Causeway Street
Room 418
Boston, MA 02222-1041
(617) 565-6850

Michigan
David Vega, Director
55 East Monroe Street
Suite 1440
Chicago, IL 60603
(312) 353-0182

Minnesota
David Vega, Director
55 East Monroe Street
Suite 1440
Chicago, IL 60603
(312) 353-0182

Mississippi
Robert M. Henderson,
Acting Director
401 West Peachtree Street,
NW
Room 1715
Atlanta, GA 30308-3516
(404) 730-3300

Missouri
David Vega, Director
55 East Monroe Street
Suite 1440
Chicago, IL 60603
(312) 353-0182

Montana
Bobby T. Jefferson, Acting
Director
1100 Commerce Street
Room 7B23
Dallas, TX 75242
(214) 767-8001

Nebraska
David Vega, Director
55 East Monroe Street
Suite 1440
Chicago, IL 60603
(312) 353-0182

Nevada
Melda Cabrera, Director
221 Main Street
Room 1280
San Francisco, CA 94105
(415) 744-3001

New Hampshire
Ronald P. Isler, Director
26 Federal Plaza
Room 3720
New York, NY 10278
(212) 264-3262

New Jersey
Ronald P. Isler, Director
26 Federal Plaza
Room 3720
New York, NY 10278
(212) 264-3262

New Mexico
Bobby T. Jefferson, Acting
Director
1100 Commerce Street
Room 7B23
Dallas, TX 75242
(214) 767-8001

New York
Ronald P. Isler, Director
26 Federal Plaza
Room 3720
New York, NY 10278
(212) 264-3262

North Carolina
Robert M. Henderson,
Acting Director
401 West Peachtree Street,
NW
Room 1715
Atlanta, GA 30308-3516
(404) 730-3300

North Dakota
Bobby T. Jefferson, Acting
Director
1100 Commerce Street
Room 7B23
Dallas, TX 75242
(214) 767-8001

Ohio
David Vega, Director
55 East Monroe Street
Suite 1440
Chicago, IL 60603
(312) 353-0182

Oklahoma
Bobby T. Jefferson, Acting
Director
1100 Commerce Street
Room 7B23
Dallas, TX 75242
(214) 767-8001

Oregon
Melda Cabrera, Director
221 Main Street
Room 1280
San Francisco, CA 94105
(415) 744-3001

Pennsylvania
Ronald P. Isler, Director
26 Federal Plaza
Room 3720
New York, NY 10278
(212) 264-3262

Alfonso Jackson, District
Officer
Federal Office Building
Room 10128
600 Arch Street
Philadelphia, PA 19106
(215) 597-9236

Puerto Rico
Ronald P. Isler, Director
26 Federal Plaza
Room 3720
New York, NY 10278
(212) 264-3262

Rhode Island
Ronald P. Isler, Director
26 Federal Plaza
Room 3720
New York, NY 10278
(212) 264-3262

South Carolina
Robert M. Henderson,
Acting Director
401 West Peachtree Street,
NW
Room 1715
Atlanta, GA 30308-3516
(404) 730-3300

South Dakota
Bobby T. Jefferson, Acting
Director
1100 Commerce Street
Room 7B23
Dallas, TX 75242
(214) 767-8001

Tennessee
Robert M. Henderson,
Acting Director
401 West Peachtree Street,
NW
Room 1715
Atlanta, GA 30308-3516
(404) 730-3300

Texas
Bobby T. Jefferson, Acting
Director
1100 Commerce Street
Room 7B23
Dallas, TX 75242
(214) 767-8001

Utah
Bobby T. Jefferson, Acting
Director
1100 Commerce Street
Room 7B23
Dallas, TX 75242
(214) 767-8001

Vermont
Ronald P. Isler, Director
26 Federal Plaza
Room 3720
New York, NY 10278
(212) 264-3262

Virginia
Ronald P. Isler, Director
26 Federal Plaza
Room 3720
New York, NY 10278
(212) 264-3262

Virgin Islands
Ronald P. Isler, Director
26 Federal Plaza
Room 3720
New York, NY 10278
(212) 264-3262

Washington
Melda Cabrera, Director
221 Main Street
Room 1280
San Francisco, CA 94105
(415) 744-3001

West Virginia
Ronald P. Isler, Director
26 Federal Plaza
Room 3720
New York, NY 10278
(212) 264-3262

Wisconsin
David Vega, Director
55 East Monroe Street
Suite 1440
Chicago, IL 60603
(312) 353-0182

Wyoming
Bobby T. Jefferson, Acting
Director
1100 Commerce Street
Room 7B23
Dallas, TX 75242
(214) 767-8001

WOMEN'S SPECIAL EMPLOYMENT ASSISTANCE

Department of Labor
Women's Bureau
Office of the Secretary
Room S3305
Washington, DC 20210
(202) 219-6606

Description: Advisory services/counseling and dissemination of technical information for expansion, training, and employment opportunities for women, especially in new technology and nontraditional occupations. Available to any individual (especially women) located in the United States or its territories.
$ Given: Not available
Application Information: Requests made to appropriate Department of Labor, Women's Bureau, regional office.
Deadline: None
Contact: Dora E. Carrington, above address, and/or Regional Administrator in respective state

Alabama
Delores L. Crockett,
Regional Administrator
1371 Peachtree Street, NE
Room 323
Atlanta, GA 30367
(404) 347-4461

Alaska
Regional Administrator
1111 Third Avenue
Room 885
Seattle, WA 98101-3211
(206) 553-1534

Arizona
Madeline Mixer, Regional
Administrator
71 Stevenson Street
Room 927
San Francisco, CA 94105
(415) 774-6679

Arkansas
Evelyn Smith, Regional
Administrator
Federal Building
Suite 731
525 Griffin Street
Dallas, TX 75202
(214) 767-6985

California
Madeline Mixer, Regional
Administrator
71 Stevenson Street
Room 927
San Francisco, CA 94105
(415) 774-6679

Colorado
Oleta Crain, Regional
Administrator
Federal Office Building
Room 1452
1801 California Street
Suite 905
Denver, CO 80202-2614
(303) 391-6755

Connecticut
Regional Administrator
One Congress Street
11th Floor
Boston, MA 02214
(617) 565-1988

Delaware
Regional Administrator
Gateway Building
Room 2450
3535 Market Street
Philadelphia, PA 19104
(215) 596-1184

District of Columbia
Regional Administrator
Gateway Building
Room 2450
3535 Market Street
Philadelphia, PA 19104
(215) 596-1184

Florida
Delores L. Crockett,
Regional Administrator
1371 Peachtree Street, NE
Room 323
Atlanta, GA 30367
(404) 347-4461

Georgia
Delores L. Crockett,
Regional Administrator
1371 Peachtree Street, NE
Room 323
Atlanta, GA 30367
(404) 347-4461

Hawaii
Madeline Mixer, Regional
Administrator
71 Stevenson Street
Room 927
San Francisco, CA 94105
(415) 774-6679

Idaho
Regional Administrator
1111 Third Avenue
Room 885
Seattle, WA 98101-3211
(206) 553-1534

Illinois
Sandra K. Frank, Regional
Administrator
230 South Dearborn Street
Room 1022
Chicago, IL 60604
(312) 353-6985

Indiana
Sandra K. Frank, Regional
Administrator
230 South Dearborn Street
Room 1022
Chicago, IL 60604
(312) 353-6985

Iowa
Rose A. Kemp, Regional
Administrator
Federal Building
Room 2511
911 Walnut Street
Kansas City, MO 64106
(816) 426-6108

Kansas
Rose A. Kemp, Regional
Administrator
Federal Building
Room 2511
911 Walnut Street
Kansas City, MO 64106
(816) 426-6108

Kentucky
Delores L. Crockett,
Regional Administrator
1371 Peachtree Street, NE
Room 323
Atlanta, GA 30367
(404) 347-4461

Louisiana
Evelyn Smith, Regional
Administrator
Federal Building
Suite 731
525 Griffin Street
Dallas, TX 75202
(214) 767-6985

Maine
Regional Administrator
One Congress Street
11th Floor
Boston, MA 02214
(617) 565-1988

Maryland
Regional Administrator
Gateway Building
Room 2450
3535 Market Street
Philadelphia, PA 19104
(215) 596-1184

Massachusetts
Regional Administrator
One Congress Street
11th Floor
Boston, MA 02214
(617) 565-1988

Michigan
Sandra K. Frank, Regional
Administrator
230 South Dearborn Street
Room 1022
Chicago, IL 60604
(312) 353-6985

Minnesota
Sandra K. Frank, Regional
Administrator
230 South Dearborn Street
Room 1022
Chicago, IL 60604
(312) 353-6985

Mississippi
Delores L. Crockett,
Regional Administrator
1371 Peachtree Street, NE
Room 323
Atlanta, GA 30367
(404) 347-4461

Missouri
Rose A. Kemp, Regional
Administrator
Federal Building
Room 2511
911 Walnut Street
Kansas City, MO 64106
(816) 426-6108

Montana
Oleta Crain, Regional
Administrator
Federal Office Building
Room 1452
1801 California Street
Suite 905
Denver, CO 80202-2614
(303) 391-6755

Nebraska
Rose A. Kemp, Regional
Administrator
Federal Building
Room 2511
911 Walnut Street
Kansas City, MO 64106
(816) 426-6108

Nevada
Madeline Mixer, Regional
Administrator
71 Stevenson Street
Room 927
San Francisco, CA 94105
(415) 774-6679

New Hampshire
Regional Administrator
One Congress Street
11th Floor
Boston, MA 02214
(617) 565-1988

New Jersey
Mary C. Murphree,
Regional Administrator
201 Varick Street
Room 601
New York, NY 10014
(212) 337-2389

New Mexico
Evelyn Smith, Regional
Administrator
Federal Building
Suite 731
525 Griffin Street
Dallas, TX 75202
(214) 767-6985

New York
Mary C. Murphree,
Regional Administrator
201 Varick Street
Room 601
New York, NY 10014
(212) 337-2389

North Carolina
Delores L. Crockett,
Regional Administrator
1371 Peachtree Street, NE
Room 323
Atlanta, GA 30367
(404) 347-4461

North Dakota
Oleta Crain, Regional
Administrator
Federal Office Building
Room 1452
1801 California Street
Suite 905
Denver, CO 80202-2614
(303) 391-6755

Ohio
Sandra K. Frank, Regional
Administrator
230 South Dearborn Street
Room 1022
Chicago, IL 60604
(312) 353-6985

Oklahoma
Evelyn Smith, Regional
Administrator
Federal Building
Suite 731
525 Griffin Street
Dallas, TX 75202
(214) 767-6985

Oregon
Regional Administrator
1111 Third Avenue
Room 885
Seattle, WA 98101-3211
(206) 553-1534

Pennsylvania
Regional Administrator
Gateway Building
Room 2450
3535 Market Street
Philadelphia, PA 19104
(215) 596-1184

Puerto Rico
Mary C. Murphree,
Regional Administrator
201 Varick Street
Room 601
New York, NY 10014
(212) 337-2389

Rhode Island
Regional Administrator
One Congress Street
11th Floor
Boston, MA 02214
(617) 565-1988

South Carolina
Delores L. Crockett,
Regional Administrator
1371 Peachtree Street, NE
Room 323
Atlanta, GA 30367
(404) 347-4461

South Dakota
Oleta Crain, Regional
Administrator
Federal Office Building
Room 1452
1801 California Street
Suite 905
Denver, CO 80202-2614
(303) 391-6755

Tennessee
Delores L. Crockett,
Regional Administrator
1371 Peachtree Street, NE
Room 323
Atlanta, GA 30367
(404) 347-4461

Texas
Evelyn Smith, Regional
Administrator
Federal Building
Suite 731
525 Griffin Street
Dallas, TX 75202
(214) 767-6985

Utah
Oleta Crain, Regional
Administrator
Federal Office Building
Room 1452
1801 California Street
Suite 905
Denver, CO 80202-2614
(303) 391-6755

Vermont
Regional Administrator
One Congress Street
11th Floor
Boston, MA 02214
(617) 565-1988

Virginia
Regional Administrator
Gateway Building
Room 2450
3535 Market Street
Philadelphia, PA 19104
(215) 596-1184

Virgin Islands
Mary C. Murphree,
Regional Administrator
201 Varick Street
Room 601
New York, NY 10014
(212) 337-2389

Washington
Regional Administrator
1111 Third Avenue
Room 885
Seattle, WA 98101-3211
(206) 553-1534

West Virginia
Regional Administrator
Gateway Building
Room 2450
3535 Market Street
Philadelphia, PA 19104
(215) 596-1184

Wisconsin
Sandra K. Frank, Regional
Administrator
230 South Dearborn Street
Room 1022
Chicago, IL 60604
(312) 353-6985

Wyoming
Oleta Crain, Regional
Administrator
Federal Office Building
Room 1452
1801 California Street
Suite 905
Denver, CO 80202-2614
(303) 391-6755

Housing

Assistance is widely available from the federal government for owners and builders of housing units for the following:

1. *Assistance* to owners and builders of multifamily projects, low- or moderate-income projects, and nursing homes and housing for the elderly; funds are available for restoration, maintenance, or construction
2. *Guaranteed insured loans* to businesses for provision of mortgage insurance for rental units or single-room-occupancy units or for development of condominium projects, manufactured-home parks, or rental housing in urban renewal areas
3. *Loans* to individuals for financing home improvements, repairs, or home purchases or for refinancing building units

You will need to consult the list of addresses in this chapter for your nearest local or regional Housing and Urban Development office.

MANUFACTURED-HOME LOAN INSURANCE—FINANCING PURCHASE OF MANUFACTURED HOMES AS PRINCIPAL RESIDENCES OF BORROWERS

Department of Housing and Urban Development (HUD)
Title I Insurance Division
Washington, DC 20410
(202) 755-7400

Description: Guaranteed/insured loans to all persons to make possible reasonable financing of home purchases. Buyers must intend to use homes as principal place of residence.
$ Given: Through September 30, 1993: 440,974 loans approved for $7.9 billion; FY 93: 17,418 loans insured with value of $430,714,194; maximum loan: $48,600.
Application Information: Apply through HUD-approved lender or dealer.
Deadline: None
Contact: Director, above address

MORTGAGE INSURANCE—EXPERIMENTAL HOMES

Department of Housing and Urban Development (HUD)
Policy Development and Research
Division of Affordable-Housing Research and Technology
451 Seventh Street, SW
Washington, DC 20410
(202) 708-4370

Description: Guaranteed/insured loans to home builders for providing mortgage insurance for homes incorporating new or untried construction concepts that may reduce housing costs, raise living standards, and improve neighborhood design.
$ Given: To date, 600 units insured for $10 million
Application Information: Submit application to local HUD field office.
Deadline: Established on a case-by-case basis at local HUD field office
Contact: Nearest local HUD field office

Alabama
Heager Hill, Acting State Coordinator
600 Beacon Parkway West
Suite 300
Birmingham, AL 35209-3144
(205) 290-7617

Leon Jacobs, Director
Chicago Office of Indian Programs
77 West Jackson Boulevard
24th Floor
Chicago, IL 60604-3507
(312) 231-1282

Alaska
Arlene Patton, Manager
University Plaza Building
949 East 36th Avenue
Suite 401
Anchorage, AK 99508-4135
(907) 271-4170
Fax: (907) 271-3667

Martin Knight, Director
University Plaza Building
Anchorage Indian Housing
Division
949 East 36th Avenue
Suite 401
Anchorage, AK 99508-4135
(907) 271-4633

American Samoa
Gordon Y. Furutani, Acting
State Coordinator
7 Waterfront Plaza
500 Ala Moana Boulevard
Room 500
Honolulu, HI 96813-4918
(808) 541-1323
Fax: (808) 541-3146

Arizona
Dwight A. Peterson, Acting
State Coordinator
Two Arizona Center
400 North Fifth Street
Suite 1600
Phoenix, AZ 85004-2361
(602) 379-4434
Fax: (602) 379-3985

Sharon Atwell, Acting Area
Coordinator
33 North Stone Avenue
Room 700
Tucson, AZ 85701-1467
(602) 670-6237
Fax: (602) 670-6207

Charles Ming, Acting Area
Coordinator
1615 West Olympic
Boulevard
Los Angeles, CA 90015-
3801
(213) 251-7122
Fax: (213) 251-7096

Raphael Mecham, Director
HUD Indian Programs
Office
400 North Fifth Street
Suite 1650
Phoenix, AZ 85004-2361
(602) 379-4156
Fax: (602) 379-3101

Arkansas
John T. Suskie, Acting State
Coordinator
TCBY Tower
425 West Capitol Avenue
Suite 900
Little Rock, AR 72201-3488
(501) 324-5931
Fax: (501) 324-5900

Jim Cook, Acting Director
Oklahoma City Office of
Indian Programs
500 West Main Street
Oklahoma City, OK 73102-
2233

California
(San Francisco Regional
Office)
Arthur Agnos, Secretary's
Representative
Phillip Burton Federal
Building and U.S.
Courthouse
P.O. Box 36003
450 Golden Gate Avenue
San Francisco, CA 94102-
3448
(415) 556-4752
Fax: (415) 556-4176

(South California)
Charles Ming, Acting Area
Coordinator
1615 West Olympic
Boulevard
Los Angeles, CA 90015-3801
(213) 251-7122
Fax: (213) 251-7096

(Fresno)
Willie Mae Haskin, Acting
Area Coordinator
1630 East Shaw Avenue
Fresno, CA 93710-8193
(209) 487-5033
Fax: (209) 487-5344

(Northeast California)
Paul Pradia, Acting Area
Coordinator
777 12th Street
Suite 200
Sacramento, CA 95814-
1997
(916) 551-1351
Fax: (916) 551-2899

(Imperial and San Diego
Counties)
Charles J. Wilson, Acting
Area Coordinator
Mission City Corporate
Center
Suite 300
2365 Northside Drive
San Diego, CA 92108-2712
(619) 557-5310
Fax: (619) 557-6296

(Orange, Riverside, and San
Bernadino Counties, for
home mortgages)
Samuel Sandoval, Acting
Area Coordinator
3 Hutton Centre
Suite 500
Santa Ana, CA 92707-5764
(714) 957-7333
Fax: (714) 957-1903

Raphael Mecham, Director
HUD Indian Programs
Office
400 North Fifth Street
Suite 1650
Phoenix, AZ 85004-2361
(602) 379-4156
Fax: (602) 379-3101

Colorado
(Denver Regional Office)
Anthony Hernandez,
Secretary's Representative
HUD—Denver Office
633 17th Street
Denver, CO 80202-3607
(303) 844-4513
Fax: (303) 844-2475

Vernon Haragara, Director
Denver Office of Indian
Programs
Executive Tower Building
1405 Curtis Street
Denver, CO 80202-2349
(303) 844-2963

Connecticut
Robert S. Donovon, Deputy
Manager
330 Main Street
Hartford, CT 06106-1860
(203) 240-4523
Fax: (203) 240-4674

Leon Jacobs, Director
Chicago Office of Indian
Programs
77 West Jackson Boulevard
24th Floor
Chicago, IL 60604-3507
(312) 231-1282

Delaware
A. David Sharbaugh, Acting
State Coordinator
824 Market Street
Suite 850
Wilmington, DE 19801-3016
(302) 573-6300
Fax: (302) 573-6259

Leon Jacobs, Director
Chicago Office of Indian
Programs
77 West Jackson Boulevard
24th Floor
Chicago, IL 60604-3507
(312) 231-1282

District of Columbia
Jessica Franklin, Acting
State Coordinator
Union Center Plaza, Phase II
820 First Street, NE
Suite 300
Washington, DC 20002-
4205
(202) 275-9200
Fax: (202) 275-0779

Florida
James T. Chaplin, State
Coordinator
Southern Bell Tower
Suite 2200
301 West Bay Street
Jacksonville, FL 32202-5121
(904) 232-2626
Fax: (904) 232-3759

(South Florida)
Orlando T. Lorie, Acting
Area Coordinator
Gables 1 Tower
1320 South Dixie Highway
Coral Gables, FL 33146-
2911
(305) 662-4500
Fax: (305) 662-4519

(Central Florida, Western
Counties—Citrus, Sumter,
Hernando, Pasco, Manatee,
Hardee, Highlands, DeSoto,
Sarasota, Charlotte, Olaoes,
Hendry, Lake Okeechobee)
George A. Milburn Jr.,
Acting Area Coordinator
Timberlake Federal Building
Annex
501 East Polk Street
Tampa, FL 33602-3945
(813) 228-2501
Fax: (813) 228-2431

(Central Florida, Eastern
Counties—Volusia, Lake,
Seminole, Orange, Brevard,
Osceola, Indian River,
Okeechobee, St. Lucie)
M. Jeanette Porter, Acting
Area Coordinator
Langley Building
3751 Maguire Boulevard
Suite 270
Orlando, FL 32803-3032
(407) 648-6441
Fax: (407) 648-6310

Leon Jacobs, Director
Chicago Office of Indian
Programs
77 West Jackson Boulevard
24th Floor
Chicago, IL 60604-3507
(312) 231-1282

Georgia
(Atlanta Regional Office)
Davey L. Gibson, Secretary's
Representative
Regional Housing
Commissioner
Richard B. Russell Federal
Building
75 Spring Street, SW
Atlanta, GA 30303-3388
(404) 331-5136
Fax: (404) 331-0845

Leon Jacobs, Director
Chicago Office of Indian
Programs
77 West Jackson Boulevard
24th Floor
Chicago, IL 60604-3507
(312) 231-1282

Guam
Gordon Y. Furutani, Acting
State Coordinator
7 Waterfront Plaza
500 Ala Moana Boulevard
Room 500
Honolulu, HI 96813-4918
(808) 541-1323
Fax: (808) 541-3146

Hawaii
Gordon Y. Furutani, Acting
State Coordinator
7 Waterfront Plaza
500 Ala Moana Boulevard
Room 500
Honolulu, HI 96813-4918
(808) 541-1323
Fax: (808) 541-3146

Idaho
(North Idaho)
Gary Rogers, Acting Area
Coordinator
Farm Credit Bank Building
Eighth Floor East
West 601 First Avenue
Spokane, WA 99204-0317
(509) 353-2510

(West-Central Idaho)
Gary Gillespie, Acting State
Coordinator
Suite 220
Park IV
800 Park Boulevard
Boise, ID 83712-7743
(208) 334-1990
Fax: (208) 334-9648

(South Idaho)
Richard C. Brinck, Acting
State Coordinator
Cascade Building
520 SW Sixth Avenue
Portland, OR 97204-1596
(503) 221-2561

Jerry Leslie, Director
Seattle Office of Indian
Programs
Seattle Federal Office
Building
909 First Avenue
Suite 200
Seattle, WA 98104-1000
(206) 220-5270

Illinois
(Chicago Regional Office)
Edwin Eisendrath,
Secretary's Representative
Regional Housing
Commissioner
Ralph Metcalfe Federal
Building
77 West Jackson Boulevard
Chicago, IL 60604-3507
(312) 353-5680
Fax: (312) 353-0121

(Central and South Illinois)
William Fattick, Acting Area
Coordinator
509 West Capitol
Suite 206
Springfield, IL 62704-1906
(217) 492-4085
Fax: (217) 492-4971

Leon Jacobs, Director
Chicago Office of Indian
Programs
77 West Jackson Boulevard
24th Floor
Chicago, IL 60604-3507
(312) 231-1282

Indiana
J. Nicholas Shelley, Acting
State Coordinator
151 North Delaware Street
Indianapolis, IN 46204-
2526
(317) 226-6303
Fax: (317) 226-6317

Iowa
William R. McNarney,
Acting State Coordinator
HUD—Des Moines Office
Federal Building
Room 239
210 Walnut Street
Des Moines, IA 50309-2155
(515) 284-4512
Fax: (515) 284-4743

Roger M. Massey, Acting
State Coordinator
Executive Tower Center
10909 Mill Valley Road
Omaha, NE 68154-3955
(402) 492-3101
Fax: (402) 492-3150

Leon Jacobs, Director
Chicago Office of Indian
Programs
77 West Jackson Boulevard
24th Floor
Chicago, IL 60604-3507
(312) 231-1282

Kansas
Joseph O'Hern, Secretary's
Representative
Regional Housing
Commissioner
HUD—Kansas City Regional
Office
Gateway Tower II
400 State Avenue
Room 200
Kansas City, KS 66101-2406
(913) 551-5462
Fax: (913) 551-5416

Jim Cook, Acting Director
Oklahoma City Office of
Indian Programs
500 West Main Street
Oklahoma City, OK 73102-
2233

Kentucky
Verna V. Van Ness, Acting
State Coordinator
601 West Broadway
P.O. Box 1044
Louisville, KY 40201-1044
(502) 582-5251
Fax: (502) 582-6074

Leon Jacobs, Director
Chicago Office of Indian
Programs
77 West Jackson Boulevard
24th Floor
Chicago, IL 60604-3507
(312) 231-1282

Louisiana
Robert Vasquez, Acting
State Coordinator
Fisk Federal Building
1661 Canal Street
New Orleans, LA 70112-1887
(504) 589-7200
Fax: (504) 589-2917

(North Louisiana)
Ben Wiley, Acting Area
Coordinator
401 Edwards Street
500 Fannin Street
Shreveport, LA 71101-3077
(318) 266-5385

Jim Cook, Acting Director
Oklahoma City Office of
Indian Programs
500 West Main Street
Oklahoma City, OK 73102-
2233

Maine
Richard Young, Acting State
Coordinator
Casco Northern Bank
Building
23 Main Street
Bangor, ME 04401-6394
(207) 945-0467
Fax: (207) 945-0533

David B. Harrity, Acting
State Coordinator
Norris Cotton Federal
Building
275 Chester Street
Manchester, NH 03103-2487
(603) 666-7681
Fax: (603) 666-7736

Leon Jacobs, Director
Chicago Office of Indian
Programs
77 West Jackson Boulevard
24th Floor
Chicago, IL 60604-3507
(312) 231-1282

Maryland
(Except Montgomery and
Prince Georges Counties)
Maxine Saunders, Acting
State Coordinator
City Crescent Building
10 South Howard Street
Fifth Floor
Baltimore, MD 21201
(301) 962-2520

(Montgomery and Prince
Georges Counties)
Jessica Franklin, Acting
State Coordinator
Union Center Plaza, Phase II
820 First Street, NE
Suite 300
Washington, DC 20002-
4205
(202) 275-9200
Fax: (202) 275-0779

Leon Jacobs, Director
Chicago Office of Indian
Programs
77 West Jackson Boulevard
24th Floor
Chicago, IL 60604-3507
(312) 231-1282

Massachusetts
(Boston Regional Office)
Mary Lou Crane, Secretary's
Representative
Thomas P. O'Neill Jr.
Federal Building
10 Causeway Street
Room 375
Boston, MA 02222-1092
(617) 565-5234
Fax: (617) 565-5168

Leon Jacobs, Director
Chicago Office of Indian
Programs
77 West Jackson Boulevard
24th Floor
Chicago, IL 60604-3507
(312) 231-1282

Michigan
Harry I. Sharrott, Acting
State Coordinator
Patrick V. McNamara
Federal Building
477 Michigan Avenue
Detroit, MI 48226-2592
(313) 226-7900
Fax: (313) 226-4394

(East Michigan)
Gary T. LeVine, Acting Area
Coordinator
605 North Saginaw Street
Suite 200
Flint, MI 48502-1953
(313) 766-5112
Fax: (313) 766-5122

(West and North Michigan)
Ronald Weston, Acting Area
Coordinator
Northbrook Building, # II
2922 Fuller Avenue, NE
Grand Rapids, MI 49505-
3499
(616) 456-2100
Fax: (616) 456-2191

Leon Jacobs, Director
Chicago Office of Indian
Programs
77 West Jackson Boulevard
24th Floor
Chicago, IL 60604-3507
(312) 231-1282

Minnesota
Thomas Feeney, Acting State
Coordinator
220 Second Street South
Bridge Place Building
Minneapolis, MN 55401-
2195
(612) 370-3000
Fax: (612) 370-3220

Leon Jacobs, Director
Chicago Office of Indian
Programs
77 West Jackson Boulevard
24th Floor
Chicago, IL 60604-3507
(312) 231-1282

Mississippi
Sandra Freeman, Acting
State Coordinator
Koger Building
Dr. A. H. McCoy Federal
Building
100 West Capitol Street
Room 910
Jackson, MS 39269-1096
(601) 965-5308
(601) 965-4773

Leon Jacobs, Director
Chicago Office of Indian
Programs
77 West Jackson Boulevard
24th Floor
Chicago, IL 60604-3507
(312) 231-1282

Missouri
Kenneth G. Lange, Acting
Area Coordinator
1222 Spruce Street
Room 3207
St. Louis, MO 63103-2836
(314) 539-6560
Fax: (314) 539-6575

Jim Cook, Acting Director
Oklahoma City Office of
Indian Programs
500 West Main Street
Oklahoma City, OK 73102-
2233

Montana
Gerard Boone, Acting State
Coordinator
Federal Office Building,
Drawer 10095
301 South Park
Room 340
Helena, MT 59626-0095
(406) 449-5205
Fax: (406) 449-5207

Vernon Haragara, Director
Denver Office of Indian
Programs
Executive Tower Building
1405 Curtis Street
Denver, CO 80202-2349
(303) 844-2963

Nebraska
Roger M. Massey, Acting
State Coordinator
Executive Tower Center
10909 Mill Valley Road
Omaha, NE 68154-3955
(402) 492-3101
Fax: (402) 492-3150

Vernon Haragara, Director
Denver Office of Indian
Programs
Executive Tower Building
1405 Curtis Street
Denver, CO 80202-2349
(303) 844-2963

Nevada
Andrew D. Whitten Jr.,
Acting Area Coordinator
1575 DeLucchi Lane
Room 114
P.O. Box 30050
Reno, NV 89502-6581
(702) 784-5356
Fax: (702) 784-5066

Benjamin Davis, Acting
State Coordinator
1500 East Tropicana Avenue
Second Floor
Las Vegas, NV 89119-6516
(702) 388-6500
Fax: (702) 388-6736

Raphael Mecham, Director
HUD Indian Programs
Office
400 North Fifth Street
Suite 1650
Phoenix, AZ 85004-2361
(602) 379-4156
Fax: (602) 379-3101

New Hampshire
David B. Harrity, Acting
State Coordinator
Norris Cotton Federal
Building
275 Chestnut Street
Manchester, NH 03103-
2487
(603) 666-7681
Fax: (603) 666-7736

Leon Jacobs, Director
Chicago Office of Indian
Programs
77 West Jackson Boulevard
24th Floor
Chicago, IL 60604-3507
(312) 231-1282

New Jersey
(North New Jersey)
Diane Johnson, Acting State
Coordinator
One Newark Center
13th Floor
Newark, NJ 07102-5260
(201) 622-7900
Fax: (201) 645-6239

(South New Jersey)
Elmer Roy, Acting Area
Coordinator
Hudson Building
Second Floor
800 Hudson Square
Camden, NJ 08102-1156
(609) 757-5081
Fax: (609) 757-5373

Leon Jacobs, Director
Chicago Office of Indian
Programs
77 West Jackson Boulevard
24th Floor
Chicago, IL 60604-3507
(312) 231-1282

New Mexico
Michael R. Griego, Acting
State Coordinator
625 Truman Street, NW
Albuquerque, NM 87110-
6443
(505) 262-6463

Clarence D. Babers, Acting
Area Coordinator
525 Griffin Street
Room 860
Dallas, TX 75202-5007
(214) 767-8359
Fax: (214) 767-8973

Raphael Mecham, Director
HUD Indian Programs
Office
400 North Fifth Street
Suite 1650
Phoenix, AZ 85004-2361
(602) 379-4156
Fax: (602) 379-3101

New York
(New York Regional Office)
Jose Cintron, Secretary's
Representative
26 Federal Plaza
New York, NY 10278-0068
(212) 264-6500
Fax: (212) 264-0246

(North New York)
John Petricco, Acting Area
Coordinator
52 Corporate Circle
Albany, NY 12203-5121
(518) 464-4200
Fax: (518) 464-4300

(West New York)
Joseph Lynch, Acting Area
Coordinator
465 Main Street
Lafayette Court
Fifth Floor
Buffalo, NY 14203-1780
(716) 846-5755
Fax: (716) 846-5752

Leon Jacobs, Director
Chicago Office of Indian
Programs
77 West Jackson Boulevard
24th Floor
Chicago, IL 60604-3507
(312) 231-1282

North Carolina
Larry J. Parker, Acting State
Coordinator
2306 West Meadowview
Road
Koger Building
Greensboro, NC 27407-
3707
(919) 547-4001
Fax: (919) 547-4015

Leon Jacobs, Director
Chicago Office of Indian
Programs
77 West Jackson Boulevard
24th Floor
Chicago, IL 60604-3507
(312) 231-1282

North Dakota
Keith Elliott, Acting State
Coordinator
HUD—Fargo Office
Federal Building
657 Second Avenue, North
Fargo, ND 58108-2483
(701) 239-5136
Fax: (701) 783-5249

Vernon Haragara, Director
Denver Office of Indian
Programs
Executive Tower Building
1405 Curtis Street
Denver, CO 80202-2349
(303) 844-2963

Ohio
Robert W. Dolin, Acting
State Coordinator
HUD—Columbus Office
200 North High Street
Columbus, OH 43215-2499
(614) 469-5737
Fax: (614) 469-2432

(North Ohio)
Philip Ginconia, Acting Area
Coordinator
1350 Euclid Avenue
Fifth Floor
Cleveland, OH 44115-1815
(216) 552-4065
Fax: (216) 522-2975

(Southwest Ohio)
William Harris, Acting Area
Coordinator
Federal Office Building
Room 9002
550 Main Street
Cincinnati, OH 45202-3253
(513) 684-2884
Fax: (513) 684-6224

Leon Jacobs, Director
Chicago Office of Indian
Programs
77 West Jackson Boulevard
24th Floor
Chicago, IL 60604-3507
(312) 231-1282

Oklahoma
Katie Worsham, Acting State
Coordinator
500 West Main Street
Oklahoma City, OK 73102-
2233

(East Oklahoma)
James S. Colgan, Acting
Area Coordinator
1516 South Boston Avenue
Room 110
Tulsa, OK 74119-4032
(918) 581-7435
Fax: (918) 581-7440

Jim Cook, Acting Director
Oklahoma City Office of
Indian Programs
500 West Main Street
Oklahoma City, OK 73102-
2233

Oregon
Richard C. Brinck, Acting
State Coordinator
Cascade Building
520 SW Sixth Avenue
Portland, OR 97204-1596
(503) 326-2561
Fax: (503) 326-3097

Jerry Leslie, Director
Seattle Office of Indian
Programs
Seattle Federal Office
Building
909 First Avenue
Suite 200
Seattle, WA 98104-1000
(206) 220-5270

Panama Canal Zone
Rosa Villalonga, Acting
State Coordinator
159 Carlos E. Chardon
Avenue
San Juan, PR 00918-1804
(809) 766-6121
Fax: (809) 498-5201

Pennsylvania
(Philadelphia Regional
Office)
Karen A. Miller, Secretary's
Representative
Regional Housing
Commissioner
Liberty Square Building
105 South Seventh Street
Philadelphia, PA 19106-3392
(215) 597-2560
Fax: (215) 597-9627

(West Pennsylvania)
Choice Edwards, Acting
Area Coordinator
412 Old Post Office
Courthouse Building
Seventh Avenue and Grant
Street
Pittsburgh, PA 15219-1906
(412) 644-6428
Fax: (412) 644-6499

Leon Jacobs, Director
Chicago Office of Indian
Programs
77 West Jackson Boulevard
24th Floor
Chicago, IL 60604-3507
(312) 231-1282

Puerto Rico
Rosa Villalonga, Acting
State Coordinator
159 Carlos E. Chardon
Avenue
San Juan, PR 00918-1804
(809) 766-6121
Fax: (809) 498-5201

Rhode Island
Michael Dziok, Acting State
Coordinator
Room 303
John O. Pastore Federal
Building and U.S. Post
Office
Kennedy Plaza
Providence, RI 02903-1785
(401) 528-5351
Fax: (401) 528-5312

Leon Jacobs, Director
Chicago Office of Indian
Programs
77 West Jackson Boulevard
24th Floor
Chicago, IL 60604-3507
(312) 231-1282

South Carolina
Ted B. Freeman, Acting
State Coordinator
Strom Thurmond Federal
Building
1835 Assembly Street
Columbia, SC 29201-2480
(803) 765-5592
Fax: (803) 765-5515

Leon Jacobs, Director
Chicago Office of Indian
Programs
77 West Jackson Boulevard
24th Floor
Chicago, IL 60604-3507
(312) 231-1282

South Dakota
Don Olson, Acting State
Coordinator
Suite I-201
2400 West 49th Street
Sioux Falls, SD 57105-6558
(605) 330-4223
Fax: (605) 330-4465

Vernon Haragara, Director
Denver Office of Indian
Programs
Executive Tower Building
1405 Curtis Street
Denver, CO 80202-2349
(303) 844-2963

Tennessee
Mark Brezina, Acting Area
Coordinator
John J. Duncan Federal
Building
Third Floor
710 Locust Street, SW
Knoxville, TN 37902-2526
(615) 545-4384
Fax: (615) 545-4569

(West Tennessee)
Bob Atkins, Acting Area
Coordinator
One Memphis Place
200 Jefferson Avenue
Suite 1200
Memphis, TN 38103-2335
(901) 544-3367
Fax: (901) 544-3697

(Central Tennessee)
John H. Fisher, Acting State
Coordinator
251 Cumberland Bend Drive
Nashville, TN 37228-1803
(615) 736-5213
Fax: (615) 736-2018

Leon Jacobs, Director
Chicago Office of Indian
Programs
77 West Jackson Boulevard
24th Floor
Chicago, IL 60604-3507
(312) 231-1282

Texas
(Fort Worth Regional
Office)
Stephen Weatherforce,
Secretary's Representative
1600 Throckmorton
P.O. Box 2905
Fort Worth, TX 76113-2905
(817) 885-5401
Fax: (817) 885-5629

(East, North, and West
Texas)
Clarence D. Babers, Acting
Area Coordinator
525 Griffin Street
Room 860
Dallas, TX 75202-5007
(214) 767-8359
Fax: (214) 767-8973

(Northwest Texas)
Henry E. Whitney, Acting
Area Coordinator
Federal Office Building
1205 Texas Avenue
Lubbock, TX 79401-4093
(806) 743-7265

(Southwest Texas)
A. Cynthia Leon, Acting
Area Coordinator
Washington Square Building
800 Dolorosa Street
San Antonio, TX 78207-
4563
(512) 229-6800

(East-Central Texas)
George Rodriguez, Acting
Area Coordinator
Norfolk Tower
2211 Norfolk
Room 200
Houston, TX 77098-4096
(713) 653-3274

(Bowie County)
John T. Suskie, Acting State
Coordinator
TCBY Tower
425 West Capitol Avenue
Suite 900
Little Rock, AR 72201-3488
(501) 324-5931
Fax: (501) 324-5900

(Five Counties in East
Texas)
Ben Wiley, Acting Area
Coordinator
401 Edwards Street
500 Fannin Street
Shreveport, LA 71101-3107
(318) 266-5385

Jim Cook, Acting Director
Oklahoma City Office of
Indian Programs
500 West Main Street
Oklahoma City, OK 73102-
2233

Utah
Richard Bell, Acting State
Coordinator
Suite 550
257 Tower Building
257 East, 200 South
Salt Lake City, UT 84111-
2048
(801) 524-5379
Fax: (801) 524-5701

Vernon Haragara, Director
Denver Office of Indian
Programs
Executive Tower Building
1405 Curtis Street
Denver, CO 80202-2349
(303) 844-2963

Vermont
William Peters, Acting State
Coordinator
Federal Building
Room 244
11 Elmwood Avenue
P.O. Box 879
Burlington, VT 05402-0879
(802) 951-6290
Fax: (802) 951-6298

David B. Harrity, Acting
State Coordinator
Norris Cotton Federal
Building
275 Chester Street
Manchester, NH 03103-
2487
(603) 666-7681
Fax: (603) 666-7736

Leon Jacobs, Director
Chicago Office of Indian
Programs
77 West Jackson Boulevard
24th Floor
Chicago, IL 60604-3507
(312) 231-1282

Virginia
(North Virginia)
Jessica Franklin, Acting
State Coordinator
Union Center Plaza, Phase II
820 First Street, NE
Suite 300
Washington, DC 20002-
4205
(202) 275-9200
Fax: (202) 275-0779

(South Virginia)
Mary Ann Wilson, Acting
State Coordinator
P.O. Box 90331
3600 West Broad Street
Richmond, VA 23230-0331
(804) 278-4507

Leon Jacobs, Director
Chicago Office of Indian
Programs
77 West Jackson Boulevard
24th Floor
Chicago, IL 60604-3507
(312) 231-1282

Virgin Islands
Rosa Villalonga, Acting
State Coordinator
159 Carlos E. Chardon
Avenue
San Juan, PR 00918-1804
(809) 766-6121
Fax: (809) 498-5201

Washington
(Seattle Regional Office)
Bob Santos, Secretary's
Representative
Regional Housing
Commissioner
Seattle Federal Office
Building
Suite 200
909 First Avenue
Seattle, WA 98104-1000
(206) 220-5101
Fax: (206) 220-5133

(Clark, Klickitat, and
Skamania Counties)
Richard C. Brinck, Acting
State Coordinator
Cascase Building
520 SW Sixth Avenue
Portland, OR 97204-1596
(503) 326-2561
Fax: (503) 326-3097

(East Washington)
Gary Rogers, Acting Area
Coordinator
Eighth Floor East
Farm Credit Bank Building
West 601 First Avenue
Spokane, WA 99204-0317
(509) 353-2510

Jerry Leslie, Director
Seattle Office of Indian
Programs
Seattle Federal Office
Building
909 First Avenue
Suite 200
Seattle, WA 98104-1000
(206) 220-5270

West Virginia
Fred Roncaglione, Acting
State Coordinator
405 Capitol Street
Suite 708
Charleston, WV 25301-
1795
(304) 347-7000
Fax: (304) 347-7050

Choice Edwards, Acting
Area Coordinator
412 Old Post Office
Courthouse Building
Seventh Avenue and Grant
Street
Pittsburgh, PA 15219-1906
(412) 644-6428
Fax: (412) 644-6499

Leon Jacobs, Director
Chicago Office of Indian
Programs
77 West Jackson Boulevard
24th Floor
Chicago, IL 60604-3507
(312) 231-1282

Wisconsin
Delbert F. Reynolds, Acting
State Coordinator
Henry S. Reuss Federal
Plaza
310 West Wisconsin Avenue
Milwaukee, WI 53203-2289
(414) 297-3214
Fax: (414) 297-3947

Leon Jacobs, Director
Chicago Office of Indian
Programs
77 West Jackson Boulevard
24th Floor
Chicago, IL 60604-3507
(312) 231-1282

Wyoming
William Garrett, Acting
State Coordinator
4225 Federal Office Building
100 East B Street
P.O. Box 120
Casper, WY 82602-1918
(307) 261-5252
Fax: (307) 261-5251

Vernon Haragara, Director
Denver Office of Indian
Programs
Executive Tower Building
1405 Curtis Street
Denver, CO 80202-2349
(303) 844-2963

MORTGAGE INSURANCE—EXPERIMENTAL PROJECTS OTHER THAN HOUSING

Department of Housing and
Urban Development (HUD)
Policy Development and
Research
Division of Affordable
Housing Research and
Technology
451 Seventh Street, SW
Washington, DC 20410
(202) 708-4370

Description: Guaranteed/insured loans to builders/owners of group medical facilities incorporating experimental building methods intended to reduce housing costs, raise living standards, and improve neighborhood design. Applicants must prove that new technology represents an acceptable risk to HUD.
$ Given: To date, 5,000 units insured for $100 million; average: $2.3 million per project
Application Information: Initial conference with local HUD field office, followed by formal application.
Deadline: Established on a case-by-case basis at local HUD field office
Contact: Nearest local HUD field office

Alabama
Heager Hill, Acting State
Coordinator
600 Beacon Parkway West
Suite 300
Birmingham, AL 35209-3144
(205) 290-7617

Leon Jacobs, Director
Chicago Office of Indian
Programs
77 West Jackson Boulevard
24th Floor
Chicago, IL 60604-3507
(312) 231-1282

Alaska
Arlene Patton, Manager
University Plaza Building
949 East 36th Avenue
Suite 401
Anchorage, AK 99508-4135
(907) 271-4170
Fax: (907) 271-3667

Martin Knight, Director
Anchorage Indian Housing
Division
949 East 36th Avenue
Suite 401
Anchorage, AK 99508-4135
(907) 271-4633

American Samoa
Gordon Y. Furutani, Acting
State Coordinator
7 Waterfront Plaza
500 Ala Moana Boulevard
Room 500
Honolulu, HI 96813-4918
(808) 541-1323
Fax: (808) 541-3146

Arizona
Dwight A. Peterson, Acting
State Coordinator
Two Arizona Center
400 North Fifth Street
Suite 1600
Phoenix, AZ 85004-2361
(602) 379-4434
Fax: (602) 379-3985

Sharon Atwell, Acting Area
Coordinator
33 North Stone Avenue
Room 700
Tucson, AZ 85701-1467
(602) 670-6237
Fax: (602) 670-6207

Charles Ming, Acting Area
Coordinator
1615 West Olympic
Boulevard
Los Angeles, CA 90015-
3801
(213) 251-7122
Fax: (213) 251-7096

Raphael Mecham, Director
HUD Indian Programs
Office
400 North Fifth Street
Suite 1650
Phoenix, AZ 85004-2361
(602) 379-4156
Fax: (602) 379-3101

Arkansas
John T. Suskie, Acting State
Coordinator
TCBY Tower
425 West Capitol Avenue
Suite 900
Little Rock, AR 72201-3488
(501) 324-5931
Fax: (501) 324-5900

Jim Cook, Acting Director
Oklahoma City Office of
Indian Programs
500 West Main Street
Oklahoma City, OK 73102-
2233

California
(San Francisco Regional
Office)
Arthur Agnos, Secretary's
Representative
Phillip Burton Federal
Building and U.S.
Courthouse
P.O. Box 36003
450 Golden Gate Avenue
San Francisco, CA 94102-
3448
(415) 556-4752
Fax: (415) 556-4176

(South California)
Charles Ming, Acting Area
Coordinator
1615 West Olympic
Boulevard
Los Angeles, CA 90015-3801
(213) 251-7122
Fax: (213) 251-7096

(Fresno)
Willie Mae Haskin, Acting
Area Coordinator
1630 East Shaw Avenue
Fresno, CA 93710-8193
(209) 487-5033
Fax: (209) 487-5344

(Northeast California)
Paul Pradia, Acting Area
Coordinator
777 12th Street
Suite 200
Sacramento, CA 95814-
1997
(916) 551-1351
Fax: (916) 551-2899

(Imperial and San Diego
Counties)
Charles J. Wilson, Acting
Area Coordinator
Mission City Corporate
Center
Suite 300
2365 Northside Drive
San Diego, CA 92108-2712
(619) 557-5310
Fax: (619) 557-6296

(Orange, Riverside, and San
Bernadino Counties, for
home mortgages)
Samuel Sandoval, Acting
Area Coordinator
3 Hutton Centre
Suite 500
Santa Ana, CA 92707-5764
(714) 957-7333
Fax: (714) 957-1903

Raphael Mecham, Director
HUD Indian Programs
Office
400 North Fifth Street
Suite 1650
Phoenix, AZ 85004-2361
(602) 379-4156
Fax: (602) 379-3101

Colorado
(Denver Regional Office)
Anthony Hernandez,
Secretary's Representative
HUD—Denver Office
633 17th Street
Denver, CO 80202-3607
(303) 844-4513
Fax: (303) 844-2475

Vernon Haragara, Director
Denver Office of Indian
Programs
Executive Tower Building
1405 Curtis Street
Denver, CO 80202-2349
(303) 844-2963

Connecticut
Robert S. Donovon, Deputy
Manager
330 Main Street
Hartford, CT 06106-1860
(203) 240-4523
Fax: (203) 240-4674

Leon Jacobs, Director
Chicago Office of Indian
Programs
77 West Jackson Boulevard
24th Floor
Chicago, IL 60604-3507
(312) 231-1282

Delaware
A. David Sharbaugh, Acting
State Coordinator
824 Market Street
Suite 850
Wilmington, DE 19801-
3016
(302) 573-6300
Fax: (302) 573-6259

Leon Jacobs, Director
Chicago Office of Indian
Programs
77 West Jackson Boulevard
24th Floor
Chicago, IL 60604-3507
(312) 231-1282

District of Columbia
Jessica Franklin, Acting
State Coordinator
Union Center Plaza, Phase II
820 First Street, NE
Suite 300
Washington, DC 20002-
4205
(202) 275-9200
Fax: (202) 275-0779

Florida
James T. Chaplin, State
Coordinator
Southern Bell Tower
Suite 2200
301 West Bay Street
Jacksonville, FL 32202-5121
(904) 232-2626
Fax: (904) 232-3759

(South Florida)
Orlando T. Lorie, Acting
Area Coordinator
Gables 1 Tower
1320 South Dixie Highway
Coral Gables, FL 33146-
2911
(305) 662-4500
Fax: (305) 662-4519

(Central Florida, Western
Counties—Citrus, Sumter,
Hernando, Pasco, Manatee,
Hardee, Highlands, DeSoto,
Sarasota, Charlotte, Olaoes,
Hendry, Lake Okeechobee)
George A. Milburn Jr.,
Acting Area Coordinator
Timberlake Federal Building
Annex
501 East Polk Street
Tampa, FL 33602-3945
(813) 228-2501
Fax: (813) 228-2431

(Central Florida, Eastern
Counties—Volusia, Lake,
Seminole, Orange, Brevard,
Osceola, Indian River,
Okeechobee, St. Lucie)
M. Jeanette Porter, Acting
Area Coordinator
Langley Building
3751 Maguire Boulevard
Suite 270
Orlando, FL 32803-3032
(407) 648-6441
Fax: (407) 648-6310

Leon Jacobs, Director
Chicago Office of Indian
Programs
77 West Jackson Boulevard
24th Floor
Chicago, IL 60604-3507
(312) 231-1282

Georgia
(Atlanta Regional Office)
Davey L. Gibson, Secretary's
Representative
Regional Housing
Commissioner
Richard B. Russell Federal
Building
75 Spring Street, SW
Atlanta, GA 30303-3388
(404) 331-5136
Fax: (404) 331-0845

Leon Jacobs, Director
Chicago Office of Indian
Programs
77 West Jackson Boulevard
24th Floor
Chicago, IL 60604-3507
(312) 231-1282

Guam
Gordon Y. Furutani, Acting
State Coordinator
7 Waterfront Plaza
500 Ala Moana Boulevard
Room 500
Honolulu, HI 96813-4918
(808) 541-1323
Fax: (808) 541-3146

Hawaii
Gordon Y. Furutani, Acting
State Coordinator
7 Waterfront Plaza
500 Ala Moana Boulevard
Room 500
Honolulu, HI 96813-4918
(808) 541-1323
Fax: (808) 541-3146

Idaho
(North Idaho)
Gary Rogers, Acting Area
Coordinator
Farm Credit Bank Building
Eighth Floor East
West 601 First Avenue
Spokane, WA 99204-0317
(509) 353-2510

(West-Central Idaho)
Gary Gillespie, Acting State
Coordinator
Suite 220
Park IV
800 Park Boulevard
Boise, ID 83712-7743
(208) 334-1990
Fax: (208) 334-9648

(South Idaho)
Richard C. Brinck, Acting
State Coordinator
Cascade Building
520 SW Sixth Avenue
Portland, OR 97204-1596
(503) 221-2561

Jerry Leslie, Director
Seattle Office of Indian
Programs
Seattle Federal Office
Building
909 First Avenue
Suite 200
Seattle, WA 98104-1000
(206) 220-5270

Illinois
(Chicago Regional Office)
Edwin Eisendrath,
Secretary's Representative
Regional Housing
Commissioner
Ralph Metcalfe Federal
Building
77 West Jackson Boulevard
Chicago, IL 60604-3507
(312) 353-5680
Fax: (312) 353-0121

(Central and South Illinois)
William Fattick, Acting Area
Coordinator
509 West Capitol
Suite 206
Springfield, IL 62704-1906
(217) 492-4085
Fax: (217) 492-4971

Leon Jacobs, Director
Chicago Office of Indian
Programs
77 West Jackson Boulevard
24th Floor
Chicago, IL 60604-3507
(312) 231-1282

Indiana
J. Nicholas Shelley, Acting
State Coordinator
151 North Delaware Street
Indianapolis, IN 46204-
2526
(317) 226-6303
Fax: (317) 226-6317

Iowa
William R. McNarney,
Acting State Coordinator
HUD—Des Moines Office
Federal Building
Room 239
210 Walnut Street
Des Moines, IA 50309-2155
(515) 284-4512
Fax: (515) 284-4743

Roger M. Massey, Acting
State Coordinator
Executive Tower Center
10909 Mill Valley Road
Omaha, NE 68154-3955
(402) 492-3101
Fax: (402) 492-3150

Leon Jacobs, Director
Chicago Office of Indian
Programs
77 West Jackson Boulevard
24th Floor
Chicago, IL 60604-3507
(312) 231-1282

Kansas
Joseph O'Hern, Secretary's
Representative
Regional Housing
Commissioner
HUD—Kansas City Regional
Office
Gateway Tower II
400 State Avenue
Room 200
Kansas City, KS 66101-2406
(913) 551-5462
Fax: (913) 551-5416

Jim Cook, Acting Director
Oklahoma City Office of
Indian Programs
500 West Main Street
Oklahoma City, OK 73102-
2233

Kentucky
Verna V. Van Ness, Acting
State Coordinator
601 West Broadway
P.O. Box 1044
Louisville, KY 40201-1044
(502) 582-5251
Fax: (502) 582-6074

Leon Jacobs, Director
Chicago Office of Indian
Programs
77 West Jackson Boulevard
24th Floor
Chicago, IL 60604-3507
(312) 231-1282

Louisiana
Robert Vasquez, Acting
State Coordinator
Fisk Federal Building
1661 Canal Street
New Orleans, LA 70112-1887
(504) 589-7200
Fax: (504) 589-2917

(North Louisiana)
Ben Wiley, Acting Area
Coordinator
401 Edwards Street
500 Fannin Street
Shreveport, LA 71101-3077
(318) 266-5385

Jim Cook, Acting Director
Oklahoma City Office of
Indian Programs
500 West Main Street
Oklahoma City, OK 73102-
2233

Maine
Richard Young, Acting State
Coordinator
Casco Northern Bank
Building
23 Main Street
Bangor, ME 04401-6394
(207) 945-0467
Fax: (207) 945-0533

David B. Harrity, Acting
State Coordinator
Norris Cotton Federal
Building
275 Chester Street
Manchester, NH 03103-
2487
(603) 666-7681
Fax: (603) 666-7736

Leon Jacobs, Director
Chicago Office of Indian
Programs
77 West Jackson Boulevard
24th Floor
Chicago, IL 60604-3507
(312) 231-1282

Maryland
(Except Montgomery and
Prince Georges Counties)
Maxine Saunders, Acting
State Coordinator
City Crescent Building
10 South Howard Street
Fifth Floor
Baltimore, MD 21201
(301) 962-2520

(Montgomery and Prince
Georges Counties)
Jessica Franklin, Acting
State Coordinator
Union Center Plaza, Phase II
820 First Street, NE
Suite 300
Washington, DC 20002-
4205
(202) 275-9200
Fax: (202) 275-0779

Leon Jacobs, Director
Chicago Office of Indian
Programs
77 West Jackson Boulevard
24th Floor
Chicago, IL 60604-3507
(312) 231-1282

Massachusetts
(Boston Regional Office)
Mary Lou Crane, Secretary's
Representative
Thomas P. O'Neill Jr.
Federal Building
10 Causeway Street
Room 375
Boston, MA 02222-1092
(617) 565-5234
Fax: (617) 565-5168

Leon Jacobs, Director
Chicago Office of Indian
Programs
77 West Jackson Boulevard
24th Floor
Chicago, IL 60604-3507
(312) 231-1282

Michigan
Harry I. Sharrott, Acting
State Coordinator
Patrick V. McNamara
Federal Building
477 Michigan Avenue
Detroit, MI 48226-2592
(313) 226-7900
Fax: (313) 226-4394

(East Michigan)
Gary T. LeVine, Acting Area
Coordinator
605 North Saginaw Street
Suite 200
Flint, MI 48502-1953
(313) 766-5112
Fax: (313) 766-5122

(West and North Michigan)
Ronald Weston, Acting Area
Coordinator
Northbrook Building, # II
2922 Fuller Avenue, NE
Grand Rapids, MI 49505-
3499
(616) 456-2100
Fax: (616) 456-2191

Leon Jacobs, Director
Chicago Office of Indian
Programs
77 West Jackson Boulevard
24th Floor
Chicago, IL 60604-3507
(312) 231-1282

Minnesota
Thomas Feeney, Acting State
Coordinator
220 Second Street South
Bridge Place Building
Minneapolis, MN 55401-
2195
(612) 370-3000
Fax: (612) 370-3220

Leon Jacobs, Director
Chicago Office of Indian
Programs
77 West Jackson Boulevard
24th Floor
Chicago, IL 60604-3507
(312) 231-1282

Mississippi
Sandra Freeman, Acting
State Coordinator
Koger Building
Dr. A. H. McCoy Federal
Building
100 West Capitol Street
Room 910
Jackson, MS 39269-1096
(601) 965-5308
Fax: (601) 965-4773

Leon Jacobs, Director
Chicago Office of Indian
Programs
77 West Jackson Boulevard
24th Floor
Chicago, IL 60604-3507
(312) 231-1282

Missouri
Kenneth G. Lange, Acting
Area Coordinator
1222 Spruce Street
Room 3207
St. Louis, MO 63103-2836
(314) 539-6560
Fax: (314) 539-6575

Jim Cook, Acting Director
Oklahoma City Office of
Indian Programs
500 West Main Street
Oklahoma City, OK 73102-
2233

Montana
Gerard Boone, Acting State
Coordinator
Federal Office Building,
Drawer 10095
301 South Park
Room 340
Helena, MT 59626-0095
(406) 449-5205
Fax: (406) 449-5207

Vernon Haragara, Director
Denver Office of Indian
Programs
Executive Tower Building
1405 Curtis Street
Denver, CO 80202-2349
(303) 844-2963

Nebraska
Roger M. Massey, Acting
State Coordinator
Executive Tower Center
10909 Mill Valley Road
Omaha, NE 68154-3955
(402) 492-3101
Fax: (402) 492-3150

Vernon Haragara, Director
Denver Office of Indian
Programs
Executive Tower Building
1405 Curtis Street
Denver, CO 80202-2349
(303) 844-2963

Nevada
Andrew D. Whitten Jr.,
Acting Area Coordinator
1575 DeLucchi Lane
Room 114
P.O. Box 30050
Reno, NV 89502-6581
(702) 784-5356
Fax: (702) 784-5066

Benjamin Davis, Acting
State Coordinator
1500 East Tropicana Avenue
Second Floor
Las Vegas, NV 89119-6516
(702) 388-6500
Fax: (702) 388-6736

Raphael Mecham, Director
HUD Indian Programs
Office
400 North Fifth Street
Suite 1650
Phoenix, AZ 85004-2361
(602) 379-4156
Fax: (602) 379-3101

New Hampshire
David B. Harrity, Acting
State Coordinator
Norris Cotton Federal
Building
275 Chestnut Street
Manchester, NH 03103-
2487
(603) 666-7681
Fax: (603) 666-7736

Leon Jacobs, Director
Chicago Office of Indian
Programs
77 West Jackson Boulevard
24th Floor
Chicago, IL 60604-3507
(312) 231-1282

New Jersey
(North New Jersey)
Diane Johnson, Acting State
Coordinator
One Newark Center
13th Floor
Newark, NJ 07102-5260
(201) 622-7900
Fax: (201) 645-6239

(South New Jersey)
Elmer Roy, Acting Area
Coordinator
Hudson Building
Second Floor
800 Hudson Square
Camden, NJ 08102-1156
(609) 757-5081
Fax: (609) 757-5373

Leon Jacobs, Director
Chicago Office of Indian
Programs
77 West Jackson Boulevard
24th Floor
Chicago, IL 60604-3507
(312) 231-1282

New Mexico
Michael R. Griego, Acting
State Coordinator
625 Truman Street, NW
Albuquerque, NM 87110-6443
(505) 262-6463

Clarence D. Babers, Acting
Area Coordinator
525 Griffin Street
Room 860
Dallas, TX 75202-5007
(214) 767-8359
Fax: (214) 767-8973

Raphael Mecham, Director
HUD Indian Programs
Office
400 North Fifth Street
Suite 1650
Phoenix, AZ 85004-2361
(602) 379-4156
Fax: (602) 379-3101

New York
(New York Regional Office)
Jose Cintron, Secretary's
Representative
26 Federal Plaza
New York, NY 10278-0068
(212) 264-6500
Fax: (212) 264-0246

(North New York)
John Petricco, Acting Area
Coordinator
52 Corporate Circle
Albany, NY 12203-5121
(518) 464-4200
Fax: (518) 464-4300

(West New York)
Joseph Lynch, Acting Area
Coordinator
465 Main Street
Lafayette Court
Fifth Floor
Buffalo, NY 14203-1780
(716) 846-5755
Fax: (716) 846-5752

Leon Jacobs, Director
Chicago Office of Indian
Programs
77 West Jackson Boulevard
24th Floor
Chicago, IL 60604-3507
(312) 231-1282

North Carolina
Larry J. Parker, Acting State
Coordinator
2306 West Meadowview
Road
Koger Building
Greensboro, NC 27407-3707
(919) 547-4001
Fax: (919) 547-4015

Leon Jacobs, Director
Chicago Office of Indian
Programs
77 West Jackson Boulevard
24th Floor
Chicago, IL 60604-3507
(312) 231-1282

North Dakota
Keith Elliott, Acting State
Coordinator
HUD—Fargo Office
Federal Building
657 Second Avenue, North
Fargo, ND 58108-2483
(701) 239-5136
Fax: (701) 783-5249

Vernon Haragara, Director
Denver Office of Indian
Programs
Executive Tower Building
1405 Curtis Street
Denver, CO 80202-2349
(303) 844-2963

Ohio
Robert W. Dolin, Acting
State Coordinator
HUD—Columbus Office
200 North High Street
Columbus, OH 43215-2499
(614) 469-5737
Fax: (614) 469-2432

(North Ohio)
Philip Ginconia, Acting Area
Coordinator
1350 Euclid Avenue
Fifth Floor
Cleveland, OH 44115-1815
(216) 552-4065
Fax: (216) 522-2975

(Southwest Ohio)
William Harris, Acting Area
Coordinator
Federal Office Building
Room 9002
550 Main Street
Cincinnati, OH 45202-3253
(513) 684-2884
Fax: (513) 684-6224

Leon Jacobs, Director
Chicago Office of Indian
Programs
77 West Jackson Boulevard
24th Floor
Chicago, IL 60604-3507
(312) 231-1282

Oklahoma
Katie Worsham, Acting State
Coordinator
500 West Main Street
Oklahoma City, OK 73102-
2233

(East Oklahoma)
James S. Colgan, Acting
Area Coordinator
1516 South Boston Avenue
Room 110
Tulsa, OK 74119-4032
(918) 581-7435
Fax: (918) 581-7440

Jim Cook, Acting Director
Oklahoma City Office of
Indian Programs
500 West Main Street
Oklahoma City, OK 73102-
2233

Oregon
Richard C. Brinck, Acting
State Coordinator
Cascade Building
520 SW Sixth Avenue
Portland, OR 97204-1596
(503) 326-2561
Fax: (503) 326-3097

Jerry Leslie, Director
Seattle Office of Indian
Programs
Seattle Federal Office
Building
909 First Avenue
Suite 200
Seattle, WA 98104-1000
(206) 220-5270

Panama Canal Zone
Rosa Villalonga, Acting
State Coordinator
159 Carlos E. Chardon
Avenue
San Juan, PR 00918-1804
(809) 766-6121
Fax: (809) 498-5201

Pennsylvania
(Philadelphia Regional
Office)
Karen A. Miller, Secretary's
Representative
Regional Housing
Commissioner
Liberty Square Building
105 South Seventh Street
Philadelphia, PA 19106-
3392
(215) 597-2560
Fax: (215) 597-9627

(West Pennsylvania)
Choice Edwards, Acting
Area Coordinator
412 Old Post Office
Courthouse Building
Seventh Avenue and Grant
Street
Pittsburgh, PA 15219-1906
(412) 644-6428
Fax: (412) 644-6499

Leon Jacobs, Director
Chicago Office of Indian
Programs
77 West Jackson Boulevard
24th Floor
Chicago, IL 60604-3507
(312) 231-1282

Puerto Rico
Rosa Villalonga, Acting
State Coordinator
159 Carlos E. Chardon
Avenue
San Juan, PR 00918-1804
(809) 766-6121
Fax: (809) 498-5201

Rhode Island
Michael Dziok, Acting State
Coordinator
Room 303
John O. Pastore Federal
Building and U.S. Post
Office
Kennedy Plaza
Providence, RI 02903-1785
(401) 528-5351
Fax: (401) 528-5312

Leon Jacobs, Director
Chicago Office of Indian
Programs
77 West Jackson Boulevard
24th Floor
Chicago, IL 60604-3507
(312) 231-1282

South Carolina
Ted B. Freeman, Acting
State Coordinator
Strom Thurmond Federal
Building
1835 Assembly Street
Columbia, SC 29201-2480
(803) 765-5592
Fax: (803) 765-5515

Leon Jacobs, Director
Chicago Office of Indian
Programs
77 West Jackson Boulevard
24th Floor
Chicago, IL 60604-3507
(312) 231-1282

South Dakota
Don Olson, Acting State
Coordinator
Suite I-201
2400 West 49th Street
Sioux Falls, SD 57105-6558
(605) 330-4223
Fax: (605) 330-4465

Vernon Haragara, Director
Denver Office of Indian
Programs
Executive Tower Building
1405 Curtis Street
Denver, CO 80202-2349
(303) 844-2963

Tennessee
Mark Brezina, Acting Area
Coordinator
John J. Duncan Federal
Building
Third Floor
710 Locust Street, SW
Knoxville, TN 37902-2526
(615) 545-4384
Fax: (615) 545-4569

(West Tennessee)
Bob Atkins, Acting Area
Coordinator
One Memphis Place
200 Jefferson Avenue
Suite 1200
Memphis, TN 38103-2335
(901) 544-3367
Fax: (901) 544-3697

(Central Tennessee)
John H. Fisher, Acting State
Coordinator
251 Cumberland Bend Drive
Nashville, TN 37228-1803
(615) 736-5213
Fax: (615) 736-2018

Leon Jacobs, Director
Chicago Office of Indian
Programs
77 West Jackson Boulevard
24th Floor
Chicago, IL 60604-3507
(312) 231-1282

Texas
(Fort Worth Regional
Office)
Stephen Weatherforce,
Secretary's Representative
1600 Throckmorton
P.O. Box 2905
Fort Worth, TX 76113-2905
(817) 885-5401
Fax: (817) 885-5629

(East, North, and West
Texas)
Clarence D. Babers, Acting
Area Coordinator
525 Griffin Street
Room 860
Dallas, TX 75202-5007
(214) 767-8359
Fax: (214) 767-8973

(Northwest Texas)
Henry E. Whitney, Acting
Area Coordinator
Federal Office Building
1205 Texas Avenue
Lubbock, TX 79401-4093
(806) 743-7265

(Southwest Texas)
A. Cynthia Leon, Acting
Area Coordinator
Washington Square Building
800 Dolorosa Street
San Antonio, TX 78207-
4563
(512) 229-6800

(East-Central Texas)
George Rodriguez, Acting
Area Coordinator
Norfolk Tower
2211 Norfolk
Room 200
Houston, TX 77098-4096
(713) 653-3274

(Bowie County)
John T. Suskie, Acting State
Coordinator
TCBY Tower
425 West Capitol Avenue
Suite 900
Little Rock, AR 72201-3488
(501) 324-5931
Fax: (501) 324-5900

(Five Counties in East
Texas)
Ben Wiley, Acting Area
Coordinator
401 Edwards Street
500 Fannin Street
Shreveport, LA 71101-3107
(318) 266-5385

Jim Cook, Acting Director
Oklahoma City Office of
Indian Programs
500 West Main Street
Oklahoma City, OK 73102-
2233

Utah
Richard Bell, Acting State
Coordinator
257 Tower Building
257 East, 200 South
Salt Lake City, UT 84111-
2048
(801) 524-5379
Fax: (801) 524-5701

Vernon Haragara, Director
Denver Office of Indian
Programs
Executive Tower Building
1405 Curtis Street
Denver, CO 80202-2349
(303) 844-2963

Vermont
William Peters, Acting State
Coordinator
Federal Building
Room 244
11 Elmwood Avenue
P.O. Box 879
Burlington, VT 05402-0879
(802) 951-6290
Fax: (802) 951-6298

David B. Harrity, Acting
State Coordinator
Norris Cotton Federal
Building
275 Chester Street
Manchester, NH 03103-
2487
(603) 666-7681
Fax: (603) 666-7736

Leon Jacobs, Director
Chicago Office of Indian
Programs
77 West Jackson Boulevard
24th Floor
Chicago, IL 60604-3507
(312) 231-1282

Virginia
(North Virginia)
Jessica Franklin, Acting
State Coordinator
Union Center Plaza, Phase II
820 First Street, NE
Suite 300
Washington, DC 20002-
4205
(202) 275-9200
Fax: (202) 275-0779

(South Virginia)
Mary Ann Wilson, Acting
State Coordinator
P.O. Box 90331
3600 West Broad Street
Richmond, VA 23230-0331
(804) 278-4507

Leon Jacobs, Director
Chicago Office of Indian
Programs
77 West Jackson Boulevard
24th Floor
Chicago, IL 60604-3507
(312) 231-1282

Virgin Islands
Rosa Villalonga, Acting
State Coordinator
159 Carlos E. Chardon
Avenue
San Juan, PR 00918-1804
(809) 766-6121
Fax: (809) 498-5201

Washington
(Seattle Regional Office)
Bob Santos, Secretary's
Representative
Regional Housing
Commissioner
Seattle Federal Office
Building
Suite 200
909 First Avenue
Seattle, WA 98104-1000
(206) 220-5101
Fax: (206) 220-5133

(Clark, Klickitat, and
Skamania Counties)
Richard C. Brinck, Acting
State Coordinator
Cascase Building
520 SW Sixth Avenue
Portland, OR 97204-1596
(503) 326-2561
Fax: (503) 326-3097

(East Washington)
Gary Rogers, Acting Area
Coordinator
Eighth Floor East
Farm Credit Bank Building
West 601 First Avenue
Spokane, WA 99204-0317
(509) 353-2510

Jerry Leslie, Director
Seattle Office of Indian
Programs
Seattle Federal Office
Building
909 First Avenue
Suite 200
Seattle, WA 98104-1000
(206) 220-5270

West Virginia
Fred Roncaglione, Acting
State Coordinator
405 Capitol Street
Suite 708
Charleston, WV 25301-
1795
(304) 347-7000
Fax: (304) 347-7050

Choice Edwards, Acting
Area Coordinator
412 Old Post Office
Courthouse Building
Seventh Avenue and Grant
Street
Pittsburgh, PA 15219-1906
(412) 644-6428
Fax: (412) 644-6499

Leon Jacobs, Director
Chicago Office of Indian
Programs
77 West Jackson Boulevard
24th Floor
Chicago, IL 60604-3507
(312) 231-1282

Wisconsin
Delbert F. Reynolds, Acting
State Coordinator
Henry S. Reuss Federal
Plaza
310 West Wisconsin Avenue
Milwaukee, WI 53203-2289
(414) 297-3214
Fax: (414) 297-3947

Leon Jacobs, Director
Chicago Office of Indian
Programs
77 West Jackson Boulevard
24th Floor
Chicago, IL 60604-3507
(312) 231-1282

Wyoming
William Garrett, Acting
State Coordinator
4225 Federal Office Building
100 East B Street
P.O. Box 120
Casper, WY 82602-1918
(307) 261-5252
Fax: (307) 261-5251

Vernon Haragara, Director
Denver Office of Indian
Programs
Executive Tower Building
1405 Curtis Street
Denver, CO 80202-2349
(303) 844-2963

MORTGAGE INSURANCE—EXPERIMENTAL RENTAL HOUSING

Department of Housing and
Urban Development (HUD)
Policy Development and
Research
Division of Affordable
Housing Research and
Technology
451 Seventh Street, SW
Washington, DC 20410
(202) 708-4370

Description: Guaranteed/insured loans to builders/owners for
construction or rehabilitation of multifamily housing
facilities incorporating experimental building methods
designed to reduce housing costs, raise living standards, and
improve neighborhood design. Applicants must prove that
new technology represents an acceptable risk to HUD.
$ Given: To date, 5,000 units insured for $100 million;
average: $2.3 million per project
Application Information: Initial conference with local HUD
field office followed by formal application.
Deadline: Established on a case-by-case basis at local HUD
field office.
Contact: Nearest local HUD field office

Alabama
Heager Hill, Acting State
Coordinator
600 Beacon Parkway West
Suite 300
Birmingham, AL 35209-
3144
(205) 290-7617

Leon Jacobs, Director
Chicago Office of Indian
Programs
77 West Jackson Boulevard
24th Floor
Chicago, IL 60604-3507
(312) 231-1282

Alaska
Arlene Patton, Manager
University Plaza Building
949 East 36th Avenue
Suite 401
Anchorage, AK 99508-4135
(907) 271-4170
Fax: (907) 271-3667

Martin Knight, Director
Anchorage Indian Housing
Division
949 East 36th Avenue
Suite 401
Anchorage, AK 99508-4135
(907) 271-4633

American Samoa
Gordon Y. Furutani, Acting
State Coordinator
7 Waterfront Plaza
500 Ala Moana Boulevard
Room 500
Honolulu, HI 96813-4918
(808) 541-1323
Fax: (808) 541-3146

Arizona
Dwight A. Peterson, Acting
State Coordinator
Two Arizona Center
400 North Fifth Street
Suite 1600
Phoenix, AZ 85004-2361
(602) 379-4434
Fax: (602) 379-3985

Sharon Atwell, Acting Area
Coordinator
33 North Stone Avenue
Room 700
Tucson, AZ 85701-1467
(602) 670-6237
Fax: (602) 670-6207

Charles Ming, Acting Area
Coordinator
1615 West Olympic
Boulevard
Los Angeles, CA 90015-
3801
(213) 251-7122
Fax: (213) 251-7096

Raphael Mecham, Director
HUD Indian Programs
Office
400 North Fifth Street
Suite 1650
Phoenix, AZ 85004-2361
(602) 379-4156
Fax: (602) 379-3101

Arkansas
John T. Suskie, Acting State
Coordinator
TCBY Tower
425 West Capitol Avenue
Suite 900
Little Rock, AR 72201-3488
(501) 324-5931
Fax: (501) 324-5900

Jim Cook, Acting Director
Oklahoma City Office of
Indian Programs
500 West Main Street
Oklahoma City, OK 73102-
2233

California
(San Francisco Regional
Office)
Arthur Agnos, Secretary's
Representative
Phillip Burton Federal
Building and U.S.
Courthouse
P.O. Box 36003
450 Golden Gate Avenue
San Francisco, CA 94102-
3448
(415) 556-4752
Fax: (415) 556-4176

(South California)
Charles Ming, Acting Area
Coordinator
1615 West Olympic
Boulevard
Los Angeles, CA 90015-3801
(213) 251-7122
Fax: (213) 251-7096

(Fresno)
Willie Mae Haskin, Acting
Area Coordinator
1630 East Shaw Avenue
Fresno, CA 93710-8193
(209) 487-5033
Fax: (209) 487-5344

(Northeast California)
Paul Pradia, Acting Area
Coordinator
777 12th Street
Suite 200
Sacramento, CA 95814-1997
(916) 551-1351
Fax: (916) 551-2899

(Imperial and San Diego
Counties)
Charles J. Wilson, Acting
Area Coordinator
Mission City Corporate
Center
Suite 300
2365 Northside Drive
San Diego, CA 92108-2712
(619) 557-5310
Fax: (619) 557-6296

(Orange, Riverside, and San
Bernadino Counties, for
home mortgages)
Samuel Sandoval, Acting
Area Coordinator
3 Hutton Centre
Suite 500
Santa Ana, CA 92707-5764
(714) 957-7333
Fax: (714) 957-1903

Raphael Mecham, Director
HUD Indian Programs
Office
400 North Fifth Street
Suite 1650
Phoenix, AZ 85004-2361
(602) 379-4156
Fax: (602) 379-3101

Colorado
(Denver Regional Office)
Anthony Hernandez,
Secretary's Representative
HUD—Denver Office
633 17th Street
Denver, CO 80202-3607
(303) 844-4513
Fax: (303) 844-2475

Vernon Haragara, Director
Denver Office of Indian
Programs
Executive Tower Building
1405 Curtis Street
Denver, CO 80202-2349
(303) 844-2963

Connecticut
Robert S. Donovon, Deputy
Manager
330 Main Street
Hartford, CT 06106-1860
(203) 240-4523
Fax: (203) 240-4674

Leon Jacobs, Director
Chicago Office of Indian
Programs
77 West Jackson Boulevard
24th Floor
Chicago, IL 60604-3507
(312) 231-1282

Delaware
A. David Sharbaugh, Acting
State Coordinator
824 Market Street
Suite 850
Wilmington, DE 19801-
3016
(302) 573-6300
Fax: (302) 573-6259

Leon Jacobs, Director
Chicago Office of Indian
Programs
77 West Jackson Boulevard
24th Floor
Chicago, IL 60604-3507
(312) 231-1282

District of Columbia
Jessica Franklin, Acting
State Coordinator
Union Center Plaza, Phase II
820 First Street, NE
Suite 300
Washington, DC 20002-
4205
(202) 275-9200
Fax: (202) 275-0779

Florida
James T. Chaplin, State
Coordinator
Southern Bell Tower
Suite 2200
301 West Bay Street
Jacksonville, FL 32202-5121
(904) 232-2626
Fax: (904) 232-3759

(South Florida)
Orlando T. Lorie, Acting
Area Coordinator
Gables 1 Tower
1320 South Dixie Highway
Coral Gables, FL 33146-
2911
(305) 662-4500
Fax: (305) 662-4519

(Central Florida, Western
Counties—Citrus, Sumter,
Hernando, Pasco, Manatee,
Hardee, Highlands, DeSoto,
Sarasota, Charlotte, Olaoes,
Hendry, Lake Okeechobee)
George A. Milburn Jr.,
Acting Area Coordinator
Timberlake Federal Building
Annex
501 East Polk Street
Tampa, FL 33602-3945
(813) 228-2501
Fax: (813) 228-2431

(Central Florida, Eastern
Counties—Volusia, Lake,
Seminole, Orange, Brevard,
Osceola, Indian River,
Okeechobee, St. Lucie)
M. Jeanette Porter, Acting
Area Coordinator
Langley Building
3751 Maguire Boulevard
Suite 270
Orlando, FL 32803-3032
(407) 648-6441
Fax: (407) 648-6310

Leon Jacobs, Director
Chicago Office of Indian
Programs
77 West Jackson Boulevard
24th Floor
Chicago, IL 60604-3507
(312) 231-1282

Georgia
(Atlanta Regional Office)
Davey L. Gibson, Secretary's
Representative
Regional Housing
Commissioner
Richard B. Russell Federal
Building
75 Spring Street, SW
Atlanta, GA 30303-3388
(404) 331-5136
Fax: (404) 331-0845

Leon Jacobs, Director
Chicago Office of Indian
Programs
77 West Jackson Boulevard
24th Floor
Chicago, IL 60604-3507
(312) 231-1282

Guam
Gordon Y. Furutani, Acting
State Coordinator
7 Waterfront Plaza
500 Ala Moana Boulevard
Room 500
Honolulu, HI 96813-4918
(808) 541-1323
Fax: (808) 541-3146

Hawaii
Gordon Y. Furutani, Acting
State Coordinator
7 Waterfront Plaza
500 Ala Moana Boulevard
Room 500
Honolulu, HI 96813-4918
(808) 541-1323
Fax: (808) 541-3146

Idaho
(North Idaho)
Gary Rogers, Acting Area
Coordinator
Farm Credit Bank Building
Eighth Floor East
West 601 First Avenue
Spokane, WA 99204-0317
(509) 353-2510

(West-Central Idaho)
Gary Gillespie, Acting State
Coordinator
Suite 220
Park IV
800 Park Boulevard
Boise, ID 83712-7743
(208) 334-1990
Fax: (208) 334-9648

(South Idaho)
Richard C. Brinck, Acting
State Coordinator
Cascade Building
520 SW Sixth Avenue
Portland, OR 97204-1596
(503) 221-2561

Jerry Leslie, Director
Seattle Office of Indian
Programs
Seattle Federal Office
Building
909 First Avenue
Suite 200
Seattle, WA 98104-1000
(206) 220-5270

Illinois
(Chicago Regional Office)
Edwin Eisendrath,
Secretary's Representative
Regional Housing
Commissioner
Ralph Metcalfe Federal
Building
77 West Jackson Boulevard
Chicago, IL 60604-3507
(312) 353-5680
Fax: (312) 353-0121

(Central and South Illinois)
William Fattick, Acting Area
Coordinator
509 West Capitol
Suite 206
Springfield, IL 62704-1906
(217) 492-4085
Fax: (217) 492-4971

Leon Jacobs, Director
Chicago Office of Indian
Programs
77 West Jackson Boulevard
24th Floor
Chicago, IL 60604-3507
(312) 231-1282

Indiana
J. Nicholas Shelley, Acting
State Coordinator
151 North Delaware Street
Indianapolis, IN 46204-
2526
(317) 226-6303
Fax: (317) 226-6317

Iowa
William R. McNarney,
Acting State Coordinator
HUD—Des Moines Office
Federal Building
Room 239
210 Walnut Street
Des Moines, IA 50309-2155
(515) 284-4512
Fax: (515) 284-4743

Roger M. Massey, Acting
State Coordinator
Executive Tower Center
10909 Mill Valley Road
Omaha, NE 68154-3955
(402) 492-3101
Fax: (402) 492-3150

Leon Jacobs, Director
Chicago Office of Indian
Programs
77 West Jackson Boulevard
24th Floor
Chicago, IL 60604-3507
(312) 231-1282

Kansas
Joseph O'Hern, Secretary's
Representative
Regional Housing
Commissioner
HUD—Kansas City Regional
Office
Gateway Tower II
400 State Avenue
Room 200
Kansas City, KS 66101-2406
(913) 551-5462
Fax: (913) 551-5416

Jim Cook, Acting Director
Oklahoma City Office of
Indian Programs
500 West Main Street
Oklahoma City, OK 73102-
2233

Kentucky
Verna V. Van Ness, Acting
State Coordinator
601 West Broadway
P.O. Box 1044
Louisville, KY 40201-1044
(502) 582-5251
Fax: (502) 582-6074

Leon Jacobs, Director
Chicago Office of Indian
Programs
77 West Jackson Boulevard
24th Floor
Chicago, IL 60604-3507
(312) 231-1282

Louisiana
Robert Vasquez, Acting
State Coordinator
Fisk Federal Building
1661 Canal Street
New Orleans, LA 70112-
1887
(504) 589-7200
Fax: (504) 589-2917

(North Louisiana)
Ben Wiley, Acting Area
Coordinator
401 Edwards Street
500 Fannin Street
Shreveport, LA 71101-3077
(318) 266-5385

Jim Cook, Acting Director
Oklahoma City Office of
Indian Programs
500 West Main Street
Oklahoma City, OK 73102-
2233

Maine
Richard Young, Acting State
Coordinator
Casco Northern Bank
Building
23 Main Street
Bangor, ME 04401-6394
(207) 945-0467
Fax: (207) 945-0533

David B. Harrity, Acting
State Coordinator
Norris Cotton Federal
Building
275 Chester Street
Manchester, NH 03103-
2487
(603) 666-7681
Fax: (603) 666-7736

Leon Jacobs, Director
Chicago Office of Indian
Programs
77 West Jackson Boulevard
24th Floor
Chicago, IL 60604-3507
(312) 231-1282

Maryland
(Except Montgomery and
Prince Georges Counties)
Maxine Saunders, Acting
State Coordinator
City Crescent Building
10 South Howard Street
Fifth Floor
Baltimore, MD 21201
(301) 962-2520

(Montgomery and Prince
Georges Counties)
Jessica Franklin, Acting
State Coordinator
Union Center Plaza, Phase II
820 First Street, NE
Suite 300
Washington, DC 20002-
4205
(202) 275-9200
Fax: (202) 275-0779

Leon Jacobs, Director
Chicago Office of Indian
Programs
77 West Jackson Boulevard
24th Floor
Chicago, IL 60604-3507
(312) 231-1282

Massachusetts
(Boston Regional Office)
Mary Lou Crane, Secretary's
Representative
Thomas P. O'Neill Jr.
Federal Building
10 Causeway Street
Room 375
Boston, MA 02222-1092
(617) 565-5234
Fax: (617) 565-5168

Leon Jacobs, Director
Chicago Office of Indian
Programs
77 West Jackson Boulevard
24th Floor
Chicago, IL 60604-3507
(312) 231-1282

Michigan
Harry I. Sharrott, Acting
State Coordinator
Patrick V. McNamara
Federal Building
477 Michigan Avenue
Detroit, MI 48226-2592
(313) 226-7900
Fax: (313) 226-4394

(Eastern Michigan)
Gary T. LeVine, Acting Area
Coordinator
605 North Saginaw Street
Suite 200
Flint, MI 48502-1953
(313) 766-5112
Fax: (313) 766-5122

(Wester and Northern
Michigan)
Ronald Weston, Acting Area
Coordinator
Northbrook Building, # II
2922 Fuller Avenue, NE
Grand Rapids, MI 49505-
3499
(616) 456-2100
Fax: (616) 456-2191

Leon Jacobs, Director
Chicago Office of Indian
Programs
77 West Jackson Boulevard
24th Floor
Chicago, IL 60604-3507
(312) 231-1282

Minnesota
Thomas Feeney, Acting State
Coordinator
220 Second Street South
Bridge Place Building
Minneapolis, MN 55401-
2195
(612) 370-3000
Fax: (612) 370-3220

Leon Jacobs, Director
Chicago Office of Indian
Programs
77 West Jackson Boulevard
24th Floor
Chicago, IL 60604-3507
(312) 231-1282

Mississippi
Sandra Freeman, Acting
State Coordinator
Koger Building
Dr. A. H. McCoy Federal
Building
100 West Capitol Street
Room 910
Jackson, MS 39269-1096
(601) 965-5308
Fax: (601) 965-4773

Leon Jacobs, Director
Chicago Office of Indian
Programs
77 West Jackson Boulevard
24th Floor
Chicago, IL 60604-3507
(312) 231-1282

Missouri
Kenneth G. Lange, Acting
Area Coordinator
1222 Spruce Street
Room 3207
St. Louis, MO 63103-2836
(314) 539-6560
Fax: (314) 539-6575

Jim Cook, Acting Director
Oklahoma City Office of
Indian Programs
500 West Main Street
Oklahoma City, OK 73102-
2233

Montana
Gerard Boone, Acting State
Coordinator
Federal Office Building,
Drawer 10095
301 South Park
Room 340
Helena, MT 59626-0095
(406) 449-5205
Fax: (406) 449-5207

Vernon Haragara, Director
Denver Office of Indian
Programs
Executive Tower Building
1405 Curtis Street
Denver, CO 80202-2349
(303) 844-2963

Nebraska
Roger M. Massey, Acting
State Coordinator
Executive Tower Center
10909 Mill Valley Road
Omaha, NE 68154-3955
(402) 492-3101
Fax: (402) 492-3150

Vernon Haragara, Director
Denver Office of Indian
Programs
Executive Tower Building
1405 Curtis Street
Denver, CO 80202-2349
(303) 844-2963

Nevada
Andrew D. Whitten Jr.,
Acting Area Coordinator
1575 DeLucchi Lane
Room 114
P.O. Box 30050
Reno, NV 89502-6581
(702) 784-5356
Fax: (702) 784-5066

Benjamin Davis, Acting
State Coordinator
1500 East Tropicana Avenue
Second Floor
Las Vegas, NV 89119-6516
(702) 388-6500
Fax: (702) 388-6736

Raphael Mecham, Director
HUD Indian Programs
Office
400 North Fifth Street
Suite 1650
Phoenix, AZ 85004-2361
(602) 379-4156
Fax: (602) 379-3101

New Hampshire
David B. Harrity, Acting
State Coordinator
Norris Cotton Federal
Building
275 Chestnut Street
Manchester, NH 03103-
2487
(603) 666-7681
Fax: (603) 666-7736

Leon Jacobs, Director
Chicago Office of Indian
Programs
77 West Jackson Boulevard
24th Floor
Chicago, IL 60604-3507
(312) 231-1282

New Jersey
(North New Jersey)
Diane Johnson, Acting State
Coordinator
One Newark Center
13th Floor
Newark, NJ 07102-5260
(201) 622-7900
Fax: (201) 645-6239

(South New Jersey)
Elmer Roy, Acting Area
Coordinator
Hudson Building
Second Floor
800 Hudson Square
Camden, NJ 08102-1156
(609) 757-5081
Fax: (609) 757-5373

Leon Jacobs, Director
Chicago Office of Indian
Programs
77 West Jackson Boulevard
24th Floor
Chicago, IL 60604-3507
(312) 231-1282

New Mexico
Michael R. Griego, Acting
State Coordinator
625 Truman Street, NW
Albuquerque, NM 87110-
6443
(505) 262-6463

Clarence D. Babers, Acting
Area Coordinator
525 Griffin Street
Room 860
Dallas, TX 75202-5007
(214) 767-8359
Fax: (214) 767-8973

Raphael Mecham, Director
HUD Indian Programs
Office
400 North Fifth Street
Suite 1650
Phoenix, AZ 85004-2361
(602) 379-4156
Fax: (602) 379-3101

New York
(New York Regional Office)
Jose Cintron, Secretary's
Representative
26 Federal Plaza
New York, NY 10278-0068
(212) 264-6500
Fax: (212) 264-0246

(North New York)
John Petricco, Acting Area
Coordinator
52 Corporate Circle
Albany, NY 12203-5121
(518) 464-4200
Fax: (518) 464-4300

(West New York)
Joseph Lynch, Acting Area
Coordinator
465 Main Street
Lafayette Court
Fifth Floor
Buffalo, NY 14203-1780
(716) 846-5755
Fax: (716) 846-5752

Leon Jacobs, Director
Chicago Office of Indian
Programs
77 West Jackson Boulevard
24th Floor
Chicago, IL 60604-3507
(312) 231-1282

North Carolina
Larry J. Parker, Acting State
Coordinator
2306 West Meadowview
Road
Koger Building
Greensboro, NC 27407-
3707
(919) 547-4001
Fax: (919) 547-4015

Leon Jacobs, Director
Chicago Office of Indian
Programs
77 West Jackson Boulevard
24th Floor
Chicago, IL 60604-3507
(312) 231-1282

North Dakota
Keith Elliott, Acting State
Coordinator
HUD—Fargo Office
Federal Building
657 Second Avenue, North
Fargo, ND 58108-2483
(701) 239-5136
Fax: (701) 783-5249

Vernon Haragara, Director
Denver Office of Indian
Programs
Executive Tower Building
1405 Curtis Street
Denver, CO 80202-2349
(303) 844-2963

Ohio
Robert W. Dolin, Acting
State Coordinator
HUD—Columbus Office
200 North High Street
Columbus, OH 43215-2499
(614) 469-5737
Fax: (614) 469-2432

(North Ohio)
Philip Ginconia, Acting Area
Coordinator
1350 Euclid Avenue
Fifth Floor
Cleveland, OH 44115-1815
(216) 552-4065
Fax: (216) 522-2975

(Southwest Ohio)
William Harris, Acting Area
Coordinator
Federal Office Building
Room 9002
550 Main Street
Cincinnati, OH 45202-3253
(513) 684-2884
Fax: (513) 684-6224

Leon Jacobs, Director
Chicago Office of Indian
Programs
77 West Jackson Boulevard
24th Floor
Chicago, IL 60604-3507
(312) 231-1282

Oklahoma
Edwin I. Gardner, Acting
State Coordinator
500 West Main Street
200 NW Fifth Street
Oklahoma City, OK 73102-
2233
(405) 231-4181
Fax: (405) 231-4648

(East Oklahoma)
James S. Colgan, Acting
Area Coordinator
1516 South Boston Avenue
Room 110
Tulsa, OK 74119-4032
(918) 581-7435
Fax: (918) 581-7440

Jim Cook, Acting Director
Oklahoma City Office of
Indian Programs
500 West Main Street
Oklahoma City, OK 73102-
2233

Oregon
Richard C. Brinck, Acting
State Coordinator
Cascade Building
520 SW Sixth Avenue
Portland, OR 97204-1596
(503) 326-2561
Fax: (503) 326-3097

Jerry Leslie, Director
Seattle Office of Indian
Programs
Seattle Federal Office
Building
909 First Avenue
Suite 200
Seattle, WA 98104-1000
(206) 220-5270

Panama Canal Zone
Rosa Villalonga, Acting
State Coordinator
159 Carlos E. Chardon
Avenue
San Juan, PR 00918-1804
(809) 766-6121
Fax: (809) 498-5201

Pennsylvania
(Philadelphia Regional
Office)
Karen A. Miller, Secretary's
Representative
Regional Housing
Commissioner
Liberty Square Building
105 South Seventh Street
Philadelphia, PA 19106-
3392
(215) 597-2560
Fax: (215) 597-9627

(West Pennsylvania)
Choice Edwards, Acting
Area Coordinator
412 Old Post Office
Courthouse Building
Seventh Avenue and Grant
Street
Pittsburgh, PA 15219-1906
(412) 644-6428
Fax: (412) 644-6499

Leon Jacobs, Director
Chicago Office of Indian
Programs
77 West Jackson Boulevard
24th Floor
Chicago, IL 60604-3507
(312) 231-1282

Puerto Rico
Rosa Villalonga, Acting
State Coordinator
159 Carlos E. Chardon
Avenue
San Juan, PR 00918-1804
(809) 766-6121
Fax: (809) 498-5201

Rhode Island
Michael Dziok, Acting State
Coordinator
Room 303
John O. Pastore Federal
Building and U.S. Post
Office
Kennedy Plaza
Providence, RI 02903-1785
(401) 528-5351
Fax: (401) 528-5312

Leon Jacobs, Director
Chicago Office of Indian
Programs
77 West Jackson Boulevard
24th Floor
Chicago, IL 60604-3507
(312) 231-1282

South Carolina
Ted B. Freeman, Acting
State Coordinator
Strom Thurmond Federal
Building
1835 Assembly Street
Columbia, SC 29201-2480
(803) 765-5592
Fax: (803) 765-5515

Leon Jacobs, Director
Chicago Office of Indian
Programs
77 West Jackson Boulevard
24th Floor
Chicago, IL 60604-3507
(312) 231-1282

South Dakota
Don Olson, Acting State
Coordinator
Suite I-201
2400 West 49th Street
Sioux Falls, SD 57105-6558
(605) 330-4223
Fax: (605) 330-4465

Vernon Haragara, Director
Denver Office of Indian
Programs
Executive Tower Building
1405 Curtis Street
Denver, CO 80202-2349
(303) 844-2963

Tennessee
Mark Brezina, Acting Area
Coordinator
John J. Duncan Federal
Building
Third Floor
710 Locust Street, SW
Knoxville, TN 37902-2526
(615) 545-4384
Fax: (615) 545-4569

(West Tennessee)
Bob Atkins, Acting Area
Coordinator
One Memphis Place
200 Jefferson Avenue
Suite 1200
Memphis, TN 38103-2335
(901) 544-3367
Fax: (901) 544-3697

(Central Tennessee)
John H. Fisher, Acting State
Coordinator
251 Cumberland Bend Drive
Nashville, TN 37228-1803
(615) 736-5213
Fax: (615) 736-2018

Leon Jacobs, Director
Chicago Office of Indian
Programs
77 West Jackson Boulevard
24th Floor
Chicago, IL 60604-3507
(312) 231-1282

Texas
(Fort Worth Regional
Office)
Stephen Weatherforce,
Secretary's Representative
1600 Throckmorton
P.O. Box 2905
Fort Worth, TX 76113-2905
(817) 885-5401
Fax: (817) 885-5629

(East, North, and West
Texas)
Clarence D. Babers, Acting
Area Coordinator
525 Griffin Street
Room 860
Dallas, TX 75202-5007
(214) 767-8359
Fax: (214) 767-8973

(Northwest Texas)
Henry E. Whitney, Acting
Area Coordinator
Federal Office Building
1205 Texas Avenue
Lubbock, TX 79401-4093
(806) 743-7265

(Southwest Texas)
A. Cynthia Leon, Acting
Area Coordinator
Washington Square Building
800 Dolorosa Street
San Antonio, TX 78207-
4563
(512) 229-6800

(East-Central Texas)
George Rodriguez, Acting
Area Coordinator
Norfolk Tower
2211 Norfolk
Room 200
Houston, TX 77098-4096
(713) 653-3274

(Bowie County)
John T. Suskie, Acting State
Coordinator
TCBY Tower
425 West Capitol Avenue
Suite 900
Little Rock, AR 72201-3488
(501) 324-5931
Fax: (501) 324-5900

(Five Counties in East
Texas)
Ben Wiley, Acting Area
Coordinator
401 Edwards Street
500 Fannin Street
Shreveport, LA 71101-3107
(318) 266-5385

Jim Cook, Acting Director
Oklahoma City Office of
Indian Programs
500 West Main Street
Oklahoma City, OK 73102-
2233

Utah
Richard Bell, Acting State
Coordinator
257 Tower Building
257 East, 200 South
Salt Lake City, UT 84111-
2048
(801) 524-5379
Fax: (801) 524-5701

Vernon Haragara, Director
Denver Office of Indian
Programs
Executive Tower Building
1405 Curtis Street
Denver, CO 80202-2349
(303) 844-2963

Vermont
William Peters, Acting State
Coordinator
Federal Building
Room 244
11 Elmwood Avenue
P.O. Box 879
Burlington, VT 05402-0879
(802) 951-6290
Fax: (802) 951-6298

David B. Harrity, Acting
State Coordinator
Norris Cotton Federal
Building
275 Chester Street
Manchester, NH 03103-
2487
(603) 666-7681
Fax: (603) 666-7736

Leon Jacobs, Director
Chicago Office of Indian
Programs
77 West Jackson Boulevard
24th Floor
Chicago, IL 60604-3507
(312) 231-1282

Virginia
(North Virginia)
Jessica Franklin, Acting
State Coordinator
Union Center Plaza, Phase II
820 First Street, NE
Suite 300
Washington, DC 20002-
4205
(202) 275-9200
Fax: (202) 275-0779

(South Virginia)
Mary Ann Wilson, Acting
State Coordinator
P.O. Box 90331
3600 West Broad Street
Richmond, VA 23230-0331
(804) 278-4507

Leon Jacobs, Director
Chicago Office of Indian
Programs
77 West Jackson Boulevard
24th Floor
Chicago, IL 60604-3507
(312) 231-1282

Virgin Islands
Rosa Villalonga, Acting
State Coordinator
159 Carlos E. Chardon
Avenue
San Juan, PR 00918-1804
(809) 766-6121
Fax: (809) 498-5201

Washington
(Seattle Regional Office)
Bob Santos, Secretary's
Representative
Regional Housing
Commissioner
Seattle Federal Office
Building
Suite 200
909 First Avenue
Seattle, WA 98104-1000
(206) 220-5101
Fax: (206) 220-5133

(Clark, Klickitat, and
Skamania Counties)
Richard C. Brinck, Acting
State Coordinator
Cascase Building
520 SW Sixth Avenue
Portland, OR 97204-1596
(503) 326-2561
Fax: (503) 326-3097

(East Washington)
Gary Rogers, Acting Area
Coordinator
Eighth Floor East
Farm Credit Bank Building
West 601 First Avenue
Spokane, WA 99204-0317
(509) 353-2510

Jerry Leslie, Director
Seattle Office of Indian
Programs
Seattle Federal Office
Building
909 First Avenue
Suite 200
Seattle, WA 98104-1000
(206) 220-5270

West Virginia
Fred Roncaglione, Acting
State Coordinator
405 Capitol Street
Suite 708
Charleston, WV 25301-
1795
(304) 347-7000
Fax: (304) 347-7050

Choice Edwards, Acting
Area Coordinator
412 Old Post Office
Courthouse Building
Seventh Avenue and Grant
Street
Pittsburgh, PA 15219-1906
(412) 644-6428
Fax: (412) 644-6499

Leon Jacobs, Director
Chicago Office of Indian
Programs
77 West Jackson Boulevard
24th Floor
Chicago, IL 60604-3507
(312) 231-1282

Wisconsin
Delbert F. Reynolds, Acting
State Coordinator
Henry S. Reuss Federal
Plaza
310 West Wisconsin Avenue
Milwaukee, WI 53203-2289
(414) 297-3214
Fax: (414) 297-3947

Leon Jacobs, Director
Chicago Office of Indian
Programs
77 West Jackson Boulevard
24th Floor
Chicago, IL 60604-3507
(312) 231-1282

Wyoming
William Garrett, Acting
State Coordinator
4225 Federal Office Building
100 East B Street
P.O. Box 120
Casper, WY 82602-1918
(307) 261-5252
Fax: (307) 261-5251

Vernon Haragara, Director
Denver Office of Indian
Programs
Executive Tower Building
1405 Curtis Street
Denver, CO 80202-2349
(303) 844-2963

MORTGAGE INSURANCE—NURSING HOMES, INTERMEDIATE CARE FACILITIES, AND BOARD AND CARE HOMES

Department of Housing and
Urban Development (HUD)
Policy and Procedures
Division
Office of Insured
Multifamily Housing
Development
Washington, DC 20412
(202) 708-2556

Description: Guaranteed/insured loans to investors, builders, developers, and corporations for making possible the construction and rehabilitation of nursing homes and the like. Applicants must be licensed or regulated by the state.
$ Given: $1.0 billion in insured mortgages est. nationwide FY 95
Application Information: Initial conference at local HUD field office followed by formal application.
Deadline: Established on a case-by-case basis, mutually agreed to at initial conference.
Contact: Nearest local HUD field office

Alabama
Heager Hill, Acting State
Coordinator
600 Beacon Parkway West
Suite 300
Birmingham, AL 35209-
3144
(205) 290-7617

Leon Jacobs, Director
Chicago Office of Indian
Programs
77 West Jackson Boulevard
24th Floor
Chicago, IL 60604-3507
(312) 231-1282

Alaska
Arlene Patton, Manager
University Plaza Building
949 East 36th Avenue
Suite 401
Anchorage, AK 99508-4135
(907) 271-4170
Fax: (907) 271-3667

Martin Knight, Director
Anchorage Indian Housing
Division
949 East 36th Avenue
Suite 401
Anchorage, AK 99508-4135
(907) 271-4633

American Samoa
Gordon Y. Furutani, Acting
State Coordinator
7 Waterfront Plaza
500 Ala Moana Boulevard
Room 500
Honolulu, HI 96813-4918
(808) 541-1323
Fax: (808) 541-3146

Arizona
Dwight A. Peterson, Acting
State Coordinator
Two Arizona Center
400 North Fifth Street
Suite 1600
Phoenix, AZ 85004-2361
(602) 379-4434
Fax: (602) 379-3985

Sharon Atwell, Acting Area
Coordinator
33 North Stone Avenue
Room 700
Tucson, AZ 85701-1467
(602) 670-6237
Fax: (602) 670-6207

Charles Ming, Acting Area
Coordinator
1615 West Olympic
Boulevard
Los Angeles, CA 90015-
3801
(213) 251-7122
Fax: (213) 251-7096

Raphael Mecham, Director
HUD Indian Programs
Office
400 North Fifth Street
Suite 1650
Phoenix, AZ 85004-2361
(602) 379-4156
Fax: (602) 379-3101

Arkansas
John T. Suskie, Acting State
Coordinator
TCBY Tower
425 West Capitol Avenue
Suite 900
Little Rock, AR 72201-3488
(501) 324-5931
Fax: (501) 324-5900

Jim Cook, Acting Director
Oklahoma City Office of
Indian Programs
500 West Main Street
Oklahoma City, OK 73102-
2233

California
(San Francisco Regional
Office)
Arthur Agnos, Secretary's
Representative
Phillip Burton Federal
Building and U.S.
Courthouse
P.O. Box 36003
450 Golden Gate Avenue
San Francisco, CA 94102-
3448
(415) 556-4752
Fax: (415) 556-4176

(South California)
Charles Ming, Acting Area
Coordinator
1615 West Olympic
Boulevard
Los Angeles, CA 90015-
3801
(213) 251-7122
Fax: (213) 251-7096

(Fresno)
Willie Mae Haskin, Acting
Area Coordinator
1630 East Shaw Avenue
Fresno, CA 93710-8193
(209) 487-5033
Fax: (209) 487-5344

(Northeast California)
Paul Pradia, Acting Area
Coordinator
777 12th Street
Suite 200
Sacramento, CA 95814-
1997
(916) 551-1351
Fax: (916) 551-2899

(Imperial and San Diego
Counties)
Charles J. Wilson, Acting
Area Coordinator
Mission City Corporate
Center
Suite 300
2365 Northside Drive
San Diego, CA 92108-2712
(619) 557-5310
Fax: (619) 557-6296

(Orange, Riverside, and San
Bernadino Counties, for
home mortgages)
Samuel Sandoval, Acting
Area Coordinator
3 Hutton Centre
Suite 500
Santa Ana, CA 92707-5764
(714) 957-7333
Fax: (714) 957-1903

Raphael Mecham, Director
HUD Indian Programs
Office
400 North Fifth Street
Suite 1650
Phoenix, AZ 85004-2361
(602) 379-4156
Fax: (602) 379-3101

Colorado
(Denver Regional Office)
Anthony Hernandez,
Secretary's Representative
HUD—Denver Office
633 17th Street
Denver, CO 80202-3607
(303) 844-4513
Fax: (303) 844-2475

Vernon Haragara, Director
Denver Office of Indian
Programs
Executive Tower Building
1405 Curtis Street
Denver, CO 80202-2349
(303) 844-2963

Connecticut
Robert S. Donovon, Deputy
Manager
330 Main Street
Hartford, CT 06106-1860
(203) 240-4523
Fax: (203) 240-4674

Leon Jacobs, Director
Chicago Office of Indian
Programs
77 West Jackson Boulevard
24th Floor
Chicago, IL 60604-3507
(312) 231-1282

Delaware
A. David Sharbaugh, Acting
State Coordinator
824 Market Street
Suite 850
Wilmington, DE 19801-3016
(302) 573-6300
Fax: (302) 573-6259

Leon Jacobs, Director
Chicago Office of Indian
Programs
77 West Jackson Boulevard
24th Floor
Chicago, IL 60604-3507
(312) 231-1282

District of Columbia
Jessica Franklin, Acting
State Coordinator
Union Center Plaza, Phase II
820 First Street, NE
Suite 300
Washington, DC 20002-4205
(202) 275-9200
Fax: (202) 275-0779

Florida
James T. Chaplin, State Coordinator
Southern Bell Tower
Suite 2200
301 West Bay Street
Jacksonville, FL 32202-5121
(904) 232-2626
Fax: (904) 232-3759

(South Florida)
Orlando T. Lorie, Acting Area Coordinator
Gables 1 Tower
1320 South Dixie Highway
Coral Gables, FL 33146-2911
(305) 662-4500
Fax: (305) 662-4519

(Central Florida, Western Counties—Citrus, Sumter, Hernando, Pasco, Manatee, Hardee, Highlands, DeSoto, Sarasota, Charlotte, Olaoes, Hendry, Lake Okeechobee)
George A. Milburn Jr., Acting Area Coordinator
Timberlake Federal Building Annex
501 East Polk Street
Tampa, FL 33602-3945
(813) 228-2501
Fax: (813) 228-2431

(Central Florida, Eastern Counties—Volusia, Lake, Seminole, Orange, Brevard, Osceola, Indian River, Okeechobee, St. Lucie)
M. Jeanette Porter, Acting Area Coordinator
Langley Building
3751 Maguire Boulevard
Suite 270
Orlando, FL 32803-3032
(407) 648-6441
Fax: (407) 648-6310

Leon Jacobs, Director
Chicago Office of Indian Programs
77 West Jackson Boulevard
24th Floor
Chicago, IL 60604-3507
(312) 231-1282

Georgia
(Atlanta Regional Office)
Davey L. Gibson, Secretary's Representative
Regional Housing Commissioner
Richard B. Russell Federal Building
75 Spring Street, SW
Atlanta, GA 30303-3388
(404) 331-5136
Fax: (404) 331-0845

Leon Jacobs, Director
Chicago Office of Indian Programs
77 West Jackson Boulevard
24th Floor
Chicago, IL 60604-3507
(312) 231-1282

Guam
Gordon Y. Furutani, Acting State Coordinator
7 Waterfront Plaza
500 Ala Moana Boulevard
Room 500
Honolulu, HI 96813-4918
(808) 541-1323
Fax: (808) 541-3146

Hawaii
Gordon Y. Furutani, Acting State Coordinator
7 Waterfront Plaza
500 Ala Moana Boulevard
Room 500
Honolulu, HI 96813-4918
(808) 541-1323
Fax: (808) 541-3146

Idaho
(North Idaho)
Gary Rogers, Acting Area Coordinator
Farm Credit Bank Building
Eighth Floor East
West 601 First Avenue
Spokane, WA 99204-0317
(509) 353-2510

(West-Central Idaho)
Gary Gillespie, Acting State Coordinator
Suite 220
Park IV
800 Park Boulevard
Boise, ID 83712-7743
(208) 334-1990
Fax: (208) 334-9648

(South Idaho)
Richard C. Brinck, Acting State Coordinator
Cascade Building
520 SW Sixth Avenue
Portland, OR 97204-1596
(503) 221-2561

Jerry Leslie, Director
Seattle Office of Indian Programs
Seattle Federal Office Building
909 First Avenue
Suite 200
Seattle, WA 98104-1000
(206) 220-5270

Illinois
(Chicago Regional Office)
Edwin Eisendrath, Secretary's Representative
Regional Housing Commissioner
Ralph Metcalfe Federal Building
77 West Jackson Boulevard
Chicago, IL 60604-3507
(312) 353-5680
Fax: (312) 353-0121

(Central and South Illinois)
William Fattick, Acting Area
Coordinator
509 West Capitol
Suite 206
Springfield, IL 62704-1906
(217) 492-4085
Fax: (217) 492-4971

Leon Jacobs, Director
Chicago Office of Indian
Programs
77 West Jackson Boulevard
24th Floor
Chicago, IL 60604-3507
(312) 231-1282

Indiana
J. Nicholas Shelley, Acting
State Coordinator
151 North Delaware Street
Indianapolis, IN 46204-
2526
(317) 226-6303
Fax: (317) 226-6317

Iowa
William R. McNarney,
Acting State Coordinator
HUD—Des Moines Office
Federal Building
Room 239
210 Walnut Street
Des Moines, IA 50309-2155
(515) 284-4512
Fax: (515) 284-4743

Roger M. Massey, Acting
State Coordinator
Executive Tower Center
10909 Mill Valley Road
Omaha, NE 68154-3955
(402) 492-3101
Fax: (402) 492-3150

Leon Jacobs, Director
Chicago Office of Indian
Programs
77 West Jackson Boulevard
24th Floor
Chicago, IL 60604-3507
(312) 231-1282

Kansas
Joseph O'Hern, Secretary's
Representative
Regional Housing
Commissioner
HUD—Kansas City Regional
Office
Gateway Tower II
400 State Avenue
Room 200
Kansas City, KS 66101-2406
(913) 551-5462
Fax: (913) 551-5416

Jim Cook, Acting Director
Oklahoma City Office of
Indian Programs
500 West Main Street
Oklahoma City, OK 73102-
2233

Kentucky
Verna V. Van Ness, Acting
State Coordinator
601 West Broadway
P.O. Box 1044
Louisville, KY 40201-1044
(502) 582-5251
Fax: (502) 582-6074

Leon Jacobs, Director
Chicago Office of Indian
Programs
77 West Jackson Boulevard
24th Floor
Chicago, IL 60604-3507
(312) 231-1282

Louisiana
Robert Vasquez, Acting
State Coordinator
Fisk Federal Building
1661 Canal Street
New Orleans, LA 70112-
1887
(504) 589-7200
Fax: (504) 589-2917

(North Louisiana)
Ben Wiley, Acting Area
Coordinator
401 Edwards Street
500 Fannin Street
Shreveport, LA 71101-3107
(318) 266-5385

Jim Cook, Acting Director
Oklahoma City Office of
Indian Programs
500 West Main Street
Oklahoma City, OK 73102-
2233

Maine
Richard Young, Acting State
Coordinator
Casco Northern Bank
Building
23 Main Street
Bangor, ME 04401-6394
(207) 945-0467
Fax: (207) 945-0533

David B. Harrity, Acting
State Coordinator
Norris Cotton Federal
Building
275 Chester Street
Manchester, NH 03103-
2487
(603) 666-7681
Fax: (603) 666-7736

Leon Jacobs, Director
Chicago Office of Indian
Programs
77 West Jackson Boulevard
24th Floor
Chicago, IL 60604-3507
(312) 231-1282

Maryland
(Except Montgomery and
Prince Georges Counties)
Maxine Saunders, Acting
State Coordinator
City Crescent Building
10 South Howard Street
Fifth Floor
Baltimore, MD 21201
(301) 962-2520

(Montgomery and Prince
Georges Counties)
Jessica Franklin, Acting
State Coordinator
Union Center Plaza, Phase II
820 First Street, NE
Suite 300
Washington, DC 20002-
4205
(202) 275-9200
Fax: (202) 275-0779

Leon Jacobs, Director
Chicago Office of Indian
Programs
77 West Jackson Boulevard
24th Floor
Chicago, IL 60604-3507
(312) 231-1282

Massachusetts
(Boston Regional Office)
Mary Lou Crane, Secretary's
Representative
Thomas P. O'Neill Jr.
Federal Building
10 Causeway Street
Room 375
Boston, MA 02222-1092
(617) 565-5234
Fax: (617) 565-5168

Leon Jacobs, Director
Chicago Office of Indian
Programs
77 West Jackson Boulevard
24th Floor
Chicago, IL 60604-3507
(312) 231-1282

Michigan
Harry I. Sharrott, Acting
State Coordinator
Patrick V. McNamara
Federal Building
477 Michigan Avenue
Detroit, MI 48226-2592
(313) 226-7900
Fax: (313) 226-4394

(East Michigan)
Gary T. LeVine, Acting Area
Coordinator
605 North Saginaw Street
Suite 200
Flint, MI 48502-1953
(313) 766-5112
Fax: (313) 766-5122

(West and North Michigan)
Ronald Weston, Acting Area
Coordinator
Northbrook Building, # II
2922 Fuller Avenue, NE
Grand Rapids, MI 49505-
3499
(616) 456-2100
Fax: (616) 456-2191

Leon Jacobs, Director
Chicago Office of Indian
Programs
77 West Jackson Boulevard
24th Floor
Chicago, IL 60604-3507
(312) 231-1282

Minnesota
Thomas Feeney, Acting State
Coordinator
220 Second Street South
Bridge Place Building
Minneapolis, MN 55401-
2195
(612) 370-3000
Fax: (612) 370-3220

Leon Jacobs, Director
Chicago Office of Indian
Programs
77 West Jackson Boulevard
24th Floor
Chicago, IL 60604-3507
(312) 231-1282

Mississippi
Sandra Freeman, Acting
State Coordinator
Koger Building
Dr. A. H. McCoy Federal
Building
100 West Capitol Street
Room 910
Jackson, MS 39269-1096
(601) 965-5308
Fax: (601) 965-4773

Leon Jacobs, Director
Chicago Office of Indian
Programs
77 West Jackson Boulevard
24th Floor
Chicago, IL 60604-3507
(312) 231-1282

Missouri
Kenneth G. Lange, Acting
Area Coordinator
1222 Spruce Street
Room 3207
St. Louis, MO 63103-2836
(314) 539-6560
Fax: (314) 539-6575

Jim Cook, Acting Director
Oklahoma City Office of
Indian Programs
500 West Main Street
Oklahoma City, OK 73102-
2233

Montana
Gerard Boone, Acting State
Coordinator
Federal Office Building,
Drawer 10095
301 South Park
Room 340
Helena, MT 59626-0095
(406) 449-5205
Fax: (406) 449-5207

Vernon Haragara, Director
Denver Office of Indian
Programs
Executive Tower Building
1405 Curtis Street
Denver, CO 80202-2349
(303) 844-2963

Nebraska
Roger M. Massey, Acting
State Coordinator
Executive Tower Center
10909 Mill Valley Road
Omaha, NE 68154-3955
(402) 492-3101
Fax: (402) 492-3150

Vernon Haragara, Director
Denver Office of Indian
Programs
Executive Tower Building
1405 Curtis Street
Denver, CO 80202-2349
(303) 844-2963

Nevada
Andrew D. Whitten Jr.,
Acting Area Coordinator
1575 DeLucchi Lane
Room 114
P.O. Box 30050
Reno, NV 89502-6581
(702) 784-5356
Fax: (702) 784-5066

Benjamin Davis, Acting
State Coordinator
1500 East Tropicana Avenue
Second Floor
Las Vegas, NV 89119-6516
(702) 388-6500
Fax: (702) 388-6736

Raphael Mecham, Director
HUD Indian Programs
Office
400 North Fifth Street
Suite 1650
Phoenix, AZ 85004-2361
(602) 379-4156
Fax: (602) 379-3101

New Hampshire
David B. Harrity, Acting
State Coordinator
Norris Cotton Federal
Building
275 Chestnut Street
Manchester, NH 03103-
2487
(603) 666-7681
Fax: (603) 666-7736

Leon Jacobs, Director
Chicago Office of Indian
Programs
77 West Jackson Boulevard
24th Floor
Chicago, IL 60604-3507
(312) 231-1282

New Jersey
(North New Jersey)
Diane Johnson, Acting State
Coordinator
One Newark Center
13th Floor
Newark, NJ 07102-5260
(201) 622-7900
Fax: (201) 645-6239

(South New Jersey)
Elmer Roy, Acting Area
Coordinator
Hudson Building
Second Floor
800 Hudson Square
Camden, NJ 08102-1156
(609) 757-5081
Fax: (609) 757-5373

Leon Jacobs, Director
Chicago Office of Indian
Programs
77 West Jackson Boulevard
24th Floor
Chicago, IL 60604-3507
(312) 231-1282

New Mexico
Michael R. Griego, Acting
State Coordinator
625 Truman Street, NW
Albuquerque, NM 87110-
6443
(505) 262-6463

Clarence D. Babers, Acting
Area Coordinator
525 Griffin Street
Room 860
Dallas, TX 75202-5007
(214) 767-8359
Fax: (214) 767-8973

Raphael Mecham, Director
HUD Indian Programs
Office
400 North Fifth Street
Suite 1650
Phoenix, AZ 85004-2361
(602) 379-4156
Fax: (602) 379-3101

New York
(New York Regional Office)
Jose Cintron, Secretary's
Representative
26 Federal Plaza
New York, NY 10278-0068
(212) 264-6500
Fax: (212) 264-0246

(North New York)
John Petricco, Acting Area
Coordinator
52 Corporate Circle
Albany, NY 12203-5121
(518) 464-4200
Fax: (518) 464-4300

(West New York)
Joseph Lynch, Acting Area
Coordinator
465 Main Street
Lafayette Court
Fifth Floor
Buffalo, NY 14203-1780
(716) 846-5755
Fax: (716) 846-5752

Leon Jacobs, Director
Chicago Office of Indian
Programs
77 West Jackson Boulevard
24th Floor
Chicago, IL 60604-3507
(312) 231-1282

North Carolina
Larry J. Parker, Acting State
Coordinator
2306 West Meadowview
Road
Koger Building
Greensboro, NC 27407-
3707
(919) 547-4001
Fax: (919) 547-4015

Leon Jacobs, Director
Chicago Office of Indian
Programs
77 West Jackson Boulevard
24th Floor
Chicago, IL 60604-3507
(312) 231-1282

North Dakota
Keith Elliott, Acting State
Coordinator
HUD—Fargo Office
Federal Building
657 Second Avenue, North
Fargo, ND 58108-2483
(701) 239-5136
Fax: (701) 783-5249

Vernon Haragara, Director
Denver Office of Indian
Programs
Executive Tower Building
1405 Curtis Street
Denver, CO 80202-2349
(303) 844-2963

Ohio
Robert W. Dolin, Acting
State Coordinator
HUD—Columbus Office
200 North High Street
Columbus, OH 43215-2499
(614) 469-5737
Fax: (614) 469-2432

(North Ohio)
Philip Ginconia, Acting Area
Coordinator
1350 Euclid Avenue
Fifth Floor
Cleveland, OH 44115-1815
(216) 552-4065
Fax: (216) 522-2975

(Southwest Ohio)
William Harris, Acting Area
Coordinator
Federal Office Building
Room 9002
550 Main Street
Cincinnati, OH 45202-3253
(513) 684-2884
Fax: (513) 684-6224

Leon Jacobs, Director
Chicago Office of Indian
Programs
77 West Jackson Boulevard
24th Floor
Chicago, IL 60604-3507
(312) 231-1282

Oklahoma
Katie Worsham, Acting State
Coordinator
500 West Main Street
Oklahoma City, OK 73102-
2233

(East Oklahoma)
James S. Colgan, Acting
Area Coordinator
1516 South Boston Avenue
Room 110
Tulsa, OK 74119-4032
(918) 581-7435
Fax: (918) 581-7440

Jim Cook, Acting Director
Oklahoma City Office of
Indian Programs
500 West Main Street
Oklahoma City, OK 73102-
2233

Oregon
Richard C. Brinck, Acting
State Coordinator
Cascade Building
520 SW Sixth Avenue
Portland, OR 97204-1596
(503) 326-2561
Fax: (503) 326-3097

Jerry Leslie, Director
Seattle Office of Indian
Programs
Seattle Federal Office
Building
909 First Avenue
Suite 200
Seattle, WA 98104-1000
(206) 220-5270

Panama Canal Zone
Rosa Villalonga, Acting
State Coordinator
159 Carlos E. Chardon
Avenue
San Juan, PR 00918-1804
(809) 766-6121
Fax: (809) 498-5201

Pennsylvania
(Philadelphia Regional
Office)
Karen A. Miller, Secretary's
Representative
Regional Housing
Commissioner
Liberty Square Building
105 South Seventh Street
Philadelphia, PA 19106-
3392
(215) 597-2560
Fax: (215) 597-9627

(West Pennsylvania)
Choice Edwards, Acting
Area Coordinator
412 Old Post Office
Courthouse Building
Seventh Avenue and Grant
Street
Pittsburgh, PA 15219-1906
(412) 644-6428
Fax: (412) 644-6499

Leon Jacobs, Director
Chicago Office of Indian
Programs
77 West Jackson Boulevard
24th Floor
Chicago, IL 60604-3507
(312) 231-1282

Puerto Rico
Rosa Villalonga, Acting
State Coordinator
159 Carlos E. Chardon
Avenue
San Juan, PR 00918-1804
(809) 766-6121
Fax: (809) 498-5201

Rhode Island
Michael Dziok, Acting State
Coordinator
Room 303
John O. Pastore Federal
Building and U.S. Post
Office
Kennedy Plaza
Providence, RI 02903-1785
(401) 528-5351
Fax: (401) 528-5312

Leon Jacobs, Director
Chicago Office of Indian
Programs
77 West Jackson Boulevard
24th Floor
Chicago, IL 60604-3507
(312) 231-1282

South Carolina
Ted B. Freeman, Acting
State Coordinator
Strom Thurmond Federal
Building
1835 Assembly Street
Columbia, SC 29201-2480
(803) 765-5592
Fax: (803) 765-5515

Leon Jacobs, Director
Chicago Office of Indian
Programs
77 West Jackson Boulevard
24th Floor
Chicago, IL 60604-3507
(312) 231-1282

South Dakota
Don Olson, Acting State
Coordinator
Suite I-201
2400 West 49th Street
Sioux Falls, SD 57105-6558
(605) 330-4223
Fax: (605) 330-4465

Vernon Haragara, Director
Denver Office of Indian
Programs
Executive Tower Building
1405 Curtis Street
Denver, CO 80202-2349
(303) 844-2963

Tennessee
Mark Brezina, Acting Area
Coordinator
John J. Duncan Federal
Building
Third Floor
710 Locust Street, SW
Knoxville, TN 37902-2526
(615) 545-4384
Fax: (615) 545-4569

(West Tennessee)
Bob Atkins, Acting Area
Coordinator
One Memphis Place
200 Jefferson Avenue
Suite 1200
Memphis, TN 38103-2335
(901) 544-3367
Fax: (901) 544-3697

(Central Tennessee)
John H. Fisher, Acting State
Coordinator
251 Cumberland Bend Drive
Nashville, TN 37228-1803
(615) 736-5213
Fax: (615) 736-2018

Leon Jacobs, Director
Chicago Office of Indian
Programs
77 West Jackson Boulevard
24th Floor
Chicago, IL 60604-3507
(312) 231-1282

Texas
(Fort Worth Regional
Office)
Stephen Weatherforce,
Secretary's Representative
1600 Throckmorton
P.O. Box 2905
Fort Worth, TX 76113-2905
(817) 885-5401
Fax: (817) 885-5629

(East, North, and West
Texas)
Clarence D. Babers, Acting
Area Coordinator
525 Griffin Street
Room 860
Dallas, TX 75202-5007
(214) 767-8359
Fax: (214) 767-8973

(Northwest Texas)
Henry E. Whitney, Acting
Area Coordinator
Federal Office Building
1205 Texas Avenue
Lubbock, TX 79401-4093
(806) 743-7265

(Southwest Texas)
A. Cynthia Leon, Acting
Area Coordinator
Washington Square Building
800 Dolorosa Street
San Antonio, TX 78207-
4563
(512) 229-6800

(East-Central Texas)
George Rodriguez, Acting
Area Coordinator
Norfolk Tower
2211 Norfolk
Room 200
Houston, TX 77098-4096
(713) 653-3274

(Bowie County)
John T. Suskie, Acting State
Coordinator
TCBY Tower
425 West Capitol Avenue
Suite 900
Little Rock, AR 72201-3488
(501) 324-5931
Fax: (501) 324-5900

(Five Counties in East
Texas)
Ben Wiley, Acting Area
Coordinator
401 Edwards Street
500 Fannin Street
Shreveport, LA 71101-3107
(318) 266-5385

Jim Cook, Acting Director
Oklahoma City Office of
Indian Programs
500 West Main Street
Oklahoma City, OK 73102-
2233

Utah
Richard Bell, Acting State
Coordinator
257 Tower Building
257 East, 200 South
Salt Lake City, UT 84111-
2048
(801) 524-5379
Fax: (801) 524-5701

Vernon Haragara, Director
Denver Office of Indian
Programs
Executive Tower Building
1405 Curtis Street
Denver, CO 80202-2349
(303) 844-2963

Vermont
William Peters, Acting State
Coordinator
Federal Building
Room 244
11 Elmwood Avenue
P.O. Box 879
Burlington, VT 05402-0879
(802) 951-6290
Fax: (802) 951-6298

David B. Harrity, Acting
State Coordinator
Norris Cotton Federal
Building
275 Chester Street
Manchester, NH 03103-
2487
(603) 666-7681
Fax: (603) 666-7736

Leon Jacobs, Director
Chicago Office of Indian
Programs
77 West Jackson Boulevard
24th Floor
Chicago, IL 60604-3507
(312) 231-1282

Virginia
(North Virginia)
Jessica Franklin, Acting
State Coordinator
Union Center Plaza, Phase II
820 First Street, NE
Suite 300
Washington, DC 20002-4205
(202) 275-9200
Fax: (202) 275-0779

(South Virginia)
Mary Ann Wilson, Acting
State Coordinator
P.O. Box 90331
3600 West Broad Street
Richmond, VA 23230-0331
(804) 278-4507

Leon Jacobs, Director
Chicago Office of Indian
Programs
77 West Jackson Boulevard
24th Floor
Chicago, IL 60604-3507
(312) 231-1282

Virgin Islands
Rosa Villalonga, Acting
State Coordinator
159 Carlos E. Chardon
Avenue
San Juan, PR 00918-1804
(809) 766-6121
Fax: (809) 498-5201

Washington
(Seattle Regional Office)
Bob Santos, Secretary's
Representative
Regional Housing
Commissioner
Seattle Federal Office Building
Suite 200
909 First Avenue
Seattle, WA 98104-1000
(206) 220-5101
Fax: (206) 220-5133

(Clark, Klickitat, and
Skamania Counties)
Richard C. Brinck, Acting
State Coordinator
Cascase Building
520 SW Sixth Avenue
Portland, OR 97204-1596
(503) 326-2561
Fax: (503) 326-3097

(East Washington)
Gary Rogers, Acting Area
Coordinator
Eighth Floor East
Farm Credit Bank Building
West 601 First Avenue
Spokane, WA 99204-0317
(509) 353-2510

Jerry Leslie, Director
Seattle Office of Indian
Programs
Seattle Federal Office Building
909 First Avenue
Suite 200
Seattle, WA 98104-1000
(206) 220-5270

West Virginia
Fred Roncaglione, Acting
State Coordinator
405 Capitol Street
Suite 708
Charleston, WV 25301-1795
(304) 347-7000
Fax: (304) 347-7050

Choice Edwards, Acting
Area Coordinator
412 Old Post Office
Courthouse Building
Seventh Avenue and Grant
Street
Pittsburgh, PA 15219-1906
(412) 644-6428
Fax: (412) 644-6499

Leon Jacobs, Director
Chicago Office of Indian
Programs
77 West Jackson Boulevard
24th Floor
Chicago, IL 60604-3507
(312) 231-1282

Wisconsin
Delbert F. Reynolds, Acting
State Coordinator
Henry S. Reuss Federal Plaza
310 West Wisconsin Avenue
Milwaukee, WI 53203-2289
(414) 297-3214
Fax: (414) 297-3947

Leon Jacobs, Director
Chicago Office of Indian
Programs
77 West Jackson Boulevard
24th Floor
Chicago, IL 60604-3507
(312) 231-1282

Wyoming
William Garrett, Acting
State Coordinator
4225 Federal Office Building
100 East B Street
P.O. Box 120
Casper, WY 82602-1918
(307) 261-5252
Fax: (307) 261-5251

Vernon Haragara, Director
Denver Office of Indian
Programs
Executive Tower Building
1405 Curtis Street
Denver, CO 80202-2349
(303) 844-2963

MORTGAGE INSURANCE—RENTAL AND COOPERATIVE HOUSING FOR MODERATE-INCOME FAMILIES AND ELDERLY, MARKET INTEREST RATE

Department of Housing and
Urban Development (HUD)
Policies and Procedures
Division
Office of Uninsured
Multifamily Housing
Development
Washington, DC 20412
(202) 708-2556

Description: Guaranteed/insured loans to profit-motivated sponsors, buildersellers, and others for providing good-quality rental or cooperative housing for moderate-income families and the elderly and handicapped. Housing must consist of five or more units. There are various other restrictions.

$ Given: Through September 30, 1993, 9,633 projects with 1.0 million units valued at $27.4 billion; FY 93 $407 million for 60 projects; FY 95 est. $445 million

Application Information: Initial conference with local HUD field office before submission of formal proposal.

Deadline: Established on a case-by-case basis at local HUD field office.

Contact: Nearest local HUD field office

Alabama
Heager Hill, Acting State
Coordinator
600 Beacon Parkway West
Suite 300
Birmingham, AL 35209-3144
(205) 290-7617

Leon Jacobs, Director
Chicago Office of Indian
Programs
77 West Jackson Boulevard
24th Floor
Chicago, IL 60604-3507
(312) 231-1282

Alaska
Arlene Patton, Manager
University Plaza Building
949 East 36th Avenue
Suite 401
Anchorage, AK 99508-4135
(907) 271-4170
Fax: (907) 271-3667

Martin Knight, Director
Anchorage Indian Housing
Division
949 East 36th Avenue
Suite 401
Anchorage, AK 99508-4135
(907) 271-4633

American Samoa
Gordon Y. Furutani, Acting
State Coordinator
7 Waterfront Plaza
500 Ala Moana Boulevard
Room 500
Honolulu, HI 96813-4918
(808) 541-1323
Fax: (808) 541-3146

Arizona
Dwight A. Peterson, Acting
State Coordinator
Two Arizona Center
400 North Fifth Street
Suite 1600
Phoenix, AZ 85004-2361
(602) 379-4434
Fax: (602) 379-3985

Sharon Atwell, Acting Area
Coordinator
33 North Stone Avenue
Room 700
Tucson, AZ 85701-1467
(602) 670-6237
Fax: (602) 670-6207

Charles Ming, Acting Area
Coordinator
1615 West Olympic
Boulevard
Los Angeles, CA 90015-3801
(213) 251-7122
Fax: (213) 251-7096

Raphael Mecham, Director
HUD Indian Programs
Office
400 North Fifth Street
Suite 1650
Phoenix, AZ 85004-2361
(602) 379-4156
Fax: (602) 379-3101

Arkansas
John T. Suskie, Acting State
Coordinator
TCBY Tower
425 West Capitol Avenue
Suite 900
Little Rock, AR 72201-3488
(501) 324-5931
Fax: (501) 324-5900

Jim Cook, Acting Director
Oklahoma City Office of
Indian Programs
500 West Main Street
Oklahoma City, OK 73102-
2233

California
(San Francisco Regional
Office)
Arthur Agnos, Secretary's
Representative
Phillip Burton Federal
Building and U.S.
Courthouse
P.O. Box 36003
450 Golden Gate Avenue
San Francisco, CA 94102-
3448
(415) 556-4752
Fax: (415) 556-4176

(South California)
Charles Ming, Acting Area
Coordinator
1615 West Olympic
Boulevard
Los Angeles, CA 90015-
3801
(213) 251-7122
Fax: (213) 251-7096

(Fresno)
Willie Mae Haskin, Acting
Area Coordinator
1630 East Shaw Avenue
Fresno, CA 93710-8193
(209) 487-5033
Fax: (209) 487-5344

(Northeast California)
Paul Pradia, Acting Area
Coordinator
777 12th Street
Suite 200
Sacramento, CA 95814-
1997
(916) 551-1351
Fax: (916) 551-2899

(Imperial and San Diego
Counties)
Charles J. Wilson, Acting
Area Coordinator
Mission City Corporate
Center
Suite 300
2365 Northside Drive
San Diego, CA 92108-2712
(619) 557-5310
Fax: (619) 557-6296

(Orange, Riverside, and San
Bernadino Counties, for
home mortgages)
Samuel Sandoval, Acting
Area Coordinator
3 Hutton Centre
Suite 500
Santa Ana, CA 92707-5764
(714) 957-7333
Fax: (714) 957-1903

Raphael Mecham, Director
HUD Indian Programs
Office
400 North Fifth Street
Suite 1650
Phoenix, AZ 85004-2361
(602) 379-4156
Fax: (602) 379-3101

Colorado
(Denver Regional Office)
Anthony Hernandez,
Secretary's Representative
HUD—Denver Office
633 17th Street
Denver, CO 80202-3607
(303) 844-4513
Fax: (303) 844-2475

Vernon Haragara, Director
Denver Office of Indian
Programs
Executive Tower Building
1405 Curtis Street
Denver, CO 80202-2349
(303) 844-2963

Connecticut
Robert S. Donovon, Deputy
Manager
330 Main Street
Hartford, CT 06106-1860
(203) 240-4523
Fax: (203) 240-4674

Leon Jacobs, Director
Chicago Office of Indian
Programs
77 West Jackson Boulevard
24th Floor
Chicago, IL 60604-3507
(312) 231-1282

Delaware
A. David Sharbaugh, Acting
State Coordinator
824 Market Street
Suite 850
Wilmington, DE 19801-3016
(302) 573-6300
Fax: (302) 573-6259

Leon Jacobs, Director
Chicago Office of Indian
Programs
77 West Jackson Boulevard
24th Floor
Chicago, IL 60604-3507
(312) 231-1282

District of Columbia
Jessica Franklin, Acting
State Coordinator
Union Center Plaza, Phase II
820 First Street, NE
Suite 300
Washington, DC 20002-4205
(202) 275-9200
Fax: (202) 275-0779

Florida
James T. Chaplin, State
Coordinator
Southern Bell Tower
Suite 2200
301 West Bay Street
Jacksonville, FL 32202-5121
(904) 232-2626
Fax: (904) 232-3759

(South Florida)
Orlando T. Lorie, Acting
Area Coordinator
Gables 1 Tower
1320 South Dixie Highway
Coral Gables, FL 33146-
2911
(305) 662-4500
Fax: (305) 662-4519

(Central Florida, Western
Counties—Citrus, Sumter,
Hernando, Pasco, Manatee,
Hardee, Highlands, DeSoto,
Sarasota, Charlotte, Olaoes,
Hendry, Lake Okeechobee)
George A. Milburn Jr.,
Acting Area Coordinator
Timberlake Federal Building
Annex
501 East Polk Street
Tampa, FL 33602-3945
(813) 228-2501
Fax: (813) 228-2431

(Central Florida, Eastern
Counties—Volusia, Lake,
Seminole, Orange, Brevard,
Osceola, Indian River,
Okeechobee, St. Lucie)
M. Jeanette Porter, Acting
Area Coordinator
Langley Building
3751 Maguire Boulevard
Suite 270
Orlando, FL 32803-3032
(407) 648-6441
Fax: (407) 648-6310

Leon Jacobs, Director
Chicago Office of Indian
Programs
77 West Jackson Boulevard
24th Floor
Chicago, IL 60604-3507
(312) 231-1282

Georgia
(Atlanta Regional Office)
Davey L. Gibson, Secretary's
Representative
Regional Housing
Commissioner
Richard B. Russell Federal
Building
75 Spring Street, SW
Atlanta, GA 30303-3388
(404) 331-5136
Fax: (404) 331-0845

Leon Jacobs, Director
Chicago Office of Indian
Programs
77 West Jackson Boulevard
24th Floor
Chicago, IL 60604-3507
(312) 231-1282

Guam
Gordon Y. Furutani, Acting
State Coordinator
7 Waterfront Plaza
500 Ala Moana Boulevard
Room 500
Honolulu, HI 96813-4918
(808) 541-1323
Fax: (808) 541-3146

Hawaii
Gordon Y. Furutani, Acting
State Coordinator
7 Waterfront Plaza
500 Ala Moana Boulevard
Room 500
Honolulu, HI 96813-4918
(808) 541-1323
Fax: (808) 541-3146

Idaho
(North Idaho)
Gary Rogers, Acting Area
Coordinator
Farm Credit Bank Building
Eighth Floor East
West 601 First Avenue
Spokane, WA 99204-0317
(509) 353-2510

(West-Central Idaho)
Gary Gillespie, Acting State
Coordinator
Suite 220
Park IV
800 Park Boulevard
Boise, ID 83712-7743
(208) 334-1990
Fax: (208) 334-9648

(South Idaho)
Richard C. Brinck, Acting
State Coordinator
Cascade Building
520 SW Sixth Avenue
Portland, OR 97204-1596
(503) 221-2561

Jerry Leslie, Director
Seattle Office of Indian
Programs
Seattle Federal Office
Building
909 First Avenue
Suite 200
Seattle, WA 98104-1000
(206) 220-5270

Illinois
(Chicago Regional Office)
Edwin Eisendrath,
Secretary's Representative
Regional Housing
Commissioner
Ralph Metcalfe Federal
Building
77 West Jackson Boulevard
Chicago, IL 60604-3507
(312) 353-5680
Fax: (312) 353-0121

(Central and South Illinois)
William Fattick, Acting Area
Coordinator
509 West Capitol
Suite 206
Springfield, IL 62704-1906
(217) 492-4085
Fax: (217) 492-4971

Leon Jacobs, Director
Chicago Office of Indian
Programs
77 West Jackson Boulevard
24th Floor
Chicago, IL 60604-3507
(312) 231-1282

Indiana
J. Nicholas Shelley, Acting
State Coordinator
151 North Delaware Street
Indianapolis, IN 46204-
2526
(317) 226-6303
Fax: (317) 226-6317

Iowa
William R. McNarney,
Acting State Coordinator
HUD—Des Moines Office
Federal Building
Room 239
210 Walnut Street
Des Moines, IA 50309-2155
(515) 284-4512
Fax: (515) 284-4743

Roger M. Massey, Acting
State Coordinator
Executive Tower Center
10909 Mill Valley Road
Omaha, NE 68154-3955
(402) 492-3101
Fax: (402) 492-3150

Leon Jacobs, Director
Chicago Office of Indian
Programs
77 West Jackson Boulevard
24th Floor
Chicago, IL 60604-3507
(312) 231-1282

Kansas
Joseph O'Hern, Secretary's
Representative
Regional Housing
Commissioner
HUD—Kansas City Regional
Office
Gateway Tower II
400 State Avenue
Room 200
Kansas City, KS 66101-2406
(913) 551-5462
Fax: (913) 551-5416

Jim Cook, Acting Director
Oklahoma City Office of
Indian Programs
500 West Main Street
Oklahoma City, OK 73102-
2233

Kentucky
Verna V. Van Ness, Acting
State Coordinator
601 West Broadway
P.O. Box 1044
Louisville, KY 40201-1044
(502) 582-5251
Fax: (502) 582-6074

Leon Jacobs, Director
Chicago Office of Indian
Programs
77 West Jackson Boulevard
24th Floor
Chicago, IL 60604-3507
(312) 231-1282

Louisiana
Robert Vasquez, Acting
State Coordinator
Fisk Federal Building
1661 Canal Street
New Orleans, LA 70112-
1887
(504) 589-7200
Fax: (504) 589-2917

(North Louisiana)
Ben Wiley, Acting Area
Coordinator
401 Edwards Street
500 Fannin Street
Shreveport, LA 71101-3107
(318) 266-5385

Jim Cook, Acting Director
Oklahoma City Office of
Indian Programs
500 West Main Street
Oklahoma City, OK 73102-
2233

Maine
Richard Young, Acting State
Coordinator
Casco Northern Bank
Building
23 Main Street
Bangor, ME 04401-6394
(207) 945-0467
Fax: (207) 945-0533

David B. Harrity, Acting
State Coordinator
Norris Cotton Federal
Building
275 Chester Street
Manchester, NH 03103-
2487
(603) 666-7681
Fax: (603) 666-7736

Leon Jacobs, Director
Chicago Office of Indian
Programs
77 West Jackson Boulevard
24th Floor
Chicago, IL 60604-3507
(312) 231-1282

Maryland
(Except Montgomery and
Prince Georges Counties)
Maxine Saunders, Acting
State Coordinator
City Crescent Building
10 South Howard Street
Fifth Floor
Baltimore, MD 21201
(301) 962-2520

(Montgomery and Prince
Georges Counties)
Jessica Franklin, Acting
State Coordinator
Union Center Plaza, Phase II
820 First Street, NE
Suite 300
Washington, DC 20002-
4205
(202) 275-9200
Fax: (202) 275-0779

Leon Jacobs, Director
Chicago Office of Indian
Programs
77 West Jackson Boulevard
24th Floor
Chicago, IL 60604-3507
(312) 231-1282

Massachusetts
(Boston Regional Office)
Mary Lou Crane, Secretary's
Representative
Thomas P. O'Neill Jr.
Federal Building
10 Causeway Street
Room 375
Boston, MA 02222-1092
(617) 565-5234
Fax: (617) 565-5168

Leon Jacobs, Director
Chicago Office of Indian
Programs
77 West Jackson Boulevard
24th Floor
Chicago, IL 60604-3507
(312) 231-1282

Michigan
Harry I. Sharrott, Acting
State Coordinator
Patrick V. McNamara
Federal Building
477 Michigan Avenue
Detroit, MI 48226-2592
(313) 226-7900
Fax: (313) 226-4394

(East Michigan)
Gary T. LeVine, Acting Area
Coordinator
605 North Saginaw Street
Suite 200
Flint, MI 48502-1953
(313) 766-5112
Fax: (313) 766-5122

(West and North Michigan)
Ronald Weston, Acting Area
Coordinator
Northbrook Building, # II
2922 Fuller Avenue, NE
Grand Rapids, MI 49505-
3499
(616) 456-2100
Fax: (616) 456-2191

Leon Jacobs, Director
Chicago Office of Indian
Programs
77 West Jackson Boulevard
24th Floor
Chicago, IL 60604-3507
(312) 231-1282

Minnesota
Thomas Feeney, Acting State
Coordinator
220 Second Street South
Bridge Place Building
Minneapolis, MN 55401-
2195
(612) 370-3000
Fax: (612) 370-3220

Leon Jacobs, Director
Chicago Office of Indian
Programs
77 West Jackson Boulevard
24th Floor
Chicago, IL 60604-3507
(312) 231-1282

Mississippi
Sandra Freeman, Acting
State Coordinator
Koger Building
Dr. A. H. McCoy Federal
Building
100 West Capitol Street
Room 910
Jackson, MS 39269-1096
(601) 965-5308
Fax: (601) 965-4773

Leon Jacobs, Director
Chicago Office of Indian
Programs
77 West Jackson Boulevard
24th Floor
Chicago, IL 60604-3507
(312) 231-1282

Missouri
Kenneth G. Lange, Acting
Area Coordinator
1222 Spruce Street
Room 3207
St. Louis, MO 63103-2836
(314) 539-6560
Fax: (314) 539-6575

Jim Cook, Acting Director
Oklahoma City Office of
Indian Programs
500 West Main Street
Oklahoma City, OK 73102-
2233

Montana
Gerard Boone, Acting State
Coordinator
Federal Office Building,
Drawer 10095
301 South Park
Room 340
Helena, MT 59626-0095
(406) 449-5205
Fax: (406) 449-5207

Vernon Haragara, Director
Denver Office of Indian
Programs
Executive Tower Building
1405 Curtis Street
Denver, CO 80202-2349
(303) 844-2963

Nebraska
Roger M. Massey, Acting
State Coordinator
Executive Tower Center
10909 Mill Valley Road
Omaha, NE 68154-3955
(402) 492-3101
Fax: (402) 492-3150

Vernon Haragara, Director
Denver Office of Indian
Programs
Executive Tower Building
1405 Curtis Street
Denver, CO 80202-2349
(303) 844-2963

Nevada
Andrew D. Whitten Jr.,
Acting Area Coordinator
1575 DeLucchi Lane
Room 114
P.O. Box 30050
Reno, NV 89502-6581
(702) 784-5356
Fax: (702) 784-5066

Benjamin Davis, Acting
State Coordinator
1500 East Tropicana Avenue
Second Floor
Las Vegas, NV 89119-6516
(702) 388-6500
Fax: (702) 388-6736

Raphael Mecham, Director
HUD Indian Programs
Office
400 North Fifth Street
Suite 1650
Phoenix, AZ 85004-2361
(602) 379-4156
Fax: (602) 379-3101

New Hampshire
David B. Harrity, Acting
State Coordinator
Norris Cotton Federal
Building
275 Chestnut Street
Manchester, NH 03103-
2487
(603) 666-7681
Fax: (603) 666-7736

Leon Jacobs, Director
Chicago Office of Indian
Programs
77 West Jackson Boulevard
24th Floor
Chicago, IL 60604-3507
(312) 231-1282

New Jersey
(North New Jersey)
Diane Johnson, Acting State
Coordinator
One Newark Center
13th Floor
Newark, NJ 07102-5260
(201) 622-7900
Fax: (201) 645-6239

(South New Jersey)
Elmer Roy, Acting Area
Coordinator
Hudson Building
Second Floor
800 Hudson Square
Camden, NJ 08102-1156
(609) 757-5081
Fax: (609) 757-5373

Leon Jacobs, Director
Chicago Office of Indian
Programs
77 West Jackson Boulevard
24th Floor
Chicago, IL 60604-3507
(312) 231-1282

New Mexico
Michael R. Griego, Acting
State Coordinator
625 Truman Street, NW
Albuquerque, NM 87110-
6443
(505) 262-6463

Clarence D. Babers, Acting
Area Coordinator
525 Griffin Street
Room 860
Dallas, TX 75202-5007
(214) 767-8359
Fax: (214) 767-8973

Raphael Mecham, Director
HUD Indian Programs
Office
400 North Fifth Street
Suite 1650
Phoenix, AZ 85004-2361
(602) 379-4156
Fax: (602) 379-3101

New York
(New York Regional Office)
Jose Cintron, Secretary's
Representative
26 Federal Plaza
New York, NY 10278-0068
(212) 264-6500
Fax: (212) 264-0246

(North New York)
John Petricco, Acting Area
Coordinator
52 Corporate Circle
Albany, NY 12203-5121
(518) 464-4200
Fax: (518) 464-4300

(West New York)
Joseph Lynch, Acting Area
Coordinator
465 Main Street
Lafayette Court
Fifth Floor
Buffalo, NY 14203-1780
(716) 846-5755
Fax: (716) 846-5752

Leon Jacobs, Director
Chicago Office of Indian
Programs
77 West Jackson Boulevard
24th Floor
Chicago, IL 60604-3507
(312) 231-1282

North Carolina
Larry J. Parker, Acting State
Coordinator
2306 West Meadowview
Road
Koger Building
Greensboro, NC 27407-
3707
(919) 547-4001
Fax: (919) 547-4015

Leon Jacobs, Director
Chicago Office of Indian
Programs
77 West Jackson Boulevard
24th Floor
Chicago, IL 60604-3507
(312) 231-1282

North Dakota
Keith Elliott, Acting State
Coordinator
HUD—Fargo Office
Federal Building
657 Second Avenue, North
Fargo, ND 58108-2483
(701) 239-5136
Fax: (701) 783-5249

Vernon Haragara, Director
Denver Office of Indian
Programs
Executive Tower Building
1405 Curtis Street
Denver, CO 80202-2349
(303) 844-2963

Ohio
Robert W. Dolin, Acting
State Coordinator
HUD—Columbus Office
200 North High Street
Columbus, OH 43215-2499
(614) 469-5737
Fax: (614) 469-2432

(North Ohio)
Philip Ginconia, Acting Area
Coordinator
1350 Euclid Avenue
Fifth Floor
Cleveland, OH 44115-1815
(216) 552-4065
Fax: (216) 522-2975

(Southwest Ohio)
William Harris, Acting Area
Coordinator
Federal Office Building
Room 9002
550 Main Street
Cincinnati, OH 45202-3253
(513) 684-2884
Fax: (513) 684-6224

Leon Jacobs, Director
Chicago Office of Indian
Programs
77 West Jackson Boulevard
24th Floor
Chicago, IL 60604-3507
(312) 231-1282

Oklahoma
Katie Worsham, Acting State
Coordinator
500 West Main Street
Oklahoma City, OK 73102-
2233

(East Oklahoma)
James S. Colgan, Acting
Area Coordinator
1516 South Boston Avenue
Room 110
Tulsa, OK 74119-4032
(918) 581-7435
Fax: (918) 581-7440

Jim Cook, Acting Director
Oklahoma City Office of
Indian Programs
500 West Main Street
Oklahoma City, OK 73102-
2233

Oregon
Richard C. Brinck, Acting
State Coordinator
Cascade Building
520 SW Sixth Avenue
Portland, OR 97204-1596
(503) 326-2561
Fax: (503) 326-3097

Jerry Leslie, Director
Seattle Office of Indian
Programs
Seattle Federal Office
Building
909 First Avenue
Suite 200
Seattle, WA 98104-1000
(206) 220-5270

Panama Canal Zone
Rosa Villalonga, Acting
State Coordinator
159 Carlos E. Chardon
Avenue
San Juan, PR 00918-1804
(809) 766-6121
Fax: (809) 498-5201

Pennsylvania
(Philadelphia Regional
Office)
Karen A. Miller, Secretary's
Representative
Regional Housing
Commissioner
Liberty Square Building
105 South Seventh Street
Philadelphia, PA 19106-
3392
(215) 597-2560
Fax: (215) 597-9627

(West Pennsylvania)
Choice Edwards, Acting
Area Coordinator
412 Old Post Office
Courthouse Building
Seventh Avenue and Grant
Street
Pittsburgh, PA 15219-1906
(412) 644-6428
Fax: (412) 644-6499

Leon Jacobs, Director
Chicago Office of Indian
Programs
77 West Jackson Boulevard
24th Floor
Chicago, IL 60604-3507
(312) 231-1282

Puerto Rico
Rosa Villalonga, Acting
State Coordinator
159 Carlos E. Chardon
Avenue
San Juan, PR 00918-1804
(809) 766-6121
Fax: (809) 498-5201

Rhode Island
Michael Dziok, Acting State
Coordinator
Room 303
John O. Pastore Federal
Building and U.S. Post
Office
Kennedy Plaza
Providence, RI 02903-1785
(401) 528-5351
Fax: (401) 528-5312

Leon Jacobs, Director
Chicago Office of Indian
Programs
77 West Jackson Boulevard
24th Floor
Chicago, IL 60604-3507
(312) 231-1282

South Carolina
Ted B. Freeman, Acting
State Coordinator
Strom Thurmond Federal
Building
1835 Assembly Street
Columbia, SC 29201-2480
(803) 765-5592
Fax: (803) 765-5515

Leon Jacobs, Director
Chicago Office of Indian
Programs
77 West Jackson Boulevard
24th Floor
Chicago, IL 60604-3507
(312) 231-1282

South Dakota
Don Olson, Acting State
Coordinator
Suite I-201
2400 West 49th Street
Sioux Falls, SD 57105-6558
(605) 330-4223
Fax: (605) 330-4465

Vernon Haragara, Director
Denver Office of Indian
Programs
Executive Tower Building
1405 Curtis Street
Denver, CO 80202-2349
(303) 844-2963

Tennessee
Mark Brezina, Acting Area
Coordinator
John J. Duncan Federal
Building
Third Floor
710 Locust Street, SW
Knoxville, TN 37902-2526
(615) 545-4384
Fax: (615) 545-4569

(West Tennessee)
Bob Atkins, Acting Area
Coordinator
One Memphis Place
200 Jefferson Avenue
Suite 1200
Memphis, TN 38103-2335
(901) 544-3367
Fax: (901) 544-3697

(Central Tennessee)
John H. Fisher, Acting State
Coordinator
251 Cumberland Bend Drive
Nashville, TN 37228-1803
(615) 736-5213
Fax: (615) 736-2018

Leon Jacobs, Director
Chicago Office of Indian
Programs
77 West Jackson Boulevard
24th Floor
Chicago, IL 60604-3507
(312) 231-1282

Texas
(Fort Worth Regional
Office)
Stephen Weatherforce,
Secretary's Representative
1600 Throckmorton
P.O. Box 2905
Fort Worth, TX 76113-2905
(817) 885-5401
Fax: (817) 885-5629

(East, North, and West
Texas)
Clarence D. Babers, Acting
Area Coordinator
525 Griffin Street
Room 860
Dallas, TX 75202-5007
(214) 767-8359
Fax: (214) 767-8973

(Northwest Texas)
Henry E. Whitney, Acting
Area Coordinator
Federal Office Building
1205 Texas Avenue
Lubbock, TX 79401-4093
(806) 743-7265

(Southwest Texas)
A. Cynthia Leon, Acting
Area Coordinator
Washington Square Building
800 Dolorosa Street
San Antonio, TX 78207-4563
(512) 229-6800

(East-Central Texas)
George Rodriguez, Acting
Area Coordinator
Norfolk Tower
2211 Norfolk
Room 200
Houston, TX 77098-4096
(713) 653-3274

(Bowie County)
John T. Suskie, Acting State
Coordinator
TCBY Tower
425 West Capitol Avenue
Suite 900
Little Rock, AR 72201-3488
(501) 324-5931
Fax: (501) 324-5900

(Five Counties in East Texas)
Ben Wiley, Acting Area
Coordinator
401 Edwards Street
500 Fannin Street
Shreveport, LA 71101-3107
(318) 266-5385

Jim Cook, Acting Director
Oklahoma City Office of
Indian Programs
500 West Main Street
Oklahoma City, OK 73102-
2233

Utah
Richard Bell, Acting State
Coordinator
257 Tower Building
257 East, 200 South
Salt Lake City, UT 84111-
2048
(801) 524-5379
Fax: (801) 524-5701

Vernon Haragara, Director
Denver Office of Indian
Programs
Executive Tower Building
1405 Curtis Street
Denver, CO 80202-2349
(303) 844-2963

Vermont
William Peters, Acting State
Coordinator
Federal Building
Room 244
11 Elmwood Avenue
P.O. Box 879
Burlington, VT 05402-0879
(802) 951-6290
Fax: (802) 951-6298

David B. Harrity, Acting
State Coordinator
Norris Cotton Federal
Building
275 Chester Street
Manchester, NH 03103-
2487
(603) 666-7681
Fax: (603) 666-7736

Leon Jacobs, Director
Chicago Office of Indian
Programs
77 West Jackson Boulevard
24th Floor
Chicago, IL 60604-3507
(312) 231-1282

Virginia
(North Virginia)
Jessica Franklin, Acting
State Coordinator
Union Center Plaza, Phase II
820 First Street, NE
Suite 300
Washington, DC 20002-
4205
(202) 275-9200
Fax: (202) 275-0779

(South Virginia)
Mary Ann Wilson, Acting
State Coordinator
P.O. Box 90331
3600 West Broad Street
Richmond, VA 23230-0331
(804) 278-4507

Leon Jacobs, Director
Chicago Office of Indian
Programs
77 West Jackson Boulevard
24th Floor
Chicago, IL 60604-3507
(312) 231-1282

Virgin Islands
Rosa Villalonga, Acting
State Coordinator
159 Carlos E. Chardon
Avenue
San Juan, PR 00918-1804
(809) 766-6121
Fax: (809) 498-5201

Washington
(Seattle Regional Office)
Bob Santos, Secretary's
Representative
Regional Housing
Commissioner
Seattle Federal Office
Building
Suite 200
909 First Avenue
Seattle, WA 98104-1000
(206) 220-5101
Fax: (206) 220-5133

(Clark, Klickitat, and
Skamania Counties)
Richard C. Brinck, Acting
State Coordinator
Cascase Building
520 SW Sixth Avenue
Portland, OR 97204-1596
(503) 326-2561
Fax: (503) 326-3097

(East Washington)
Gary Rogers, Acting Area
Coordinator
Eighth Floor East
Farm Credit Bank Building
West 601 First Avenue
Spokane, WA 99204-0317
(509) 353-2510

Jerry Leslie, Director
Seattle Office of Indian
Programs
Seattle Federal Office
Building
909 First Avenue
Suite 200
Seattle, WA 98104-1000
(206) 220-5270

West Virginia
Fred Roncaglione, Acting
State Coordinator
405 Capitol Street
Suite 708
Charleston, WV 25301-
1795
(304) 347-7000
Fax: (304) 347-7050

Choice Edwards, Acting
Area Coordinator
412 Old Post Office
Courthouse Building
Seventh Avenue and Grant
Street
Pittsburgh, PA 15219-1906
(412) 644-6428
Fax: (412) 644-6499

Leon Jacobs, Director
Chicago Office of Indian
Programs
77 West Jackson Boulevard
24th Floor
Chicago, IL 60604-3507
(312) 231-1282

Wisconsin
Delbert F. Reynolds, Acting
State Coordinator
Henry S. Reuss Federal
Plaza
310 West Wisconsin Avenue
Milwaukee, WI 53203-2289
(414) 297-3214
Fax: (414) 297-3947

Leon Jacobs, Director
Chicago Office of Indian
Programs
77 West Jackson Boulevard
24th Floor
Chicago, IL 60604-3507
(312) 231-1282

Wyoming
William Garrett, Acting
State Coordinator
4225 Federal Office Building
100 East B Street
P.O. Box 120
Casper, WY 82602-1918
(307) 261-5252
Fax: (307) 261-5251

Vernon Haragara, Director
Denver Office of Indian
Programs
Executive Tower Building
1405 Curtis Street
Denver, CO 80202-2349
(303) 844-2963

MORTGAGE INSURANCE—TWO-YEAR OPERATING LOSS LOANS

Department of Housing and Urban Development (HUD)
Policies and Procedures Division
Office of Insured Multifamily Housing Development
Washington, DC 20412
(202) 755-2556

Description: Guaranteed/insured loans to owners of multifamily projects or facilities subject to mortgage insured or held by HUD to insure a separate loan covering operating losses during first two years after a first HUD mortgage. Limited to currently insured HUD projects and to term of mortgage.
$ Given: $19.1 million est. nationwide FY 95
Application Information: Initial conference at local HUD field office, followed by formal application.
Deadline: Three years after end of two-year operating loss period
Contact: Nearest local HUD field office

Alabama
Heager Hill, Acting State Coordinator
600 Beacon Parkway West
Suite 300
Birmingham, AL 35209-3144
(205) 290-7617

Leon Jacobs, Director
Chicago Office of Indian Programs
77 West Jackson Boulevard
24th Floor
Chicago, IL 60604-3507
(312) 231-1282

Alaska
Arlene Patton, Manager
University Plaza Building
949 East 36th Avenue
Suite 401
Anchorage, AK 99508-4135
(907) 271-4170
Fax: (907) 271-3667

Martin Knight, Director
Anchorage Indian Housing Division
949 East 36th Avenue
Suite 401
Anchorage, AK 99508-4135
(907) 271-4633

American Samoa
Gordon Y. Furutani, Acting State Coordinator
7 Waterfront Plaza
500 Ala Moana Boulevard
Room 500
Honolulu, HI 96813-4918
(808) 541-1323
Fax: (808) 541-3146

Arizona
Dwight A. Peterson, Acting State Coordinator
Two Arizona Center
400 North Fifth Street
Suite 1600
Phoenix, AZ 85004-2361
(602) 379-4434
Fax: (602) 379-3985

Sharon Atwell, Acting Area Coordinator
33 North Stone Avenue
Room 700
Tucson, AZ 85701-1467
(602) 670-6237
Fax: (602) 670-6207

Charles Ming, Acting Area Coordinator
1615 West Olympic Boulevard
Los Angeles, CA 90015-3801
(213) 251-7122
Fax: (213) 251-7096

Raphael Mecham, Director
HUD Indian Programs Office
400 North Fifth Street
Suite 1650
Phoenix, AZ 85004-2361
(602) 379-4156
Fax: (602) 379-3101

Arkansas
John T. Suskie, Acting State Coordinator
TCBY Tower
425 West Capitol Avenue
Suite 900
Little Rock, AR 72201-3488
(501) 324-5931
Fax: (501) 324-5900

Jim Cook, Acting Director
Oklahoma City Office of
Indian Programs
500 West Main Street
Oklahoma City, OK 73102-
2233

California
(San Francisco Regional
Office)
Arthur Agnos, Secretary's
Representative
Phillip Burton Federal
Building and U.S.
Courthouse
P.O. Box 36003
450 Golden Gate Avenue
San Francisco, CA 94102-
3448
(415) 556-4752
Fax: (415) 556-4176

(South California)
Charles Ming, Acting Area
Coordinator
1615 West Olympic
Boulevard
Los Angeles, CA 90015-
3801
(213) 251-7122
Fax: (213) 251-7096

(Fresno)
Willie Mae Haskin, Acting
Area Coordinator
1630 East Shaw Avenue
Fresno, CA 93710-8193
(209) 487-5033
Fax: (209) 487-5344

(Northeast California)
Paul Pradia, Acting Area
Coordinator
777 12th Street
Suite 200
Sacramento, CA 95814-
1997
(916) 551-1351
Fax: (916) 551-2899

(Imperial and San Diego
Counties)
Charles J. Wilson, Acting
Area Coordinator
Mission City Corporate
Center
Suite 300
2365 Northside Drive
San Diego, CA 92108-2712
(619) 557-5310
Fax: (619) 557-6296

(Orange, Riverside, and San
Bernadino Counties, for
home mortgages)
Samuel Sandoval, Acting
Area Coordinator
3 Hutton Centre
Suite 500
Santa Ana, CA 92707-5764
(714) 957-7333
Fax: (714) 957-1903

Raphael Mecham, Director
HUD Indian Programs
Office
400 North Fifth Street
Suite 1650
Phoenix, AZ 85004-2361
(602) 379-4156
Fax: (602) 379-3101

Colorado
(Denver Regional Office)
Anthony Hernandez,
Secretary's Representative
HUD—Denver Office
633 17th Street
Denver, CO 80202-3607
(303) 844-4513
Fax: (303) 844-2475

Vernon Haragara, Director
Denver Office of Indian
Programs
Executive Tower Building
1405 Curtis Street
Denver, CO 80202-2349
(303) 844-2963

Connecticut
Robert S. Donovon, Deputy
Manager
330 Main Street
Hartford, CT 06106-1860
(203) 240-4523
Fax: (203) 240-4674

Leon Jacobs, Director
Chicago Office of Indian
Programs
77 West Jackson Boulevard
24th Floor
Chicago, IL 60604-3507
(312) 231-1282

Delaware
A. David Sharbaugh, Acting
State Coordinator
824 Market Street
Suite 850
Wilmington, DE 19801-
3016
(302) 573-6300
Fax: (302) 573-6259

Leon Jacobs, Director
Chicago Office of Indian
Programs
77 West Jackson Boulevard
24th Floor
Chicago, IL 60604-3507
(312) 231-1282

District of Columbia
Jessica Franklin, Acting
State Coordinator
Union Center Plaza, Phase II
820 First Street, NE
Suite 300
Washington, DC 20002-
4205
(202) 275-9200
Fax: (202) 275-0779

Florida
James T. Chaplin, State
Coordinator
Southern Bell Tower
Suite 2200
301 West Bay Street
Jacksonville, FL 32202-5121
(904) 232-2626
Fax: (904) 232-3759

(South Florida)
Orlando T. Lorie, Acting
Area Coordinator
Gables 1 Tower
1320 South Dixie Highway
Coral Gables, FL 33146-
2911
(305) 662-4500
Fax: (305) 662-4519

(Central Florida, Western
Counties—Citrus, Sumter,
Hernando, Pasco, Manatee,
Hardee, Highlands, DeSoto,
Sarasota, Charlotte, Olaoes,
Hendry, Lake Okeechobee)
George A. Milburn Jr.,
Acting Area Coordinator
Timberlake Federal Building
Annex
501 East Polk Street
Tampa, FL 33602-3945
(813) 228-2501
Fax: (813) 228-2431

(Central Florida, Eastern
Counties—Volusia, Lake,
Seminole, Orange, Brevard,
Osceola, Indian River,
Okeechobee, St. Lucie)
M. Jeanette Porter, Acting
Area Coordinator
Langley Building
3751 Maguire Boulevard
Suite 270
Orlando, FL 32803-3032
(407) 648-6441
Fax: (407) 648-6310

Leon Jacobs, Director
Chicago Office of Indian
Programs
77 West Jackson Boulevard
24th Floor
Chicago, IL 60604-3507
(312) 231-1282

Georgia
(Atlanta Regional Office)
Davey L. Gibson, Secretary's
Representative
Regional Housing
Commissioner
Richard B. Russell Federal
Building
75 Spring Street, SW
Atlanta, GA 30303-3388
(404) 331-5136
Fax: (404) 331-0845

Leon Jacobs, Director
Chicago Office of Indian
Programs
77 West Jackson Boulevard
24th Floor
Chicago, IL 60604-3507
(312) 231-1282

Guam
Gordon Y. Furutani, Acting
State Coordinator
7 Waterfront Plaza
500 Ala Moana Boulevard
Room 500
Honolulu, HI 96813-4918
(808) 541-1323
Fax: (808) 541-3146

Hawaii
Gordon Y. Furutani, Acting
State Coordinator
7 Waterfront Plaza
500 Ala Moana Boulevard
Room 500
Honolulu, HI 96813-4918
(808) 541-1323
Fax: (808) 541-3146

Idaho
(North Idaho)
Gary Rogers, Acting Area
Coordinator
Farm Credit Bank Building
Eighth Floor East
West 601 First Avenue
Spokane, WA 99204-0317
(509) 353-2510

(West-Central Idaho)
Gary Gillespie, Acting State
Coordinator
Suite 220
Park IV
800 Park Boulevard
Boise, ID 83712-7743
(208) 334-1990
Fax: (208) 334-9648

(South Idaho)
Richard C. Brinck, Acting
State Coordinator
Cascade Building
520 SW Sixth Avenue
Portland, OR 97204-1596
(503) 221-2561

Jerry Leslie, Director
Seattle Office of Indian
Programs
Seattle Federal Office
Building
909 First Avenue
Suite 200
Seattle, WA 98104-1000
(206) 220-5270

Illinois
(Chicago Regional Office)
Edwin Eisendrath,
Secretary's Representative
Regional Housing
Commissioner
Ralph Metcalfe Federal
Building
77 West Jackson Boulevard
Chicago, IL 60604-3507
(312) 353-5680
Fax: (312) 353-0121

(Central and South Illinois)
William Fattick, Acting Area
Coordinator
509 West Capitol
Suite 206
Springfield, IL 62704-1906
(217) 492-4085
Fax: (217) 492-4971

Leon Jacobs, Director
Chicago Office of Indian
Programs
77 West Jackson Boulevard
24th Floor
Chicago, IL 60604-3507
(312) 231-1282

Indiana
J. Nicholas Shelley, Acting
State Coordinator
151 North Delaware Street
Indianapolis, IN 46204-
2526
(317) 226-6303
Fax: (317) 226-6317

Iowa
William R. McNarney,
Acting State Coordinator
HUD—Des Moines Office
Federal Building
Room 239
210 Walnut Street
Des Moines, IA 50309-2155
(515) 284-4512
Fax: (515) 284-4743

Roger M. Massey, Acting
State Coordinator
Executive Tower Center
10909 Mill Valley Road
Omaha, NE 68154-3955
(402) 492-3101
Fax: (402) 492-3150

Leon Jacobs, Director
Chicago Office of Indian
Programs
77 West Jackson Boulevard
24th Floor
Chicago, IL 60604-3507
(312) 231-1282

Kansas
Joseph O'Hern, Secretary's
Representative
Regional Housing
Commissioner
HUD—Kansas City Regional
Office
Gateway Tower II
400 State Avenue
Room 200
Kansas City, KS 66101-2406
(913) 551-5462
Fax: (913) 551-5416

Jim Cook, Acting Director
Oklahoma City Office of
Indian Programs
500 West Main Street
Oklahoma City, OK 73102-
2233

Kentucky
Verna V. Van Ness, Acting
State Coordinator
601 West Broadway
P.O. Box 1044
Louisville, KY 40201-1044
(502) 582-5251
Fax: (502) 582-6074

Leon Jacobs, Director
Chicago Office of Indian
Programs
77 West Jackson Boulevard
24th Floor
Chicago, IL 60604-3507
(312) 231-1282

Louisiana
Robert Vasquez, Acting
State Coordinator
Fisk Federal Building
1661 Canal Street
New Orleans, LA 70112-
1887
(504) 589-7200
Fax: (504) 589-2917

(North Louisiana)
Ben Wiley, Acting Area
Coordinator
401 Edwards Street
500 Fannin Street
Shreveport, LA 71101-3107
(318) 266-5385

Jim Cook, Acting Director
Oklahoma City Office of
Indian Programs
500 West Main Street
Oklahoma City, OK 73102-
2233

Maine
Richard Young, Acting State
Coordinator
Casco Northern Bank
Building
23 Main Street
Bangor, ME 04401-6394
(207) 945-0467
Fax: (207) 945-0533

David B. Harrity, Acting
State Coordinator
Norris Cotton Federal
Building
275 Chester Street
Manchester, NH 03103-
2487
(603) 666-7681
Fax: (603) 666-7736

Leon Jacobs, Director
Chicago Office of Indian
Programs
77 West Jackson Boulevard
24th Floor
Chicago, IL 60604-3507
(312) 231-1282

Maryland
(Except Montgomery and
Prince Georges Counties)
Maxine Saunders, Acting
State Coordinator
City Crescent Building
10 South Howard Street
Fifth Floor
Baltimore, MD 21201
(301) 962-2520

(Montgomery and Prince
Georges Counties)
Jessica Franklin, Acting
State Coordinator
Union Center Plaza, Phase II
820 First Street, NE
Suite 300
Washington, DC 20002-
4205
(202) 275-9200
Fax: (202) 275-0779

Leon Jacobs, Director
Chicago Office of Indian
Programs
77 West Jackson Boulevard
24th Floor
Chicago, IL 60604-3507
(312) 231-1282

Massachusetts
(Boston Regional Office)
Mary Lou Crane, Secretary's
Representative
Thomas P. O'Neill Jr.
Federal Building
10 Causeway Street
Room 375
Boston, MA 02222-1092
(617) 565-5234
Fax: (617) 565-5168

Leon Jacobs, Director
Chicago Office of Indian
Programs
77 West Jackson Boulevard
24th Floor
Chicago, IL 60604-3507
(312) 231-1282

Michigan
Harry I. Sharrott, Acting
State Coordinator
Patrick V. McNamara
Federal Building
477 Michigan Avenue
Detroit, MI 48226-2592
(313) 226-7900
Fax: (313) 226-4394

(East Michigan)
Gary T. LeVine, Acting Area
Coordinator
605 North Saginaw Street
Suite 200
Flint, MI 48502-1953
(313) 766-5112
Fax: (313) 766-5122

(West and North Michigan)
Ronald Weston, Acting Area
Coordinator
Northbrook Building, # II
2922 Fuller Avenue, NE
Grand Rapids, MI 49505-
3499
(616) 456-2100
Fax: (616) 456-2191

Leon Jacobs, Director
Chicago Office of Indian
Programs
77 West Jackson Boulevard
24th Floor
Chicago, IL 60604-3507
(312) 231-1282

Minnesota
Thomas Feeney, Acting State
Coordinator
220 Second Street South
Bridge Place Building
Minneapolis, MN 55401-
2195
(612) 370-3000
Fax: (612) 370-3220

Leon Jacobs, Director
Chicago Office of Indian
Programs
77 West Jackson Boulevard
24th Floor
Chicago, IL 60604-3507
(312) 231-1282

Mississippi
Sandra Freeman, Acting
State Coordinator
Koger Building
Dr. A. H. McCoy Federal
Building
100 West Capitol Street
Room 910
Jackson, MS 39269-1096
(601) 965-5308
Fax: (601) 965-4773

Leon Jacobs, Director
Chicago Office of Indian
Programs
77 West Jackson Boulevard
24th Floor
Chicago, IL 60604-3507
(312) 231-1282

Missouri
Kenneth G. Lange, Acting
Area Coordinator
1222 Spruce Street
Room 3207
St. Louis, MO 63103-2836
(314) 539-6560
Fax: (314) 539-6575

Jim Cook, Acting Director
Oklahoma City Office of
Indian Programs
500 West Main Street
Oklahoma City, OK 73102-
2233

Montana
Gerard Boone, Acting State
Coordinator
Federal Office Building,
Drawer 10095
301 South Park
Room 340
Helena, MT 59626-0095
(406) 449-5205
Fax: (406) 449-5207

Vernon Haragara, Director
Denver Office of Indian
Programs
Executive Tower Building
1405 Curtis Street
Denver, CO 80202-2349
(303) 844-2963

Nebraska
Roger M. Massey, Acting
State Coordinator
Executive Tower Center
10909 Mill Valley Road
Omaha, NE 68154-3955
(402) 492-3101
Fax: (402) 492-3150

Vernon Haragara, Director
Denver Office of Indian
Programs
Executive Tower Building
1405 Curtis Street
Denver, CO 80202-2349
(303) 844-2963

Nevada
Andrew D. Whitten Jr.,
Acting Area Coordinator
1575 DeLucchi Lane
Room 114
P.O. Box 30050
Reno, NV 89502-6581
(702) 784-5356
Fax: (702) 784-5066

Benjamin Davis, Acting
State Coordinator
1500 East Tropicana Avenue
Second Floor
Las Vegas, NV 89119-6516
(702) 388-6500
Fax: (702) 388-6736

Raphael Mecham, Director
HUD Indian Programs
Office
400 North Fifth Street
Suite 1650
Phoenix, AZ 85004-2361
(602) 379-4156
Fax: (602) 379-3101

New Hampshire
David B. Harrity, Acting
State Coordinator
Norris Cotton Federal
Building
275 Chestnut Street
Manchester, NH 03103-
2487
(603) 666-7681
Fax: (603) 666-7736

Leon Jacobs, Director
Chicago Office of Indian
Programs
77 West Jackson Boulevard
24th Floor
Chicago, IL 60604-3507
(312) 231-1282

New Jersey
(North New Jersey)
Diane Johnson, Acting State
Coordinator
One Newark Center
13th Floor
Newark, NJ 07102-5260
(201) 622-7900
Fax: (201) 645-6239

(South New Jersey)
Elmer Roy, Acting Area
Coordinator
Hudson Building
Second Floor
800 Hudson Square
Camden, NJ 08102-1156
(609) 757-5081
Fax: (609) 757-5373

Leon Jacobs, Director
Chicago Office of Indian
Programs
77 West Jackson Boulevard
24th Floor
Chicago, IL 60604-3507
(312) 231-1282

New Mexico
Michael R. Griego, Acting
State Coordinator
625 Truman Street, NW
Albuquerque, NM 87110-
6443
(505) 262-6463

Clarence D. Babers, Acting
Area Coordinator
525 Griffin Street
Room 860
Dallas, TX 75202-5007
(214) 767-8359
Fax: (214) 767-8973

Raphael Mecham, Director
HUD Indian Programs
Office
400 North Fifth Street
Suite 1650
Phoenix, AZ 85004-2361
(602) 379-4156
Fax: (602) 379-3101

New York
(New York Regional Office)
Jose Cintron, Secretary's
Representative
26 Federal Plaza
New York, NY 10278-0068
(212) 264-6500
Fax: (212) 264-0246

(North New York)
John Petricco, Acting Area
Coordinator
52 Corporate Circle
Albany, NY 12203-5121
(518) 464-4200
Fax: (518) 464-4300

(West New York)
Joseph Lynch, Acting Area
Coordinator
465 Main Street
Lafayette Court
Fifth Floor
Buffalo, NY 14203-1780
(716) 846-5755
Fax: (716) 846-5752

Leon Jacobs, Director
Chicago Office of Indian
Programs
77 West Jackson Boulevard
24th Floor
Chicago, IL 60604-3507
(312) 231-1282

North Carolina
Larry J. Parker, Acting State
Coordinator
2306 West Meadowview
Road
Koger Building
Greensboro, NC 27407-
3707
(919) 547-4001
Fax: (919) 547-4015

Leon Jacobs, Director
Chicago Office of Indian
Programs
77 West Jackson Boulevard
24th Floor
Chicago, IL 60604-3507
(312) 231-1282

North Dakota
Keith Elliott, Acting State
Coordinator
HUD—Fargo Office
Federal Building
657 Second Avenue, North
Fargo, ND 58108-2483
(701) 239-5136
Fax: (701) 783-5249

Vernon Haragara, Director
Denver Office of Indian
Programs
Executive Tower Building
1405 Curtis Street
Denver, CO 80202-2349
(303) 844-2963

Ohio
Robert W. Dolin, Acting
State Coordinator
HUD—Columbus Office
200 North High Street
Columbus, OH 43215-2499
(614) 469-5737
Fax: (614) 469-2432

(North Ohio)
Philip Ginconia, Acting Area
Coordinator
1350 Euclid Avenue
Fifth Floor
Cleveland, OH 44115-1815
(216) 552-4065
Fax: (216) 522-2975

(Southwest Ohio)
William Harris, Acting Area
Coordinator
Federal Office Building
Room 9002
550 Main Street
Cincinnati, OH 45202-3253
(513) 684-2884
Fax: (513) 684-6224

Leon Jacobs, Director
Chicago Office of Indian
Programs
77 West Jackson Boulevard
24th Floor
Chicago, IL 60604-3507
(312) 231-1282

Oklahoma
Katie Worsham, Acting State
Coordinator
500 West Main Street
Oklahoma City, OK 73102-
2233

(East Oklahoma)
James S. Colgan, Acting
Area Coordinator
1516 South Boston Avenue
Room 110
Tulsa, OK 74119-4032
(918) 581-7435
Fax: (918) 581-7440

Jim Cook, Acting Director
Oklahoma City Office of
Indian Programs
500 West Main Street
Oklahoma City, OK 73102-
2233

Oregon
Richard C. Brinck, Acting
State Coordinator
Cascade Building
520 SW Sixth Avenue
Portland, OR 97204-1596
(503) 326-2561
Fax: (503) 326-3097

Jerry Leslie, Director
Seattle Office of Indian
Programs
Seattle Federal Office
Building
909 First Avenue
Suite 200
Seattle, WA 98104-1000
(206) 220-5270

Panama Canal Zone
Rosa Villalonga, Acting
State Coordinator
159 Carlos E. Chardon
Avenue
San Juan, PR 00918-1804
(809) 766-6121
Fax: (809) 498-5201

Pennsylvania
(Philadelphia Regional
Office)
Karen A. Miller, Secretary's
Representative
Regional Housing
Commissioner
Liberty Square Building
105 South Seventh Street
Philadelphia, PA 19106-
3392
(215) 597-2560
Fax: (215) 597-9627

(West Pennsylvania)
Choice Edwards, Acting
Area Coordinator
412 Old Post Office
Courthouse Building
Seventh Avenue and Grant
Street
Pittsburgh, PA 15219-1906
(412) 644-6428
Fax: (412) 644-6499

Leon Jacobs, Director
Chicago Office of Indian
Programs
77 West Jackson Boulevard
24th Floor
Chicago, IL 60604-3507
(312) 231-1282

Puerto Rico
Rosa Villalonga, Acting
State Coordinator
159 Carlos E. Chardon
Avenue
San Juan, PR 00918-1804
(809) 766-6121
Fax: (809) 498-5201

Rhode Island
Michael Dziok, Acting State
Coordinator
Room 303
John O. Pastore Federal
Building and U.S. Post
Office
Kennedy Plaza
Providence, RI 02903-1785
(401) 528-5351
Fax: (401) 528-5312

Leon Jacobs, Director
Chicago Office of Indian
Programs
77 West Jackson Boulevard
24th Floor
Chicago, IL 60604-3507
(312) 231-1282

South Carolina
Ted B. Freeman, Acting
State Coordinator
Strom Thurmond Federal
Building
1835 Assembly Street
Columbia, SC 29201-2480
(803) 765-5592
Fax: (803) 765-5515

Leon Jacobs, Director
Chicago Office of Indian
Programs
77 West Jackson Boulevard
24th Floor
Chicago, IL 60604-3507
(312) 231-1282

South Dakota
Don Olson, Acting State
Coordinator
Suite I-201
2400 West 49th Street
Sioux Falls, SD 57105-6558
(605) 330-4223
Fax: (605) 330-4465

Vernon Haragara, Director
Denver Office of Indian
Programs
Executive Tower Building
1405 Curtis Street
Denver, CO 80202-2349
(303) 844-2963

Tennessee
Mark Brezina, Acting Area
Coordinator
John J. Duncan Federal
Building
Third Floor
710 Locust Street, SW
Knoxville, TN 37902-2526
(615) 545-4384
Fax: (615) 545-4569

(West Tennessee)
Bob Atkins, Acting Area
Coordinator
One Memphis Place
200 Jefferson Avenue
Suite 1200
Memphis, TN 38103-2335
(901) 544-3367
Fax: (901) 544-3697

(Central Tennessee)
John H. Fisher, Acting State
Coordinator
251 Cumberland Bend Drive
Nashville, TN 37228-1803
(615) 736-5213
Fax: (615) 736-2018

Leon Jacobs, Director
Chicago Office of Indian
Programs
77 West Jackson Boulevard
24th Floor
Chicago, IL 60604-3507
(312) 231-1282

Texas
(Fort Worth Regional
Office)
Stephen Weatherforce,
Secretary's Representative
1600 Throckmorton
P.O. Box 2905
Fort Worth, TX 76113-2905
(817) 885-5401
Fax: (817) 885-5629

(East, North, and West
Texas)
Clarence D. Babers, Acting
Area Coordinator
525 Griffin Street
Room 860
Dallas, TX 75202-5007
(214) 767-8359
Fax: (214) 767-8973

(Northwest Texas)
Henry E. Whitney, Acting
Area Coordinator
Federal Office Building
1205 Texas Avenue
Lubbock, TX 79401-4093
(806) 743-7265

(Southwest Texas)
A. Cynthia Leon, Acting
Area Coordinator
Washington Square Building
800 Dolorosa Street
San Antonio, TX 78207-
4563
(512) 229-6800

(East-Central Texas)
George Rodriguez, Acting
Area Coordinator
Norfolk Tower
2211 Norfolk
Room 200
Houston, TX 77098-4096
(713) 653-3274

(Bowie County)
John T. Suskie, Acting State
Coordinator
TCBY Tower
425 West Capitol Avenue
Suite 900
Little Rock, AR 72201-3488
(501) 324-5931
Fax: (501) 324-5900

(Five Counties in East
Texas)
Ben Wiley, Acting Area
Coordinator
401 Edwards Street
500 Fannin Street
Shreveport, LA 71101-3107
(318) 266-5385

Jim Cook, Acting Director
Oklahoma City Office of
Indian Programs
500 West Main Street
Oklahoma City, OK 73102-
2233

Utah
Richard Bell, Acting State
Coordinator
257 Tower Building
257 East, 200 South
Salt Lake City, UT 84111-
2048
(801) 524-5379
Fax: (801) 524-5701

Vernon Haragara, Director
Denver Office of Indian
Programs
Executive Tower Building
1405 Curtis Street
Denver, CO 80202-2349
(303) 844-2963

Vermont
William Peters, Acting State
Coordinator
Federal Building
Room 244
11 Elmwood Avenue
P.O. Box 879
Burlington, VT 05402-0879
(802) 951-6290
Fax: (802) 951-6298

David B. Harrity, Acting
State Coordinator
Norris Cotton Federal
Building
275 Chester Street
Manchester, NH 03103-
2487
(603) 666-7681
Fax: (603) 666-7736

Leon Jacobs, Director
Chicago Office of Indian
Programs
77 West Jackson Boulevard
24th Floor
Chicago, IL 60604-3507
(312) 231-1282

Virginia
(North Virginia)
Jessica Franklin, Acting
State Coordinator
Union Center Plaza, Phase II
820 First Street, NE
Suite 300
Washington, DC 20002-
4205
(202) 275-9200
Fax: (202) 275-0779

(South Virginia)
Mary Ann Wilson, Acting
State Coordinator
P.O. Box 90331
3600 West Broad Street
Richmond, VA 23230-0331
(804) 278-4507

Leon Jacobs, Director
Chicago Office of Indian
Programs
77 West Jackson Boulevard
24th Floor
Chicago, IL 60604-3507
(312) 231-1282

Virgin Islands
Rosa Villalonga, Acting
State Coordinator
159 Carlos E. Chardon
Avenue
San Juan, PR 00918-1804
(809) 766-6121
Fax: (809) 498-5201

Washington
(Seattle Regional Office)
Bob Santos, Secretary's
Representative
Regional Housing
Commissioner
Seattle Federal Office
Building
Suite 200
909 First Avenue
Seattle, WA 98104-1000
(206) 220-5101
Fax: (206) 220-5133

(Clark, Klickitat, and
Skamania Counties)
Richard C. Brinck, Acting
State Coordinator
Cascase Building
520 SW Sixth Avenue
Portland, OR 97204-1596
(503) 326-2561
Fax: (503) 326-3097

(East Washington)
Gary Rogers, Acting Area
Coordinator
Eighth Floor East
Farm Credit Bank Building
West 601 First Avenue
Spokane, WA 99204-0317
(509) 353-2510

Jerry Leslie, Director
Seattle Office of Indian
Programs
Seattle Federal Office Building
909 First Avenue
Suite 200
Seattle, WA 98104-1000
(206) 220-5270

West Virginia
Fred Roncaglione, Acting
State Coordinator
405 Capitol Street
Suite 708
Charleston, WV 25301-1795
(304) 347-7000
Fax: (304) 347-7050

Choice Edwards, Acting
Area Coordinator
412 Old Post Office
Courthouse Building
Seventh Avenue and Grant
Street
Pittsburgh, PA 15219-1906
(412) 644-6428
Fax: (412) 644-6499

Leon Jacobs, Director
Chicago Office of Indian
Programs
77 West Jackson Boulevard
24th Floor
Chicago, IL 60604-3507
(312) 231-1282

Wisconsin
Delbert F. Reynolds, Acting
State Coordinator
Henry S. Reuss Federal Plaza
310 West Wisconsin Avenue
Milwaukee, WI 53203-2289
(414) 297-3214
Fax: (414) 297-3947

Leon Jacobs, Director
Chicago Office of Indian
Programs
77 West Jackson Boulevard
24th Floor
Chicago, IL 60604-3507
(312) 231-1282

Wyoming
William Garrett, Acting
State Coordinator
4225 Federal Office Building
100 East B Street
P.O. Box 120
Casper, WY 82602-1918
(307) 261-5252
Fax: (307) 261-5251

Vernon Haragara, Director
Denver Office of Indian
Programs
Executive Tower Building
1405 Curtis Street
Denver, CO 80202-2349
(303) 844-2963

OPERATING ASSISTANCE FOR TROUBLED MULTIFAMILY HOUSING PROJECTS
(Flexible Subsidy Fund/Troubled Projects)

Department of Housing and
Urban Development (HUD)
Office of Multifamily
Housing Management
Washington, DC 20420
(202) 708-3730

Description: Direct payments for specific use to profit-motivated, limited dividend, and cooperative owners for restoring or maintaining physical and financial upkeep of certain approved low- to moderate-income projects. Restricted to certain projects approved by HUD. Assurance must be gained from local government that real estate taxes will be assessed in a normal manner and that assistance is not inconsistent with local plans and priorities.
$ Given: $128.5 million est. nationwide FY 95; average: $830,000 per project
Application Information: Projects identified by HUD as needing aid are asked to submit appropriate documentation.
Deadline: None
Contact: Chief, loan management branch of local HUD field office

Alabama
Heager Hill, Acting State
Coordinator
600 Beacon Parkway West
Suite 300
Birmingham, AL 35209-3144
(205) 290-7617

Leon Jacobs, Director
Chicago Office of Indian
Programs
77 West Jackson Boulevard
24th Floor
Chicago, IL 60604-3507
(312) 231-1282

Alaska
Arlene Patton, Manager
University Plaza Building
949 East 36th Avenue
Suite 401
Anchorage, AK 99508-4135
(907) 271-4170
Fax: (907) 271-3667

Martin Knight, Director
Anchorage Indian Housing
Division
949 East 36th Avenue
Suite 401
Anchorage, AK 99508-4135
(907) 271-4633

American Samoa
Gordon Y. Furutani, Acting
State Coordinator
7 Waterfront Plaza
500 Ala Moana Boulevard
Room 500
Honolulu, HI 96813-4918
(808) 541-1323
Fax: (808) 541-3146

Arizona
Dwight A. Peterson, Acting
State Coordinator
Two Arizona Center
400 North Fifth Street
Suite 1600
Phoenix, AZ 85004-2361
(602) 379-4434
Fax: (602) 379-3985

Sharon Atwell, Acting Area
Coordinator
33 North Stone Avenue
Room 700
Tucson, AZ 85701-1467
(602) 670-6237
Fax: (602) 670-6207

Charles Ming, Acting Area
Coordinator
1615 West Olympic
Boulevard
Los Angeles, CA 90015-3801
(213) 251-7122
Fax: (213) 251-7096

Raphael Mecham, Director
HUD Indian Programs
Office
400 North Fifth Street
Suite 1650
Phoenix, AZ 85004-2361
(602) 379-4156
Fax: (602) 379-3101

Arkansas
John T. Suskie, Acting State
Coordinator
TCBY Tower
425 West Capitol Avenue
Suite 900
Little Rock, AR 72201-3488
(501) 324-5931
Fax: (501) 324-5900

Jim Cook, Acting Director
Oklahoma City Office of
Indian Programs
500 West Main Street
Oklahoma City, OK 73102-
2233

California
(San Francisco Regional
Office)
Arthur Agnos, Secretary's
Representative
Phillip Burton Federal
Building and U.S.
Courthouse
P.O. Box 36003
450 Golden Gate Avenue
San Francisco, CA 94102-
3448
(415) 556-4752
Fax: (415) 556-4176

(South California)
Charles Ming, Acting Area
Coordinator
1615 West Olympic
Boulevard
Los Angeles, CA 90015-
3801
(213) 251-7122
Fax: (213) 251-7096

(Fresno)
Willie Mae Haskin, Acting
Area Coordinator
1630 East Shaw Avenue
Fresno, CA 93710-8193
(209) 487-5033
Fax: (209) 487-5344

(Northeast California)
Paul Pradia, Acting Area
Coordinator
777 12th Street
Suite 200
Sacramento, CA 95814-
1997
(916) 551-1351
Fax: (916) 551-2899

(Imperial and San Diego
Counties)
Charles J. Wilson, Acting
Area Coordinator
Mission City Corporate
Center
Suite 300
2365 Northside Drive
San Diego, CA 92108-2712
(619) 557-5310
Fax: (619) 557-6296

(Orange, Riverside, and San
Bernadino Counties, for
home mortgages)
Samuel Sandoval, Acting
Area Coordinator
3 Hutton Centre
Suite 500
Santa Ana, CA 92707-5764
(714) 957-7333
Fax: (714) 957-1903

Raphael Mecham, Director
HUD Indian Programs
Office
400 North Fifth Street
Suite 1650
Phoenix, AZ 85004-2361
(602) 379-4156
Fax: (602) 379-3101

Colorado
(Denver Regional Office)
Anthony Hernandez,
Secretary's Representative
HUD—Denver Office
633 17th Street
Denver, CO 80202-3607
(303) 844-4513
Fax: (303) 844-2475

Vernon Haragara, Director
Denver Office of Indian
Programs
Executive Tower Building
1405 Curtis Street
Denver, CO 80202-2349
(303) 844-2963

Connecticut
Robert S. Donovon, Deputy
Manager
330 Main Street
Hartford, CT 06106-1860
(203) 240-4523
Fax: (203) 240-4674

Leon Jacobs, Director
Chicago Office of Indian
Programs
77 West Jackson Boulevard
24th Floor
Chicago, IL 60604-3507
(312) 231-1282

Delaware
A. David Sharbaugh, Acting
State Coordinator
824 Market Street
Suite 850
Wilmington, DE 19801-3016
(302) 573-6300
Fax: (302) 573-6259

Leon Jacobs, Director
Chicago Office of Indian
Programs
77 West Jackson Boulevard
24th Floor
Chicago, IL 60604-3507
(312) 231-1282

District of Columbia
Jessica Franklin, Acting
State Coordinator
Union Center Plaza, Phase II
820 First Street, NE
Suite 300
Washington, DC 20002-4205
(202) 275-9200
Fax: (202) 275-0779

Florida
James T. Chaplin, State
Coordinator
Southern Bell Tower
Suite 2200
301 West Bay Street
Jacksonville, FL 32202-5121
(904) 232-2626
Fax: (904) 232-3759

(South Florida)
Orlando T. Lorie, Acting
Area Coordinator
Gables 1 Tower
1320 South Dixie Highway
Coral Gables, FL 33146-
2911
(305) 662-4500
Fax: (305) 662-4519

(Central Florida, Western
Counties—Citrus, Sumter,
Hernando, Pasco, Manatee,
Hardee, Highlands, DeSoto,
Sarasota, Charlotte, Olaoes,
Hendry, Lake Okeechobee)
George A. Milburn Jr.,
Acting Area Coordinator
Timberlake Federal Building
Annex
501 East Polk Street
Tampa, FL 33602-3945
(813) 228-2501
Fax: (813) 228-2431

(Central Florida, Eastern
Counties—Volusia, Lake,
Seminole, Orange, Brevard,
Osceola, Indian River,
Okeechobee, St. Lucie)
M. Jeanette Porter, Acting
Area Coordinator
Langley Building
3751 Maguire Boulevard
Suite 270
Orlando, FL 32803-3032
(407) 648-6441
Fax: (407) 648-6310

Leon Jacobs, Director
Chicago Office of Indian
Programs
77 West Jackson Boulevard
24th Floor
Chicago, IL 60604-3507
(312) 231-1282

Georgia
(Atlanta Regional Office)
Davey L. Gibson, Secretary's
Representative
Regional Housing
Commissioner
Richard B. Russell Federal
Building
75 Spring Street, SW
Atlanta, GA 30303-3388
(404) 331-5136
Fax: (404) 331-0845

Leon Jacobs, Director
Chicago Office of Indian
Programs
77 West Jackson Boulevard
24th Floor
Chicago, IL 60604-3507
(312) 231-1282

Guam
Gordon Y. Furutani, Acting
State Coordinator
7 Waterfront Plaza
500 Ala Moana Boulevard
Room 500
Honolulu, HI 96813-4918
(808) 541-1323
Fax: (808) 541-3146

Hawaii
Gordon Y. Furutani, Acting
State Coordinator
7 Waterfront Plaza
500 Ala Moana Boulevard
Room 500
Honolulu, HI 96813-4918
(808) 541-1323
Fax: (808) 541-3146

Idaho
(North Idaho)
Gary Rogers, Acting Area
Coordinator
Farm Credit Bank Building
Eighth Floor East
West 601 First Avenue
Spokane, WA 99204-0317
(509) 353-2510

(West-Central Idaho)
Gary Gillespie, Acting State
Coordinator
Suite 220
Park IV
800 Park Boulevard
Boise, ID 83712-7743
(208) 334-1990
Fax: (208) 334-9648

(South Idaho)
Richard C. Brinck, Acting
State Coordinator
Cascade Building
520 SW Sixth Avenue
Portland, OR 97204-1596
(503) 221-2561

Jerry Leslie, Director
Seattle Office of Indian
Programs
Seattle Federal Office
Building
909 First Avenue
Suite 200
Seattle, WA 98104-1000
(206) 220-5270

Illinois
(Chicago Regional Office)
Edwin Eisendrath,
Secretary's Representative
Regional Housing
Commissioner
Ralph Metcalfe Federal
Building
77 West Jackson Boulevard
Chicago, IL 60604-3507
(312) 353-5680
Fax: (312) 353-0121

(Central and South Illinois)
William Fattick, Acting Area
Coordinator
509 West Capitol
Suite 206
Springfield, IL 62704-1906
(217) 492-4085
Fax: (217) 492-4971

Leon Jacobs, Director
Chicago Office of Indian
Programs
77 West Jackson Boulevard
24th Floor
Chicago, IL 60604-3507
(312) 231-1282

Indiana
J. Nicholas Shelley, Acting
State Coordinator
151 North Delaware Street
Indianapolis, IN 46204-
2526
(317) 226-6303
Fax: (317) 226-6317

Iowa
William R. McNarney,
Acting State Coordinator
HUD—Des Moines Office
Federal Building
Room 239
210 Walnut Street
Des Moines, IA 50309-2155
(515) 284-4512
Fax: (515) 284-4743

Roger M. Massey, Acting
State Coordinator
Executive Tower Center
10909 Mill Valley Road
Omaha, NE 68154-3955
(402) 492-3101
Fax: (402) 492-3150

Leon Jacobs, Director
Chicago Office of Indian
Programs
77 West Jackson Boulevard
24th Floor
Chicago, IL 60604-3507
(312) 231-1282

Kansas
Joseph O'Hern, Secretary's
Representative
Regional Housing
Commissioner
HUD—Kansas City Regional
Office
Gateway Tower II
400 State Avenue
Room 200
Kansas City, KS 66101-2406
(913) 551-5462
Fax: (913) 551-5416

Jim Cook, Acting Director
Oklahoma City Office of
Indian Programs
500 West Main Street
Oklahoma City, OK 73102-
2233

Kentucky
Verna V. Van Ness, Acting
State Coordinator
601 West Broadway
P.O. Box 1044
Louisville, KY 40201-1044
(502) 582-5251
Fax: (502) 582-6074

Leon Jacobs, Director
Chicago Office of Indian
Programs
77 West Jackson Boulevard
24th Floor
Chicago, IL 60604-3507
(312) 231-1282

Louisiana
Robert Vasquez, Acting
State Coordinator
Fisk Federal Building
1661 Canal Street
New Orleans, LA 70112-
1887
(504) 589-7200
Fax: (504) 589-2917

(North Louisiana)
Ben Wiley, Acting Area
Coordinator
401 Edwards Street
500 Fannin Street
Shreveport, LA 71101-3107
(318) 266-5385

Jim Cook, Acting Director
Oklahoma City Office of
Indian Programs
500 West Main Street
Oklahoma City, OK 73102-
2233

Maine
Richard Young, Acting State
Coordinator
Casco Northern Bank
Building
23 Main Street
Bangor, ME 04401-6394
(207) 945-0467
Fax: (207) 945-0533

David B. Harrity, Acting
State Coordinator
Norris Cotton Federal
Building
275 Chester Street
Manchester, NH 03103-
2487
(603) 666-7681
Fax: (603) 666-7736

Leon Jacobs, Director
Chicago Office of Indian
Programs
77 West Jackson Boulevard
24th Floor
Chicago, IL 60604-3507
(312) 231-1282

Maryland
(Except Montgomery and
Prince Georges Counties)
Maxine Saunders, Acting
State Coordinator
City Crescent Building
10 South Howard Street
Fifth Floor
Baltimore, MD 21201
(301) 962-2520

(Montgomery and Prince
Georges Counties)
Jessica Franklin, Acting
State Coordinator
Union Center Plaza, Phase II
820 First Street, NE
Suite 300
Washington, DC 20002-
4205
(202) 275-9200
Fax: (202) 275-0779

Leon Jacobs, Director
Chicago Office of Indian
Programs
77 West Jackson Boulevard
24th Floor
Chicago, IL 60604-3507
(312) 231-1282

Massachusetts
(Boston Regional Office)
Mary Lou Crane, Secretary's
Representative
Thomas P. O'Neill Jr.
Federal Building
10 Causeway Street
Room 375
Boston, MA 02222-1092
(617) 565-5234
Fax: (617) 565-5168

Leon Jacobs, Director
Chicago Office of Indian
Programs
77 West Jackson Boulevard
24th Floor
Chicago, IL 60604-3507
(312) 231-1282

Michigan
Harry I. Sharrott, Acting
State Coordinator
Patrick V. McNamara
Federal Building
477 Michigan Avenue
Detroit, MI 48226-2592
(313) 226-7900
Fax: (313) 226-4394

(East Michigan)
Gary T. LeVine, Acting Area
Coordinator
605 North Saginaw Street
Suite 200
Flint, MI 48502-1953
(313) 766-5112
Fax: (313) 766-5122

(West and North Michigan)
Ronald Weston, Acting Area
Coordinator
Northbrook Building, # II
2922 Fuller Avenue, NE
Grand Rapids, MI 49505-
3499
(616) 456-2100
Fax: (616) 456-2191

Leon Jacobs, Director
Chicago Office of Indian
Programs
77 West Jackson Boulevard
24th Floor
Chicago, IL 60604-3507
(312) 231-1282

Minnesota
Thomas Feeney, Acting State
Coordinator
220 Second Street South
Bridge Place Building
Minneapolis, MN 55401-
2195
(612) 370-3000
Fax: (612) 370-3220

Leon Jacobs, Director
Chicago Office of Indian
Programs
77 West Jackson Boulevard
24th Floor
Chicago, IL 60604-3507
(312) 231-1282

Mississippi
Sandra Freeman, Acting
State Coordinator
Koger Building
Dr. A. H. McCoy Federal
Building
100 West Capitol Street
Room 910
Jackson, MS 39269-1096
(601) 965-5308
Fax: (601) 965-4773

Leon Jacobs, Director
Chicago Office of Indian
Programs
77 West Jackson Boulevard
24th Floor
Chicago, IL 60604-3507
(312) 231-1282

Missouri
Kenneth G. Lange, Acting
Area Coordinator
1222 Spruce Street
Room 3207
St. Louis, MO 63103-2836
(314) 539-6560
Fax: (314) 539-6575

Jim Cook, Acting Director
Oklahoma City Office of
Indian Programs
500 West Main Street
Oklahoma City, OK 73102-
2233

Montana
Gerard Boone, Acting State
Coordinator
Federal Office Building,
Drawer 10095
301 South Park
Room 340
Helena, MT 59626-0095
(406) 449-5205
Fax: (406) 449-5207

Vernon Haragara, Director
Denver Office of Indian
Programs
Executive Tower Building
1405 Curtis Street
Denver, CO 80202-2349
(303) 844-2963

Nebraska
Roger M. Massey, Acting
State Coordinator
Executive Tower Center
10909 Mill Valley Road
Omaha, NE 68154-3955
(402) 492-3101
Fax: (402) 492-3150

Vernon Haragara, Director
Denver Office of Indian
Programs
Executive Tower Building
1405 Curtis Street
Denver, CO 80202-2349
(303) 844-2963

Nevada
Andrew D. Whitten Jr.,
Acting Area Coordinator
1575 DeLucchi Lane
Room 114
P.O. Box 30050
Reno, NV 89502-6581
(702) 784-5356
Fax: (702) 784-5066

Benjamin Davis, Acting
State Coordinator
1500 East Tropicana Avenue
Second Floor
Las Vegas, NV 89119-6516
(702) 388-6500
Fax: (702) 388-6736

Raphael Mecham, Director
HUD Indian Programs
Office
400 North Fifth Street
Suite 1650
Phoenix, AZ 85004-2361
(602) 379-4156
Fax: (602) 379-3101

New Hampshire
David B. Harrity, Acting
State Coordinator
Norris Cotton Federal
Building
275 Chestnut Street
Manchester, NH 03103-
2487
(603) 666-7681
Fax: (603) 666-7736

Leon Jacobs, Director
Chicago Office of Indian
Programs
77 West Jackson Boulevard
24th Floor
Chicago, IL 60604-3507
(312) 231-1282

New Jersey
(North New Jersey)
Diane Johnson, Acting State
Coordinator
One Newark Center
13th Floor
Newark, NJ 07102-5260
(201) 622-7900
Fax: (201) 645-6239

(South New Jersey)
Elmer Roy, Acting Area
Coordinator
Hudson Building
Second Floor
800 Hudson Square
Camden, NJ 08102-1156
(609) 757-5081
Fax: (609) 757-5373

Leon Jacobs, Director
Chicago Office of Indian
Programs
77 West Jackson Boulevard
24th Floor
Chicago, IL 60604-3507
(312) 231-1282

New Mexico
Michael R. Griego, Acting
State Coordinator
625 Truman Street, NW
Albuquerque, NM 87110-
6443
(505) 262-6463

Clarence D. Babers, Acting
Area Coordinator
525 Griffin Street
Room 860
Dallas, TX 75202-5007
(214) 767-8359
Fax: (214) 767-8973

Raphael Mecham, Director
HUD Indian Programs
Office
400 North Fifth Street
Suite 1650
Phoenix, AZ 85004-2361
(602) 379-4156
Fax: (602) 379-3101

New York
(New York Regional Office)
Jose Cintron, Secretary's
Representative
26 Federal Plaza
New York, NY 10278-0068
(212) 264-6500
Fax: (212) 264-0246

(North New York)
John Petricco, Acting Area
Coordinator
52 Corporate Circle
Albany, NY 12203-5121
(518) 464-4200
Fax: (518) 464-4300

(West New York)
Joseph Lynch, Acting Area
Coordinator
465 Main Street
Lafayette Court
Fifth Floor
Buffalo, NY 14203-1780
(716) 846-5755
Fax: (716) 846-5752

Leon Jacobs, Director
Chicago Office of Indian
Programs
77 West Jackson Boulevard
24th Floor
Chicago, IL 60604-3507
(312) 231-1282

North Carolina
Larry J. Parker, Acting State
Coordinator
2306 West Meadowview
Road
Koger Building
Greensboro, NC 27407-
3707
(919) 547-4001
Fax: (919) 547-4015

Leon Jacobs, Director
Chicago Office of Indian
Programs
77 West Jackson Boulevard
24th Floor
Chicago, IL 60604-3507
(312) 231-1282

North Dakota
Keith Elliott, Acting State
Coordinator
HUD—Fargo Office
Federal Building
657 Second Avenue, North
Fargo, ND 58108-2483
(701) 239-5136
Fax: (701) 783-5249

Vernon Haragara, Director
Denver Office of Indian
Programs
Executive Tower Building
1405 Curtis Street
Denver, CO 80202-2349
(303) 844-2963

Ohio
Robert W. Dolin, Acting
State Coordinator
HUD—Columbus Office
200 North High Street
Columbus, OH 43215-2499
(614) 469-5737
Fax: (614) 469-2432

(North Ohio)
Philip Ginconia, Acting Area
Coordinator
1350 Euclid Avenue
Fifth Floor
Cleveland, OH 44115-1815
(216) 552-4065
Fax: (216) 522-2975

(Southwest Ohio)
William Harris, Acting Area
Coordinator
Federal Office Building
Room 9002
550 Main Street
Cincinnati, OH 45202-3253
(513) 684-2884
Fax: (513) 684-6224

Leon Jacobs, Director
Chicago Office of Indian
Programs
77 West Jackson Boulevard
24th Floor
Chicago, IL 60604-3507
(312) 231-1282

Oklahoma
Katie Worsham, Acting State
Coordinator
500 West Main Street
Oklahoma City, OK 73102-
2233

(East Oklahoma)
James S. Colgan, Acting
Area Coordinator
1516 South Boston Avenue
Room 110
Tulsa, OK 74119-4032
(918) 581-7435
Fax: (918) 581-7440

Jim Cook, Acting Director
Oklahoma City Office of
Indian Programs
500 West Main Street
Oklahoma City, OK 73102-
2233

Oregon
Richard C. Brinck, Acting
State Coordinator
Cascade Building
520 SW Sixth Avenue
Portland, OR 97204-1596
(503) 326-2561
Fax: (503) 326-3097

Jerry Leslie, Director
Seattle Office of Indian
Programs
Seattle Federal Office
Building
909 First Avenue
Suite 200
Seattle, WA 98104-1000
(206) 220-5270

Panama Canal Zone
Rosa Villalonga, Acting
State Coordinator
159 Carlos E. Chardon
Avenue
San Juan, PR 00918-1804
(809) 766-6121
Fax: (809) 498-5201

Pennsylvania
(Philadelphia Regional
Office)
Karen A. Miller, Secretary's
Representative
Regional Housing
Commissioner
Liberty Square Building
105 South Seventh Street
Philadelphia, PA 19106-
3392
(215) 597-2560
Fax: (215) 597-9627

(West Pennsylvania)
Choice Edwards, Acting
Area Coordinator
412 Old Post Office
Courthouse Building
Seventh Avenue and Grant
Street
Pittsburgh, PA 15219-1906
(412) 644-6428
Fax: (412) 644-6499

Leon Jacobs, Director
Chicago Office of Indian
Programs
77 West Jackson Boulevard
24th Floor
Chicago, IL 60604-3507
(312) 231-1282

Puerto Rico
Rosa Villalonga, Acting
State Coordinator
159 Carlos E. Chardon
Avenue
San Juan, PR 00918-1804
(809) 766-6121
Fax: (809) 498-5201

Rhode Island
Michael Dziok, Acting State
Coordinator
Room 303
John O. Pastore Federal
Building and U.S. Post
Office
Kennedy Plaza
Providence, RI 02903-1785
(401) 528-5351
Fax: (401) 528-5312

Leon Jacobs, Director
Chicago Office of Indian
Programs
77 West Jackson Boulevard
24th Floor
Chicago, IL 60604-3507
(312) 231-1282

South Carolina
Ted B. Freeman, Acting
State Coordinator
Strom Thurmond Federal
Building
1835 Assembly Street
Columbia, SC 29201-2480
(803) 765-5592
Fax: (803) 765-5515

Leon Jacobs, Director
Chicago Office of Indian
Programs
77 West Jackson Boulevard
24th Floor
Chicago, IL 60604-3507
(312) 231-1282

South Dakota
Don Olson, Acting State
Coordinator
Suite I-201
2400 West 49th Street
Sioux Falls, SD 57105-6558
(605) 330-4223
Fax: (605) 330-4465

Vernon Haragara, Director
Denver Office of Indian
Programs
Executive Tower Building
1405 Curtis Street
Denver, CO 80202-2349
(303) 844-2963

Tennessee
Mark Brezina, Acting Area
Coordinator
John J. Duncan Federal
Building
Third Floor
710 Locust Street, SW
Knoxville, TN 37902-2526
(615) 545-4384
Fax: (615) 545-4569

(West Tennessee)
Bob Atkins, Acting Area
Coordinator
One Memphis Place
200 Jefferson Avenue
Suite 1200
Memphis, TN 38103-2335
(901) 544-3367
Fax: (901) 544-3697

(Central Tennessee)
John H. Fisher, Acting State
Coordinator
251 Cumberland Bend Drive
Nashville, TN 37228-1803
(615) 736-5213
Fax: (615) 736-2018

Leon Jacobs, Director
Chicago Office of Indian
Programs
77 West Jackson Boulevard
24th Floor
Chicago, IL 60604-3507
(312) 231-1282

Texas
(Fort Worth Regional
Office)
Stephen Weatherforce,
Secretary's Representative
1600 Throckmorton
P.O. Box 2905
Fort Worth, TX 76113-2905
(817) 885-5401
Fax: (817) 885-5629

(East, North, and West
Texas)
Clarence D. Babers, Acting
Area Coordinator
525 Griffin Street
Room 860
Dallas, TX 75202-5007
(214) 767-8359
Fax: (214) 767-8973

(Northwest Texas)
Henry E. Whitney, Acting
Area Coordinator
Federal Office Building
1205 Texas Avenue
Lubbock, TX 79401-4093
(806) 743-7265

(Southwest Texas)
A. Cynthia Leon, Acting
Area Coordinator
Washington Square Building
800 Dolorosa Street
San Antonio, TX 78207-
4563
(512) 229-6800

(East-Central Texas)
George Rodriguez, Acting
Area Coordinator
Norfolk Tower
2211 Norfolk
Room 200
Houston, TX 77098-4096
(713) 653-3274

(Bowie County)
John T. Suskie, Acting State
Coordinator
TCBY Tower
425 West Capitol Avenue
Suite 900
Little Rock, AR 72201-3488
(501) 324-5931
Fax: (501) 324-5900

(Five Counties in East
Texas)
Ben Wiley, Acting Area
Coordinator
401 Edwards Street
500 Fannin Street
Shreveport, LA 71101-3107
(318) 266-5385

Jim Cook, Acting Director
Oklahoma City Office of
Indian Programs
500 West Main Street
Oklahoma City, OK 73102-
2233

Utah
Richard Bell, Acting State
Coordinator
257 Tower Building
257 East, 200 South
Room 550
Salt Lake City, UT 84111-
2048
(801) 524-5379
Fax: (801) 524-5701

Vernon Haragara, Director
Denver Office of Indian
Programs
Executive Tower Building
1405 Curtis Street
Denver, CO 80202-2349
(303) 844-2963

Vermont
William Peters, Acting State
Coordinator
Federal Building
Room 244
11 Elmwood Avenue
P.O. Box 879
Burlington, VT 05402-0879
(802) 951-6290
Fax: (802) 951-6298

David B. Harrity, Acting
State Coordinator
Norris Cotton Federal
Building
275 Chester Street
Manchester, NH 03103-
2487
(603) 666-7681
Fax: (603) 666-7736

Leon Jacobs, Director
Chicago Office of Indian
Programs
77 West Jackson Boulevard
24th Floor
Chicago, IL 60604-3507
(312) 231-1282

Virginia
(North Virginia)
Jessica Franklin, Acting
State Coordinator
Union Center Plaza, Phase II
820 First Street, NE
Suite 300
Washington, DC 20002-
4205
(202) 275-9200
Fax: (202) 275-0779

(South Virginia)
Mary Ann Wilson, Acting
State Coordinator
P.O. Box 90331
3600 West Broad Street
Richmond, VA 23230-0331
(804) 278-4507

Leon Jacobs, Director
Chicago Office of Indian
Programs
77 West Jackson Boulevard
24th Floor
Chicago, IL 60604-3507
(312) 231-1282

Virgin Islands
Rosa Villalonga, Acting
State Coordinator
159 Carlos E. Chardon
Avenue
San Juan, PR 00918-1804
(809) 766-6121
Fax: (809) 498-5201

Washington
(Seattle Regional Office)
Bob Santos, Secretary's
Representative
Regional Housing
Commissioner
Seattle Federal Office
Building
Suite 200
909 First Avenue
Seattle, WA 98104-1000
(206) 220-5101
Fax: (206) 220-5133

(Clark, Klickitat, and
Skamania Counties)
Richard C. Brinck, Acting
State Coordinator
Cascase Building
520 SW Sixth Avenue
Portland, OR 97204-1596
(503) 326-2561
Fax: (503) 326-3097

(East Washington)
Gary Rogers, Acting Area
Coordinator
Eighth Floor East
Farm Credit Bank Building
West 601 First Avenue
Spokane, WA 99204-0317
(509) 353-2510

Jerry Leslie, Director
Seattle Office of Indian
Programs
Seattle Federal Office
Building
909 First Avenue
Suite 200
Seattle, WA 98104-1000
(206) 220-5270

West Virginia
Fred Roncaglione, Acting
State Coordinator
405 Capitol Street
Suite 708
Charleston, WV 25301-
1795
(304) 347-7000
Fax: (304) 347-7050

Choice Edwards, Acting
Area Coordinator
412 Old Post Office
Courthouse Building
Seventh Avenue and Grant
Street
Pittsburgh, PA 15219-1906
(412) 644-6428
Fax: (412) 644-6499

Leon Jacobs, Director
Chicago Office of Indian
Programs
77 West Jackson Boulevard
24th Floor
Chicago, IL 60604-3507
(312) 231-1282

Wisconsin
Delbert F. Reynolds, Acting
State Coordinator
Henry S. Reuss Federal
Plaza
310 West Wisconsin Avenue
Milwaukee, WI 53203-2289
(414) 297-3214
Fax: (414) 297-3947

Leon Jacobs, Director
Chicago Office of Indian
Programs
77 West Jackson Boulevard
24th Floor
Chicago, IL 60604-3507
(312) 231-1282

Wyoming
William Garrett, Acting
State Coordinator
4225 Federal Office Building
100 East B Street
P.O. Box 120
Casper, WY 82602-1918
(307) 261-5252
Fax: (307) 261-5251

Vernon Haragara, Director
Denver Office of Indian
Programs
Executive Tower Building
1405 Curtis Street
Denver, CO 80202-2349
(303) 844-2963

PROPERTY IMPROVEMENT LOAN INSURANCE FOR IMPROVING ALL EXISTING STRUCTURES AND BUILDING OF NEW NONRESIDENTIAL STRUCTURES

**Department of Housing and
Urban Development (HUD)**
Title I Insurance Division
Room B-133
Washington, DC 20410
(800) 733-4663
(202) 755-7400

Description: Guaranteed/insured loans to eligible borrowers for facilitating the financing of home improvements and the construction of nonresidential structures. Maximum loan for one-family dwelling is $25,000; maximum for multifamily dwelling is $12,000 per unit, not to exceed $60,000.
$ Given: $1.3 billion est. nationwide FY 95
Application Information: Borrower applies directly through insured lender or lender's approved dealer.
Deadline: None
Contact: Director, above address, for program information

REHABILITATION MORTGAGE INSURANCE

**Department of Housing and
Urban Development (HUD)**
Single-Family Development
Division
Office of Insured Single-
Family Housing
Washington, DC 20410
(202) 708-2720

Description: Guaranteed/insured loans to individual purchasers and investors for purchasing, repairing, improving, and refinancing existing structures more than one year old. Rehabilitation costs must be at least $5,000. Condominiums are not acceptable.
$ Given: $201.3 million est. FY 95; $233.6 million for 4,540 units FY 93
Application Information: Submit application through HUD-approved lending institution.
Deadline: None
Contact: Director, above address; persons are encouraged to communicate with local HUD field office.

Alabama
Heager Hill, Acting State
Coordinator
600 Beacon Parkway West
Suite 300
Birmingham, AL 35209-
3144
(205) 290-7617

Leon Jacobs, Director
Chicago Office of Indian
Programs
77 West Jackson Boulevard
24th Floor
Chicago, IL 60604-3507
(312) 231-1282

Alaska
Arlene Patton, Manager
University Plaza Building
949 East 36th Avenue
Suite 401
Anchorage, AK 99508-4135
(907) 271-4170
Fax: (907) 271-3667

Martin Knight, Director
Anchorage Indian Housing
Division
949 East 36th Avenue
Suite 401
Anchorage, AK 99508-4135
(907) 271-4633

American Samoa
Gordon Y. Furutani, Acting
State Coordinator
7 Waterfront Plaza
500 Ala Moana Boulevard
Room 500
Honolulu, HI 96813-4918
(808) 541-1323
Fax: (808) 541-3146

Arizona
Dwight A. Peterson, Acting
State Coordinator
Two Arizona.Center
400 North Fifth Street
Suite 1600
Phoenix, AZ 85004-2361
(602) 379-4434
Fax: (602) 379-3985

Sharon Atwell, Acting Area
Coordinator
33 North Stone Avenue
Room 700
Tucson, AZ 85701-1467
(602) 670-6237
Fax: (602) 670-6207

Charles Ming, Acting Area
Coordinator
1615 West Olympic
Boulevard
Los Angeles, CA 90015-
3801
(213) 251-7122
Fax: (213) 251-7096

Raphael Mecham, Director
HUD Indian Programs
Office
400 North Fifth Street
Suite 1650
Phoenix, AZ 85004-2361
(602) 379-4156
Fax: (602) 379-3101

Arkansas
John T. Suskie, Acting State
Coordinator
TCBY Tower
425 West Capitol Avenue
Suite 900
Little Rock, AR 72201-3488
(501) 324-5931
Fax: (501) 324-5900

Jim Cook, Acting Director
Oklahoma City Office of
Indian Programs
500 West Main Street
Oklahoma City, OK 73102-
2233

California
(San Francisco Regional
Office)
Arthur Agnos, Secretary's
Representative
Phillip Burton Federal
Building and U.S.
Courthouse
P.O. Box 36003
450 Golden Gate Avenue
San Francisco, CA 94102-
3448
(415) 556-4752
Fax: (415) 556-4176

(South California)
Charles Ming, Acting Area
Coordinator
1615 West Olympic
Boulevard
Los Angeles, CA 90015-
3801
(213) 251-7122
Fax: (213) 251-7096

(Fresno)
Willie Mae Haskin, Acting
Area Coordinator
1630 East Shaw Avenue
Fresno, CA 93710-8193
(209) 487-5033
Fax: (209) 487-5344

(Northeast California)
Paul Pradia, Acting Area
Coordinator
777 12th Street
Suite 200
Sacramento, CA 95814-
1997
(916) 551-1351
Fax: (916) 551-2899

(Imperial and San Diego
Counties)
Charles J. Wilson, Acting
Area Coordinator
Mission City Corporate
Center
Suite 300
2365 Northside Drive
San Diego, CA 92108-2712
(619) 557-5310
Fax: (619) 557-6296

(Orange, Riverside, and San
Bernadino Counties, for
home mortgages)
Samuel Sandoval, Acting
Area Coordinator
3 Hutton Centre
Suite 500
Santa Ana, CA 92707-5764
(714) 957-7333
Fax: (714) 957-1903

Raphael Mecham, Director
HUD Indian Programs
Office
400 North Fifth Street
Suite 1650
Phoenix, AZ 85004-2361
(602) 379-4156
Fax: (602) 379-3101

Colorado
(Denver Regional Office)
Anthony Hernandez,
Secretary's Representative
HUD—Denver Office
633 17th Street
Denver, CO 80202-3607
(303) 844-4513
Fax: (303) 844-2475

Vernon Haragara, Director
Denver Office of Indian
Programs
Executive Tower Building
1405 Curtis Street
Denver, CO 80202-2349
(303) 844-2963

Connecticut
Robert S. Donovon, Deputy
Manager
330 Main Street
Hartford, CT 06106-1860
(203) 240-4523
Fax: (203) 240-4674

Leon Jacobs, Director
Chicago Office of Indian
Programs
77 West Jackson Boulevard
24th Floor
Chicago, IL 60604-3507
(312) 231-1282

Delaware
A. David Sharbaugh, Acting
State Coordinator
824 Market Street
Suite 850
Wilmington, DE 19801-
3016
(302) 573-6300
Fax: (302) 573-6259

Leon Jacobs, Director
Chicago Office of Indian
Programs
77 West Jackson Boulevard
24th Floor
Chicago, IL 60604-3507
(312) 231-1282

District of Columbia
Jessica Franklin, Acting
State Coordinator
Union Center Plaza, Phase II
820 First Street, NE
Suite 300
Washington, DC 20002-
4205
(202) 275-9200
Fax: (202) 275-0779

Florida
James T. Chaplin, State
Coordinator
Southern Bell Tower
Suite 2200
301 West Bay Street
Jacksonville, FL 32202-5121
(904) 232-2626
Fax: (904) 232-3759

(South Florida)
Orlando T. Lorie, Acting
Area Coordinator
Gables 1 Tower
1320 South Dixie Highway
Coral Gables, FL 33146-
2911
(305) 662-4500
Fax: (305) 662-4519

(Central Florida, Western
Counties—Citrus, Sumter,
Hernando, Pasco, Manatee,
Hardee, Highlands, DeSoto,
Sarasota, Charlotte, Olaoes,
Hendry, Lake Okeechobee)
George A. Milburn Jr.,
Acting Area Coordinator
Timberlake Federal Building
Annex
501 East Polk Street
Tampa, FL 33602-3945
(813) 228-2501
Fax: (813) 228-2431

(Central Florida, Eastern
Counties—Volusia, Lake,
Seminole, Orange, Brevard,
Osceola, Indian River,
Okeechobee, St. Lucie)
M. Jeanette Porter, Acting
Area Coordinator
Langley Building
3751 Maguire Boulevard
Suite 270
Orlando, FL 32803-3032
(407) 648-6441
Fax: (407) 648-6310

Leon Jacobs, Director
Chicago Office of Indian
Programs
77 West Jackson Boulevard
24th Floor
Chicago, IL 60604-3507
(312) 231-1282

Georgia
(Atlanta Regional Office)
Davey L. Gibson, Secretary's
Representative
Regional Housing
Commissioner
Richard B. Russell Federal
Building
75 Spring Street, SW
Atlanta, GA 30303-3388
(404) 331-5136
Fax: (404) 331-0845

Leon Jacobs, Director
Chicago Office of Indian
Programs
77 West Jackson Boulevard
24th Floor
Chicago, IL 60604-3507
(312) 231-1282

Guam
Gordon Y. Furutani, Acting
State Coordinator
7 Waterfront Plaza
500 Ala Moana Boulevard
Room 500
Honolulu, HI 96813-4918
(808) 541-1323
Fax: (808) 541-3146

Hawaii
Gordon Y. Furutani, Acting
State Coordinator
7 Waterfront Plaza
500 Ala Moana Boulevard
Room 500
Honolulu, HI 96813-4918
(808) 541-1323
Fax: (808) 541-3146

Idaho
(North Idaho)
Gary Rogers, Acting Area
Coordinator
Farm Credit Bank Building
Eighth Floor East
West 601 First Avenue
Spokane, WA 99204-0317
(509) 353-2510

(West-Central Idaho)
Gary Gillespie, Acting State
Coordinator
Suite 220
Park IV
800 Park Boulevard
Boise, ID 83712-7743
(208) 334-1990
Fax: (208) 334-9648

(South Idaho)
Richard C. Brinck, Acting
State Coordinator
Cascade Building
520 SW Sixth Avenue
Portland, OR 97204-1596
(503) 221-2561

Jerry Leslie, Director
Seattle Office of Indian
Programs
Seattle Federal Office
Building
909 First Avenue
Suite 200
Seattle, WA 98104-1000
(206) 220-5270

Illinois
(Chicago Regional Office)
Edwin Eisendrath,
Secretary's Representative
Regional Housing
Commissioner
Ralph Metcalfe Federal
Building
77 West Jackson Boulevard
Chicago, IL 60604-3507
(312) 353-5680
Fax: (312) 353-0121

(Central and South Illinois)
William Fattick, Acting Area
Coordinator
509 West Capitol
Suite 206
Springfield, IL 62704-1906
(217) 492-4085
Fax: (217) 492-4971

Leon Jacobs, Director
Chicago Office of Indian
Programs
77 West Jackson Boulevard
24th Floor
Chicago, IL 60604-3507
(312) 231-1282

Indiana
J. Nicholas Shelley, Acting
State Coordinator
151 North Delaware Street
Indianapolis, IN 46204-
2526
(317) 226-6303
Fax: (317) 226-6317

Iowa
William R. McNarney,
Acting State Coordinator
HUD—Des Moines Office
Federal Building
Room 239
210 Walnut Street
Des Moines, IA 50309-2155
(515) 284-4512
Fax: (515) 284-4743

Roger M. Massey, Acting
State Coordinator
Executive Tower Center
10909 Mill Valley Road
Omaha, NE 68154-3955
(402) 492-3101
Fax: (402) 492-3150

Leon Jacobs, Director
Chicago Office of Indian
Programs
77 West Jackson Boulevard
24th Floor
Chicago, IL 60604-3507
(312) 231-1282

Kansas
Joseph O'Hern, Secretary's
Representative
Regional Housing
Commissioner
HUD—Kansas City Regional
Office
Gateway Tower II
400 State Avenue
Room 200
Kansas City, KS 66101-2406
(913) 551-5462
Fax: (913) 551-5416

Jim Cook, Acting Director
Oklahoma City Office of
Indian Programs
500 West Main Street
Oklahoma City, OK 73102-
2233

Kentucky
Verna V. Van Ness, Acting
State Coordinator
601 West Broadway
P.O. Box 1044
Louisville, KY 40201-1044
(502) 582-5251
Fax: (502) 582-6074

Leon Jacobs, Director
Chicago Office of Indian
Programs
77 West Jackson Boulevard
24th Floor
Chicago, IL 60604-3507
(312) 231-1282

Louisiana
Robert Vasquez, Acting
State Coordinator
Fisk Federal Building
1661 Canal Street
New Orleans, LA 70112-
1887
(504) 589-7200
Fax: (504) 589-2917

(North Louisiana)
Ben Wiley, Acting Area
Coordinator
401 Edwards Street
500 Fannin Street
Shreveport, LA 71101-3107
(318) 266-5385

Jim Cook, Acting Director
Oklahoma City Office of
Indian Programs
500 West Main Street
Oklahoma City, OK 73102-
2233

Maine
Richard Young, Acting State
Coordinator
Casco Northern Bank
Building
23 Main Street
Bangor, ME 04401-6394
(207) 945-0467
Fax: (207) 945-0533

David B. Harrity, Acting
State Coordinator
Norris Cotton Federal
Building
275 Chester Street
Manchester, NH 03103-
2487
(603) 666-7681
Fax: (603) 666-7736

Leon Jacobs, Director
Chicago Office of Indian
Programs
77 West Jackson Boulevard
24th Floor
Chicago, IL 60604-3507
(312) 231-1282

Maryland
(Except Montgomery and
Prince Georges Counties)
Maxine Saunders, Acting
State Coordinator
City Crescent Building
10 South Howard Street
Fifth Floor
Baltimore, MD 21201
(301) 962-2520

(Montgomery and Prince
Georges Counties)
Jessica Franklin, Acting
State Coordinator
Union Center Plaza, Phase II
820 First Street, NE
Suite 300
Washington, DC 20002-
4205
(202) 275-9200
Fax: (202) 275-0779

Leon Jacobs, Director
Chicago Office of Indian
Programs
77 West Jackson Boulevard
24th Floor
Chicago, IL 60604-3507
(312) 231-1282

Massachusetts
(Boston Regional Office)
Mary Lou Crane, Secretary's
Representative
Thomas P. O'Neill Jr.
Federal Building
10 Causeway Street
Room 375
Boston, MA 02222-1092
(617) 565-5234
Fax: (617) 565-5168

Leon Jacobs, Director
Chicago Office of Indian
Programs
77 West Jackson Boulevard
24th Floor
Chicago, IL 60604-3507
(312) 231-1282

Michigan
Harry I. Sharrott, Acting
State Coordinator
Patrick V. McNamara
Federal Building
477 Michigan Avenue
Detroit, MI 48226-2592
(313) 226-7900
Fax: (313) 226-4394

(East Michigan)
Gary T. LeVine, Acting Area
Coordinator
605 North Saginaw Street
Suite 200
Flint, MI 48502-1953
(313) 766-5112
Fax: (313) 766-5122

(West and North Michigan)
Ronald Weston, Acting Area
Coordinator
Northbrook Building, # II
2922 Fuller Avenue, NE
Grand Rapids, MI 49505-
3499
(616) 456-2100
Fax: (616) 456-2191

Leon Jacobs, Director
Chicago Office of Indian
Programs
77 West Jackson Boulevard
24th Floor
Chicago, IL 60604-3507
(312) 231-1282

Minnesota
Thomas Feeney, Acting State
Coordinator
220 Second Street South
Bridge Place Building
Minneapolis, MN 55401-
2195
(612) 370-3000
Fax: (612) 370-3220

Leon Jacobs, Director
Chicago Office of Indian
Programs
77 West Jackson Boulevard
24th Floor
Chicago, IL 60604-3507
(312) 231-1282

Mississippi
Sandra Freeman, Acting
State Coordinator
Koger Building
Dr. A. H. McCoy Federal
Building
100 West Capitol Street
Room 910
Jackson, MS 39269-1096
(601) 965-5308
Fax: (601) 965-4773

Leon Jacobs, Director
Chicago Office of Indian
Programs
77 West Jackson Boulevard
24th Floor
Chicago, IL 60604-3507
(312) 231-1282

Missouri
Kenneth G. Lange, Acting
Area Coordinator
1222 Spruce Street
Room 3207
St. Louis, MO 63103-2836
(314) 539-6560
Fax: (314) 539-6575

Jim Cook, Acting Director
Oklahoma City Office of
Indian Programs
500 West Main Street
Oklahoma City, OK 73102-
2233

Montana
Gerard Boone, Acting State
Coordinator
Federal Office Building,
Drawer 10095
301 South Park
Room 340
Helena, MT 59626-0095
(406) 449-5205
Fax: (406) 449-5207

Vernon Haragara, Director
Denver Office of Indian
Programs
Executive Tower Building
1405 Curtis Street
Denver, CO 80202-2349
(303) 844-2963

Nebraska
Roger M. Massey, Acting
State Coordinator
Executive Tower Center
10909 Mill Valley Road
Omaha, NE 68154-3955
(402) 492-3101
Fax: (402) 492-3150

Vernon Haragara, Director
Denver Office of Indian
Programs
Executive Tower Building
1405 Curtis Street
Denver, CO 80202-2349
(303) 844-2963

Nevada
Andrew D. Whitten Jr.,
Acting Area Coordinator
1575 DeLucchi Lane
Room 114
P.O. Box 30050
Reno, NV 89502-6581
(702) 784-5356
Fax: (702) 784-5066

Benjamin Davis, Acting
State Coordinator
1500 East Tropicana Avenue
Second Floor
Las Vegas, NV 89119-6516
(702) 388-6500
Fax: (702) 388-6736

Raphael Mecham, Director
HUD Indian Programs
Office
400 North Fifth Street
Suite 1650
Phoenix, AZ 85004-2361
(602) 379-4156
Fax: (602) 379-3101

New Hampshire
David B. Harrity, Acting
State Coordinator
Norris Cotton Federal
Building
275 Chestnut Street
Manchester, NH 03103-
2487
(603) 666-7681
Fax: (603) 666-7736

Leon Jacobs, Director
Chicago Office of Indian
Programs
77 West Jackson Boulevard
24th Floor
Chicago, IL 60604-3507
(312) 231-1282

New Jersey
(North New Jersey)
Diane Johnson, Acting State
Coordinator
One Newark Center
13th Floor
Newark, NJ 07102-5260
(201) 622-7900
Fax: (201) 645-6239

(South New Jersey)
Elmer Roy, Acting Area
Coordinator
Hudson Building
Second Floor
800 Hudson Square
Camden, NJ 08102-1156
(609) 757-5081
Fax: (609) 757-5373

Leon Jacobs, Director
Chicago Office of Indian
Programs
77 West Jackson Boulevard
24th Floor
Chicago, IL 60604-3507
(312) 231-1282

New Mexico
Michael R. Griego, Acting
State Coordinator
625 Truman Street, NW
Albuquerque, NM 87110-
6443
(505) 262-6463

Clarence D. Babers, Acting
Area Coordinator
525 Griffin Street
Room 860
Dallas, TX 75202-5007
(214) 767-8359
Fax: (214) 767-8973

Raphael Mecham, Director
HUD Indian Programs
Office
400 North Fifth Street
Suite 1650
Phoenix, AZ 85004-2361
(602) 379-4156
Fax: (602) 379-3101

New York
(New York Regional Office)
Jose Cintron, Secretary's
Representative
26 Federal Plaza
New York, NY 10278-0068
(212) 264-6500
Fax: (212) 264-0246

(North New York)
John Petricco, Acting Area
Coordinator
52 Corporate Circle
Albany, NY 12203-5121
(518) 464-4200
Fax: (518) 464-4300

(West New York)
Joseph Lynch, Acting Area
Coordinator
465 Main Street
Lafayette Court
Fifth Floor
Buffalo, NY 14203-1780
(716) 846-5755
Fax: (716) 846-5752

Leon Jacobs, Director
Chicago Office of Indian
Programs
77 West Jackson Boulevard
24th Floor
Chicago, IL 60604-3507
(312) 231-1282

North Carolina
Larry J. Parker, Acting State
Coordinator
2306 West Meadowview
Road
Koger Building
Greensboro, NC 27407-
3707
(919) 547-4001
Fax: (919) 547-4015

Leon Jacobs, Director
Chicago Office of Indian
Programs
77 West Jackson Boulevard
24th Floor
Chicago, IL 60604-3507
(312) 231-1282

North Dakota
Keith Elliott, Acting State
Coordinator
HUD—Fargo Office
Federal Building
657 Second Avenue, North
Fargo, ND 58108-2483
(701) 239-5136
Fax: (701) 783-5249

Vernon Haragara, Director
Denver Office of Indian
Programs
Executive Tower Building
1405 Curtis Street
Denver, CO 80202-2349
(303) 844-2963

Ohio
Robert W. Dolin, Acting
State Coordinator
HUD—Columbus Office
200 North High Street
Columbus, OH 43215-2499
(614) 469-5737
Fax: (614) 469-2432

(North Ohio)
Philip Ginconia, Acting Area
Coordinator
1350 Euclid Avenue
Fifth Floor
Cleveland, OH 44115-1815
(216) 552-4065
Fax: (216) 522-2975

(Southwest Ohio)
William Harris, Acting Area
Coordinator
Federal Office Building
Room 9002
550 Main Street
Cincinnati, OH 45202-3253
(513) 684-2884
Fax: (513) 684-6224

Leon Jacobs, Director
Chicago Office of Indian
Programs
77 West Jackson Boulevard
24th Floor
Chicago, IL 60604-3507
(312) 231-1282

Oklahoma
Katie Worsham, Acting State
Coordinator
500 West Main Street
Oklahoma City, OK 73102-
2233

(East Oklahoma)
James S. Colgan, Acting
Area Coordinator
1516 South Boston Avenue
Room 110
Tulsa, OK 74119-4032
(918) 581-7435
Fax: (918) 581-7440

Jim Cook, Acting Director
Oklahoma City Office of
Indian Programs
500 West Main Street
Oklahoma City, OK 73102-
2233

Oregon
Richard C. Brinck, Acting
State Coordinator
Cascade Building
520 SW Sixth Avenue
Portland, OR 97204-1596
(503) 326-2561
Fax: (503) 326-3097

Jerry Leslie, Director
Seattle Office of Indian
Programs
Seattle Federal Office
Building
909 First Avenue
Suite 200
Seattle, WA 98104-1000
(206) 220-5270

Panama Canal Zone
Rosa Villalonga, Acting
State Coordinator
159 Carlos E. Chardon
Avenue
San Juan, PR 00918-1804
(809) 766-6121
Fax: (809) 498-5201

Pennsylvania
(Philadelphia Regional
Office)
Karen A. Miller, Secretary's
Representative
Regional Housing
Commissioner
Liberty Square Building
105 South Seventh Street
Philadelphia, PA 19106-
3392
(215) 597-2560
Fax: (215) 597-9627

(West Pennsylvania)
Choice Edwards, Acting
Area Coordinator
412 Old Post Office
Courthouse Building
Seventh Avenue and Grant
Street
Pittsburgh, PA 15219-1906
(412) 644-6428
Fax: (412) 644-6499

Leon Jacobs, Director
Chicago Office of Indian
Programs
77 West Jackson Boulevard
24th Floor
Chicago, IL 60604-3507
(312) 231-1282

Puerto Rico
Rosa Villalonga, Acting
State Coordinator
159 Carlos E. Chardon
Avenue
San Juan, PR 00918-1804
(809) 766-6121
Fax: (809) 498-5201

Rhode Island
Michael Dziok, Acting State
Coordinator
Room 303
John O. Pastore Federal
Building and U.S. Post
Office
Kennedy Plaza
Providence, RI 02903-1785
(401) 528-5351
Fax: (401) 528-5312

Leon Jacobs, Director
Chicago Office of Indian
Programs
77 West Jackson Boulevard
24th Floor
Chicago, IL 60604-3507
(312) 231-1282

South Carolina
Ted B. Freeman, Acting
State Coordinator
Strom Thurmond Federal
Building
1835 Assembly Street
Columbia, SC 29201-2480
(803) 765-5592
Fax: (803) 765-5515

Leon Jacobs, Director
Chicago Office of Indian
Programs
77 West Jackson Boulevard
24th Floor
Chicago, IL 60604-3507
(312) 231-1282

South Dakota
Don Olson, Acting State
Coordinator
Suite I-201
2400 West 49th Street
Sioux Falls, SD 57105-6558
(605) 330-4223
Fax: (605) 330-4465

Vernon Haragara, Director
Denver Office of Indian
Programs
Executive Tower Building
1405 Curtis Street
Denver, CO 80202-2349
(303) 844-2963

Tennessee
Mark Brezina, Acting Area
Coordinator
John J. Duncan Federal
Building
Third Floor
710 Locust Street, SW
Knoxville, TN 37902-2526
(615) 545-4384
Fax: (615) 545-4569

(West Tennessee)
Bob Atkins, Acting Area
Coordinator
One Memphis Place
200 Jefferson Avenue
Suite 1200
Memphis, TN 38103-2335
(901) 544-3367
Fax: (901) 544-3697

(Central Tennessee)
John H. Fisher, Acting State
Coordinator
251 Cumberland Bend Drive
Nashville, TN 37228-1803
(615) 736-5213
Fax: (615) 736-2018

Leon Jacobs, Director
Chicago Office of Indian
Programs
77 West Jackson Boulevard
24th Floor
Chicago, IL 60604-3507
(312) 231-1282

Texas
(Fort Worth Regional
Office)
Stephen Weatherforce,
Secretary's Representative
1600 Throckmorton
P.O. Box 2905
Fort Worth, TX 76113-2905
(817) 885-5401
Fax: (817) 885-5629

(East, North, and West
Texas)
Clarence D. Babers, Acting
Area Coordinator
525 Griffin Street
Room 860
Dallas, TX 75202-5007
(214) 767-8359
Fax: (214) 767-8973

(Northwest Texas)
Henry E. Whitney, Acting
Area Coordinator
Federal Office Building
1205 Texas Avenue
Lubbock, TX 79401-4093
(806) 743-7265

(Southwest Texas)
A. Cynthia Leon, Acting
Area Coordinator
Washington Square Building
800 Dolorosa Street
San Antonio, TX 78207-
4563
(512) 229-6800

(East-Central Texas)
George Rodriguez, Acting
Area Coordinator
Norfolk Tower
2211 Norfolk
Room 200
Houston, TX 77098-4096
(713) 653-3274

(Bowie County)
John T. Suskie, Acting State
Coordinator
TCBY Tower
425 West Capitol Avenue
Suite 900
Little Rock, AR 72201-3488
(501) 324-5931
Fax: (501) 324-5900

(Five Counties in East
Texas)
Ben Wiley, Acting Area
Coordinator
401 Edwards Street
500 Fannin Street
Shreveport, LA 71101-3107
(318) 266-5385

Jim Cook, Acting Director
Oklahoma City Office of
Indian Programs
500 West Main Street
Oklahoma City, OK 73102-
2233

Utah
Richard Bell, Acting State
Coordinator
257 Tower Building
257 East, 200 South
Salt Lake City, UT 84111-
2048
(801) 524-5379
Fax: (801) 524-5701

Vernon Haragara, Director
Denver Office of Indian
Programs
Executive Tower Building
1405 Curtis Street
Denver, CO 80202-2349
(303) 844-2963

Vermont
William Peters, Acting State
Coordinator
Federal Building
Room 244
11 Elmwood Avenue
P.O. Box 879
Burlington, VT 05402-0879
(802) 951-6290
Fax: (802) 951-6298

David B. Harrity, Acting
State Coordinator
Norris Cotton Federal
Building
275 Chester Street
Manchester, NH 03103-
2487
(603) 666-7681
Fax: (603) 666-7736

Leon Jacobs, Director
Chicago Office of Indian
Programs
77 West Jackson Boulevard
24th Floor
Chicago, IL 60604-3507
(312) 231-1282

Virginia
(North Virginia)
Jessica Franklin, Acting
State Coordinator
Union Center Plaza, Phase II
820 First Street, NE
Suite 300
Washington, DC 20002-
4205
(202) 275-9200
Fax: (202) 275-0779

(South Virginia)
Mary Ann Wilson, Acting
State Coordinator
P.O. Box 90331
3600 West Broad Street
Richmond, VA 23230-0331
(804) 278-4507

Leon Jacobs, Director
Chicago Office of Indian
Programs
77 West Jackson Boulevard
24th Floor
Chicago, IL 60604-3507
(312) 231-1282

Virgin Islands
Rosa Villalonga, Acting
State Coordinator
159 Carlos E. Chardon
Avenue
San Juan, PR 00918-1804
(809) 766-6121
Fax: (809) 498-5201

Washington
(Seattle Regional Office)
Bob Santos, Secretary's
Representative
Regional Housing
Commissioner
Seattle Federal Office
Building
Suite 200
909 First Avenue
Seattle, WA 98104-1000
(206) 220-5101
Fax: (206) 220-5133

(Clark, Klickitat, and
Skamania Counties)
Richard C. Brinck, Acting
State Coordinator
Cascase Building
520 SW Sixth Avenue
Portland, OR 97204-1596
(503) 326-2561
Fax: (503) 326-3097

(East Washington)
Gary Rogers, Acting Area
Coordinator
Eighth Floor East
Farm Credit Bank Building
West 601 First Avenue
Spokane, WA 99204-0317
(509) 353-2510

Jerry Leslie, Director
Seattle Office of Indian
Programs
Seattle Federal Office
Building
909 First Avenue
Suite 200
Seattle, WA 98104-1000
(206) 220-5270

West Virginia
Fred Roncaglione, Acting
State Coordinator
405 Capitol Street
Suite 708
Charleston, WV 25301-
1795
(304) 347-7000
Fax: (304) 347-7050

Choice Edwards, Acting
Area Coordinator
412 Old Post Office
Courthouse Building
Seventh Avenue and Grant
Street
Pittsburgh, PA 15219-1906
(412) 644-6428
Fax: (412) 644-6499

Leon Jacobs, Director
Chicago Office of Indian
Programs
77 West Jackson Boulevard
24th Floor
Chicago, IL 60604-3507
(312) 231-1282

Wisconsin
Delbert F. Reynolds, Acting
State Coordinator
Henry S. Reuss Federal
Plaza
310 West Wisconsin Avenue
Milwaukee, WI 53203-2289
(414) 297-3214
Fax: (414) 297-3947

Leon Jacobs, Director
Chicago Office of Indian
Programs
77 West Jackson Boulevard
24th Floor
Chicago, IL 60604-3507
(312) 231-1282

Wyoming
William Garrett, Acting
State Coordinator
4225 Federal Office Building
100 East B Street
P.O. Box 120
Casper, WY 82602-1918
(307) 261-5252
Fax: (307) 261-5251

Vernon Haragara, Director
Denver Office of Indian
Programs
Executive Tower Building
1405 Curtis Street
Denver, CO 80202-2349
(303) 844-2963

Bibliography

Catalog of Federal Domestic Assistance. Washington, DC: U.S. Government Printing Office, 1995; published annually.

The United States Government Manual. The Office of the Federal Register. Describes the broad responsibilities of all the major federal government departments and agencies. It does not list grant programs specifically but does list various publications that are offered by each agency. If you know that an agency does give grants—and many do—you can find useful information about them in some of these publications. You can contact the relevant agencies to have your name put on their mailing lists for program information.

- To find your local U.S. Government Bookstore, call: (202) 512-0132

- To order U.S. government publications by mail, write to:

U.S. Government Printing Office
Superintendent of Documents
Washington, DC 20402

- For general information about U.S. government programs, contact the Federal Information Center nearest you. The main office is:

Federal Information Center
P.O. Box 600
Cumberland, MD 21501-0600
(301) 722-9098

You can also access general information through the *Federal Assistance Programs Retrieval System* (FAPRS). There are designated access points in each state where you can ask for a computer search of the database. You can also access the database through some commercial computer-network companies.

- For more information on FAPRS, contact:

  Federal Domestic Assistance Catalog Staff
  General Services Administration
  Reporters Building, Ground Floor
  300 Seventh Street, SW
  Washington, DC 20407
  (800) 669-8331
  (202) 708-5126

- For literature on federal business loans, contact:

  The Director
  Loan Policy and Procedures Branch
  Small Business Administration (SBA)
  409 Third Street, SW
  Washington, DC 20416
  (202) 205-6570

Index